Children's Literature Review

Guide to Gale Literary Criticism Series

For criticism on	Consult these Gale series
Authors now living or who died after December 31, 1999	*CONTEMPORARY LITERARY CRITICISM (CLC)*
Authors who died between 1900 and 1999	*TWENTIETH-CENTURY LITERARY CRITICISM (TCLC)*
Authors who died between 1800 and 1899	*NINETEENTH-CENTURY LITERATURE CRITICISM (NCLC)*
Authors who died between 1400 and 1799	*LITERATURE CRITICISM FROM 1400 TO 1800 (LC)* *SHAKESPEAREAN CRITICISM (SC)*
Authors who died before 1400	*CLASSICAL AND MEDIEVAL LITERATURE CRITICISM (CMLC)*
Authors of books for children and young adults	*CHILDREN'S LITERATURE REVIEW (CLR)*
Dramatists	*DRAMA CRITICISM (DC)*
Poets	*POETRY CRITICISM (PC)*
Short story writers	*SHORT STORY CRITICISM (SSC)*
Literary topics and movements	*HARLEM RENAISSANCE: A GALE CRITICAL COMPANION (HR)* *THE BEAT GENERATION: A GALE CRITICAL COMPANION (BG)*
Asian American writers of the last two hundred years	*ASIAN AMERICAN LITERATURE (AAL)*
Black writers of the past two hundred years	*BLACK LITERATURE CRITICISM (BLC)* *BLACK LITERATURE CRITICISM SUPPLEMENT (BLCS)*
Hispanic writers of the late nineteenth and twentieth centuries	*HISPANIC LITERATURE CRITICISM (HLC)* *HISPANIC LITERATURE CRITICISM SUPPLEMENT (HLCS)*
Native North American writers and orators of the eighteenth, nineteenth, and twentieth centuries	*NATIVE NORTH AMERICAN LITERATURE (NNAL)*
Major authors from the Renaissance to the present	*WORLD LITERATURE CRITICISM, 1500 TO THE PRESENT (WLC)* *WORLD LITERATURE CRITICISM SUPPLEMENT (WLCS)*

ISSN 0362-4145

volume 94

Children's Literature Review

Excerpts from Reviews, Criticism, and Commentary on Books for Children and Young People

Allison Marion
Project Editor

GALE®

THOMSON
GALE™

Detroit • New York • San Diego • San Francisco • Cleveland • New Haven, Conn. • Waterville, Maine • London • Munich

THOMSON
GALE

Children's Literature Review, Vol. 94

Project Editor
Allison Marion

Editorial
Tom Burns, Jenny Cromie, Kathy D. Darrow, Jeffrey W. Hunter, Michael L. LaBlanc, Rebecca Long, Lemma Shomali

Permissions
Margaret Chamberlain, Lori Hines

Imaging and Multimedia
Dean Dauphinais, Robert Duncan, Leitha Etheridge-Sims, Mary K. Grimes, Lezlie Light, Dan Newell, David G. Oblender, Christine O'Bryan, Kelly A. Quin, Luke Rademacher

Composition and Electronic Capture
Carolyn A. Roney

Manufacturing
Lori Kessler

For more information, contact
The Gale Group, Inc.
27500 Drake Rd.
Farmington Hills, MI 48331-3535
Or you can visit our internet site at
http://www.gale.com

LIBRARY OF CONGRESS CATALOG CARD NUMBER 76-643301

ISBN 0-7876-6787-0
ISSN 0362-4145

Printed in the United States of America
10 9 8 7 6 5 4 3 2 1

Contents

Preface

Literature for children and young adults has evolved into both a respected branch of creative writing and a successful industry. Currently, books for young readers are considered among the most popular segments of publishing. Criticism of juvenile literature is instrumental in recording the literary or artistic development of the creators of children's books as well as the trends and controversies that result from changing values or attitudes about young people and their literature. Designed to provide a permanent, accessible record of this ongoing scholarship, *Children's Literature Review* (*CLR*) presents parents, teachers, and librarians—those responsible for bringing children and books together—with the opportunity to make informed choices when selecting reading materials for the young. In addition, *CLR* provides researchers of children's literature with easy access to a wide variety of critical information from English-language sources in the field. Users will find balanced overviews of the careers of the authors and illustrators of the books that children and young adults are reading; these entries, which contain excerpts from published criticism in books and periodicals, assist users by sparking ideas for papers and assignments and suggesting supplementary and classroom reading. Ann L. Kalkhoff, president and editor of *Children's Book Review Service Inc.,* writes that "*CLR* has filled a gap in the field of children's books, and it is one series that will never lose its validity or importance."

Scope of the Series

Each volume of *CLR* profiles the careers of a selection of authors and illustrators of books for children and young adults from preschool through high school. Author lists in each volume reflect:

- an international scope
- representation of authors of all eras
- the variety of genres covered by children's and/or YA literature: picture books, fiction, nonfiction, poetry, folklore, and drama

Although the focus of the series is on authors new to *CLR,* entries will be updated as the need arises.

Organization of the Book

A *CLR* entry consists of the following elements:

- The **Author Heading** consists of the author's name followed by birth and death dates. The portion of the name outside the parentheses denotes the form under which the author is most frequently published. If the author wrote consistently under a pseudonym, the pseudonym will be listed in the author heading and the author's actual name given in parentheses on the first line of the biographical and critical information. Also located here are any name variations under which an author wrote, including transliterated forms for authors whose native languages use non-roman alphabets. Uncertain birth or death dates are indicated by question marks.
- A **Portrait of the Author** is included when available.
- The **Author Introduction** contains information designed to introduce an author to *CLR* users by presenting an overview of the author's themes and styles, biographical facts that relate to the author's literary career or critical responses to the author's works, and information about major awards and prizes the author has received. The introduction begins by identifying the nationality of the author and by listing genres in which s/he has written for children and young adults. Introductions also list a group of representative titles for which the author or illustrator being profiled is best known; this section, which begins with the words "major works include," follows the genre line

of the introduction. For seminal figures, a listing of major works about the author follows when appropriate, highlighting important biographies about the author or illustrator that are not excerpted in the entry. The centered heading "Introduction" announces the body of the text.

- **Criticism** is located in three sections: **Author Commentary** (when available) **General Commentary** (when available), and **Title Commentary** (commentary on specific titles).

  The **Author Commentary** presents background material written by the author or by an interviewer. This commentary may cover a specific work or several works. Author commentary on more than one work appears after the author introduction, while commentary on an individual book follows the title entry heading.

  The **General Commentary** consists of critical excerpts that consider more than one work by the author or illustrator being profiled. General commentary is preceded by the critic's name in boldface type or, in the case of unsigned criticism, by the title of the journal. *CLR* also features entries that emphasize general criticism on the oeuvre of an author or illustrator. When appropriate, a selection of reviews is included to supplement the general commentary.

  The **Title Commentary** begins with the title entry headings, which precede the criticism on a title and cite publication information on the work being reviewed. Title headings list the title of the work as it appeared in its first English-language edition. The first English-language publication date of each work (unless otherwise noted) is listed in parentheses following the title. Differing U.S. and British titles follow the publication date within parentheses. When a work is written by an individual other than the one being profiled, as is the case when illustrators are featured, the parenthetical material following the title cites the author of the work before listing its publication date.

Entries in each title commentary section consist of critical excerpts on the author's individual works, arranged chronologically by publication date. The entries generally contain two to seven reviews per title, depending on the stature of the book and the amount of criticism it has generated. The editors select titles that reflect the entire scope of the author's literary contribution, covering each genre and subject. An effort is made to reprint criticism that represents the full range of each title's reception, from the year of its initial publication to current assessments. Thus, the reader is provided with a record of the author's critical history. Publication information (such as publisher names and book prices) and parenthetical numerical references (such as footnotes or page and line references to specific editions of works) have been deleted at the discretion of the editors to provide smoother reading of the text.

- A complete **Bibliographical Citation** of the original essay or book precedes each piece of criticism.

- Selected excerpts are preceded by brief **Annotations,** which provide information on the critic or work of criticism to enhance the reader's understanding of the excerpt.

- Numerous **Illustrations** are featured in *CLR.* For entries on illustrators, an effort has been made to include illustrations that reflect the characteristics discussed in the criticism. Entries on authors who do not illustrate their own works my include photographs and other illustrative material pertinent to their careers.

Special Features: Entries on Illustrators

Entries on authors who are also illustrators will occasionally feature commentary on selected works illustrated but not written by the author being profiled. These works are strongly associated with the illustrator and have received critical acclaim for their art. By including critical comment on works of this type, the editors wish to provide a more complete representation of the artist's career. Criticism on these works has been chosen to stress artistic, rather than literary, contributions. Title entry headings for works illustrated by the author being profiled are arranged chronologically within the entry by date of publication and include notes identifying the author of the illustrated work. In order to provide easier access for users, all titles illustrated by the subject of the entry are boldfaced.

CLR also includes entries on prominent illustrators who have contributed to the field of children's literature. These entries are designed to represent the development of the illustrator as an artist rather than as a literary stylist. The illustrator's section is organized like that of an author, with two exceptions: the introduction presents an overview of the illustrator's styles and techniques rather than outlining his or her literary background, and the commentary written by the illustrator on his or her works is called "Illustrator's Commentary" rather than "Author's Commentary." All titles of books containing illustrations by the artist being profiled are highlighted in boldface type.

Indexes

A **Cumulative Author Index** lists all of the authors who have appeared in *CLR* with cross-references to the biographical, autobiographical, and literary criticism series published by the Gale Group. A complete list of these sources is found facing the first page of the Author Index. The index also includes birth and death dates and cross-references between pseudonyms and actual names.

A **Cumulative Nationality Index** lists all authors featured in *CLR* by nationality, followed by the number of the *CLR* volume in which their entry appears.

A **Cumulative Title Index** lists all author titles covered in *CLR*. Each title is followed by the author's name and corresponding volume and page numbers where commentary on the work is located.

Citing *Children's Literature Review*

When citing criticism reprinted in the Literary Criticism Series, students should provide complete bibliographic information so that the cited essay can be located in the original print or electronic source. Students who quote directly from reprinted criticism may use any accepted bibliographic format, such as University of Chicago Press style or Modern Language Association style.

The examples below follow recommendations for preparing a bibliography set forth in *The Chicago Manual of Style,* 14th ed. (Chicago: The University of Chicago Press, 1993); the first example pertains to material drawn from periodicals, the second to material reprinted from books.

Frederick, Heather Vogel. "Cynthia Rylant: A Quiet and Reflective Craft." *Publishers Weekly* 244, no. 29 (21 July 1997): 178-79. Reprinted in *Children's Literature Review.* Vol. 86, edited by Scot Peacock, 124-26. Detroit: Gale, 2003.

Strong, Pauline T. "Playing Indian in the Nineties: *Pocahontas* and *The Indian in the Cupboard." In Hollywood's Indian: The Portrayal of the Native American in Film,* edited by Peter C. Rollins and John E. O'Connor, 73-81. Lexington: The University Press of Kentucky, 1998. Reprinted in *Children's Literature Review.* Vol. 86, edited by Scot Peacock, 124-26. Detroit: Gale, 2003.

The examples below follow recommendations for preparing a works cited list set forth in the *MLA Handbook for Writers of Research Papers,* 5th ed. (New York: The Modern Language Association of America, 1999); the first example pertains to material drawn from periodicals, the second to material reprinted from books.

Frederick, Heather Vogel. "Cynthia Rylant: A Quiet and Reflective Craft." *Publishers Weekly* 244. 29 (21 July 1997): 178-79. Reprinted in *Children's Literature Review.* Ed. Scot Peacock. Vol. 86. Detroit: Gale, 2003. 124-26.

Strong, Pauline T. "Playing Indian in the Nineties: *Pocahontas* and *The Indian in the Cupboard." Hollywood's Indian: The Portrayal of the Native American in Film.* Eds. Peter C. Rollins and John E. O'Connor. Lexington: The University Press of Kentucky, 1998. 73-81. Reprinted in *Children's Literature Review.* Ed. Scot Peacock. Vol. 86. Detroit: Gale, 2003. 124-26.

Suggestions are Welcome

In response to various suggestions, several features have been added to *CLR* since the beginning of the series, including author entries on retellers of traditional literature as well as those who have been the first to record oral tales and other folklore; entries on prominent illustrators featuring commentary on their styles and techniques; entries on authors whose works are considered controversial; occasional entries devoted to criticism on a single work or a series of works; sections in author introductions that list major works by and about the author or illustrator being profiled; explanatory notes that provide information on the critic or work of criticism to enhance the usefulness of the excerpt; more extensive illustrative material, such as holographs of manuscript pages and photographs of people and places pertinent to the careers of the authors and artists; a cumulative nationality index for easy access to authors by nationality; and occasional guest essays written specifically for *CLR* by prominent critics on subjects of their choice.

Readers who wish to suggest new features, topics, or authors to appear in future volumes, or who have other suggestions or comments are cordially invited to call, write, or fax the Managing Editor:

Managing Editor, Literary Criticism Series
The Gale Group
27500 Drake Road
Farmington Hills, MI 48331-3535
1-800-347-4253 (GALE)
Fax: 248-699-8054

Acknowledgments

The editors wish to thank the copyright holders of the excerpted criticism included in this volume and the permissions managers of many book and magazine publishing companies for assisting us in securing reproduction rights. We are also grateful to the staffs of the Detroit Public Library, the Library of Congress, the University of Detroit Mercy Library, Wayne State University Purdy/Kresge Library Complex, and the University of Michigan Libraries for making their resources available to us. Following is a list of the copyright holders who have granted us permission to reproduce material in this volume of *CLR*. Every effort has been made to trace copyright, but if omissions have been made, please let us know.

COPYRIGHTED EXCERPTS IN *CLR*, VOLUME 94, WERE REPRODUCED FROM THE FOLLOWING PERIODICALS:

Book, July-August, 2003. Copyright 2003 West Egg Communications LLC. Reproduced by permission.—***Book Links,*** v. 9, January, 2000; v. 9, March 2000; v. 10, December, 2000-January, 2001; April-May, 2002; v. 12, December, 2002-January, 2003. Copyright 2000, 2002 American Library Association. Reproduced by permission.—***Booklist,*** v. 61, February 15, 1965; v. 70, June 1, 1974; v. 88, February 1, 1992; v. 89, April 1, 1993; v. 91, November 15, 1994; v. 91, March 1, 1995; v. 92, April 1, 1996; v. 93, November 1, 1996; v. 94, September 15, 1997; v. 94, January 1, 1998; v. 94, July, 1998; v. 95, November 1, 1998; April 1, 1999; April 15, 1999; November 1, 1999; January 1, 2000; v. 96, January 1-15, 2000; v. 96, July, 2000; v. 97, September 15, 2000; v. 97, November 15, 2000; v. 97, February 15, 2001; v. 98, July, 2002; v. 98, August, 2002; v. 99, September 1, 2002; v. 99, July, 2003. Copyright © 1965, 1974, 1992, 1993, 1994, 1995, 1996, 1997, 1998, 1999, 2000, 2001, 2002, 2003 by the American Library Association. Reproduced by permission.—***Bulletin of the Center for Children's Books,*** v. 18, January, 1965; v. 23, November, 1969; v. 52, March, 1999; v. 53, May, 2000; v. 53, July-August, 2000; v. 54, September, 2000; v. 54, February, 2001. Copyright 1965, 1969, 1999, 2000, 2001 by The Board of Trustees of the University of Illinois. Reproduced by permission.—***Childhood Education,*** v. 78, Mid-Summer, 2002. Copyright © 2002 by the Association. Reproduced by permission of the Association for Childhood Education International, 17904 Georgia Avenue, Suite 215, Olney, MD.—***Children's Literature,*** v. 25, 1997. Copyright © 1997 by Hollins College. All rights reserved. Reproduced by permission.—***English Journal,*** v. 58, March, 1969. Copyright © 1969 by the National Council of Teachers of English. Reproduced by permission of the publisher and the author.—***The Georgia Review,*** v. 19, Spring, 1965. Copyright © 1965 by the University of Georgia. Reproduced by permission. —***The Hebrew University Studies in Literature,*** v. 9, Spring, 1981. Copyright © 1981 by HSL. Reproduced by permission.—***The Horn Book Guide,*** v. 1, Spring, 1990; v. 4, Spring, 1993; v. 5, Spring, 1994; v. 5, Spring, 1994; v. 8, Spring, 1997; v. 10, Spring, 1999; v. 10, Fall, 1999; v. 11, Spring, 2000; v. 11, Fall, 2000; v. 12, Spring, 2001; v. 12, no. 2, Fall, 2001. Copyright, 1989, 1992, 1993, 1997, 1999, 2000, 2001 by The Horn Book, Inc., 11 Beacon St., Suite 1000, Boston, MA 02108. All rights reserved. Reproduced by permission.—***The Horn Book Magazine,*** v. 41, April, 1965; v. 66, March, 1990; v. 64, May, 1991; v. 68, May, 1992; v. 71, March-April, 1995; v. 72, July-August, 1996; v. 75, September-October, 1999; v. 75, November, 1999; v. 76, May-June, 2000; v. 76, November-December, 2000; v. 77, September-October, 2001; v. 78, July-August, 2002. Copyright, 1965, 1990, 1991, 1992, 1995, 1996, 1999, 2000, 2001, 2002 by The Horn Book, Inc., 11 Beacon St., Suite 1000, Boston, MA 02108. All rights reserved. Reproduced by permission.—***Kirkus Reviews,*** v. 37, July 1, 1969; v. 37, October 1, 1969; v. 39, August 15, 1971; v. 40, July 1, 1972; v. 41, August 15, 1973; v. 42, May 1, 1974; v. 64, September 15, 1986; July 15, 1999; August 1, 1999; December 15, 1999; April 15, 2000; September 1, 2000; January 1, 2001; June 15, 2001; July 1, 2001. Copyright © 1969, 1971, 1972, 1973, 1974, 1986, 1999, 2000, 2001 The Kirkus Service, Inc. All rights reserved. Reproduced by permission of the publisher, Kirkus Reviews, and Kirkus Associates, L.P.—***Language Arts,*** v. 79, September, 2001; v. 79, March, 2002. Copyright 2001, 2002 National Council of Teachers of English Conference on College Composition and Communications. Reproduced by permission of the publisher.—***Library Journal,*** v. 91, March 15, 1966; v. 93, March 15, 1968; v. 94, September 15, 1969; v. 97, October 15, 1972; v. 98, November 15, 1973; v. 99, July, 1974. Copyright © 1966, 1968, 1969, 1972, 1974, by Reed Elsevier, USA. Reproduced by permission.—***The Lion and the Unicorn,*** v. 21, 1997. © 1997 The Johns Hopkins University Press. Reproduced by permission.—***The New York Times Book Review,*** February 23, 1936; October 29, 1939; January 24, 1965; March 24, 1968; November 9, 1969; December 3, 1972. © 1936, renewed 1964; 1936, renewed 1967; 1965, 1968, 1969, 1972. Reproduced by permission.—***Publishers Weekly,*** v. 193, April 1, 1968; v. 196, August 4, 1969; v. 196, September 22, 1969; v. 198, July 27, 1970; v. 202, July 10, 1972; v. 204, July 30, 1973; v. 205, April 29, 1974; v. 214, November 13, 1978; v. 218, October 10, 1980; v. 220, August 7, 1981. Copyright © 1968, 1969, 1970, 1972, 1973, 1974, 1978, 1980, 1981 by Xerox Corporation. Reproduced from ***Publishers Weekly,*** published by R. R. Bowker Company, a Xerox company, by permission./ v. 237, December 14, 1990; v. 237, December 21, 1990; v. 239, June 15, 1992; v. 240, April 19, 1993; v. 240, July 26, 1993; v. 242, January 16, 1995; v.

243, August 26, 1996; v. 243, December 30, 1996; v. 244, September 29, 1997; v. 244, October 6, 1997; May 3, 1999; September 27, 1999; March 13, 2000; June 5, 2000; November 6, 2000; v. 248, January 1, 2001; v. 248, July 30, 2001; v. 248, September 24, 2001; v. 249, April 8, 2002; v. 250, June 30, 2003; v. 250, July 21, 2003. Copyright 1990, 1992, 1993, 1995, 1996, 1997, 1999, 2000, 2001, 2002, 2003 by Reed Publishing USA. Reproduced from ***Publishers Weekly,*** published by the Bowker Magazine Group of Cahners Publishing Co., a division of Reed Publishing USA., by permission.—***The Reading Teacher,*** v. 54, March, 2001. Copyright International Reading Association, 2001. Reproduced with permission of the International Reading Association.—***Scholastic Scope,*** v. 50, April 8-22, 2002. Copyright 2002 Scholastic Inc. Reproduced by permission.—***School Library Journal,*** v. 34, May, 1988; v. 35, October, 1988; v. 36, April, 1990; v. 37, February, 1991; v. 38, April, 1992; v. 38, August, 1992; v. 39, April, 1993; v. 39, September, 1993; v. 41, January, 1995; v. 41, March, 1995; v. 42, September 1996; v. 42, October, 1996; v. 43, October 10, 1997; v. 43, November, 1997; v. 44, April, 1998; v. 44, September, 1998; v. 45, April, 1999; May, 1999; September, 1999; v. 45, December, 1999; March, 2000; May, 2000; July, 2000; September, 2000; v. 46, October, 2000; v. 46, December, 2000; February, 2001; March, 2001; August, 2001; v. 47, October, 2001; v. 48, May, 2002; v. 48, July, 2002. Copyright © 1988, 1990, 1991, 1992, 1993, 1995, 1996, 1997, 1998, 1999, 2000, 2001, 2002. Reproduced from ***School Library Journal,*** a Cahners/R. R. Bowker Publication. Reproduced by permission.—***Sewanee Review,*** v. 57, 1949. Copyright © 1949, renewed 1986 by The University of the South. Reproduced with permission of the editor.—***Studies in the Novel,*** v. 24, Spring, 1992. Copyright 1992 by North Texas State University. Reproduced by permission.—***Texas Studies in Literature and Language: A Journal of the Humanities,*** v. 7, Winter, 1966 for "Mute Choirboys and Angelic Pigs: The Fable in Lord of the Flies" by J.D. O'Hara. Copyright © 1966 by the University of Texas Press. Reproduced by permission of the publisher and the author.—***The Times Literary Supplement,*** n. 3501, April 3, 1969; n. 3536, December 4, 1969; n. 3734, September 28, 1973. Copyright The Times Supplements Limited, 1969, 1973. Reproduced from ***The Times Literary Supplement*** by permission.—***The Virginia Kirkus Service,*** v. 34, February 15, 1966 for a review of "What Color is Love" in The Virginia Kirkus Service. Copyright © 1966 Virginia Kirkus Service, Inc. Reproduced by permission of the publisher, The Virginia Kirkus Service and Kirkus Associates, L.P.

COPYRIGHTED EXCERPTS IN *CLR,* VOLUME 94, WERE REPRODUCED FROM THE FOLLOWING BOOKS:

Boyd, S. J. From ***The Novels of William Golding.*** St. Martin's Press, 1988. Copyright © 1988 S. J. Boyd. All rights reserved. Reprinted by permission of St. Martin's Press, LLC. —Cox, C. B. From "On 'Lord of the Flies'," in ***William Golding: Novels, 1954-67.*** Edited by Norman Page. Macmillan, 1985. Copyright © Norman Page 1985. All rights reserved. Reproduced by permission.—Crawford, Paul. From ***Politics and History in William Golding: The World Turned Upside Down.*** University of Missouri Press, 2002. Copyright © 2002 by The Curators of the University of Missouri. All rights reserved. Reproduced by permission.—Dick, Bernard F. From ***William Golding.*** Revised edition. Twayne Publishers, 1987. Copyright © 1987 by G. K. Hall & Co. All rights reserved. Reproduced by permission of The Gale Group.—Dickson, L. L. From ***The Modern Allegories of William Golding.*** University of South Florida Press, 1990. Copyright © 1990 by the Board of Regents of the State of Florida. Reproduced by permission of the University Press of Florida.—Friedman, Lawrence S. From ***William Golding.*** Frederick Ungar, 1993. Copyright © 1993 by Lawrence S. Friedman. All rights reserved. Reproduced by permission.—Hynes, Samuel. From ***William Golding: Columbia Essays on Modern Writers.*** Columbia University Press, 1968. Reproduced by permission of Columbia University Press.—Hodson, Leighton. From ***William Golding.*** Oliver and Boyd, 1969. Copyright © 1969 by Leighton Hodson. Reproduced by permission of the author. —Johnston, Arnold. From ***Of Earth and Darkness: The Novels of William Golding.*** University of Missouri Press, 1980. Copyright © 1980 by The Curators of the University of Missouri. All rights reserved. Reproduced by permission.—Marsden, Madonna. From "Gentle Truths for Gentle Readers: The Fiction of Elizabeth Goudge," in ***Images of Women in Fiction: Feminist Perspectives.*** Edited by Susan Koppelman Cornillon. Bowling Green University Popular Press, 1972. Copyright © 1972 by the Bowling Green University Popular Press. Reproduced by permission of the Literary Estate of Madonna Marsden.—McDonald, Megan. "Biography: Seeing the Inside," February 27, 2002, www.meganmcdonald.net August 9, 2003. Reproduced by permission of the author.—McDonald, Megan. "An interview with Megan McDonald," February 27, 2002, www.meganmcdonald.net/about.htm, August 9, 2003. Reproduced by permission of the author.—Oldsey, Bernard S. and Stanley Weintraub. From ***The Art of William Golding.*** Harcourt, Brace & World, Inc., 1965. Copyright © 1965 by Bernard S. Oldsey and Stanley Weintraub. Reproduced by permission of Coward McCann, a division of Penguin Putnam Inc.—Olsen, Kirstin. From ***Understanding Lord of the Flies: A Student Casebook to Issues, Sources, and Historical Documents.*** Greenwood Press, 2000. Copyright © 2000 by Kirstin Olsen. All rights reserved. Reproduced by permission of Greenwood Publishing Group, Inc., Westport, CT.—Tiger, Virginia. From ***William Golding: The Dark Fields of Discovery.*** Calder & Boyars, 1974. Copyright © Virginia Tiger 1974. All rights reserved. Reproduced by permission.—Vandergrift, Kay. "Learning About Janet S. Wong," April 16, 1997, www.scils.rutgers.edu, August 9, 2003. Reproduced by permission of the author.—Wong, Janet. "Poems & Stories," 1999, www.janetwong.com. August 9, 2003. Copyright © 1999 Janet S. Wong. All rights reserved. Reproduced by permission.

PHOTOGRAPHS AND ILLUSTRATIONS APPEARING IN *CLR*, VOLUME 94, WERE RECEIVED FROM THE FOLLOWING SOURCES:

Anglund, Joan Walsh, illustrator. From an illustration in ***Love Is a Special Way of Feeling*** by Joan Walsh Anglund. Harcourt, 1960. Copyright © 1960, renewed 1988 by Joan Walsh Anglund. Reproduced by permission of Harcourt, Inc.—Golding, William, photograph. AP/Wide World Photos. Reproduced by permission.—Goudge, Elizabeth, photograph. AP/Wide World Photos. Reproduced by permission.— McDonald, Megan, photograph by Michele McDonald. Reproduced by permission.

Gale Literature Product Advisory Board

The members of the Gale Group Literature Product Advisory Board—reference librarians from public and academic library systems—represent a cross-section of our customer base and offer a variety of informed perspectives on both the presentation and content of our literature products. Advisory board members assess and define such quality issues as the relevance, currency, and usefulness of the author coverage, critical content, and literary topics included in our series; evaluate the layout, presentation, and general quality of our printed volumes; provide feedback on the criteria used for selecting authors and topics covered in our series; provide suggestions for potential enhancements to our series; identify any gaps in our coverage of authors or literary topics, recommending authors or topics for inclusion; analyze the appropriateness of our content and presentation for various user audiences, such as high school students, undergraduates, graduate students, librarians, and educators; and offer feedback on any proposed changes/enhancements to our series. We wish to thank the following advisors for their advice throughout the year.

Joan Walsh Anglund
1926-

American children's writer and illustrator.

INTRODUCTION

Anglund became popular in the 1960s for her unique style of illustrations featuring round-faced children without mouths or noses. Many readers have equated Anglund's cherubic figures with the virtues of innocence and chastity, with some commenting that Anglund's artwork inspires unexpected feelings of nostalgia and emotionalism. Anglund has written more than ninety children's books—including picture books, children's poetry, lullabies, religious verses and prayers—as well as composing her own adult poetry and providing illustrations for contemporary authors. Her books have been translated into several languages, published in over fourteen countries, and have sold more than forty million copies worldwide.

BIOGRAPHICAL INFORMATION

Anglund was born on January 3, 1926, in Hinsdale, Illinois, the daughter of Thomas F. Anglund, a commercial artist, and Mildred Pfiefer Walsh, a painter. In 1944 she attended the Chicago Art Institute, later transferring to the American Academy of Art in 1945. While studying in Chicago, she became an apprentice commercial artist under the tutelage of Adele Roth. She met Robert Anglund and the couple was married in 1947. Anglund's literary career began after she was inspired to write by a group of neighborhood children playing near her home. While watching the children, she wrote the text for *A Friend Is Someone Who Likes You* (1958). Many of her illustrations are based on people and places from her own life—particularly her two children, Joy and Todd. As the popularity of her children's works continued to grow, Anglund's artwork began appearing on a wide range of consumer merchandise, including dolls, plates, greeting cards, notebooks, ceramics, calendars, prints, and Christmas ornaments. Beginning in 1979, Anglund started writing and illustrating a special quarterly segment for *Good Housekeeping* magazine and her artwork has since been featured in *Ladies Home Journal, Woman's Day* and *Family Circle.*

MAJOR WORKS

Anglund's picture books, which typically present tales promoting Christian values or retellings of classic fables, have attracted a large popular audience. *A Friend Is Someone Who Likes You* and *Do You Love Someone?* (1971) both focus on convincing children that love, friendship, and loyalty are essential to a young person's happiness. Anglund wrote *A Child's Book of Old Nursery Rhymes* (1973) for her grandchild, collecting a variety of traditional nursery songs and rhymes and accompanying them with her own distinct illustrations. A similar work, *The Joan Walsh Anglund Story Book* (1978) presents selections of folktales, poems, and lullabies, targeted towards a preschool audience. *A Gift of Love* (1980), one of Anglund's best-selling works, is an anthology collection, including reprints of *A Friend Is Someone Who Likes You, Love Is a Special Way of Feeling* (1960), *Christmas Is a Time of Giving* (1961), *What Color Is Love?* (1966) and *Do You Love Someone?* These five works all examine Anglund's recurring fascination with love, innocence, and the emotional development of children, while presenting some of Anglund's most popular illustrations from her career thus far.

Anglund is also an accomplished children's poet and *The Joan Walsh Anglund Book of Poetry* (1987) presents thirty-six of the author's original poems. The poems offer lyrical reflections on images and emotions from a child's perspective, discussing animals, special places, and seasons of the year. In 1996 Anglund published an additional collection, *Poems of Childhood,* which features a twenty-six poem cycle, following a group of children as they play throughout the year. Anglund has also released several popular seasonal children's works, including *Christmas Is Love* (1988) in which her famously mouthless children are depicted against holiday settings. In *A Christmas Sampler: A New Collection of Holiday Treasures* (2001) Anglund includes examinations of traditional carols, customs, and historical festivals, a selection of original poems, and a recipe for gingerbread cookies.

CRITICAL RECEPTION

Anglund has developed a devoted following among readers and her books have become a popular choice as a gift for children, particularly during the holidays. Many commentators have lauded Anglund's evocative and engaging illustrative style, noting her skill at inspiring warm emotional responses through her renderings of childhood innocence. In the *Publishers Weekly* review of *The Joan Walsh Anglund Story Book,* the critic commented that the collection "boasts the singularly effective paintings, in lovely shades, that make Anglund instantly recognizable and popular." However, most critics and scholars have reacted negatively towards Anglund's writing ability, faulting the author for being overly sentimental, predictable, and condescending. Though such reviewers acknowledge Anglund's commercial appeal, they have argued that her works should not be included in library collections, deeming them more worthy of mass-market bookstores and gift shops.

AWARDS

A Friend Is Someone Who Likes You was selected as one of ten best illustrated books of 1958 by the *New York Times.*

PRINCIPAL WORKS

A Friend Is Someone Who Likes You (picture book) 1958
The Brave Cowboy (picture book) 1959
Look Out the Window (children's book) 1959
Love Is a Special Way of Feeling (picture book) 1960
Christmas Is a Time of Giving (picture book) 1961
Cowboy and His Friend (picture book) 1961
Cowboy's Secret Life (picture book) 1963
Spring Is a New Beginning (children's book) 1963
Childhood Is a Time of Innocence (children's book) 1964
What Color Is Love? (picture book) 1966
A Is for Always (picture book) 1968
Morning Is a Little Child (picture book) 1969
A Slice of Snow (adult poetry) 1970
Do You Love Someone? (picture book) 1971
The Cowboy's Christmas (picture book) 1972
A Child's Book of Old Nursery Rhymes (picture book) 1973
The Joan Walsh Anglund Storybook (picture book) 1978
Almost a Rainbow: A Book of Poems (children's poetry) 1980
**A Gift of Love* (picture book) 1980
Rainbow Love (children's book) 1982
A Christmas Book (children's book) 1983
Christmas Candy Book (children's book) 1983
The Circle of the Spirit (children's book) 1983
The Joan Walsh Anglund Coloring Book (coloring book) 1984
The Joan Walsh Anglund Book of Poetry (children's poetry) 1987
Christmas Is Love (children's poetry) 1988
A Little Book of Poems and Prayers (children's poetry and prayers) 1989
A Child's Year (picture book) 1992
Love Is a Baby (children's poetry) 1992
A Bedtime Book (children's book) 1993
Peace is a Circle of Love (children's poetry) 1993
Joan Walsh Anglund's Mother Goose Pop-Up Book (picture book) 1995
Little Angels' Alphabet of Love (picture book) 1996
Poems of Childhood (picture book) 1996
Sweet Dreams: Three Sleepytime Books of Poems, Prayers, and Lullabies (picture book) 1996
Little Angels' Book of Christmas (picture book) 1997
In All Thy Ways—A Book of Bible Verses (religious verses) 1999
A Christmas Sampler: A New Collection of Holiday Treasures (anthology) 2001

*Includes *A Friend Is Someone Who Likes You, Love Is a Special Way of Feeling, Christmas Is a Time of Giving, What Color Is Love* and *Do You Love Someone?*

TITLE COMMENTARY

THE BRAVE COWBOY (1959)

***Publishers Weekly* (review date 6 November 2000)**

SOURCE: "Children's Notes." *Publishers Weekly* 247, no. 45 (6 November 2000): 93.

First published in 1959, Joan Walsh Anglund's ***The Brave Cowboy*** looks as spiffy as ever. Her pen-and-ink drawings inventively utilize the color red to fill out the boy's imagination. For his "ride across the prairie," the boy—suited up in boots, holster, bandanna and cowboy hat—sits backward on a high stool, while Anglund fills in the outline of a horse in red; a "fair maiden in distress" is the boy's cat, stranded on a tree limb (again red lines overlay the image of a girl in curls and bonnet). (*ages 4-8*)

Horn Book Guide (review date fall 2001)

SOURCE: *Horn Book Guide* 12, no. 2 (fall 2001): 246.

A little boy in cowboy gear pretends he is rounding up rustlers and roping steers [***The Brave Cowboy***]. The boy and his real world are drawn in detailed black line, while the imaginary bank robbers, horses, and covered wagons are drawn in red. Despite the over-sweetness of Anglund's drawings and the somewhat condescending tone, the book still manages to have child appeal.

🕮 *WHAT COLOR IS LOVE?* (1966)

***Kirkus Reviews* (review date 15 February 1966)**

SOURCE: *Kirkus Reviews* 34, no. 4 (15 February 1966): 177.

As in the previous Anglund books, ***A Friend Is Someone Who Likes You, Childhood Is a Time of Innocence, Love Is a Special Way of Feeling,*** the title [***What Color is Love?***] identifies a thoughty thought not to be faulted by any right thinker. The illustrations are of the thoroughly familiar Anglund children, a style that might be called post-Hummel marzipan. Some are drawn in color and some are in black and white and all the children are posed against a text that runs to—"In a garden all the flowers are different colors, but they live happily together . . . side by side." The skin tones employed are not distinct. There is one child shown who might be Chinese or just suffering a touch of jaundice. Two more are rather dark but considerably lighter than the average Sicilian. The total effect brings to mind the book review attributed to Abraham Lincoln: "People who like this sort of thing will find this the sort of thing they like." The market is as assured as it is for red velvet valentines bearing the word "Mother" in gold.

Patricia H. Allen and E. Louise Davis (review date 15 March 1966)

SOURCE: Allen, Patricia H., and E. Louise Davis. *Library Journal* 91, no. 6 (15 March 1966): 1687.

PreS-K Pointing out that "an apple is red," "the sun is yellow," etc., Mrs. Anglund goes on to say [in ***What Color Is Love?***] that "in a garden all the flowers are different colors, but they live happily together side by side." After similar sentiments about the animals and the birds living happily together, she says, "In our world all the people are different colors, and, sometimes, they live happily together side by side" and "Color is something we see with our eyes, but love is something we see with our heart." She ends the book with "And, if I asked you, could you tell me what color is love?" In this little book with illustrations in her usual style, the message is obvious to the adult, but is it really needed for little children, most of whom have not yet learned about prejudice? Purchase where the other Anglund books are popular.

🕮 *A IS FOR ALWAYS* (1968)

Della Thomas (review date 15 March 1968)

SOURCE: Thomas, Della. *Library Journal* 93, no. 6 (15 March 1968): 1301.

Gr 1-3—Miniature in format (slightly more than 3" × 4"), enclosed in a slipcase, and decorated with demure, apple-cheeked moppets, this ABC [***A Is for Always***] is obviously a gift item rather than a library book. "A-Always; B-Be; C-Courteous," constitute the first three pages, after which the book proceeds through 23 other positive traits from "determined" to "zestful." Each page contains, in addition to the characteristic word, a large, ornamental initial letter, in or on which one or more wide-eyed children—in sailor suits, aprons, mob caps, and other quaint attire—climb, recline, perch, and, generally, entwine themselves. A typical Anglund product, the book will, no doubt, be requested by her considerable following. Libraries may wish to stock it in spite of shelving problems and standards for alphabet books.

George A. Woods (review date 24 March 1968)

SOURCE: Woods, George A. *New York Times Book Review* (24 March 1968): 38.

For Ages 3 to 6. A is for Anglund, Joan Walsh, who has a new book, ***A Is for Always.*** B is for best-selling; her ***Love Is a Special Way of Feeling*** and ***A Friend Is Someone Who Likes You*** have had a combined sales of over a million and a half copies. C is for children, the very young, for whom her books are intended although there is some dispute about this. The charm, the idealism and precise delicacy of many of her books catch the older eye and heart, it is said, in-

An illustration from Love Is a Special Way of Feeling *(1960).*

stead of being serviceable and entertaining to the child. ***A Is for Always,*** a small alphabet book, won't resolve the argument. It has the same, familiar Anglund-style moppets twined, draped, nestled on letters of the alphabet. The one word text for each page represents abstract virtues—"obedient," "patient," "quick," etc. No adult would turn those things down.

Publishers Weekly **(review date 1 April 1968)**

SOURCE: *Publishers Weekly* 193, no. 14 (1 April 1968): 39.

(3-7) Rev up your cash registers! Here's a new Anglund [***A Is for Always***]! There's nothing new to say about an Anglund. And there's no need to say *anything* to confirmed Anglund-philes; the news there's a new Anglund will bring them running. (A fringe benefit: keep this one within your reach. If your grown-up party starts to go flat, you can revive it by asking what qualities your guests would choose to match the alphabet. Would they go along with Mrs. Anglund's choice of Virtue, portrayed as a bride, for V? Or would they choose Vice? A black-humor Anglund alphabet would be a pretty funny thing to contemplate—and a highly improbable one.)

MORNING IS A LITTLE CHILD (1969)

Kirkus Reviews **(review date 1 July 1969)**

SOURCE: *Kirkus Reviews* 37, no. 13 (1 July 1969): 669.

Once more with *feeling*. The author's [***Morning Is a Little Child***] puffed-cheek, pastel pretties in a selection of verses, many concerned with times of the day and year, and just an many with currant buns and ladybugs and best friends.

Publishers Weekly **(review date 4 August 1969)**

SOURCE: *Publishers Weekly* 196, no. 5 (4 August 1969): 49.

(4-up) Good news for Anglund buffs; she has a new book [***Morning Is a Little Child***] for them. A book of verses, illustrated with the unique Anglund illustrations of small, clean boys and girls, of small clean pink and blue landscapes.

Sada Fretz (review date 15 September 1969)

SOURCE: Fretz, Sada. *Library Journal* 94, no. 16 (15 September 1969): 3194.

PreS-Gr 1—Mrs. Anglund's latest product [***Morning Is a Little Child***] differs from her previous, similarly entitled works in size (at 7½" × 9¾", it is larger than its pocket-sized predecessors) and form (brief, simple rhymes replace brief, simple prose). But the saccharine text and cloying pictures (the same featureless moppets, gnarled trees and quaint details) are all too familiar. The rhymes—about such basic subjects as the seasons, times of day, and tiny animals—attempt to recreate the simple, wondering tones of childhood. Instead, the concepts are trite, the phrasing artificially old-fashioned, and the pat final lines dismally anticlimactic: "I stay within my garden small, / I do not wander past my wall, / but sometimes, when the moon is late, / I wonder what's beyond my gate." Grandmothers and aunties who found the author's previous works just adorable, will lap up this one too; but children should be spared its boredom potential.

Ramona Weeks (review date 9 November 1969)

SOURCE: Weeks, Ramona. "Focus on Seasons, Sounds and Rites of Passage." *New York Times Book Review* (9 November 1969): 46.

Morning Is a Little Child is ripe with spondees, trochees and rocking lambs. In this vita-candy world the prevailing mood is optimism, unflagging and anthropomorphic "Morning glories climb my wall / with small green hands / and never fall." Mrs. Anglund is more successful when she is being whimsical; here her nosegays of old-fashioned children, their menageries and pull toys, are stifled by a message: "The duty of children is fun!" The book is certain to be popular, but I'd like to register my preference for Anglund books in the squeeze-box format.

A SLICE OF SNOW (1970)

Publishers Weekly **(review date 27 July 1970)**

SOURCE: *Publishers Weekly* 198, no. 4 (27 July 1970): 73.

This is the second book of poems for adults [***A Slice of Snow: A Book of Poems***] by the beloved author-illustrator of a host of children's books. The first was ***A Cup of Snow*** (1967). Extended comment on this author's fragile charm would be irrelevant. Poems are memorable or they are more or less than poems. An austerely simple statement like Mrs. Anglund's "For every murder I allow, I am the victim," is memorable on the mature level because it is not diminished by a thought too much, nor a syllable. The same is true of "It is when we earn love least that we need it most." Notably the simplicity of the book's design benefits from the restrained use, in perfect miniatures, of the author's decorative line drawings.

DO YOU LOVE SOMEONE? (1971)

Kirkus Reviews (review date 15 August 1971)

SOURCE: *Kirkus Reviews* 39, no. 16 (15 August 1971): 869.

Elementary psychology for the easily assured [in ***Do You Love Someone?***], complacently stating that everyone needs to feel special and the best way to be important is to be loved. But the pictures belie any such avowal of individual worth; the children therein are the same faceless, interchangeable gumdrops Mrs. Anglund has catered for years. *3-5*

THE COWBOY'S CHRISTMAS (1972)

Kirkus Reviews (review date 1 July 1972)

SOURCE: *Kirkus Reviews* 40, no. 13 (1 July 1972): 719.

If you've seen the other ***Cowboy*** books the title alone [***The Cowboy's Christmas***] should tell you all you need to know about this one: how the cowboy is especially good throughout December, how on Christmas eve he goes to bed "to dream a Very Special Dream," and how the next morning he awakens to presents and "a Very Merry Christmas"—accompanied throughout all the coyly capitalized activities by his imaginary friend Bear, drawn in red beside the black reality. Isn't it time we stopped stuffing Mrs. Anglund's stocking? *4-5*

Publishers Weekly (review date 10 July 1972)

SOURCE: *Publishers Weekly* 202, no. 2 (10 July 1972): 46.

(3-7) In the "brave cowboy's" latest adventures [***The Cowboy's Christmas***], he and his pretend friend (the huge bear) are preparing for Christmas. Although they are very busy—making presents and decorations, wrapping things, writing lists, wishing for special gifts—they are never cross or disobedient from the first of December throughout the next 25 days. Mrs. Anglund has drawn the boy in black-and-white and his make-believe bear in red, as in her previous books in this series. An appropriate gift for the preschooler.

Alice Miller Bregman (review date 15 October 1972)

SOURCE: Bregman, Alice Miller. "Cashing in on Christmas: Christmas Books for 1972." *Library Journal* 97, no. 18 (15 October 1972): 3467-470.

Christmas comes earlier and earlier every year. The department stores can hardly wait for the day after Thanksgiving to put up their Christmas decorations, and for children's book publishers, Christmas now begins in August. This year's offerings are as torpid and enervating as a long day on a sunny August beach.

One cooling thought is that fewer publishers are cashing in on Christmas this year—there are only 14 titles, but with only a few exceptions they are as mediocre as most of last year's 22. Maybe someone overheard the three-year-old who, while sitting through a boring Christmas sermon, removed the toy watch she'd found in her stocking that morning, threw it three pews in front of her and said in a carrying voice, "Mommy, mommy! Baby Jesus stole my watch!" (For that expression of boredom, read, "Mommy, mommy! Someone's stolen the fun from Christmas!")

Only three titles this year offer any sensitivity to Christmas spirit. The rest are tedious, commercially produced and promoted pieces of merchandise.

The worst example this year is Joan Walsh Anglund's ***The Christmas Cowboy.*** Stressing the spirit of hypocrisy—"But not matter how Busy he was, the cowboy was never cross . . . he was never fretful. Somehow, the cowboy was Especially Polite. . . . Somehow, the cowboy always seemed to be helpful lately"—Cowboy is busy the whole month of December doing good things so that he'll get lots of presents on the 25th. His imaginary friend, Bear, pictured in red throughout, imitates everything cowboy does. This dainty piece of preciousness leads up to cowboy making sure to send "a Very Merry Christmas" message to all while Bear holds up "Merry Christmas" signs in several languages. In this bit of marshmallow fluff, as usual, none of Anglund's pictured children have complete facial characteristics (no noses or mouths) while all the animals do. Perhaps this means that children should be seen and not heard; at any rate, this Anglund offering should not be seen at all. PreS-Grl.

Sidney Long (review date 3 December 1972)

SOURCE: Long, Sidney. ". . . And a Partridge in a Pear Tree." *New York Times Book Review* (3 December 1972): 8.

Another book which seems to slide right out of the nineteen-fifties and into this Christmas season is ***The Cowboy's Christmas*** (Ages 3 to 7) by Joan Walsh Anglund. Mrs. Anglund's style doesn't vary much. The text says things like, "Once there was a cowboy . . . who was Especially Busy" and there is a line drawing of a little boy dressed in a cowboy outfit hanging a Christmas calendar with the help of his imaginary friend, Bear. You can tell that Bear is imaginary because he is outlined in red. There are some mice outlined in red, also. Though there is not much excitement in watching the brave cowboy and Bear complete their Christmas preparation, the small size and sweet sentiment of the book may mean that it will be stuffed into a lot of Christmas stockings.

***Times Literary Supplement* (review date 28 September 1973)**

SOURCE: *Times Literary Supplement* no. 3734 (28 September 1973): 1126.

Joan Walsh Anglund is a liberal and enthusiastic purveyor of Simple Sentiment, and her cute drawings of kids with no mouths or noses may not be every parent's (or child's) cup of tea, but this story [***The Cowboy's Christmas***] about a small cowboy's preparations for Christmas is given interest and novelty by the activities of his imaginary helpers, a large amiable bear and a band of mice, drawn in red to distinguish them from the black-and-white lines of the real world.

A CHILD'S BOOK OF OLD NURSERY RHYMES (1973)

***Publishers Weekly* (review date 30 July 1973)**

SOURCE: *Publishers Weekly* 204, no. 5 (30 July 1973): 68.

(2-up) The child who inspired ***A Friend Is Someone Who Likes You*** and set in motion the phenomenal career of her mother is now a mother herself, and grandmother Ms. Anglund has created this tiny book [***A Child's Book of Old Nursery Rhymes***] for her tiny grandchild. As in all the artist's other books, the representations of children, animals, flowers, trees and other features are uniquely Joan Walsh Anglund—enough said. Few books are as popular as hers and her new one is bound to be a best seller.

***Kirkus Reviews* (review date 15 August 1973)**

SOURCE: *Kirkus Reviews* 41, no. 16 (15 August 1973): 879.

Miss Muffett, Jack Horner, Boy Blue and twenty-three others [in ***A Child's Book of Old Nursery Rhymes***], made uniformly vacant and featureless in the familiar Anglund manner. *2-3*

***Margaret Maxwell* (review date 15 November 1973)**

SOURCE: Maxwell, Margaret. *Library Journal* 98, no. 20 (15 November 1973): 3437.

PreS-Gr 1—Twenty-six nursery rhymes [***A Child's Book of Old Nursery Rhymes***] are illustrated in the all-too-quaint, all-too-gentle, all-too-familiar Anglund style. Alert children will wonder how mouthless Miss Muffet can ingest the curds and whey she purports to be eating. Alert librarians will pass this characterless miniature book up in favor of any one of the multitude of attractive editions of Mother Goose available

THE CHRISTMAS COOKIE BOOK (1977)

***Publishers Weekly* (review date 7 August 1981)**

SOURCE: *Publishers Weekly* 220, no. 6 (7 August 1981): 78.

Determined Productions is offering the second edition of ***The Christmas Cookie Book,*** a miniature volume by Joan Walsh Anglund. Like ***A Friend Is Someone Who Likes You*** and all of Anglund's books, this book has been a longtime bestseller and is sure to appeal to customers looking for Christmas stocking stuffers. Its toothsome recipes are accompanied by quaint paintings, in color, of typical Anglund tots. for all ages.

THE JOAN WALSH ANGLUND STORY BOOK (1978)

***Publishers Weekly* (review date 13 November 1978)**

SOURCE: *Publishers Weekly* 214, no. 20 (13 November 1978): 63.

A baker's dozen of simple tales, poems and a lullabye make up the latest offering by Anglund [***The Joan Walsh Anglund Story Book***], whose books have been international best sellers since 1958. The first story tells of "A True Teddy-Bear," so dear to his little boy owner that it is worn out by hugs and kisses. The boy's mother keeps mending the toy until it becomes a droll figure of spare parts. In "The Big Brown Bag," Emily covers her head with the bag on a day when everything goes wrong and she throws tantrums. She stays hidden behind her mean mask until a dear friend soothes her hurt feelings. Each of the pieces in the book boasts the singularly effective paintings, in lovely shades, that make Anglund instantly recognizable and popular. That small price tag is an added attraction. (2-6)

A GIFT OF LOVE (1980)

Publishers Weekly (review date 10 October 1980)

SOURCE: *Publishers Weekly* 218, no. 15 (10 October 1980): 74.

Harcourt Brace Jovanovich is issuing a boxed set entitled ***A Gift of Love,*** five little books written and illustrated by Joan Walsh Anglund. These are reprints of her first and succeeding works that have been selling phenomenally for over 20 years, favorites of children and college students especially, and the package should attract shoppers during the coming holidays. Included are ***A Friend Is Someone Who Likes You, Do You Love Someone? What Color Is Love? Love Is a Special Way of Feeling*** and ***Christmas Is a Time of Giving***; (all ages).

THE JOAN WALSH ANGLUND BOOK OF POETRY (1987)

Kathleen Whalin (review date May 1988)

SOURCE: Whalin, Kathleen. *School Library Journal* 34, no. 9 (May 1988): 90-1.

PreS-Gr 1—These 36 original poems [in ***The Joan Walsh Anglund Book of Poetry***] are sweet and bland and are accompanied by Anglund's trademarked sweet watercolors of children in old-fashioned clothes. Subjects in the volume such as "bears," "a little place that I know," and "spring" have been written about with more originality by many other authors. Anglund's verses offer didactic homilies but not insight ("The birds, / they do not sing to *me,* / They sing to life! / But I may *listen!*" or "Gentle Sister, Little Brother, / do not quarrel / . . . for time is brief"). A poem is something clear and unique—skip this book.

CHRISTMAS IS LOVE (1988)

Susan Hepler (essay date October 1988)

SOURCE: Hepler, Susan. "December Holiday Book Roundup." *School Library Journal* 35, no. 2 (October 1988): 32.

Gr 1 Up—Anglund's sweet little mouthless children clothed in old-fashioned garb dance and pose in various spotlessly perfect holiday settings [In ***Christmas Is Love***]. Six rhymed couplets tell what "Christmas is": snow so white, candles bright, sugar plums tart, joy in every heart, etc. Leave this one to the purveyors of gift books.

A LITTLE BOOK OF POEMS AND PRAYERS (1989)

Horn Book Guide (review date spring 1990)

SOURCE: *Horn Book Guide* 1, no. 1 (spring 1990): 128.

K-3 Prayers and verses [***A Little Book of Poems and Prayers***] selected from a wide range of sources and cultures, most of which are more nostalgic than childlike. It is unfortunate that Anglund's "angelic" children reflect only one culture, particularly noticeable when reading the native American prayers.

A CHILD'S YEAR (1992)

Publishers Weekly (review date 15 June 1992)

SOURCE: *Publishers Weekly* 239, no. 27 (15 June 1992): 101.

The publication of . . . Little Golden Books [***A Child's Year***], released to commemorate the imprint's 50th anniversary, is indeed cause for celebration. The work of this impressive roundup of gifted authors and illustrators appears in the line's familiar format, featuring sturdy covers, a patterned foil spine and a low cover price. Each title's writing and illustrations are representative of its well-known creator's style . . . these worthy additions [are] bound to become staples of Little Golden Books's backlist. Ages 2-5.

LOVE IS A BABY (1992)

Suzanne Sigman (review date spring 1993)

SOURCE: Sigman, Suzanne. *Horn Book Guide* 4, no. 1 (spring 1993): 132.

K-3 A short inspirational book [***Love Is a Baby***] of adult interest about how precious babies are. The watercolors are sickeningly cute and depict babies without mouths.

A BEDTIME BOOK (1993)

***Publishers Weekly* (review date 26 July 1993)**

SOURCE: *Publishers Weekly* 240, no. 30 (26 July 1993): 70.

Though this collection of nine brief story-poems [***A Bedtime Book***] may find an appreciative audience among Anglund's fans, most of the entries are curiously aimless. The sole exception—and the only tale told in rhyming verse—is **"My Dragon,"** the sprightly account of a boy's friendship with a flying dragon. The bulk of the remaining pieces, all featuring Anglund's familiar, round- and empty-faced children, are facile and flat. It's difficult to imagine, for example, that any child will find comfort at bedtime from **"A Rainbow Story,"** which tells of a rainbow that no one noticed: "So, after a little while, the little rainbow got discouraged, and sadly folded away all its bright colors, and faded back up into the sky where no one could ever find it. Poor little rainbow. Poor silly people!" Ages 3-6.

Elizabeth Hanson (review date September 1993)

SOURCE: Hanson, Elizabeth. *School Library Journal* 39, no. 9 (September 1993): 204.

PreS-Gr 2—A collection of poetry and stories [***A Bedtime Book***] done in Anglund's typical, overly precious style. The title is misleading; the contents do not relate to bedtime per se. Instead, they include poems about a dragon and an apple, and selections on friendship that teeter between poetry and prose. The illustrations depict mouthless, white children rendered in pastel watercolors. The illustrator's characteristic sweetness comes out again in this book that is best suited for supermarkets and greeting-card stores.

***Horn Book Guide* (review date spring 1994)**

SOURCE: *Horn Book Guide* 5, no. 1 (spring 1994): 63.

A small collection of brief, comforting stories and poems [***A Bedtime Book***] focuses on such child-centered themes as little sisters, princesses, dragons, animals, and nature. Uninspired, but with appeal at bedtime or any quiet moment. Illustrations in pen-and-ink and soft watercolors match the tranquil mood.

PEACE IS A CIRCLE OF LOVE (1993)

***Horn Book Guide* (review date spring 1994)**

SOURCE: *Horn Book Guide* 5, no. 1 (spring 1994): 152.

K-3. Peace [in ***Peace Is a Circle of Love***] is described as "a bird that sings in the heart," a flower with love as its seed, and "a rainbow that encircles the world." These and other definitions are illustrated with children who trust, love, and forgive one another and work together to plan a better world. Anglund's precious style makes this a book about children, rather than for them. Differences in clothing indicate people from various parts of the world.

POEMS OF CHILDHOOD (1996)

***Kirkus Reviews* (review date 15 September 1996)**

SOURCE: *Kirkus Reviews* 64, no. 18 (15 September 1996): 1396.

Greeting card verses and plenty of pastels make this volume [***Poems of Childhood***] by Anglund not much different from her previous books. Simple rhymes sentimentalize seasonal activities: playing in the leaves and sledding. Others describe childhood events: the wind stealing a kite, a child's anger over a broken toy, and a birthday party. In several places the clichés wear thin. One verse about friends in "far-off places" portrays a line of children in costumes more typical of 1950s notions of a global village than the current trend toward authenticity. Another poem, about going to bed in summertime, does not improve on Robert Lewis Stevenson. The illustrations, too, show little change (other than the addition of an occasional brown face amid the rosy cheeks), with few realistic portrayals of children. The book is strictly for collectors: Most readers need something more than two dots for eyes, for true human expression includes smiles and frowns—or at least noses and mouths. *(3-7)*

Horn Book Guide (review date spring 1997)

SOURCE: *Horn Book Guide* 8, no. 1 (spring 1997): 151.

K-3 These twenty-six vapid poems [***Poems of Childhood***] with predictable rhythms and rhymes present an overly sweet view of children playing throughout the year and offer no new or fresh insights into childhood. Anglund's illustrations show her signature featureless children.

LITTLE ANGELS' ALPHABET OF LOVE (1996)

Publishers Weekly (review date 30 December 1996)

SOURCE: *Publishers Weekly* 243, no. 52 (30 December 1996): 68.

Joan Walsh Anglund's ***Little Angels' Alphabet of Love*** recites the ABCs from "Always" to "Zest," and comes with a small pink envelope for mailing. The illustrations feature Anglund's trademark children, with wide-set dot eyes and no mouths, wearing no more than a pair of wings and an occasional discreet swath of ribbon. (all ages)

IN ALL THY WAYS: A BOOK OF BIBLE VERSES (1999)

Publishers Weekly (review date 27 September 1999)

SOURCE: "Children's Religion Notes." *Publishers Weekly* 246, no. 39 (27 September 1999): 98.

Also in a small format, Joan Walsh Anglund's ***In All Thy Ways: A Book of Bible Verses*** will satisfy the artist's legions of admirers. Her button-eyed children show up in quaint attire (sailor suits for boys, dresses with petticoats, pantaloons and pinafores for girls); they pose in embraces and other quiet moments. A line or so of verse from the King James Bible faces each vignette. (ages 3-8)

A CHRISTMAS SAMPLER: A NEW COLLECTION OF HOLIDAY TREASURES (2001)

Diane Roback, Jennifer M. Brown, and Jason Britton (review date 24 September 2001)

SOURCE: Roback, Diane, Jennifer M. Brown, and Jason Britton. *Publishers Weekly* 248, no. 39 (24 September 2001): 49.

Anglund's (***Christmas Is Love***) trademark chubby-cheeked children dot the pages of this small-format holiday anthology [***A Christmas Sampler: A New Collection of Holiday Treasures***]. Gathering traditional carols and customs from around the world, along with original poems (plus a recipe for gingerbread cookies), she creates idealized scenes of innocent, old-fashioned festivity, brightly bordered in red and green. Anglund's many fans will be pleased. All ages.

Virginia Walter (review date October 2001)

SOURCE: Walter, Virginia. *School Library Journal* 47, no. 10 (October 2001): 62.

PreS-Gr 2—There may be grandmothers and aunts, remembering these round-faced children with no mouths from the heyday of Anglund's popularity in the 1960s, who will welcome this collection [***A Christmas Sampler: A New Collection of Holiday Treasures***] of miscellaneous Christmas lore and customs, some poetry by the author, a recipe for gingerbread, and the lyrics to "Hark! the Herald Angels Sing" and "Jingle Bells." With its small trim size, its place on the first page for the name of the person to whom it is given, and its sentimental illustrations, this looks more like a gift book than a likely addition to library collections. Bookstores will probably carry this title; libraries needn't bother.

FURTHER READING

Bibliography

Loganberry Books. "Joan Walsh Anglund." *Loganberry Books* <http://www.logan.com/loganberry/most-anglund.html

Website listing Anglund's most requested books and short biography.

Biographies

King Features Syndicate, Inc. "Joan Walsh Anglund, Renowned Illustrator and Author, Represented for Licensing By King Features." *King Features Syndicate, Inc.* <http://www.kingfeatures.com/pressrm/rel_44_28_6_2001.htm

Short description of Anglund's career as an author and illustrator and products licensed for marketing.

———. "Joan Walsh Anglund." *King Features Syndicate, Inc.* <http://www.kingfeatures.com/license/liprop/anglund/MainB.htm

Brief biographical sketch and listing of consumer merchandise.

Criticism

Sedgwick, Eve Kosofsky. "A Poem Is Being Written." *Representations* no. 17 (winter 1987): 110-43.

Brief reference to Anglund's style of illustrations.

Times Literary Supplement (16 October 1969): 1201.

Brief review of *A Is for Always.*

Additional coverage of Anglund's life and career is contained in the following sources published by the Gale Group: *Children's Literature Review,* Vol. 1; *Contemporary Authors,* Vols. 5-8R; *Contemporary Authors New Revision Series,* Vol. 15; *Literature Resource Center*; *Major Authors and Illustrators for Children and Young Adults,* Ed. 2; and *Something about the Author,* Vol. 2.

Elizabeth Goudge
1900-1984

(Full name Elizabeth de Beauchamp Goudge) English poet, short story writer, playwright, novelist, biographer, children's writer, and editor.

INTRODUCTION

Goudge secured tremendous readership throughout her career and was particularly known for her romantic imagination, proficiency with prose, and idealism during World War II and postwar years.

BIOGRAPHICAL INFORMATION

Goudge was born in Wells, Somerset, England, on April 24, 1900, the only child of Henry Leighton, a Regius Professor of Divinity at Oxford University, and Ida de Beauchamp (Collenette) Goudge. She died April 1, 1984, near Henley-on-Thames, England, at the age of eighty-three. She annually visited her maternal grandparents, a prominent French family on the island of Guernsey. At eleven years of age, her family moved to Ely after her father was appointed a canon at the cathedral. When World War I broke out, Goudge was sent to Grassendale School, Southbourne, Hampshire. She attended Reading University School of Art for two years where she wrote her first published children's book *The Fairies' Baby and Other Stories* (1919), which was a commercial failure. From 1922 to 1932 Goudge wrote part-time and taught design and applied art in Ely and then Oxford when her father was promoted to Professor of Divinity. In 1932 she moved to a seaside bungalow at Barton, in Hampshire, with her ailing mother and began to write full-time. At the age of thirty-four, her first novel, *Island Magic* (1934), was met with success. Goudge was commissioned by literary agent Nancy Pearn to write short stories for *Strand* magazine. *The Woman's Home Companion, Ladies' Home Journal, Good Housekeeping,* and *McCall's* featured her stories for more than thirty years.

In the late 1930s Goudge suffered a nervous breakdown induced by anxiety over the illnesses of her mother and father; she found it impossible to write for some time after her father's death in the spring of 1939. She confined herself to her bedroom in Providence Cottage and endeavored to complete the novel she had abandoned after her father's death. *The Bird in the Tree* (1940) was the first of three novels to portray the Eliot family during World War I. In a more lighthearted approach, Goudge then wrote *Smoky-House* (1940), a children's novel; both books earned enough to pay for Providence Cottage. The Devonshire countryside and the necessity of funds effected a prolific period for Goudge. She published a collection of short stories, a children's book, her first best-seller in the United States, her sixth novel, *The Castle on the Hill* (1942), and *Henrietta's House* (1942), a sequel to *A City of Bells* (1936). By the time *Green Dolphin Country* (1944) was completed, Goudge was warned it might not be published due to a paper shortage. She sent it to her American publisher and was stunned to hear she had won an MGM

Literary Award for $125,000. An MGM movie titled *Green Dolphin Street* was released in October 1947 and grossed more than $5 million at the box office; the film gained an Academy Award for special effects and a nomination for cinematography. Goudge's novel *The Little White Horse* (1946) won the 1947 Carnegie Medal for outstanding children's fiction in the United Kingdom.

MAJOR WORKS

Goudge's first novel, *Island Magic* (1934), set on the Channel Island of Guernsey in the nineteenth century, examines the emotional upheavals of Andre and Rachel du Frocq through impending bankruptcy, five children, and the presence of a foreigner who ultimately reveals he is Andre's lost brother. What is known as The Torminister Trilogy—*A City of Bells, Sister of the Angels: A Christmas Story* (1939) and *Henrietta's House*—gives a romantic sense of Goudge's historical era. In the setting of a small cathedral town at the end of the Boer War, readers are introduced to Canon Fordyce, a saintly grandfather; Jocelyn Fordyce, grandson back from war; Gabriel Ferranti, an impoverished writer; and orphaned Henrietta, adopted into the family. Gabriel discovers Henrietta is the lost child of his own dead love. In the second installment, Henrietta urges a forgery artist to return to painting and he awakens her artistic abilities. Goudge focuses on the themes of second chances, rebirth, and love. In *Henrietta's House,* Hugh Anthony has a birthday celebration picnic; traveling to the picnic site, the guests have unexpected adventures. Goudge's best-known novel, *Green Dolphin Country,* involves the mistaken identity of two sisters in love with the same man. Forty years after the marriage of William and Marianne, they return from New Zealand. An unhappy Marianne reveals to William his true love—the jilted sister Marguerite who is now a nun; the three accept their life choices and reconcile.

While Goudge was at her pinnacle of recognition, *The Little White Horse* was published. The thirteen-year-old heroine, Maria Merryweather, returns to her ancestral home in an enchanted village and discovers her destiny to become the next Moon Princess. Discovering the mystic white horse helps her strengthen her own character and resolve the mysteries of the kingdom. *The Bird in the Tree* (1940), *The Herb of Grace* (1948; also known as *Pilgrim's Inn*) and *The Heart of the Family* (1953) are young adult novels known as the Damerosehay Trilogy dealing with the Eliot family who live in the marshy Hampshire Coast. The family and close community occupants unite against the love affair of David and Nadine, his uncle George's divorced wife, and they are forced to renounce their love. Six years later in the second novel, Nadine and George buy an old rural inn close to Damerosehay. A discontented Nadine spends her time refurbishing the inn; her love for David is rekindled when he comes to visit. However, she again releases David and comes to peace in a personal identity revelation. In the final novel, Nadine is a well-integrated, happy woman, and the focus shifts to the four generations of Eliots and their individual revelations into their own lives.

Set in 1912 England, *Linnets and Valerians* (1964), tells the story of four Linnet children who run away from their strict grandmother. Through their adventures, the Linnet children help in solving the mystery of the missing Valerian family members. A *Booklist* reviewer described the novel as "a story which blends fantasy with realism and has a sensitively depicted setting, unique characters, a romantic plot, and a satisfying ending." *I Saw Three Ships* (1969) is a story set in an eighteenth-century English seaport village. Polly, an orphan living with her Aunt Constantia, is eagerly awaiting Christmas. Three visitors are introduced who represent the Three Wise Men to Polly: Uncle Tom who comes home suddenly bearing gold, a French refugee who brings a jeweled rosary, and the town beggar who offers up his life. Goudge's autobiography *The Joy of the Snow* (1974) is popular with her devoted readership. Goudge recaptures happy childhood memories, her years with her companion Jessie, the love of the English countryside, and examines the philosophy in her writings. Goudge's final novel *The Child from the Sea* (1970) is a retelling of the life of Lucy Walter and her disastrous love affair with Charles II. Betrayed by her maid, she loses her husband's loyalty, is arrested, and forbidden access to her children. *Publishers Weekly* classified it as "strictly for the ladies," but the novel was on the best-seller list from October 1970 until February 1971.

CRITICAL RECEPTION

Goudge's works include forty-six titles, some of which have been translated into Danish, Dutch, French, German, Italian, Spanish, and Swedish. Most had dual publications—in Great Britain and the United States—and many remain in print. Madonna Marsden in *Images of Women in Fiction* examined

Goudge's literary reception: "What is intriguing, however, is that reviewers accord Ms. Goudge less than enthusiastic praise and academicians have totally ignored her, despite her impact on the reading habits of a substantial number of women all over the world." In *The Lion and the Unicorn,* reviewer Megan Lynn Isaac acknowledged that "In her day, however, her books for both young and old were greeted with enthusiasm and accolades." Reviewer Aileen Pippett for *Books for Younger Readers* characterized Goudge as an author who "writes with the gentleness and good humor that have long endeared her to adult readers."

AWARDS

Metro-Goldwyn-Mayer Literary Award, 1944, and Literary Guild Award, 1944, both for *Green Dolphin Street*; Carnegie Medal for outstanding children's book published in the United Kingdom, 1947, for *The Little White Horse.*

PRINCIPAL WORKS

The Fairies' Baby and Other Stories (children's book) 1919
Island Magic (young adult novel) 1934
The Middle Window (young adult novel) 1935
A City of Bells (young adult novel) 1936
Towers in the Mist (young adult novel) 1938
Sister of the Angels: A Christmas Story (juvenile novel) 1939
Smoky-House (children's novel) 1940
The Bird in the Tree (young adult novel) 1940
The Well of the Star (children's book) 1941
The Castle on the Hill (novel) 1942
Henrietta's House (juvenile novel) 1942; revised as *The Blue Hills,* 1942
Green Dolphin Country (young adult novel) 1944; published in the United States as *Green Dolphin Street*
The Little White Horse (children's novel) 1946
Songs and Verses (poetry) 1947
The Herb of Grace (young adult novel) 1948; revised as *Pilgrim's Inn,* 1948
Make-Believe (short stories) 1949
Gentian Hill (novel) 1949
The Valley of Song (children's novel) 1951
The Heart of the Family (young adult novel) (1953)
The White Witch (novel) 1958
The Dean's Watch (young adult novel) 1960
Linnets and Valerians (children's novel) 1964
A Christmas Book (children's book) 1967
I Saw Three Ships (children's book) 1969
The Child from the Sea (novel) 1970
The Lost Angel: Stories (short stories) 1971
The Joy of the Snow (autobiography) 1974

GENERAL COMMENTARY

Madonna Marsden (essay date 1972)

SOURCE: Marsden, Madonna. "Gentle Truths for Gentle Readers: The Fiction of Elizabeth Goudge." In *Images of Women in Fiction: Feminist Perspectives,* edited by Susan Koppelman Cornillon, pp. 68-78. Bowling Green, Ohio: Bowling Green University Popular Press, 1972.

[*In the following essay, Marsden examines the role of women as portrayed in Goudge's various works.*]

Elizabeth Goudge is a kind of phenomenon among contemporary British writers. She began writing in 1934 and presently has about forty-six titles to her credit, many of which have appeared on best-seller lists. Almost every book has had dual publication in both Great Britain and America, and many have appeared in foreign translations. She has been published in regular editions, gift editions, book club editions, and paperbacks. One of her novels was made into a film. Her short stories have appeared in periodicals ranging from *Senior Scholastic* to *Ladies Home Journal.* Selections from her works have been anthologized into "The Best of . . ." kinds of volumes. What is intriguing, however, is that reviewers accord Ms. Goudge less than enthusiastic praise and academicians have totally ignored her, despite her impact on the reading habits of a substantial number of women all over the world.

Obviously any conclusions drawn about the appeal of Elizabeth Goudge would have to include a statement that what she writes must be what a large segment of the public, unconcerned with aesthetic value, wants to hear. Her own estimate of her work is that it is escapist, not true to life, and therefore perhaps inartistic.

> I know that happy endings are sometimes inartistic, and certainly, not always true to life, but I can't write any other kind. I am not a serious chronicler of the very terrible contemporary scene, but just a story-teller, and there is so much tragedy about us everywhere today that we surely

> don't want it in the story books to which we turn when we are ill or unhappy, or can't go to sleep at night. We must escape somewhere.[1]

Ms. Goudge has further assessed her own appeal as largely palliative and visceral.

> I prefer writing about children, dogs, and ordinary men and women in surroundings of natural beauty. My work appeals mostly to the old and the young and those who are ill. The sick tell me my books help them to forget their aches and pains.[2]

A substantial portion of the fiction of Elizabeth Goudge *is* devoted to the escapist and the medicinal. As noted, Ms. Goudge finds herself incapable of writing a novel with an unhappy ending. Because she integrates into this plot structure elements such as distant and remote settings and romanticized historical characters, it is perhaps too easy to dismiss her as simply a huckster of nostalgia, and ignore the paradoxical fact that war, changing ideologies, and breakdowns in myth structures provide the dramatic spine of her work. Almost all of Ms. Goudge's fiction is based on a dialectic between a self-constructed imaginative form which demands a happy ending and a content drawn from a world which does not provide that kind of well-ordered material. And it seems to be her talent for creating character images who illustrate the sacrifice of truth which must be made in exchange for order which captures her audience even more than the romance and the comfort which her novels bring. Particularly the women in Ms. Goudge's novels, then, find themselves pulled between the paradigm which models their happiness around their biology, and their own experiences which indicate that the paradigm may be false. The central problem of the fiction, then, is to reconcile the truth of the individual experience to the truth of the behavioral model—in short, to gently expand the old paradigm to absorb threats to the old truths rather than to invent a new paradigm to handle a new truth.

The cosmos posited by Elizabeth Goudge is one in which there is a definite and hierarchical as well as interconnected order of things. She sees the universe as governed by a plan, and nothing happens which is not a part of that plan. Each person, plant and rock has a definite role to fulfill, and even apparent evil works towards the creation of good. Perhaps the most succinct description of Ms. Goudge's vision of the order of the universe is the following passage from ***The Castle on the Hill.*** Mr. Birley, an elderly and wise historian, tells the confused and weary heroine of the novel:

> Personal experience and the study of history have taught me to believe in a pattern. . . . And in spite of all that has befallen the world I still believe that the threads of it, ourselves, are held securely in the scheme of things by some great unconquerable spiritual power. Call it what you will—destiny, fate, the first cause, the life stream, God—it does not lose hold of a single thread. In wanton wickedness we may tangle the pattern into what looks like hopeless confusion, but in unwearied patience the power unravels the tangle, reforms the pattern, keeps it moving along to some great goal of order whose nature we cannot even guess at yet. If the threads are not lost, there can be no lasting chaos.[3]

The directing force of this universe, then, allows humanity freedom of will, but it can also direct that freedom to meet its own ends, which always prove to be positive. Confusion is only apparent, rarely real. Chaos, meaninglessness and alienation can occur only when the individual fights the natural order of the paradigm. Ms. Goudge's vision, then is in direct opposition to that of those who would posit that order is the illusion and chaos the reality. In fact, it comes close to the eighteenth-century model of the rationally ordered Great Chain of Being.

But Ms. Goudge expands the rational to also include a tinge of the mystical. The pattern metaphor indicates that the thread which breaks away from the tapestry not only mars the beauty of the tapestry, but also loses its individual meaning. The thread alone simply has no function. In the chain metaphor the link which breaks the chain has simply created two chains. For Ms. Goudge, this metaphor and the happy ending are not possible. Two incomplete paradigms pose, rather than resolve, threats to the established myths.

Within the broad paradigm, there are implications which present a model for the role of woman. This orderly, mystical, purposeful view sees woman's particular biology as the particular governor of her destiny. Therefore, her role is to marry and to produce children. This is what gives a woman her meaning. There is a range of choice for the female character, however, and it is this range which either creates a dialectic and therefore provides the basis for a kind of imaginative literature in which the female can be a central character, or which relegates the female to secondary importance because a larger issue of the paradigm is at stake.

Generally, Ms. Goudge sees the woman in Western culture as faced with five possible choices within this pattern: 1) she can accept the demands of femininity, marry, and live happily ever after; 2) marry, question the demands of femininity and become a rebel who is eventually absorbed back into the value system; 3) reject or be rejected by the demands of femininity, not marry, and be reasonably happy if she finds family surrogates; 4) reject the demands of femininity, not marry, and find happiness through a creative career; 5) reject the system entirely and be damned by her choice. For the purposes of this article, the second kind of heroine provides the most interesting focus for demonstrating the neutralizing and absorbent function of Ms. Goudge's fiction, yet all of these types provide an interesting insight into the very limited role which a woman can play in the literary imagination.

The simple heroine is of little fictional use, since though she may recognize that the female's lot in life is not as interesting or as exciting as the male's, she accepts without question the notion that because her biology governs her destiny, marriage constitutes the whole of her existence, while it is only part of a much broader concept of life for a man. In ***Gentian Hill,*** for example, Stella, the heroine, knows

> . . . by instinct that men do not want women with them all the time; they keep certain compartments in their lives for them, and do not want them overflowing into the wrong ones.[4]

As a result of their attitudes, Stella and the heroines like her are not the center of interest in the novels or short stories in which they appear. The cultural conventions of femininity which they embody offer no paradigmatic conflict upon which the artistic imagination can act. Their basic structure offers no antithesis to the accepted thesis. Their function is subordinated to some larger issue.

The heroine who marries and then finds that wifehood and motherhood do not bring the kind of satisfaction which the paradigm has promised, provides a much more interesting fictional subject, since this type can offer material for a sensitively drawn portrait of the sacrifices which the order and rigidity of the paradigm demand. The truth of her experience vs. the truth of the paradigm offers a dramatic spine which can give this type of character a place of central rather than subordinate purpose in the novel.

Although Ms. Goudge has used this type of heroine in many of her novels, her most interesting creation is Nadine Eliot, a character who appears in the trilogy of the Eliot family, ***The Bird in the Tree*** (1940), ***Pilgrim's Inn*** (1948) and ***The Heart of the Family*** (1953). But this type of heroine is too prevalent in women's fiction to ascribe the creation of her image to the psychic structure of a single author. She has appeared in literature almost from its beginning under such various guises as the "castrating woman," the "unfaithful wife," or just simply "the bitch." Basically, what this type has always represented is a kind of hermaphroditic and therefore taboo blend of male spirit with female body. Intellectually and spiritually, the hermaphrodite heroine has a penis, though physically she is a woman, and should therefore be a receptor rather than an actor. Her tragedy is that she *does* act, and that that action makes her ugly somehow.

The Bird in the Tree was not originally conceived as the opening novel of a trilogy. The story, however, met with such success that readers demanded to hear more about Nadine; an indication that perhaps this type of heroine is the perfect image of the weaknesses of the myth structure in which she operates, and therefore a creation who has an archetypal appeal despite the critical pronouncements. There is something archetypal about Nadine's quest for a self, a quest which unlike that of the male adventure hero, is somehow turned in on itself.

The Bird in the Tree opens as Nadine's three children are in the care of their grandmother, while their father is stationed in India on assignment for the Foreign Office. Nadine has taken advantage of the freedom which her husband's absence offers her and has moved from the Eliot country estate to London, where she has opened a small antique shop. This taste of freedom has convinced her that she no longer needs George.

Nadine is an embarrassment to her mother-in-law, Lucilla, because she has blotted the family honor through her willing estrangement from George, her open indifference to her children, and her desire to be economically independent. This embarrassment is intensified when Lucilla discovers that Nadine is in love with George's young nephew, David. In an attempt to break up what she considers a highly immoral and almost incestuous affair, Lucilla admits to Nadine that as a young wife she had experienced a similar rebellion against the constraints of her role. In an effort to assert some kind of active control over her life, Lucilla had an affair with a man who seemed to offer her more freedom and excitement than her husband. As they were about to run off together, however, the man realized that his duty to his vocation took precedence over his love for her. Lucilla was angered and shamed, but the experience aided her to perceive her role on a new level of awareness.

> A doctor's work is splendidly creative, I thought; building strong bodies and healthy minds; it is more creative even than the work of painter and sculptor, for he deals in flesh and blood and thought, materials that are living. It seemed to me appalling, as I thought it over, that all this should be sacrificed to his passion for a pretty woman. It was every bit as bad as that my work for my husband and children should be sacrificed to my passion for a charming man. The love of a man and woman, I saw, should never be allowed to be an end in itself; it should be the helpmate of their work.[5]

And a bit later, she tells Nadine how she came to be able to put this new awareness to work in her life:

> Love at its highest, I thought, like truth at its highest, is a creative thing. Perhaps it is action, not feeling. I was playing the part of a good wife and mother quite successfully in the outward ways, but that, I saw now, was not enough. That was not love. Creative love meant building up by quantities of small actions a habit of service that might become at last a habit of mind and feeling as well as of body. I tried, and I found it did work like that. Feeling can be compelled by action not quite as easily as action by feeling, but far more lastingly.[6]

Lucilla's advice is ludicrous on one plane and yet quite valid on another. In many ways, it resembles a formula for breakthrough to mystical awareness. Buddhists repeat common words until they become meaningless and a new level of consciousness opens up to them. Magicians use the incantation of words to evoke the real substances which they represent. Lucilla has advised Nadine to repeat common acts to achieve the same end.

The novel ***Pilgrim's Inn*** opens some six years or so after this. George and Nadine have been reconciled, and Nadine has apparently taken Lucilla's advice to heart, for she is now the mother of five-year-old twins. But her actions do not seem to have improved her feelings. The twins are aggressive, exuberant children who compel little but exhaustion from their mother. Realizing that Nadine is still unhappy, Lucilla contrives that George and his family should move to the country where she can keep a watchful eye over the situation. Against Nadine's wishes, they move to an old estate which had once been an inn for pilgrims who were journeying to the nearby monastery. Nadine becomes immersed in refurbishing the inn, finds a nurse to care for the twins, and is leading a fairly happy life until David returns to the country for a visit. Once again Nadine becomes discontented with her life and the flame of her old love for David is rekindled.

An artist who is painting Nadine's portrait notes that something impairs her real beauty from emerging. Some struggle within has, he notes, hardened her mouth and tightened her eyes.

> You know or should know, what needs cutting out of your own life. Some quite trivial thing, probably, perhaps no more than some reservation of thought. But it's enough . . . to keep you stewing in your own juice, pulled both ways and getting nowhere. Cut it out, that thought or whatever, and you're free, and probably others, too. We're so bound together in this complicated world that the spiritual condition of each one of us is as catching as the measles.[7]

Nadine has still not reconciled herself spiritually to being a woman. She still is the divided, taboo, and therefore ugly hermaphrodite.

Nadine lets go of David, repeats the outward acts which her femininity demands, and finds that acting like a woman does indeed make her content to be one. She is at peace when she realizes

> What a ridiculous fuss she was making about doing what everyone was always doing every day, every hour, every moment of their lives almost: gathering in the divided allegiance, denying it to the one thing, giving it to the other; the choice never really in doubt when to the inner beseeching of the spirit the motive is revealed. It was a process that could not end while the eventual salvation of one's soul was still a possibility, the pain of the effort merely a question of degree, but not differing moment by moment in essence. One lived, and it was so. Accept it and have done.[8]

The situation reaches a happy ending, but the dialectic has really reached no synthesis. The antithesis is simply shown to be false because it has created chaos. The original thesis is preferable apparently because it makes life more orderly. In ***The Heart of the Family,*** of course, Nadine is no longer a prominent character. She can't be because she no longer offers any imaginative possibilities. She is now a well-integrated, happy woman.

The fiction of Elizabeth Goudge finds another way to give a female character a prominent position in a novel or short story through the use of another familiar type, the spinster heroine. Once again, this type offers the promise of sustained artistic possibilities because she offers a dialectic between what the paradigm posits as her meaning and her refusal or her inability to embrace it.

Both Dolores Brown of ***The Castle on the Hill*** and Ada Gillespie, the central character in the story "A Shepherd and A Shepherdess," have found meaning in their lives by finding surrogate ways of fulfilling what the paradigm posits as their functions. Dolores devotes her life to the care of aged parents, and when they die, opens the home she has inherited from them to lonely boarders. Ada, the only girl in a large family, mothers her brothers and then their children. Both of these characters, however, find that when their functions are gone, so are their identities. Dolores is forced to evacuate her English coastal home because it is threatened by wartime invasion. Ada's nieces and nephews grow up and can take care of themselves. And both are lost until they find new substitute families in which their female biology automatically ascribes to them the nurturing function of mothers.

All of the Elizabeth Goudge heroines who find happiness without marriage are historical figures whose talents clearly indicate that they are exceptions to the rule. "Escape for Jane" is based on a true incident in the life of Jane Austen. It focuses on her rejection of marriage and the subsequent nurturance of children in favor of the nurturance of the "dreams" inside her instead. It is interesting to note that her historical reality is what allows her to do this. Her rejection of the conventional feminine road to happiness does not threaten the paradigm, because the reader retrospectively knows that her career was a part of the pattern after all. The decisions of such a heroine do not come into conflict with the truth of the paradigm because they are always retrospective and therefore no threat.

The most tragic of Ms. Goudge's heroines is Mother Skipton, the black witch in the novel ***The White Witch,*** because she has chosen to reject the paradigm and has no historical truth to mediate her decision. Her unhappiness and her failure as a woman are the results of her urge to gain power over the lives of others. As she herself admits, however, what she thought to be the truth of her own experience was not truth at all. Her failure to perceive this until it is too late is Ms. Goudge's negative variation on the presentation of that larger positive truth.

> If souls in Hell were incapable of longing they would not be in Hell. That *is* Hell—longing for what you've thrown away and can never get back. I was a woman who wanted power. Through what stages I passed from white to black witchcraft I need not tell you but they were governed by the passion to possess power over the bodies and souls of men. At last, I liked to kill. But power is a devil who turns round on you at last. You possess it, then it turns and possesses you. Then power becomes powerlessness. I am far too tired now to change my way of life.[9]

What the fiction of Elizabeth Goudge does, then, is to establish that although many women are unhappy in the roles which Western culture demands of them, the fault lies not with the paradigm, but with the individual. The threat which is posed to the social fabric by the fact of woman's discontent with the roles of wifehood and motherhood is absorbed by demonstrating that discontent carries with it the seeds of chaos and destruction. Traditional cultural paradigms, when used as a framework for this type of fiction, serve to reaffirm and reassure us of the truth of our public vision of life as objectively meaningful. Private, threatening visions which contradict this notion are neutralized by their absorption into what is publicly and conventionally considered the larger scheme of things. The fiction of Ms. Goudge absorbs and neutralizes threats to conventional femininity by neutralizing the validity of her heroines' primal, but conventionally masculine urges for quest. Activity, aggression, intellectual curiosity, lead, in almost all cases, to an intensification of unhappiness. Passive persistence in an assigned role, on the other hand, leads to the ability to accept and transcend its limitations.

Finally, then, the appeal of the novels of Elizabeth Goudge seems to rest in their ability to affirm the rightness of humanity's artificial constructs. To have them creates the necessity for sublimation, an exchange of what Freud has called "a threatened external happiness . . . for a permanent internal unhappiness, for the tension of the sense of guilt."[10] But Ms. Goudge can create a dialectic which eliminates even the guilt as a threat. Basically, her novels save us from the embarrassment of having to admit that honest anarchy may be more personally fulfilling than the organized lie. But the organized lie has always managed to find room, through popular culture, for the threats which would expose it. Bloody cultural revolutions are prevented through the bloodless ones which are gradually fought in our mass media every day.

Notes

1. This quotation can be found on the book jackets of various novels. I first saw it on the jacket of the American edition of *The Heart of the Family.*
2. James Leasor, *Author By Profession* (London: Cleaver-Hume, 1952), p. 147.
3. Elizabeth Goudge, *The Castle on the Hill* (New York: Coward-McCann, 1941), p. 128.
4. Elizabeth Goudge, *Gentian Hill* (New York: Coward-McCann, 1949), pp. 60-61.
5. Elizabeth Goudge, *The Bird in the Tree* (New York: Coward-McCann, 1940), p. 246.
6. *The Bird in the Tree,* pp. 247-248.
7. Elizabeth Goudge, *Pilgrim's Inn* (New York: Coward-McCann, 1948), pp. 153-154.
8. *Pilgrim's Inn,* p. 146.
9. Elizabeth Goudge, *The White Witch* (New York: Coward-McCann, 1958), p. 309.
10. Sigmund Freud, *Civilization And Its Discontents,* translated and edited by James Strachey (New York: W. W. Norton, 1962), p. 75.

Megan Lynn Isaac (essay date 1997)

SOURCE: Isaac, Megan Lynn. "Misplaced: The Fantasies and Fortunes of Elizabeth Goudge." *The Lion and the Unicorn* 21, no. 1 (1997): 86-111.

[*In the following essay, Isaac presents a survey of Goudge's works.*]

In Elizabeth Goudge's novel ***Linnets and Valerians,*** characters exhibit a rather extreme, if not alarming, tendency to disappear. Except for an occasional moonlit stroll in her garden, Lady Alicia has spent the past thirty years living in strict seclusion in the upstairs rooms of the genteelly decaying Valerian manor house. Ever since her son and husband were lost, she has shunned company and has been seen by no one except her faithful servant and companion Moses. Young Francis Valerian vanished mysteriously at the age of eight while playing on Lion Tor, the magnificent rock formation behind his home. His father went astray three years later while exploring the Valley of the Kings in Egypt. Ironically, Elizabeth Goudge's reputation seems to have suffered the tragedy so many of her characters struggle against; she too has been misplaced and forgotten, at least as an author of children's literature.

In her day, however, her books for both young and old were greeted with enthusiasm and accolades. Goudge's novels celebrate the every day life of her characters—usually, but not always, large families of energetic and strong-willed children. But to say that Goudge specializes in reality, is not to say that her characters are conventional or their experiences are ordinary; for Goudge, real life *is* magical. In her novels, the kingdoms of childhood joy and belief expand to envelop adults at the same time as the moral ambiguities of the grown-up world provide rich pastures for the adventurous young protagonists. Although this collapsing or confusion of worlds sometimes provides trouble for those intent on categorizing novels as "Children's," "Young Adult," or "Adult," it enables Goudge to put her uses of the magical to some unusual purposes—including the exploration of class and economic justice. Her descriptions of the rich and wild English countryside and the idiosyncratic and splendidly detailed inns, cottages, and castles in which her protagonists dwell is also one of her greatest strengths. And best of all are her wonderfully memorable characters.

In 1946 Goudge's ***The Little White Horse*** won the Carnegie Medal, by some measures the most prestigious of Commonwealth awards in the field. However, while the American counterpart, the Newbery Medal, endows its recipients with something akin to literary immortality (virtually every public and school library purchases the winning books and many bookstores devote special shelf space to decades worth of past winners), the Carnegie Medal falls, according to one scholar of its recipients, "far short of it in impact on authors, publishers, and the world at large" (Crouch 184). But even recognition from the American Library Association and reviews which range from glowing to blazing in virtually every journal from *Horn Book* to *The New York Times Book Review* have been inadequate to sustain her popularity. A quick peek at the indexes of a half-dozen of the anthologies and texts prepared for classroom use as well as a glance at some of the more prominent authors and editors of children's literature surveys like John Townsend, Roger Sale, and Cornelia Meigs reveals that she is mentioned at best in passing, and more frequently, not at all.

Goudge is herself, perhaps, in part to blame. Even her own autobiography, ***The Joy of Snow,*** fails to mention most of her children's novels. But a fuller explanation of her disappearance may be attributed to the vagaries and limitations of the term "children's literature" and its sibling "young adult literature."

Goudge was both a prolific and varied author. She was born in England in 1900, and at her death in 1984 she had published over forty volumes (not counting the many anthologies of her work). These books include poetry, plays, collections of short stories, religious studies, novels, and the aforementioned autobiography. The editor of *Twentieth Century Children's Writers* defines ten of these works as publications for children, but other critics have not always agreed. Some of the confusion is caused by the fact that almost all of Elizabeth Goudge's work features substantive child characters. As John Gough argues, "For Goudge, adults and children alike share the same driving hungers," they all struggle with freedom and obedience, good and evil, faith and belief (*Twentieth* 273).

Goudge's first novel ***Island Magic*** was marketed and reviewed as adult fiction. The book tells the story of the du Frocq family living in the Channel Islands in the late nineteenth century. Andre du Frocq struggles with his secret desire to be a poet and the impending bankruptcy of his small farm. His wife Rachell finds her own fight to save their beloved home undermined by her growing passion for another man, a different kind of threat to the family's survival. Interwoven amidst these adult concerns are the battles and hopes of the five boisterous du Frocq children. Reviewing the book upon its publication in 1936 for *The New York Times Book Review,* it was the adventures of the children which most impressed Dorthea Kingsland:

> Sensitive, passionately different from one another, they are all possessed of imaginations at once inspiring and troubling. . . . Although ***Island Magic*** is written by an English woman and about a virtually French family, there is something appealingly familiar about the book. It is as though the beloved American scenes of Louisa Alcott's *Little Women* had been transplanted into the gardens of the Channel Islands.
>
> (6-7)

From her first introduction into the literary world, Goudge has tiptoed along the borders between adult and children's writing. Many authors transform the characters and settings of their children's fiction into more adult forms. Louisa May Alcott, Maud Hart Lovelace, L. M. Montgomery, Laura Ingalls Wilder, and Madeleine L'Engle are just a few examples of writers whose novels take their heroes and heroines from childhood through marriage and whose primary audience also shifts from children to young adults and even toward "real" adults. Goudge, however, seems to be one of the few whose work runs in the opposite chronological direction. When she next wrote about the du Frocq family in the 1949 volume of loosely linked short stories entitled ***Make-Believe,*** she directed her writing more precisely toward a young audience. The topics of infidelity and financial ruin are again presented but on an entirely different level. Instead of worrying about their own family's impoverishment, this time the du Frocq children need only to concern themselves with other people's poverty and problems. The battles, boating adventures, and midnight horse theft they engage in with all the self-confidence of the legendary Robin Hood or E. Nesbit's Would-Be-Goods makes for an infinitely amusing set of eight adventures. A bookseller, misidentified murderer, orphan, miller, and cantankerous recluse all receive the dubious benefit of their attention—though it is perhaps the endangered publisher who causes the children the most distress. Raised by a father with literary ambitions, the two eldest du Frocq children realize that "to drown a man was bad enough but to drown a publisher was a crime for which there could be no expiation" (87).

Another of Goudge's early novels caused similar categorization problems. Published in 1936, ***A City of Bells*** is set in a small cathedral town. Returning to the security of his grandfather's home to recover from the mental, as much as the physical, pain of a war injury, Jocelyn Fordyce is at a loss as to how to continue his life. But Grandfather Fordyce is accustomed to ministering to the problems of the young—he has also recently taken a nearly indigent poet, Gabriel Ferranti, under his wing. As the novel unfolds, it is not, however, Grandfather Fordyce who provides the inspiration and solution to the troubled young men, as much as the orphaned Henrietta. Although the good man has generously provided the eight-year-old sprite with a home where she proves invaluable as a companion to the indefatigable Hugh Anthony (the Fordyce family's seven-year-old orphaned grandson), Henrietta still longs secretly for a family of her own. Henrietta befriends both Jocelyn and Gabriel and becomes the bridge which leads them to their own dreams. Jocelyn finds a profession and happiness with a bride. Gabriel finds an audience for his dramatic poetry and joy in the discovery that Henrietta is, in fact, the lost child of his own dead love.

The success of ***A City of Bells*** led Goudge to write a sequel in 1939 entitled ***Sister of the Angels.*** Once again, Goudge used the sequel as an opportunity to shift her focus toward children. In this book Henrietta reprises her inspirational role; this time she helps a painter turned forgery artist return to his true vocation. He in turn helps Henrietta awaken her own artistic talent. The theme of second chances and the redemptive spirit of the novel is echoed in its Christmas season setting. Although Henrietta is undoubtedly the protagonist of this novel, indeed she is the angelic figure referred to in the title, the concerns of the book are still quite mature. Consequently, at the time of its publication, this novel too was marketed, at least in the United States, as adult fiction.[1] Today, however, it is usually listed as a children's novel.[2]

In the final volume of what is sometimes called The Torminister Trilogy, Goudge focuses even more explicitly on the world of children.[3] Published in 1942, ***Henrietta's House*** takes as its point of departure an afternoon picnic in celebration of Hugh Anthony's ninth birthday.[4] In terms of narrative structure, ***Henrietta's House*** is not Goudge's strongest novel. As the guests set off in twos and threes in their separate modes of conveyance for Foxglove Combe, the site selected by Hugh Anthony for his picnic, each group becomes lost or separated from the others and falls into an unexpected adventure. As the day draws to a close, the guests all reassemble for a much belated celebration. The plotting of the novel is episodic and is perhaps a better demonstration of Goudge's skill with the short story than the novel. Yet, thematically ***Henrietta's House*** displays what are perhaps Goudge's most noteworthy accomplishments in her writing for children, her mastery of the modern fairy-tale motif and her ability to fuse conflicting, even contradictory, systems of magic, mythology, and theology into a single enchanted vision.[5]

Early in the novel Goudge reveals what might well be her own philosophy regarding the best literature for children. Henrietta stops in at Jocelyn's bookstore to deliver an invitation to the next day's party and stays to spend the afternoon helping the customers. Just before closing time a mysterious elderly gentleman arrives, but he discovers that he has lost his shopping list. When he reveals that he has been sent to fetch volumes appropriate for a young girl's library, Henrietta comes to his rescue:

> Henrietta took the books from the shelves with a certainty that quite surprised the Old Gentleman. *The Water Babies* and *Alice in Wonderland, Undine* and *The Pilarim's Progress, jackanapes* and *Little Women, The Fairchild Family* and *A Flat Iron for a Farthing, The Back of the North Wind* and *The Princess and the Curdie* followed each other into the basket with startling rapidity, followed by *Uncle Remus,* Hans Andersen, *The Swiss Family Robinson,* Andrew Lang's *Blue Fairy Book,* his Red One and his Green One, *Mary's Meadow, Lob-lie-by-the-Fire,* and *Wind in the Willows* and *The Cocky-Olly Bird.*
>
> (34)

Sure enough, as the rest of the novel unfolds, the characters find themselves in situations suspiciously reminiscent of Henrietta's twenty favorite stories. As each set of the guests arrive at the gates of a forgotten manor, they are met by the lodge keeper. The mysterious gates he guards are both the gates of heaven and the gates to all the fairy-tale kingdoms ever explored in myth, legend, or story. The extent of the generosity and graciousness with which each of the characters treats this magical figure anticipates, in classic fairy-tale and allegorical tradition, the sort of trials and adventures he or she will face. As they cross over the threshold of the gate, Goudge seamlessly shifts each character out of the everyday world and into the world of enchantment.

Only one of the novel's characters resists this transformation of everyday experience into the extraordinary. When this cantankerous Old Man has the temerity to doubt the existence of anything but the real world (he prefers the concrete radishes of his garden to the more ethereal ones of Paradise), he is quickly rebuked:

> "Behave yourself!" said Grandfather sternly, for though he loved all human souls he loved them better when they did not spit. "And don't you dare to disparage fairy tales. A fairy tale, dear sir, in relating miraculous happenings as though they were the normal events of every day, is a humble acknowledgment of the fact that this universe is a box packed full of mysteries of which we understand absolutely nothing at all; heaven alone knows what'll pop out of it next; a singing bird, the Theory of Evolution, gooseberry pie. You can wonder till you're blue in the face as to how the giraffe got his neck, or the gooseberry puffed himself out, but you don't know. You can't know. Any theory you may evolve about a giraffe's neck, my dear sir, is a fairy tale."
>
> "There ain't no fairyland," said the Old Man obstinately.
>
> "You dare to make a statement like that in a wood like this!" thundered Grandfather in ever-growing indignation. "If this is not fairyland, then I don't know what is. Fairyland and Paradise, they're the same place, and always with us."
>
> (148)

Goudge goes on to demonstrate the interchangeability of fairyland and Paradise through the adventures that each of the birthday guests experience. Young lovers find their way to Sleeping Beauty's Bower, while the more spiritually inclined discover the secret abode of a hermit even Bunyan's Christian would have admired. The most intrepid of the characters find themselves piloting a boat with a wild abandon worthy of Toad through underground caverns as mysterious as those into which Alice stumbled. Henrietta herself finds a perfect cottage in the woods, one fit for "that loving-hearted little girl who is the heroine of all the nicest fairy stories . . . Alice, Snow-White, Red-Riding-Hood, Gretchen," one designed especially to fulfill all of Henrietta's own wishes (212). In this, one of her earliest novels for children, Goudge develops a fairy tale rich with allusions that nod in recognition to the stories which have inspired her and which foreshadow the wonderful countries balanced on the threshold between the ordinary, the fantastic, and the mystical which take center stage in her later works.

Another way to think about Goudge and her audiences is to consider the category of Young Adult literature. The move to publish and study books specifically for young adults is more recent than most of Goudge's writing, but the category is appropriate for many of her novels. Goudge frequently treats the transition from the biological home to a marital one, and she also excels at combining adult's and children's concerns in one story. For young adults who welcome more mature or complex themes, but enjoy the comfortable security of children's adventures, these books are a delight. Set in late-sixteenth-century Oxford, ***Towers in the Mist*** follows the fortunes of the Leigh family, particularly Joyeuce and Grace, the two eldest daughters, as well as the scrapes and adventures of Nicholas, Faithful, Giles, and Philip—a quartet of young students of various skill and scholarly dedication. On one level the book is a wonderful piece of historical fiction reimagining the lives of some of the more dashing figures both major and minor of the English Renaissance. On another level it is a young adult romance—four teenage lovers measure the demands of their families and careers against their desire for romantic love. ***Green Dolphin Street, The Middle Window,*** and ***The Dean's Watch*** might also be considered examples of Young Adult literature.[6] The same might be said of the Damerosehay Trilogy consisting of ***The Bird in the Tree*** (1940), ***Pilgrim's Inn*** (1948),[7] and ***The Heart of the Family*** (1953). They are full of children and, like ***Henrietta's House, Pilgrim's Inn*** is shaped, at least in part, by allusion to and reconstruction of a famous childhood classic—this time *The Wind in the Willows.* Early in the novel the Eliot family moves from London to an old rural inn built centuries ago to benefit the pilgrims doing homage at the small local Abbey. As their parents struggle to work out their identities and relationships after a separation brought on by years of both historical and marital warring, the five Eliot children—Tommy, Ben, Caroline, and the twins Jerry and José—explore the woods and waterways surrounding their new home. Each of the children adopts the name of a character from Graham's novel, usually due to some parallel personality characteristics. Tommy's siblings refer to him as Toad. At Christmas time he arrives from boarding school on a secretly and illicitly acquired motorbike instead of the expected train. Embarking on the journey homeward, Tommy congratulates himself:

> Leaving so early, avoiding the cross-country journey, he'd be home by lunchtime. Give them all the shock of their lives. They'd get five more precious hours of him than they'd expected to. Jolly for them. He pulled on his leather gauntlets, bestrode his precious bike, and with a terrifying volley of backfiring and a fearful stench (the machine was exceedingly ancient), went roaring out of the yard and down the quiet country road beyond. "'Poop-poop!'" he yelled. . . .
>
> (267)

Obviously, Tommy has come by his nickname honestly. Gentler, more artistic Ben is known as Badger. Like his namesake he excels at making peace but prefers to keep to himself. Unlike Tommy, he has suffered at boarding school and is only really happy living among his family in the inn. Like Badger he is also at home in the ancient Knyghtwood which stands adjacent to the inn providing a place of magic and refuge for everyone who visits the inn. Caroline has the least affinity with the creatures from *The Wind in the Willows,* a situation perhaps due in part to the fact that Graham's novel itself includes only the scantiest roles for women.

The five-year-old twins, however, have no such problem; they drop in and out of the personas of Rat and Mole with a perfect ease, a situation which does not always bode well for the person appointed the duty of watching them. The adventuresome wanderings and burrowings so intuitively enjoyable to Rat and Mole have a tendency to be perceived as dangerous or destructive by their elders. And in their animal form they tend to out pace sluggish adult surveillance as Sally, a visitor to the inn, discovers when she volunteers to spend an afternoon in Knyghtwood with them:

> "With Jill we've been as far as the big oak," said Jerry. "And with Ben we've been as far as his

special place, where the Person is who plays the pipes, but with you we're going right deep into the Place Beyond where the Fairy Person with the Horns is."

Sally was interested. They had probably got Pan playing his pipes out of *The Wind in the Willows*; Ben had made himself a little pipe and played it in the wood sometimes, when he thought there was no one about to see and laugh at him, and they had perhaps heard his music, but where did the Place Beyond come from, and who was the Person with the Horns? . . . Jerry and José were now Rat and Mole. They ran along making little squeaking noises, and dropping now and then to all fours.

(132)

Unfortunately, Sally makes the mistake of sitting down to rest, and before she knows it the twins have disappeared.

Goudge's use of Graham's novel goes beyond these simple adaptations. She adds a new creature. The children choose the nickname "Old Beaver" for the famous artist who arrives to spend several months at the inn painting their mother's portrait and tutoring Ben. His animal designation signifies their recognition of the fact that he shares an imaginative and visionary capacity with them, but at the same time recognizes his hard working, no-nonsense approach to life. Finally, Goudge transforms the world of Graham's novel into something original and peculiarly her own. Ben decides to create a dramatization of *The Wind in the Willows* to present to his family and friends as a Christmas pageant. The production seems doomed to abysmal failure; the text defies adaptation and his actors defy direction. So instead, just two days before Christmas, Ben writes his own legend of the Knyghtwoods—a story of the long-forgotten monk who founded the local abbey, fed the creatures of the woods, and befriended a mystical white hart.[8] As in ***Henrietta's House*** the fantastical and the spiritual collapse in upon each other. The secret refuges of Rat and Mole, as well as their human counterparts and friends, are revealed through Ben's insight and imagination as ancient holy places. Paradise and fairyland are once again one and the same.

Although much of Goudge's writing is difficult to categorize in terms of audience, she has some shorter writings which can be safely understood as children's publications. ***The Fairies' Baby and Other Stories*** (1920) is not only for young people, but was written when Goudge herself was little more than one. It is long out of print and quite rare. Goudge also produced two short Christmas stories for children (her adult collections of short stories include others). The first, ***The Well of the Star*** (1941), follows the adventures of the young shepherd boy David on the first Christmas Eve. Praying at a holy well for gold to save his sick and starving family, he is hired by a caravan of three kings to lead the way to the village of Bethlehem, and there at the stable, overwhelmed by the power of the nativity scene, he is moved to give his pipe, his only and much beloved possession, as a gift to the new king. The power of the story lies less in its originality than in the character of David. Goudge creates a hero without forfeiting humor or humanity. David moves fluidly through fright when he meets the kings, joyful delight as he experiences his first ride on a camel, and awe as he stumbles upon the manger scene. But unlike many authors, Goudge does not stop at the climax of the story. She follows David home from Bethlehem humorously illustrating how quickly a transcendent experience fades:

"Where's my camel?" he asked petulantly. "When I went to Bethlehem I was the leader of a caravan, and I had three great lords with me, and servants and torches."

"Well, you haven't got them now," said Eli. "The great lords are still at Bethlehem . . . When Jacob and Tobias and I saw you there in the stable we made haste to take you home to your mother, young truant that you are."

"I don't want mother," grumbled David. "I want my camel."

Eli glanced back over his shoulder at the disagreeable little urchin dawdling at his heels. Was this the same child who had knelt in the stable wrapped in adoration? How quick can be the fall from ecstasy! "You keep your mouth shut, little son," he adjured him, "and quicken your heels; for I must get back to those sheep."

"Baa!" said David nastily, and purposely lagged behind.

(37-38)

Goudge believes in the power of mystical experiences to transform human beings into something greater than themselves, but escapes sentimentality or mawkishness by revealing a suspicion about the duration of such transformations.

Goudge treats the subject of Christmas miracles again in one of her last books, ***I Saw Three Ships*** (1969).[9] Recently orphaned Polly Flowerdew has been sent to live in a coastal village with her Aunt Dorcas and

Aunt Constantia. Confident in her belief that the three wise men will visit if only the doors are left unlatched on Christmas Eve as a sign of welcome, Polly matches wits with her much more security conscious relatives:

> "In a seaport town such as this a great many undesirable people are about at the holiday season; and as I keep telling you, dear child, the only masculine protection in this house is your poor dear grandfather's Hat in the hall". . . .
>
> They loved her and she always had her own way with them, whether they knew it or not. She intended to have it now. "The Wise Men might come," she said. "I was always expecting them at home, but they didn't come. I expect we were too far inland. They might come here. You wouldn't want to lock your door on the Wise Men, would you?"
>
> "Don't talk nonsense, child," said Dorcas impatiently. "And there *are* no wise men. I have never met a man yet who was not foolish."
>
> (11)

Discovering her aunts have gone to bed and taken the door keys with them, Polly opens the window instead. By the time dawn breaks, a sailor, a war refugee, and a beggar have all made themselves comfortable in the parlor and, wittingly or no, left a gift for the owners of the house (gifts perhaps powerful enough to restore even Aunt Dorcas' faith in the wisdom of men)! The simple story is augmented by the verses of the old Christmas carol which are woven through the text and which lend the book its title (Review of ***I Saw Three Ships***).

Aside from these short pieces of fiction, ***Smoky House*** (1940), ***The Little White Horse*** (1946), ***The Valley of Song*** (1951), and ***Linnets and Valerians*** (1964) comprise the undisputed center of Elizabeth Goudge's writing for children.[10] Most of these books have received scant scholarly attention. ***The Little White Horse*** has been discussed most frequently, perhaps due to its reputation as a Carnegie Medal recipient. One critic of Goudge's adult novels, Madonna Marsden, has summarized her work by arguing:

> Almost all of Ms. Goudge's fiction is based on a dialectic between a self-constructed imaginative form which demands a happy ending and a content drawn from a world which does not provide that kind of well-ordered material. And it seems to be her talent for creating character images who illustrate the sacrifice of truth which must be made in exchange for order which captures her audience even more than the romance and the comfort which her novels bring.
>
> (69)

Marsden is particularly concerned with demonstrating the compromises Goudge's protagonists make, particularly her women, to accommodate an English world ordered by hierarchies of gender and class, and how Goudge manages to make such compromises look desirable despite the pain her protagonists frequently suffer. Marsden's paradigm tellingly reveals a great deal about much of Goudge's fiction, but it fails to arrive at a complete account of Goudge's philosophy or ideology since her novels for children operate quite differently. In the children's fiction of Goudge, particularly the four novels listed above, it is not the individual who bends to accommodate unpleasant realities, but instead the world which is transformed by the actions of the protagonist.

One of the most interesting examples of this phenomenon can be seen in Goudge's treatment of economic inequality. Valerie Krips has argued that children's literature represents the world and responds to the social and institutional frameworks of class in telling ways (196). She points out that "The English have long been a nation of conservationists, particularly of rural England, and the close relation of preservation to the interests of property, and the propertied classes, has been noted often" (200). Instead of completely recapitulating class hierarchies in the ways Krips notes in other authors of children's literature, Goudge struggles to create a magical world and preserve mythical traditions without sacrificing equity. Despite her sheltered upbringing—her mother came from an established Guernsey Island family and her father was the Regius Professor of Divinity at Oxford University—Goudge was by no means naive about the privileges of class and the harsh realities of life. Nor was she particularly interested in shielding her readers. In many of her adult novels pain, cruelty, poverty, and despair take center stage. Yet, no such scenes of human misery haunt Goudge's children's fiction. Instead, these novels tend towards the humorously idyllic. ***Smoky House,*** for example, opens with a description of a perfect community:

> In the village of Faraway everyone was happy, not only in spring, but always, for Faraway is set in that part of England which is called the West Country, and that is a part of the world so beautiful that the people who live in it are always happy; and as happy people are always kind you could live in the village all your life long and never hear an angry voice or the sound of weeping.
>
> (14)

The village of Silverydew in ***The Little White Horse*** and the Hard in ***The Valley of Song*** are similarly blessed. Unlike many writers of fairy tales and fantasies, however, Goudge's characters work not only within a world of physical well-being, but work toward instituting economic changes that will support and sustain such a world.

At the beginning of ***Smoky House*** the five children of the Treguddick family are vehement and comfortable in their condemnation of smugglers and highwaymen. Their village has never been harmed or plundered by such disreputable characters, but they have heard tales and know the red-coated soldiers from the nearby garrison are constantly on guard against such criminals. Thus the children are genuinely stunned one sunny morning when the local squire and justice of the peace informs them that there are two opinions about smuggling:

> "Some people say it is not wrong to break bad laws. Some say the law that makes people pay customs duties on foreign goods is a bad law, and that the smugglers who break it are not doing wrong, but good."
>
> The children gaped, for they did not quite understand.
>
> ". . . as the customs duties are so heavy the foreign merchants have to charge the English merchants a great deal for their goods, and then the English merchants have to charge their customers a great deal, and that means that only rich men can buy brandy and tobacco, or silk and lace. Poor men have to go without."
>
> "How mean!" said Jane again.
>
> "Many think so," said the Squire.
>
> (96-98)

The children quickly convert to the Squire's view of smuggling (or, as he teaches them to refer to it, "free trading") and join wholeheartedly into the business when they eventually discover that not only the Squire himself, but their father as well, participates in the illicit activity. They are not, however, quite so ready to accept as honorable the practice of holding up rich travellers on the highway. Even if the Squire does give the proceeds of such ventures to the poor, ill-gotten gains breed trouble. The recipients of such money always seem mysteriously to break out into spots or suffer other minor discomforts. So a compromise of sorts is reached: the Squire takes up farming his estate to provide an income for his charitable impulses, but

> he never became absolutely and entirely good . . . he would creep out of the house and across the garden to the stables, saddle his big black horse and gallop away up on to the moors . . . And he would come back very late for supper that night, very tired and very happy . . . And next day there would be rumours all over the countryside that the-Man-with-the-Handkerchief had been seen again, that a rich traveller had been robbed up on the high moors, and that a poor traveller had had a bag of money thrown at his feet by the unseen hand of a Good Person, and had heard a voice saying from behind a heather-covered hillock, "Pick this up if you don't mind having spots."
>
> (282)

In the end of the novel, highway robbery has been curtailed, but smuggling flourishes providing all of the villagers of Faraway with enough extra-legal income to maintain prosperity for all.

In ***The Valley of Song*** Goudge employs a similar scheme of economic levelling. The novel takes place in the Hard, a small shipbuilding town nestled above one of the loveliest rivers in England. Excusing herself from school one day to enjoy the glories of spring, Tabitha discovers that the magnificent, half-built, East Indiaman currently under construction in the Yard is about to be destroyed. The East India Company has countermanded the order. Too much love and craftsmanship has, however, gone into the ship's construction, and no one can bear to see such a beautiful work of art destroyed. Tabitha, with an unquenchable faith in the possibility of miracles, leads various members of the community on quests to obtain the materials needed to finish the ship. In the magical Valley of Song organized under the architecture of the zodiac, peopled by creatures of British and Goudgian folklore, and informed by the language of the one hundred and fourth psalm, Tabitha and her companions procure the paints, sailcloth, timber, and gold-plating needed to complete the ship. And when the ship is finished and christened the *White Swan,* she belongs to all who have worked to create her:

> She would trade for the East India Company, and Captain Throckmorton would stand upon her poop in pride and glory when she sailed down the river to the sea, but she belonged to the Hard. Every man who had worked upon her had a share in her; and so had the women and children of the Hard, and the little red-roofed houses, and the marshes and the river. . . . She belonged to them all.
>
> (272)

As with the smugglers of Faraway in ***Smoky House,*** the hard work of the citizens in ***The Valley of Song*** enriches the community. The artisans, who usually only labor for wages, are rewarded in this story with a share of their product.

Goudge makes what may well be her strongest, or at least her most direct, argument for economic justice in ***The Little White Horse.*** After the death of her father, Maria Merryweather and her governess Miss Heliotrope arrive at Moonacre Manor to take up residence with a cousin, Sir Benjamin. The mysterious passageways and gardens of the estate intrigue the heroine from the moment she arrives, and her cozy little bedroom perched atop a turret wins Maria's heart completely. Despite the lovely landscape and architecture, Maria quickly perceives that all is not well at Moonacre Manor. Although she is encouraged to explore, Maria is not allowed to wander without an escort, preferably Sir Benjamin's huge dog Wrolf whose massive chest, glorious flowing mane, and queer tail with a tuft of hair on the end of it are more than enough to keep ill-wishers at a distance.[11] Maria's wish to visit Merryweather Bay and catch her first glimpse of the sea is also thwarted when she is informed that "the fishermen down there are a very rough lot" (56), and she is not to go near them. Even Moonacre Park, it turns out, is not without its hazards. The screams of a trapped hare and the ensuing battle with a poacher for possession of the animal intrude upon Maria's first survey of the neighborhood.

Gradually Maria learns the cause of all the ominous activity in the Kingdom of Moonacre. Generations ago the first Sir Wrolf Merryweather extended his holdings by appropriating Paradise Hill, rich grazing lands previously owned by the Church. Furthermore, he decided that the nearby coastal land should also be annexed to his estate. This peremptory decision resulted in a feud with Sir William Cocq de Noir, the rightful owner of the property. For a time it looked as if the conflict would be resolved when Sir William's daughter and heir agreed to marry Sir Wrolf, but the union dissolved disastrously and the young bride disappeared. Ever since, the descendants of the two men have fought and quarreled, destroying the peace of all the surrounding inhabitants. Once in each generation a young couple have the opportunity to resolve the feud, but pride and anger have always intervened. Realizing that the opportunity for reconciliation lies in her own hands and those of her childhood playfellow Robin, Maria marshals the strength of her own character and the skills of her friends to solve the mysteries of Moonacre and bring happiness to the kingdom.

Much of Maria's task involves restoring economic justice. Her ancestor Sir Wrolf stole Paradise Hill, and the first thing she needs to do is to convince Sir Benjamin to relinquish it to its true owners. Still newly arrived, Maria is uncertain how Sir Benjamin will receive such a suggestion; she decides to take a direct approach following the example of her aristocratic ancestors and command rather than request:

> "Sir Wrolf stole Paradise Hill from God," said Maria firmly. "And tomorrow Old Parson and all the children and I are going to give it back to God. It won't be yours any more."
>
> "Dear me," said Sir Benjamin.
>
> "You must give me your word, Sir," said Maria, "that you will not keep the money for yourself any more, but will give it to the poor."
>
> "My income will be considerably depleted," said Sir Benjamin in rather dry tones.
>
> "You could eat less," suggested Maria helpfully.
>
> (183)

Happily, the robust Sir Benjamin capitulates and acknowledges that instead of dieting, he could augment his income by taking up farming on his own land. Restoring Paradise Hill is, however, only half the battle. The Black Men (the descendants of Sir William Cocq de Noir, called Black William because of his crest, a black cock, and his dark eyes and hair) must also be persuaded to give up incomes garnered through theft and poaching rather than honest labor. With Robin and several resourceful animal companions, Maria storms the ancient Norman Castle deep in the woods where the Black Men dwell and proposes a new peace:

> "My ancestor, Sir Wrolf, was very wicked to try to take Black William's land away from him," went on Maria. "But he was not any more wicked than you are, poaching and stealing in the way you do."
>
> "My land is unproductive," snapped Monsieur Cocq de Noir. "We cannot rear livestock in a pinewood. Upon what am I and my men to live if we do not poach and steal?"
>
> "You should trade with the valley people," Robin piped up suddenly. "We never have any fresh fish in the valley. We're longing for it. You should sell us your fish, and we would sell you our meat and eggs and poultry."
>
> Monsieur Cocq de Noir snorted with contempt. "It would be quite impossible for a Cocq de Noir to support himself in his ancestral castle with the

dignity befitting his rank by selling fish," he said with an indignation that raised his voice gradually from an angry mutter to a shout of rage.

(220)

Instead, Monsieur Cocq de Noir proposes a series of impossible sounding conditions for Maria to fulfill before he and his band will abandon their criminal practices. Much to even her own amazement, Maria succeeds in fulfilling them, and in the conclusion of the novel, Monsieur Cocq de Noir reluctantly agrees to his half of the bargain and takes up fishing. In ***The Little White Horse*** the villagers of the Kingdom of Moonacre win happiness and financial prosperity, not because they change their ways, but instead because Sir Benjamin and Monsieur Cocq de Noir agree to quit an unjust economic system and become members of the working class themselves.[12]

In the idyllic villages of Goudge's England, squires, captains, and the rest of the gentry may share in the bounty of the fantasy, but only if they have shared in the labor and the risks. Class distinctions are not abandoned or dismantled in these children's novels, but they are undermined in favor of economic equality; the desire to preserve class in these books is balanced against a desire to preserve a form of economic justice. In Goudge's children's novels the protagonists do not, as Marsden suggests, change or modify their beliefs, instead they work to create a world which fulfills them.

If the treatment of class sets Goudge apart from many writers of fairy tales and fantasies, her treatment of gender does not. Goudge's novels for children do not always escape the sexism of her period. In ***Linnets and Valerians,*** perhaps the most delightful and neglected of her children's novels, Nan, Robert, Tim, and Betsy flee the home of their authoritarian grandmother only to find themselves at the mercy of their Uncle Ambrose, a retired school master and firm believer in discipline. Nonetheless, unlike Grandmother, he does not believe Nan or Robert are ready for boarding school or that the fleas on the children's dog Absolom are liable to cause any more problems than the four children will themselves—and so he agrees to keep them all, and they him. Outlining the educational agenda he has planned for them, Uncle Ambrose announces, "Home's the place for girls, though they should have a classical education there. I have always maintained that women would not be the featherheaded fools they are, were they given a classical education from the earliest infancy" (37-38). And unfortunately, Goudge herself seems to agree with him, at least when it comes to keeping girls at home.

In ***Linnets and Valerians*** Timothy and Robert find themselves wrestling cats the size of tigers and defending themselves amid the tree tops from what may well be the local coven of witches. Nan and Betsy's adventures all take place in homes. Betsy chases a monkey through the dark and dusty halls of Lady Alicia's manor house. Nan's discovery of the book of spells tucked away in the parlor cupboard and of Daft Davie's secret cavern abode are intriguing, but they lack much of the heart-pounding excitement of the boys' experiences. Goudge tries to present this limitation upon her heroines' activity as evidence of their common sense rather than any sort of inability. The omniscient narrator of the novel explains, "Nan did not have many ideas of her own because it was she who had to deal with what happened after Robert had had his" (7). Such statements, regardless of their intent, tend to limit the heroines to the role of caregiver. Indeed, during the course of the novel Robert successively imagines himself adopting careers as a burglar, engine driver, acrobat, actor, general, Roman emperor, and diplomat. Nan and Betsy never imagine themselves as anything other than wives and mothers. In fact, the epilogue informs the reader that Betsy grew up to produce six children and Nan two.[13] Goudge respects the courage and intelligence of her female protagonists as much as that of her male protagonists, but she routinely fails to imagine as broad a range of possible futures for her girls as her boys.

Similar problems plague many of her children's novels. In ***Smoky House*** the girls stay in the inn to guard the newly arrived contraband while their brothers race to the coast to warn the smugglers that they have been betrayed and the soldiers are hot on their heels. In ***The Valley of Song*** Tabitha is a child with special talents who can guide less gifted mortals in and out of a magical kingdom, but once they set out on their adventures, she is unable to keep pace with them. Job, Anthony, and Andrew climb the peaks of eternal mountains and journey to the bottom of the darkest seas to fulfill their quests, but Tabitha cannot follow them and returns to the green hills of Arcady to keep Julie, the only other female adventurer in the valley, company. Only when she is with Simon, her father and protector, is Tabitha able to explore the burning heart of the kingdom.[14]

Despite her limitations, Goudge is not without humor when it comes to creating models of female behavior. Throughout ***The Little White Horse*** Maria is directed by nearly every male she meets to repress the insatiable and unbecoming curiosity to which all women are apparently prey, despite the fact she has done nothing to warrant such admonishments. The most telling advice on this issue comes from Marmaduke Scarlet, the cook, who compares Maria to the other women who have formerly dwelt in Moonacre Manor:

> "You, Mistress, are of tender years; and femininity, my dear young lady, grows on a female with the passage of time, like all bad habits, and is less objectionable in the early stages. And as for your lady governess, she is a distinct improvement upon that other duenna, who resided here before with the other young mistress, and never stopped asking questions. Through the keyhole I have perceived her to be a woman of great saintliness of character."
>
> (103)

Marmaduke Scarlet unwittingly reveals that it is not curiosity which is offensive; instead it is, apparently, the verbal expression of inquisitiveness favored by women. Spying and eavesdropping are seemingly lauded as more worthy methods of gathering information than posing questions. With this sly wink to her audience at Marmaduke Scarlet's expense, Goudge is not so much retracting the argument that girls should refrain from expressing their curiosity as pointing out that few people are able to practice their principles as well as they preach them.

In spite of his less than enlightened views of women, Marmaduke Scarlet does stand as tribute to one of Goudge's finest skills—the ability to draw delightful and memorable characters. His appearance absolutely mesmerizes Maria when she wins her first invitation into his kitchen, his kingdom:

> He must, she thought, be very old, for the fringe of whisker that encircled his whole face like a ham frill was snow white, and so were his bushy eyebrows. Except for the whisker frill, his face was clean-shaven, brown as an oak-apple, and criss-crossed with hundreds of little wrinkles. His nose was so snub that there seemed very little of it; but what there was of it was evidently sensitive, for it quivered as he worked, like a rabbit's. His sense of smell, like that of all good cooks, was obviously very highly developed indeed. His large mouth was a great half-moon of generosity when he smiled, a rat-trap of determination when he shut it. His brown ears were much too big for the rest of him, but they were beautifully shaped and tapered to a delicate point, like a fawn's.
>
> (98-99)

Amazingly, Marmaduke's language is even more colorful than his appearance. Directing Maria with the authority of a ruler absolutely confident in his dominion, Marmaduke Scarlet issues instructions:[15]

> "You may take one of those dishcloths from the line, fetch yourself a stool, and give me the benefit of your assistance during those ablutions that necessarily, though unfortunately, invariably follow the exercise of the culinary art."
>
> Marmaduke Scarlet, it seemed, made up for the shortness of his stature by using very long words in conversation. It struck Maria that if she had much to do with him she would need to keep a dictionary in her pocket.
>
> (101)

Many appealing creations issue from Marmaduke's realm—plum cake, saffron cake, cherry cake, iced fairy cakes, eclairs, gingerbread, meringues, syllabub, almond fingers, rock cakes, chocolate cakes, parkin, cream horns, Devonshire splits, Cornish pasty, jam sandwiches, lemon-curd sandwiches, lettuce sandwiches, cinnamon toast, and honey toast (265), but he does not rule over the most interesting kitchen in Goudge's novels. That honor is best reserved for Ezra Oake, a little man with a wooden leg decorated with a fascinating bee carved and painted on its round polished surface. The four children of ***Linnets and Valerians*** first meet him in his kitchen "dancing in the bright moonlight, two saucepan lids held in his hands as castanets, singing as he danced" (26). Ezra orders his kingdom on an entirely different set of principles than those of the precise and immaculate Marmaduke Scarlet:

> Apart from the settle by the hearth, and the black kettle murmuring gently on top of the range, everything was in the wrong place. A basket full of a cat and six kittens was on the draining board, the dishes and plates and two pairs of boots were stacked on the table, the cuckoo clock was in the sink, the saucepans were on the floor, and the mantel piece, windowsills, and dresser were crowded with plants in pots, bast and string, and seed boxes. Some women, but no men or children might have considered this a dirty kitchen, but they would have been wrong. It was not dirty because it smelled right. It smelled of onions, herbs, geraniums, and good earth, but not dirt.
>
> (23)

Ezra's language is also as memorable as that of Marmaduke Scarlet. But while Maria is liable to benefit from the erudition and expansiveness of Marmaduke Scarlet's conversation, the potential effects of Ezra's language on Nan, Robert, Timothy, and Betsy are more difficult to judge. When badgered by the children to teach them the song he was singing when they first discovered him dancing in the moonlight, he sheepishly acknowledges that his splendid ditty was, in fact, a drinking song:

> Glory for the foamin', brimmin tankard
> Good ale an' beer,
> Champagne in the polished crystal glasses
> Sparklin' an' clear.
> Glory glory alleluja!
>
> (203)

Another vividly drawn but more difficult character also inhabits ***Linnets and Valerians.*** Moses Glory Glory Alleluja, who draws his name from a more pious version of Ezra's song, is the chef, butler, and former coachman to the reclusive Lady Alicia. The children stop in their tracks when they first meet him in the overgrown woods of the Valerian estate:

> He was a coal-black giant with a big head and long loose arms. He had a curved knife in one hand and stood a little crouched, as though ready to spring at them. Absolom growled and the children stopped dead so suddenly that Ezra, leading Rob-Roy, bumped into Timothy.
>
> "Get on then," said Ezra, annoyed. "What's come to ee? That's only Moses Glory Glory Alleluja. Don't 'urt the poor chap's feelin's now. Gentle as a dove'e be."
>
> Nan walked bravely forward, for she was a child who would not have liked to hurt the feelings of the devil himself, the others following, and the nearer they came to Moses Glory Glory Alleluja the less terrible did he appear, and when they were actually through the arch of yew and quite close to him, he was suddenly changed by some miracle of the sunlight from a figure of fear into one of the most attractive men they had ever seen. He was a Negro with white woolly hair, tall but stooped about the shoulders, his face folded into deep lines of age and kindness. His eyes were sad, but his smile, as he looked at the children, was as wide with pleasure as Ezra's own.
>
> (62-63)

Representations of people of color are not particularly common in British children's books of the 1960s, particularly in stories set at the turn of the century and authored by aging women.[16] In ***Linnets and Valerians*** Goudge develops a fully-fledged African character without entirely escaping the stereotypes and colonialist assumptions of her period.

The children's initially fearful reaction to Moses is a little difficult to fathom. They have only recently arrived in England from India, so the sight of someone of a different race than themselves ought not to be particularly upsetting. But Moses also appears suddenly and unexpectedly, and it may be surprise at his existence, as much as his appearance, that accounts for their reaction. In any case, Ezra nudges the children into more appropriate behavior and soon both Moses and the children have cheerfully accepted each other. Only Robert, the most self-involved of the children, fails to perceive Moses as an equal. Later that same afternoon Robert slips into one of his many self-aggrandizing fantasies. Pretending to be a Roman emperor about to storm a citadel, he turns to Moses and incorporates him into his fantasy; "'Slave,' he said to his coal-black Nubian standard-bearer, lead on" (91). Robert remains oblivious to the insulting and painful presumptions of his "game," but Timothy turns to look anxiously at Moses and is relieved to discover that he is still smiling amiably, his feelings unhurt by Robert's ignorance. Through her representation of Timothy's concern, Goudge demonstrates her sensitivity to the problems inherent in Robert's assumptions that Moses is best suited for the role of a slave, but in failing to correct or change Robert, Goudge seems also tacitly to permit the continuation of certain kinds of stereotyping and ignorance. Beliefs and behaviors that may seem harmless in a powerless ten-year-old will become much more dangerous should Robert continue to exercise them as an adult.

The failure of the imagination which limits Goudge in her creation of female heroines also restricts her representation of Moses. Goudge relegates him to the role of loyal retainer with as much finality as most of her heroines are assigned to the household. The long-lost Hugo Valerian purchased Moses in a slave market when he was still in his teens and brought him home to attend upon Lady Alicia and young Francis Valerian. With a typically colonialist perspective the Valerian family, if not Goudge herself, seems perfectly content with the notion that Moses will reward his rescuer with abiding loyalty and service. Years after every other servant has abandoned the estate, Moses continucs to wait upon Lady Alicia. He ex presses no interest in the family, friends, and culture he left behind in Africa—or in any other independent ambition.

Despite these limitations in his representation, as the story progresses, Moses becomes not only a friend, guide, and protector to the children, but also a role model. On their first Sunday in residence with Uncle Ambrose, the children are terrified to discover that they haven't the slightest idea how to behave in church. Much to their relief, Moses arrives and seats himself in the front pew opposite their own:

> Entering the grand pew he sat down, said a prayer with one large hand over his eyes, then laid his cane and gloves on the seat and his prayer book on the shelf in front of him, placed his hands one upon each knee and, gazing straight in front of him, turned into an ebony statue. Nan, who was nearest to the aisle on her side, gave a sigh of relief. Moses, she knew, would do everything correctly and out of the corner of her eye she would be able to watch what he did and do the same.
>
> (123)

Unlike most of the vivid and eccentric characters in Goudge's novel, Moses requires careful consideration. He is both a sympathetic and a flawed representation of an African protagonist—sympathetic in that Goudge struggles with some success to make Moses an interesting individual rather than a stereotypical black servant, but flawed in that not all of the story's child protagonists recognize this important distinction.

One of the lesser, but more delightful, aspects of Goudge's worlds are her animal heroes. Sometimes Goudge translates the barking and braying of her four-legged protagonists into English as with the wonderfully satiric voices of the dogs Sausage and Spot and the donkey Matilda in ***Smoky House.*** In ***The Little White Horse*** the virtual menagerie of animals who accompany Maria on her adventures generally manage to communicate without the benefit of words. Zachariah the cat, however, introduces a particularly fascinating form of communication. Marmaduke Scarlet explains Zachariah's unique skills to Maria:

> "Any communication which Zachariah is called upon to deliver he inscribes with his right forepaw in the ashes," he said. "Zachariah is an exceptionally gifted cat. His ancestors were worshipped as gods by the Pharaohs of ancient Egypt, so he tells me, and the blood in his veins is blue, so he tells me. The latter statement I can corroborate, for upon one occasion he had the misfortune to insinuate his nose too near the meat hatchet. " . . . Maria set down her mug of milk, ran to the hearth and looked at the ashes. They had been spread smoothly, as though with the swish of a long tail, and little pictures bearing a marked resemblance to Egyptian hieroglyphics had been traced on them.
>
> (147)

But even Zachariah cannot compete with the species introduced in ***Linnets and Valerians.*** Uncle Ambrose's owl Hector winks, hoots, or spits pellets of disagreeable undigested material at the children as the circumstances warrant—his opinions require little translation. The vicarage bees, however, are more mysterious. Ezra admonishes the children not to go near the hives in the garden until they have been properly introduced; "Bees," he tells them, "understand every word you say." (49). When he was a boy watching the sheep on the moor, Ezra stumbled into an old mine shaft. He feared he would never be found, but in the morning the vicarage bees swarmed and led a party of villagers to rescue him. Once they understand the power of the bees, the children are careful to keep an eye out for them and, sure enough, they are rewarded for their diligence by buzzing escorts when they get lost and stinging avengers when they are attacked. In Goudge's children's novels animals (and insects) frequently display more insight and wisdom than people.

Goudge's novels unfailingly include all the best aspects of fairy tales. Her language is detailed and vivid; her characters are warm and original. Good triumphs over evil and even the villains are usually redeemed. But in weaving her fantasies into the fabric of everyday life, Goudge goes beyond magical escapism and struggles to address modern concerns as well as traditional themes. One of these themes is loss. Goudge's stories almost always require the lost to be found—a lost family member, a lost ideal, a lost history. So while it may be ironic, it is not unfitting that her books have themselves been lost to many readers and critics—at least in part because of the difficulty modern scholars and publishers have had in classifying them. The solution to the problem of loss in Goudge's novels is usually found in the children who through their curiosity, their perseverance, and their wit manage to discover and recover everyone and everything that has been misplaced or gone astray. Similarly, Goudge herself needs to be rediscovered by readers, especially children, and returned to her position of prominence in their hearts and on their bookshelves.

Notes

1. A year after the publication of *Sister of the Angels,* Goudge released another book entitled *Smoky House.* In the *New York Times Book Review* of 10 November 1940 Anne T. Eaton favorably compares the boys and girls of *Smoky House* with the young people so frequently found in Goudge's previous books (10). And a quarter-page advertisement taken out by the publisher Coward McCann on page 20 of the same issue trumpets *Smoky House* as Goudge's

first book for children. The advertisement reads, "It seemed inevitable that one who loved and portrayed children so well should sooner or later write a story mainly about children."

2. *Twentieth Century Children's Writers,* for example, lists *Sister of the Angels* among Elizabeth Goudge's publications for children.

3. At least one reviewer would have been inclined to disagree with this claim. Although *Henrietta's House* is discussed as a children's novel, in a review entitled "Half-Magic" the anonymous reviewer for the *Times Literary Supplement* claimed that, "the author too often allows her interest to be riveted by the eccentric Edwardian adults who are invited to Hugh Anthony's birthday picnic, because, one feels, she is really more attracted to adults and suffers children only as a necessary adjunct to her story" (352). Although I disagree with this reviewer's conclusions, this vein of criticism does illustrate the difficulty readers of all ages have had deciding who Goudge's books are for—adults or children. Goudge herself probably found this critic's conclusions amusing, if not annoying, as she claimed herself to prefer writing, above all other things, about children and dogs (qtd. in Marsden, 69).

4. In England *Henrietta's House* was released under the title *The Blue Hills.*

5. John Gough makes a similar claim in his article "Rediscovering 'The Little White Horse'" when he says, "One of the most remarkable aspects of *The Little White Horse,* indeed, is its anticipation of the ancient-myths-come-true-in-a-modern-world fantasy genre of such writers as Garner, C. S. Lewis, Susan Cooper, Mollie Hunter, John Gordon, Penelope Lively, Penelope Farmer and William Rayner" (168).

6. *Green Dolphin Street* is even treated in Frank Magill's *Masterplots II: Juvenile and Young Adult Fiction.* John Gough (who brought this source to my attention as well as providing me with a variety of other sources and his invaluable personal insight on Goudge's work) suspects that the reason *Green Dolphin Street* is singled out for such attention has less to do with the characteristics, themes, or quality of the novel and more to do with availability. It was offered as a Book-of-the-Month-Club selection, and in 1947 it was made into a Hollywood film directed by Victor Saville and starring Lana Turner, Donna Reed, and Van Heflin. See also his discussion of Goudge's Young Adult fiction in "Rediscovering Elizabeth Goudge—Not Just a Romance Writer."

7. *Pilgrim's Inn* was published in England in 1948 under the title *The Herb of Grace.*

8. The image of the white hart is reminiscent of the title character of another one of Goudge's children's novels, *The Little White Horse.* In both his articles "Unicorns and Literature" and "Rediscovering 'The Little White Horse,'" John Gough explores the symbolic significance of these types of images in Goudge's mythological world in much greater detail.

9. Christmas stories might, in fact, be considered a sub-genre within Goudge's work. *Sister of the Angels* is an extended Christmas story. Chapter seven of *Make-Believe,* entitled "Midnight in the Stable," can stand alone as a Christmas tale, most of the seven short Christmas stories collected in the volume *The Lost Angel* (1971) are appropriate for young readers, and many of her adult anthologies, including *A Christmas Book* (1967), also contain pieces with Christmas themes.

10. *Smoky House* and *The Valley of Song* are, sadly, long out of print and often difficult to come by. Fortunately, in 1992 Yearling Classics reissued *The Little White Horse* and *Linnets and Valerians.* Although it is difficult to foresee how long these two volumes will remain in print, they are certainly much more readily available than they were even a few years ago. I am, however, skeptical about their shelf life because both books are done an injustice by misleadingly sentimental and furbelowed cover art in place of the clever and inviting illustrations with which they were originally published.

11. Wrolf, as it turns out, is not a dog at all, but rather a lion. In several ways he seems to anticipate Aslan from C. S. Lewis' *Chronicles of Narnia,* the first of which was published four years after *The Little White Horse.* Neither Wrolf nor Aslan are permanent inhabitants of the magical worlds. Wrolf comes out of the forest once every generation in anticipation of the arrival of the moon maiden who holds the potential within herself to heal the wounds of the community. Aslan also visits Narnia only sporadically, though in C. S. Lewis' stories he is himself the savior rather than the herald of one. But even the descriptions of these animals and the ways the heroines respond to them seem to

echo each other. In *The Little White Horse* Maria struggles up the steep slopes of Paradise Hill toward a ruined Abbey:

> And Wrolf did not make things easier by perpetually pushing himself against her, and fixing her with a tawny eye full of annoyance, "What *is* it Wrolf?" she demanded. "What am I doing wrong?"
>
> Wrolf, with a subdued roar at her stupidity, turned himself right across her path so that she came to a standstill, looking down upon his broad back. Then she saw what he wanted. . . . After that everything was easy. Wrolf's beautiful thick fur was soft to sit upon, and with her fingers entwined in his ruff she was able to hold herself steady. She could look about her now, and as they mounted higher see the beautiful countryside unrolling about them like a map.
>
> (155-56)

In *The Lion, the Witch, and the Wardrobe,* Susan and Lucy share a similar experience with Aslan:

> And so the girls did what they would never have dared to do without his permission but what they had longed to do ever since they first saw him—buried their cold hands in the beautiful sea of fur and stroked it and, so doing, walked with him. And presently they saw that they were going with him up the slope of the hill on which the Stone Table stood.
>
> (147-48)

Later in the novel the girls also ride on Aslan's back and watch with amazement as Narnia unfurls before them and tiny castles grow from toys to towering citadels (161-63).

More generally, Goudge and C. S. Lewis also share a talent for creating fantastic worlds which allegorically impart a version of Christian theology, though these allegories are much more fully developed in Lewis' work. In Goudge, as in Lewis, the stories do not require symbolic explication in order to be enjoyed or understood—the Christian framework merely provides another level of meaning for those aware of or searching for spiritual perspectives.

12. The book is not a perfect celebration of a working-class text as Maria is from the gentry herself and virtually all of the leadership in the battle toward a greater economic equality comes from members of the gentry, a state of affairs which still suggests a hierarchical system, but Goudge's novels do involve a much more systematic overhaul of the economic system than most children's fantasies. Similar limitations apply to *Smoky House* as well, but perhaps not to *The Valley of Song* where Tabitha, the smith's daughter, provides the inspiration and the leadership for the new economic project.

13. Such epilogues are one of the difficult weaknesses of Goudge's novels. *Linnets and Valerians, Smoky House,* and *The Little White Horse* all end with tenuously linked conclusions relating the marital and child-bearing histories of the heroines—sometimes the fates of their brothers are also included, but not always. These "happily-ever-after" epilogues provide a sense of closure and security as the story ends, but at the same time collapse all of the well-developed and interesting heroines into a uniform stereotype. These endings are particularly ironic in that one of the strengths of Goudge's adult fiction is her uncringing willingness to dissect and expose the difficult, and even painful, reality of marriage.

    Although Henrietta from the Torminister Trilogy shows talent as an artist, her devotion to her male relatives and her wish to manage her own home, suggest that her drawing will probably play second fiddle to her housekeeping. Tabitha turns suddenly shy and well behaved at the conclusion of *The Valley of Song,* though, perhaps this new behavior is only a phase. The du Frocq girls from *Make-Believe* and *Island Magic* are perhaps her only heroines to escape domestication completely. Michelle intends to become a scholar and teacher; Peronelle intends to imitate her grandfather and become a doctor—only she intends to be more effective in the practice of medicine than he is; and Jacqueline, to her mother's dismay, leans toward the convent.

14. On some levels such criticism of the treatment of gender in *The Valley of Song* might seem unfair since each of the quests undertaken by the characters is symbolically a redemptive, spiritual journey, the kind each person must always make alone. Yet, the book fails in some ways as it limits such soul-searching and sacrifice to men. For Tabitha and Julie the Valley of Song is mostly a place of joyful renewal, not one of personal growth. Blessed with innocence they are simultaneously denied experience.

15. John Gough also comments on the splendid eloquence and circumloquacity of Marmaduke Scarlet's language and the Dickensian energy of Goudge's characters ("Rediscovering 'The Little White Horse'" 169).

16. *Linnets and Valerians* is set in 1912.

Works Cited

Campbell, Alasdair K. D. "Elizabeth Goudge." *Twentieth Century Children's Writers.* Ed. Tracy Chevalier. Chicago: St. James, 1989. 388-90.

Crouch, Marcus. "Salute to Children's Literature and its Creators." *Readings About Children's Literature.* Ed. Evelyn Rose Robinson. New York: David McKay & Co., 1966. 183-87.

Eaton, Anne T., "English Countryside." Rev. of *Smoky House* by Elizabeth Goudge. *New York Times Book Review.* 10 November 1940: 10.

Goudge, Elizabeth. *A Christmas Book.* New York: Coward McCann, 1967.

———. *A City of Bells.* New York: Coward McCann, 1936.

———. *The Dean's Watch.* New York: Coward McCann, 1960.

———. *Green Dolphin Street.* New York: Coward McCann, 1944.

———. *Henrietta's House.* Illus. Lorna R. Steele. London: U of London P/Hodder & Stoughton, 1942: as *The Blue Hills.* New York: Coward McCann, 1942.

———. *I Saw Three Ships.* Illus. Margot Tomes. New York: Coward McCann, 1969.

———. *The Joy of the Snow: An Autobiography.* London: Hodder & Stoughton, 1974.

———. *Linnets and Valerians.* Illus. Ian Ribbons. 1964. New York: Dell Publishing, 1992.

———. *The Little White Horse.* Illus. C. Walter Hodges. 1946. Leicester, England: Brockhampton Press, 1973.

———. *The Lost Angel.* Illus. Shirley Hughes. New York: Coward McCann, 1971.

———. *Make-Believe.* 1949. Hampton, NH: Curley Large Print, 1994.

———. *The Middle Window.* 1935. New York: Coward McCann, 1939.

———. *Sister of the Angels.* Illus. C. Walter Hodges. New York: Coward McCann, 1939.

———. *Smoky House.* Illus. Richard Floethe. New York: Coward McCann, 1940.

———. *The Valley of Song.* Illus. Richard Floethe. New York: Coward McCann, 1951.

———. *The Well of the Star.* New York: Coward McCann, 1941.

Gough, John. "Elizabeth Goudge." *Twentieth-Century Romance and Historical Writers.* Ed. Aruna Vasuvedan. 3rd ed. London: St James Press, 1994. 273-74.

———. "Rediscovering Elizabeth Goudge—Not Just a 'Romance' Writer." *Bookbird* 34.1 (1996), forthcoming.

———. "Rediscovering 'The Little White Horse.'" *Signal* 48 (1985): 168-75.

———. "Unicorns and Literature: Elizabeth Goudge's *The Little White Horse.*" *The Junior Bookshelf* 51.3 (1987): 113-17.

"Half-Magic." Rev. of *Henrietta's House,* by Elizabeth Goudge. *Times Literary Supplement* 3 April 1969: 335.

Rev. of *I Saw Three Ships,* by Elizabeth Goudge. *Horn Book* 45 (Dec. 1969): 661.

Kingsland, Dorthea. "Happy Islanders." Rev. of *Island Magic,* by Elizabeth Goudge. *The New York Times Book Review* 23 Feb. 1936: 6-7.

Krips, Valerie. "A Notable Irrelevance: Class and Children's Fiction." *The Lion and the Unicorn* 17.2 (1993) 195-209.

Lewis, C. S. *The Lion, the Witch, and the Wardrobe.* 1950. New York: Collier Books, 1970.

Marsden, Madonna. "Gentle Truths for Gentle Readers: The Fiction of Elizabeth Goudge." *Images of Women in Fiction: Feminist Perspectives.* Ed. Susan Koppelman Cornillon. Bowling Green OH: Bowling Green U Popular P, 1972. 68-78.

Southron, Jane Spence. "A Quiet Garden." Rev. of *Sister of the Angels,* by Elizabeth Goudge. *The New York Times Review Book Review* 29 Oct. 1939: 22.

Twentieth Century Children's Writers. Ed. Tracy Chevalier. Chicago: St James Press, 1989.

TITLE COMMENTARY

ISLAND MAGIC (1934)

Dorthea Kingsland (review date 23 February 1936)

SOURCE: Kingsland, Dorthea. "Happy Islanders." *New York Times Book Review* (23 February 1936): 6-7.

Sunsets, storms, flowers and haunted lanes and gardens—these are the magic of the Island. And they play upon the lives of the gifted, impoverished du Frocq family until rare visions shine before their eyes. ***Island Magic*** is a glowing book. Sometimes it is sentimental and too artfully poetic, but it is always a glowing book. For one thing, the Island itself, magical though it may be, is a very real place. It is one of those that dot the English Channel, being, in 1888, close to the French shore in spirit as well as geography, but mixing English culture and government with its old Gallic faith and superstition. The tumbling streets of the town hum with quaint patois while Shakespeare is read in the schools; the fancies of the du Frocq children wing the spaces of English poetry while nasty French epithets trip from their tongues. To enter into this life is a gay experience. In the year 1888 the du Frocqs are struggling for existence and finding exaltation on the long disused family farm, lovely Bon Repos, where Rachell du Frocq, "in pity for tarnished beauty, had trained a passion flower over the windows and planted scarlet fuchsias on either side of the door." Both Rachell and André du Frocq had known money and social life, but she had sacrificed them for him and he for the philosophic dreams that come to him as he pores distractedly over his pigs and diseased tomatoes. Now André fears that they must even give up Bon Repos, but Rachell, borne up by second sight, compels him to forget his fears. And presently, out of a shipwreck at sea, comes the battered stranger of Rachell's vision whose destiny is to be mingled queerly and beautifully with that of Bon Repos.

Rachell has her seeings and André his dreams, but it is to the children, being children, that the choicest beauties of Bon Repos are made known. There are five du Frocq children and their names are like syllabled music—Michelle, Peronelle, Jacqueline, Colin and Colette. Sensitive, passionately different from one another, they are all possessed of imaginations at once inspiring and troubling. For Colin there are the unseen Things moving ever up and down the water lanes to the sea; for Michelle, Keats's little marble town by the wine-dark sea; for Peronelle, Browning's exuberant optimism; for Jacqueline, nunnish embroidery done for the glory of God; while fat, 5-year-old Colette hears the bell flowers ringing music and sees God upon the garden path. However, being children, ecstasy can turn with lightning swiftness into anger and pain, and when the du Frocq temper is roused, Bon Repos sways like bedlam. These laughable and pathetic moments of downfall are among the most delightful and convincing in the book.

Although ***Island Magic*** is written by an Englishwoman and about a virtually French family, there is something appealingly familiar about the book. It is as though the beloved American scenes of Louisa Alcott's "Little Women" had been transplanted into the gardens of the Channel Islands. Here are the dear old tantrums and thrills and confidences. Here again the kindly, abstracted father, the noble mother and the cluster of tremendously individual children. But temperamentally there is a vast difference between the two authors. "Invincible Louisa" bustled about dispensing humorous morality, whereas the author of ***Island Magic*** languishes in a pleasant but rather childish mysticism.

SISTER OF THE ANGELS: A CHRISTMAS STORY (1939)

Jane Spence Southron (review date 29 October 1939)

SOURCE: Southron, Jane Spence. "A Quiet Garden." *New York Times Book Review* (29 October 1939): 22.

One of the greatest rewarding pleasures connected with reviewing books of the creative kind is watching a talent of high order come to full flower. The work of the author of ***A City of Bells*** and ***The Middle Window*** has always been distinguished by integrity; that quality which the poet Gabriel Ferranti, in the present novel [***Sister of the Angels: A Christmas Story***], defines as setting apart the artist of vision from the ruck. In a ruthless age, whose violence has been reflected, often with conspicuous ability, in literature, Miss Goudge's integrity has kept her invariably true to her own vision, the vision of beauty and the joy inseparable from it. Her stories are sung from the heart. This latest one is flawlessly lovely.

The scene is again Torminster, and, except for "Fra Angelico," the name Henrietta gave to the artist who restored and completed the medieval frescoes in the chapel, the people have been met before in ***A City of Bells.*** No previous knowledge is assumed, but Miss Goudge adopts her favorite method of portraiture, revealing personality through action, sometimes apparently trivial though never really so, much as people reveal themselves in life. So, even if we thought we knew Grandfather, Grandmother, Henrietta, Hugh Anthony and Ferranti beforehand, we find ourselves learning something new about them through every moment of the emotion-charged story.

The illustrations of Torminster, its cathedral and the chapel in the crypt are an undoubted embellishment; but those dealing with the half-dozen main characters, whatever their intrinsic artistic merit, do not, unfortunately, follow the text either in spirit or in essential detail.

It is a love story, though not a story of sexual love; and it has its roots in that other story of love that began in a manager and that flowered, in medieval times, in beautiful churches, exquisite paintings and music that can still stir those whom cacophony has not deafened. There are other loves in it. The love of an erratic poet for his little "daughters; of two very old people who can still get on each other's nerves and must practice continuous mutual forbearance; the consuming love of two talented men and a gifted child for the art which means life to them. And it is invariably love that is salty with realism and wholesome with laughter.

A walled-in chapel in the crypt of the cathedral had been opened up by Grandfather and found to contain frescoes that legend attributed to a medieval monk who, stricken with leprosy, had covered three sides and the roof of the chapel with the story of the "Second Coming"; dying before he could do more than lightly block in the design for the east wall. Upon that as a foundation Miss Goudge has built up a drama whose central figure is the modern painter who has the vision and the ability to add a remarkable "First Coming" to the frescoes.

How he prostituted his genius to save those dependent on him from starving; how terribly he paid for it; how the Canon, doing good by stealth (for fear of Grandmother), and Henrietta, the adorable young painter-to-be, and Ferranti, Henrietta's father, got busy; and how a broken man was made whole again and set free to delight the world—or the sane bits left, this being a story of our own day—with his inspired imaginings must be left for the book to tell. It will also delight you with Hugh Anthony, who set the ball of the story rolling with his never-sated curiosity, and who is as full of genuine "boy" as any 10-year-old who ever ached to wear long trousers.

To read this book after a war bulletin is to slip from Hades into a happy garden.

HENRIETTA'S HOUSE (1942)

Times Literary Supplement (review date 3 April 1969)

SOURCE: "Half-Magic." *Times Literary Supplement,* no. 3501 (3 April 1969): 352.

Looked at historically, ***Henrietta's House*** by Elizabeth Goudge, published in 1945 and now appearing in a new edition, is a fragile link between the full-blooded Edwardian fantasy of E. Nesbit and the mid-twentieth-century blossoming of the giants of the landscape-fantasy school. How weak the link, how great the development a rereading of Miss Goudge's book will show. The children in the story, Henrietta and Hugh Anthony, are real enough when the focus happens to be on them but the author all too often allows her interest to be riveted by the eccentric Edwardian adults who are invited to Hugh Anthony's birthday picnic because one feels she is really more attracted to adults and suffers children only as a necessary adjunct to her story. It is an uneasy book for this reason and its pious and mincing overtones will do little to encourage a modern readership which can gorge itself on Mayne and Garner.

THE LITTLE WHITE HORSE (1946)

Terri Schmitz (review date July-August 2002)

SOURCE: Schmitz, Terri. "Safety in Numbers." *Horn Book Magazine* 78, no. 4 (July-August 2002): 425-36.

The power of a celebrity endorsement is responsible for the republication of Elizabeth Goudge's ***The Little White Horse*** (1946) and ***Linnets and Valerians*** (1964). J. K. Rowling is quoted as saying, "I absolutely adored ***The Little White Horse***"—so back into print it trots after lying for years in well-deserved oblivion. The impossibly convoluted plot involves the return of young orphan Maria Merry-weather to her ancestral home Moonacre Manor in an enchanted village in the English West Country. There she discovers that it is her destiny to become the next Moon Princess who will repair the rift that has plagued the family for centuries and brought discord and danger to the valley. Nothing makes sense in this novel, and time and again I found myself wanting to hurl it across the room—so much merry laughter, so many grins spreading from ear to ear, such a plethora of twinkling black eyes. There are mistaken identities, evil men lurking in the woods, characters who mysteriously appear and disappear, and a hidden treasure to boot. And what is there to say about a thirteen-year-old heroine who takes more than two hundred pages to realize that the large animal watching over her is not a dog but a lion (nicely paired with the horse that is really a unicorn)? To be fair, I tried to picture my ten-year-old self enjoying this book, but sincerely hope that even at that age I would have known tripe when I saw it. Imagine my relief, then, when I reluctantly picked up ***Linnets and Valerians*** to find that it's a perfectly lovely book reminiscent of E. Nesbit's family stories, with lively, appealing characters and a plot touched with just a hint of witchcraft and magic. My irritation with Rowling subsided a little, but I hope that she sticks to her own writing from now on.

SONGS AND VERSES (1947)

Leonard Unger (review date 1949)

SOURCE: Unger, Leonard. "Poets: Non-Modern, Neo-Modern, and Modern." *Sewanee Review* 57 (1949): 509-20.

Elizabeth Goudge, another Englishwoman, brings together children's poems and inspirational pieces in ***Songs and Verses.*** Miss Goudge's publishers say that her book "makes a perfect gift for any occasion," and there is a sense in which I would like to appear serious and respectful in saying that this is quite true.

LINNETS AND VALERIANS (1964)

Bulletin of the Center for Children's Books (review date January 1965)

SOURCE: *Bulletin of the Center for Children's Books* 18, no. 5 (January 1965): 74-5.

5-6 A long and elaborate story [***Linnets and Valerians***], romantic and fanciful, set in England in 1912. Four motherless children, whose father is in the Orient, are living with a stern grandmother and run away; they stumble into the home of an elderly uncle who seems gruff but has a loving heart. Nearby lives Lady Alicia; a recluse since she lost her little son and her husband, Lady Alicia warms to the four Linnet children. Predictably, the kindly "Daft Davie," who lives alone on a hill, turns out to be Lady Alicia's long-lost boy; the man that the children's father has met in Egypt turns out to be Lady Alicia's long-lost husband. Mixed with this Victorian plot are a few adult characters, quaint in Dickensian style, and a heavy dollop of fantasy. Not a smooth blending of family

Aileen Pippett (review date 24 January 1965)

SOURCE: Pippett, Aileen. *New York Times Book Review* (24 January 1965): 26.

For Ages 10 to 14. To paraphrase William Blake, "A linnet in a cage, Puts all Heaven in a rage." So, when four lively Linnet children are locked in attics by their grandmother, it is only natural that their running away, should have the happy results recorded in this charming story [***Linnets and Valerians***] set in Edwardian England. At first they land in the unwelcoming arms of Uncle Ambrose, a retired teacher who mistakenly thinks he has had enough of children to last him the rest of his life. Although a disciplinarian, he is really an old dear.

Then there is the Valerian family living near Uncle Ambrose—that is, they should have been there but they had a propensity for getting lost, so that only eccentric Lady Alicia is left. Like Uncle Ambrose she turns out to be far nicer than she pretends. There are other odd characters about, not all of them kindly. The Linnets have some strange adventures before the good magic overcomes the bad, the lost Valerians are found and everything goes on merrily thereafter.

Elizabeth Goudge writes with the gentleness and good humor that have long endeared her to adult readers. This is only the second of her many books written for children, but she is always young in heart, blending fantasy and fact with the sure touch of the born storyteller. Animals, birds, bees and flowers are also woven into the pattern of her entrancing tale.

Ian Ribbons's illustrations are strong, lively, full of movement and character.

Booklist (review date 15 February 1965)

SOURCE: *Booklist* 61, no. 12 (15 February 1965): 578.

Escaping from a strict grandmother in whose care they have been left while their father is in Egypt [***Linnets and Valerians***], the four Linnet children are taken in by unknown Uncle Ambrose, a vicar and retired schoolmaster who professes to abominate children. Their happy association with seemingly stern but understanding Uncle Ambrose and their involvement in the mystery surrounding the Valerian family are told with inimitable Goudge charm in a story which blends fantasy with realism and has a sensitively depicted setting, unique characters, a romantic plot, and a satisfying ending. Grades 5-7.

I SAW THREE SHIPS (1969)

Publishers Weekly (review date 22 September 1969)

SOURCE: *Publishers Weekly* 196, no. 12 (22 September 1969): 85.

If you have a small girl in your house, a small girl you love, you will see to it that she will have ***I Saw Three Ships*** to read this Christmas time. Elizabeth Goudge, who has already given young readers a rare and lovely story to remember, ***Linnets and Valerians,*** has now given them a Christmas story set in an old English seaport town that they will never forget. And Margot Tomes' delicious illustrations which reflect so perfectly the mood of this magical mystery, will keep it forever green in their memories.

Kirkus Reviews (review date 1 October 1969)

SOURCE: *Kirkus Reviews* 37, no. 9 (1 October 1969): 1063.

Polly is the orphaned daughter of her elderly aunts' elder brother [***I Saw Three Ships***], so perhaps it's not surprising that sometimes "they suffered from the sensation that she was older than they were." Polly however is a winsome child, "looking very demure in the long skirts of a hundred and sixty years ago," but underneath (the awkward way of dressing up the date) she is a persistent little body, as eager that the door be left open for the Three Wise Men on Christmas Eve as Aunt Constantia is that her long-gone "brother Tom should suddenly come home." Therein lies the tale, or at least the outline of it; to fill it in—i.e. represent the two other Wise Men—we have a "mad" French refugee from "something called the Terror" and one-legged Rag-and-Bones, the venerable town beggar. Uncle Tom returns bearing gold, the Frenchman brings Polly a jeweled rosary (frankincense) and the old beggar offers up his life (myrrh), while "on Christmas day in the morning . . . three ships come sailing in," carrying the Frenchman's feared-lost family and occasioning all-round rejoicing. Shaped like a picture book and laced with references to Popish Latin prayers, to decanters and chiffoniers, this wouldn't be much good for American children even if it were better. *9-11*

Bulletin of the Center for Children's Books (review date November 1969)

SOURCE: *Bulletin of the Center for Children's Books* 23, no. 3 (November 1969): 44.

5-6 An unabashedly sentimental Christmas story [***I Saw Three Ships***], set in an English coastal village at the close of the eighteenth century, the illustrations having a period flavor in their style as well as in their architectural or costume details. A small orphaned girl living with her aunts, Polly is convinced that three ships will, indeed, come sailing in on Christmas Day and that the door should be left open all night on Christmas Eve. Her aunts lock the doors, but there are three visitors in the night: a long-lost brother of the aunts, who leaves a purse of gold, a Frenchman who brings a rosary for Polly, and an old man near death. Next morning, three ships sail into the harbor, one of them carrying the wife and child the Frenchman had thought killed in the Terror. The writing style is polished, the plot patterned; although the protagonist is a child, this is not a childlike story.

Times Literary Supplement (review date 4 December 1969)

SOURCE: "Continuations and Beginnings." *Times Literary Supplement,* no. 3536 (4 December 1969): 1369.

Elizabeth Goudge almost pulls off a Christmas parable in ***I Saw Three Ships,*** a story which shows how Polly, a wilful orphan, opens up the constricted lives of her spinster aunts Dorcas and Constantia when she goes to live with them in their harbourside cottage. Polly believes that doors should be left unlatched on Christmas Eve to let in the three Wise Men—and that three ships will sail in to port on Christmas Day in the morning. They do, one bearing the long lost wife (in a blue cloak) and (golden-haired) son of a lonely Frenchman. But readers whose critical faculties are not borne away on the heady Christmas morning breeze will wish that Miss Goudge had been sterner with herself: for surely it is a let-down that there are only two strange men in the parlour when Polly awakes? (The third, a beggar, has stolen his food and fled.) Austen-ish setting, sweet, carefree and a little careless. Though decorously illustrated by Richard Kennedy (who has a fine line in spinsters of character) this slight book looks even slighter when set against the unblushing praise lavished on author ("gem-like touches of description") and artist ("marvellously illustrated") by its publisher.

THE JOY OF THE SNOW (1974)

Publishers Weekly (review date 29 April 1974)

SOURCE: *Publishers Weekly* 205, no. 17 (29 April 1974): 47.

Readers who have been faithful fans of this British novelist during her 40-year career will revel in her autobiography [***The Joy of the Snow***]. It is, as she says, an "attempt to recapture happy memories . . . to joy in people and places I have known." She begins with early memories of her childhood (what fun to find how ladies coped with washing long hair, using a bowl and pitcher), her unsatisfactory education and the faltering beginnings of her career after World War I. In this delightful account, we mingle with Ms. Goudge's family and friends, are invited to examine her philosophy and discover what writing means to her. One entertaining episode tells of the effects on her small village when her novel ***Green Dolphin Street*** was bought by an American movie company (during World War II) for what seemed to the townspeople and the author an outrageous sum.

Kirkus Reviews (review date 1 May 1974)

SOURCE: *Kirkus Reviews* 42, no. 9 (1 May 1974): 516.

Early on Miss Goudge states "The only people who will read this book [***The Joy of the Snow***] are the people who read my stories"—a characteristically unassuming and forthrightly realistic remark—it will be for them that ***The City of Bells*** still tolls. This is a partial autobiography—dealing primarily with "the rainbow days" of her childhood in Wells and later Ely where her father was offered the canonry; with her parents (a remarkable, charming and complex mother with psychic powers she declined to use) and her grandparents on the Channel Islands; with her schooling, her writing, the war and the last years lived with her good friend Jessie. Occasionally there are higher, not too much higher, reflections of a social and religious nature and on the contemporary world which she tolerates with more "compassion" and forbearance than one might have imagined. There is of course a certain jampot sweetness (we flinch at the number of times words like "tender" and "poignancies" are applied to her—cf. the publisher's release), but it would be unwise to overlook the uplift she will exert for the consciousness which has never been raised. In her case it would seem serenity has been acquired more effortlessly.

Booklist (review date 1 June 1974)

SOURCE: *Booklist* 70, no. 19 (1 June 1974): 1076.

Goudge's fans will enjoy this autobiography [***The Joy of the Snow***] which reveals her love for the beauty of English countryside and search for a purpose in life and an understanding of God. Although she has written admirable portraits of her parents and maternal grandparents, she pictures herself more clearly as a child with her fears, joys, and problems than as an adult. A chapter on ghosts and extrasensory perception will interest some readers; the author tells where ideas for some of her books originated.

Marion Amdursky (essay date July 1974)

SOURCE: Amdursky, Marion. *Library Journal* 99, no. 13 (July 1974): 1802.

A charming potpourri of reminiscences of places and people Goudge has loved, comments on being a writer, discussions of her religious beliefs (including some intriguing anecdotes and theories about ghosts and ESP), and descriptions of her Edwardian childhood. While not strictly an autobiography, the narrative [***The Joy of the Snow***] does give a clear picture of the influence of her parents and grandparents, of her homes throughout the years, and her schooling on her writing. Readers of her novels will particularly enjoy discovering the real people and places she adapted for her stories.

FURTHER READING

Criticism

Booklist 70, no. 19 (1 June 1974): 1099.
A brief reference to Goudge's autobiography *The Joy of the Snow* as limited in appeal.

Library Journal 94, no. 18 (15 October 1969): 3851.
A brief listing of Goudge's *I Saw Three Ships* evaluating reading level.

Locus 28, no. 375 (April 1992): 46.
A brief summary of the children's novel *Linnets and Valerians.*

Publishers Weekly (30 March 1992): 106.
A succinct description of *Linnets and Valerians* supplying the reading level.

Wagenknecht, Edward. "The Little Prince Rides the White Deer: Fantasy and Symbolism in Recent Literature." *College English* 7, no. 8 (May 1946): 431-37.
A reference to fantasy in Goudge's *The Blue Hills.*

Additional coverage of Goudge's life and career is contained in the following sources published by the Gale Group: *Contemporary Authors,* Vols. 5-8R, 112; *Contemporary Authors New Revision Series,* Vol. 5; *Dictionary of Literary Biography,* Vol. 191; *Major Authors and Illustrators for Children and Young Adults,* Eds. 1, 2; *St. James Guide to Children's Writers,* Vol. 5; *Something about the Author,* Vols. 2, 38; and *Twentieth-Century Romance and Historical Writers.*

Lord of the Flies

William Golding

(Full name William Gerald Golding) English novelist, short story writer, dramatist, poet, and nonfiction writer.

The following entry presents criticsm on Golding's *Lord of the Flies* (1954).

INTRODUCTION

Declared by many scholars to be one of the most important literary works of the twentieth century, *Lord of the Flies* has become a classic and is often required reading for high school students. Although the book has been compared to Daniel Defoe's *Robinson Crusoe* (1719) and Richard Hughes's *A High Wind in Jamaica* (1929), Golding's primary influence was the nineteenth-century children's classic *The Coral Island: A Tale of the Pacific* (1858) by R. M. Ballantyne. Golding's novel shares many situations, plot elements, and even character names with Ballantyne's work. *The Coral Island* relates the story of three boys stranded on a deserted island who rely on courage and resourcefulness to survive, and who emerge from the experience strengthened and matured. While Golding's tale is very similar, it is a darker, more foreboding, and ironic vision. Golding's conclusion is far from idyllic, and despite their rescue from the island, the ultimate survival of the boys in *Lord of the Flies* is not assured. Possibly rebuking the Victorian presentation of children as pure and innocent victims of adult society, Golding's children quickly strip themselves of all the trappings of a "civilized" world on the island and revert to savagery. Many scholars contend that through this novel, Golding was positing that customs commonly viewed as making up "civilization" in many cultures are merely an unnatural façade. *Lord of the Flies* also broke new ground in the young adult novel genre by utilizing poetic description and by borrowing ideas from the schools of modern anthropology and psychology. Although it can be read strictly as an adventure tale, *Lord of the Flies* contains strong themes and elemental symbolism that have prompted critics to debate the book's true meaning. Many commentators have viewed it as a religious, social, or political allegory.

PLOT AND MAJOR CHARACTERS

Lord of the Flies takes place in the context of a large scale war. A group of schoolboys have been evacuated from Great Britain, but their airplane crashes, leaving them abandoned without adult supervision on an uninhabited island. The boys set about creating a society of their own, and although they begin with an attempt to mimic the democratic, moral, and rational examples they recall from the civilized world, the group gradually deteriorates into a cruel tyranny of the strong over the weak.

A power struggle evolves between the main protagonist, Ralph, and the head choirboy, Jack. Although Ralph is originally elected leader, Jack, appointed chief hunter, labors to obtain power and support from the other boys and to undermine Ralph's authority. The boys begin to obsessively fear a beast in the dark that is allegedly hunting them—a fear that Jack uses as a means of converting Ralph's supporters into hunters. Jack and his band soon begin to exhibit a savage delight in killing for meat that turns into bloodlust ruled only by an entity the boys create—an ultimate evil, the Lord of the Flies, also called Beelzebub. Simon, an epileptic who sees visions, attempts to unearth the truth behind this Beast, only to be murdered as he is attempting to share his discovery of reality. Ralph's friend Piggy desperately tries to maintain order, but his asthma, nearsightedness, and obesity make him a frequent target for teasing and torment. He is eventually pushed from a cliff to his death by the other boys. In the conclusion, Ralph becomes hunted by the boys who all now follow Jack, and he is saved only by the timely arrival of a naval officer on the beach who restores a veneer of social order to the group.

MAJOR THEMES

The primary theme of *Lord of the Flies* focuses on the instincts for self-preservation and the underlying human potential for savagery and cruelty. Leighton Hodson has asserted that the book is about "making people become self-aware and honest with themselves about the condition they find themselves in, and the kind of life they lead." Other scholars have commented that *Lord of the Flies* examines the concept that a society represents the traits of the individuals within it. E. L. Epstein has stated that "The theme is an attempt to trace the defects of society back to the defects of human nature. The moral is that the shape of a society must depend on the ethical nature of the individual and not on any political system."

Critics have focused on many symbols within the novel, but have interpreted the symbols in different ways. One school has viewed the book purely as social commentary addressing the nature of humanity. Other scholars have discovered a multitude of biblical and religious themes, including the fall of man, the betrayal of Cain, reflections of Egyptian mythology, and the evil inherent in mankind. Some commentators have interpreted the symbolism as political, as a statement against the rise of Nazism or a criticism of the failure of other social and political structures.

Another critical faction has recognized the universality of many of the ideas presented in the tale: fear; instinct; fascination with power; corruption. Such critics have analyzed the characters themselves and the capacity for evil within them. In his presentation of the Nobel Prize in Literature to Golding, Lars Gyllensten said, "Golding inveighs against those who think that it is the political or other systems that create evil. Evil springs from the depths of man himself—it is the wickedness in human beings that creates the evil systems or that changes what from the beginning is, or could be, good into something iniquitous and destructive."

CRITICAL RECEPTION

Half a century after its publication, *Lord of the Flies* continues to elicit critical commentary and controversy. Initially, the book received mixed reviews and sold moderately well, but when issued in paperback in 1959 it became more accessible to students and sales increased. Teachers began to assign it for English literature classes with such frequency that it became part of the standard high school curriculum.

According to many critics, the characters in *Lord of the Flies* depict various aspects of society. Such scholars hold that Ralph represents civilization's inner turmoils, as he is conflicted about decisions he is forced to make. Piggy serves as a voice of reason, intellect, and order. Jack's nature is destructive, savage, and territorial and he possesses a wildness born of unleashed freedom. Simon symbolizes humanity's spiritual nature—he is brave, visionary, sacrificial. Many commentators have declared Simon as a type of Christ figure, maintaining that he is the only one on the island who fully understands what is going on and why.

Golding wrote numerous other novels, but none were embraced, celebrated, or studied more than *Lord of the Flies.* This novel, with a powerful and exciting narrative, stirring characterization, and deep, complex, and emotional themes is widely considered to be Golding's best work. *Lord of the Flies* has been praised for its structure, its ironic conclusion, and its function as fable and pure parable. It has been translated into many languages and was adapted into film in 1963 and 1990. In a 1960 study of Golding's works, C. B. Cox wrote, "*Lord of the Flies* is probably the most important novel to be published in this country in the 1950s. A story so explicitly symbolic as this might easily become fanciful and contrived, but Golding has mastered the art of writing a twentieth-century allegory . . . a gripping story which will appeal to generations of readers."

PRINCIPAL WORKS

Lord of the Flies (novel) 1954
The Inheritors (novel) 1955
Pincher Martin (novel) 1955
Free Fall (novel) 1959
The Spire (novel) 1964
The Hot Gates: And Other Occasional Pieces (nonfiction) 1965
The Pyramid (novella) 1967
**The Scorpion God* (novels) 1971
Darkness Visible (novel) 1979
Rites of Passage (novel) 1980
A Moving Target (essays) 1982
The Paper Men (novel) 1984
An Egyptian Journal (nonfiction) 1985

*Includes *Clonk, Clonk, Envoy Extraordinary, and The Scorpion God.*

TITLE COMMENTARY

C. B. Cox (essay date 1960)

SOURCE: Cox, C. B. "On *Lord of the Flies.*" In *William Golding: Novels, 1954-67,* edited by Norman Page, pp. 115-21. London: Macmillan, 1985.

[*In the following essay, originally published in 1960, Cox analyzes the plot line, finding an underlying Christian motif.*]

William Golding's ***Lord of the Flies,*** published in 1953, is a retelling in realistic terms of R. M. Ballantyne's *The Coral Island.* A group of boys, shot down during some kind of atomic war, are marooned on an island in the Pacific. In contrast to the boys in Ballantyne's story, who after a number of exciting adventures remember their time on the island as an idyllic interlude, the children in ***Lord of the Flies*** soon begin to quarrel, and their attempts to create an ordered, just society break down. On one level the story shows how intelligence (Piggy) and common sense (Ralph) will always be overthrown in society by sadism (Roger) and the lure of totalitarianism (Jack). On another, the growth of savagery in the boys demonstrates the power of original sin. Simon, the Christ figure, who tries to tell the children that their fears of a dead parachutist are illusory, is killed in a terrifying tribal dance. The Lord of the Flies is the head of a pig, which Jack puts up on a stick to placate an illusory Beast. As Simon understands, the only dangerous beast, the true Lord of the Flies, is inside the children themselves. Lord of the Flies is the Old Testament name for Beelzebub.

Lord of the Flies is probably the most important novel to be published in this country in the 1950s. A story so explicitly symbolic as this might easily become fanciful and contrived, but Golding has mastered the art of writing a twentieth-century allegory. In contrast to the medieval audience, the general reading public today does not believe that correspondences exist between the material and spiritual world, and they do not automatically expect every incident or object to have symbolic importance. No conventions of allegory exist, and the writer cannot introduce colours, animals, flowers or any of the other emblems which were available for the medieval writer. In these circumstances, many novelists have given objects an arbitrary symbolic meaning. In Iris Murdoch's *The Bell,* for example, there is no inherent reason why the bell under the lake should represent absolute values, and so her fanciful developments of plot to illustrate this meaning often appear rather forced. This type of allegory can fully succeed only if the literal sense is dramatically coherent in its own right, as in Camus's *The Plague.* There are other methods of writing twentieth-century allegory, of course, as in Kafka's use of fanciful situations to explore psychological and religious experiences; but if a story based on real life is used, then there must be no unlikely situations or fanciful embroidery. A modern audience will accept the underlying meanings only if they are conveyed in a completely convincing, true to life series of events.

To find an exciting, stimulating plot which is both dramatically credible and capable of allegorical interpretation is exceptionally difficult. The idea of placing boys alone on an island, and letting them work out archetypal patterns of human society, is a brilliant technical device, with a simple coherence which is easily understood by a modern audience. Its success is due in part to the quality of Golding's Christianity. He is neither puritan nor transcendentalist, and his religious faith is based upon his interpretation of experience, rather than upon an unquestioning acceptance of revelation. Although his four novels [sc. those written up to the time of Cox's essay—Ed.] deal with the depravity of man, he cares deeply about the condition of human life, and shows great compassion for men who suffer and men who sin. His religious sense does not make him turn from life in disgust, but proves to him the dignity and importance of human action. In development of plot, descriptions of island and sea, and treatment of character, he explores actual life to prove dramatically the authenticity of his religious viewpoint.

Lord of the Flies is a gripping story which will appeal to generations of readers. It is easy to despise the power of a good story, and to think of moral implications as an alternative to the obvious devices of surprise, suspense and climax. But to succeed, a good story needs more than sudden deaths, a terrifying chase and an unexpected conclusion. ***Lord of the Flies*** includes all these ingredients, but their exceptional force derives from Golding's faith that every detail of human life has a religious significance. This is one reason why he is unique among new writers in the '50s, and why he excels in narrative ability. Typical of the writers of the '50s is an uncertainty about human values, a fundamental doubt about whether life has any importance whatsoever. In contrast, Golding can describe friendship, guilt, pain and horror with a full sense of how deeply meaningful these can be for the individual. The terrible fire which kills the young children, the fear of Ralph as he is pursued across the island, and Piggy's fall to his death on the rocks make us feel, in their vivid detail, Golding's intense conviction that every particular of human life has a profound importance. His children are not juvenile delinquents, but human beings realising for themselves the beauty and horror of life.

This faith in the importance of our experiences in this world is reflected in Golding's vivid, imaginative style. He has a fresh, delightful response to the mystery of Nature, with its weird beauty and fantastic variety. The conch, which Ralph and Piggy discover in the lagoon and use to call the children to assemblies, is not just a symbol of order. From the beginning Golding does justice to the strange attraction of the shell, with its delicate, embossed pattern, and deep harsh note which echoes back from the pink granite of the mountain. When towards the end of the story the conch is smashed, we feel that sadness which comes when any object of exquisite beauty is broken. The symbolic meaning, that this is the end of the beauty of justice and order, is not forced upon us, but is reflected through our emotional reaction to the object itself.

In this way Golding expresses his passionate interest in both physical and moral life. His narrative style has an unusual lucidity and vitality because he never forgets the concrete in his search for symbolic action:

> Now a great wind blew the rain sideways, cascading the water from the forest trees. On the mountain-top the parachute filled and moved; the figure slid, rose to its feet, spun, swayed down through a vastness of wet air and trod with ungainly feet the tops of the high trees; falling, still falling, it sank towards the beach and the boys rushed screaming into the darkness. The parachute took the figure forward, furrowing the lagoon, and bumped it over the reef and out to sea.

With admirable simplicity this passage conveys a multitude of effects. The incident is part of an exciting story, a surprising climax to the murder of Simon; at the same time the dead parachutist is the 'beast' to the children, a symbol of adult evil, which, by their own act of killing, they have shown to be part of themselves. But the passage achieves its strong emotional impact because it is so firmly grounded in physical awareness. Water cascades from the forest trees, the parachutist 'furrows' the lagoon. These precise words describe with physical immediacy a situation which is real and dramatically poignant. And the picture of the man treading the tops of the high trees recalls the mystery of human life, with its incredible inventions, and yet also makes us feel deep compassion for the ungainly feet, the horror of death.

The island itself is boat-shaped, and the children typify all mankind on their journey through life. In the opening scenes the island has the glamour of a new-found paradise. With the green shadows from the palms and the forest sliding over his skin, Ralph is overcome by wonder. He lolls in the warm water, looking at the mirages which wrestle with the brilliance of the lagoon. But soon the terrifying fire transforms the island, and illusion gives way to reality. In nightmares the children begin to be afraid that this is not a good island; they become accustomed to the mirages, 'and ignored them, just as they ignored the miraculous, throbbing stars'. The beauty of the earthly paradise grows stale to their eyes. At the end they leave behind them 'the burning wreckage of the island', whose loveliness has been degraded by their presence.

As his attempts to discipline the boys begin to appear hopeless, Ralph, on a search for the illusory beast, sees beyond the lagoon out to open sea:

> The lagoon had protected them from the Pacific: and for some reason only Jack had gone right down to the water on the other side. Now he saw the landsman's view of the swell and it seemed like the breathing of some stupendous creature.

> Slowly the waters sank among the rocks, revealing pink tables of granite, strange growths of coral, polyp, and weed. Down, down, the waters went, whispering like the wind among the heads of the forest. There was one flat rock there, spread like a table, and the waters sucking down on the four weedy sides made them seem like cliffs. Then the sleeping leviathan breathed out—the waters rose, the weed streamed, and the water boiled over the table rock with a roar. There was no sense of the passage of waves; only this minute-long fall and rise and fall.

This creature becomes a part of Ralph's consciousness, a symbol of a reality he tries to avoid. As he watches the ceaseless, bulging passage of the deep sea waves, the remoteness and infiniteness of the ocean force themselves upon his attention. By the quiet lagoon he can dream of rescue, but the brute obtuseness of the ocean tells him he is helpless. It is significant that the two boys who are killed, Simon and Piggy, are taken back to this infinite ocean.

As the waves creep towards the body of Simon beneath the moonlight, the brilliantly realistic description of the advancing tide typifies all the beauty of the world which promises eternal reward to those who suffer:

> Along the shoreward edge of the shallows the advancing clearness was full of strange, moonbeam-bodied creatures with fiery eyes. Here and there a larger pebble clung to its own air and was covered with a coat of pearls. The tide swelled in over the rain-pitted sand and smoothed everything with a layer of silver. Now it touched the first of the stains that seeped from the broken body and the creatures made a moving patch of light as they gathered at the edge. The water rose further and dressed Simon's coarse hair with brightness. The line of his cheek silvered and the turn of his shoulder became sculptured marble. The strange, attendant creatures, with their fiery eyes and trailing vapours, busied themselves round his head. The body lifted a fraction of an inch from the sand and a bubble of air escaped from the mouth with a wet plop. Then it turned gently in the water.

Here we become aware of the Christian meaning underlying the story. For Ralph the sea typifies the insensitivity of the universe, but this is to see it from only one point of view. The multitudinous beauties of the tide promise that creation was not an accident; after our suffering and confusions are over, a healing power of great beauty will solve all problems. The advancing waves are like moon-beam-bodied creatures, gently washing the body of Simon free from all stain, and dressing him in pearls, silver and marble in token of the richness of his love for the other children. Instead of seeking to introduce ancient myths into the modern world, Golding creates his own, basing his symbols on the actual wonder of life itself. The intricate beauty of the waves is not merely a pleasing arrangement of light and matter, but an incredible manifestation of the wonder of creation, with a valid life in our consciousness. As Simon's body moves out to open sea under the delicate yet firm lifting of the tide, it seems impossible that his sacrifice has had no ultimate meaning.

The island, the sea and the sacrifice of Simon all show Ralph the truth of the human situation. His mind finds the burden of responsibility too great, and he begins to lose his power to think coherently: 'He found himself understanding the wearisomeness of this life, where every path was an improvisation and a considerable part of one's waking life was spent watching one's feet.' Jack's return to savagery, taking all the children with him, is portrayed with frightening realism. The lust for killing grows too strong, and Ralph's inadequate democratic machinery cannot keep it in check. Behind their painted faces, the children can feel a security, a lack of personal responsibility for the evil they perpetrate, and this desire explains the growth of Jack's prestige. When he tells them they will not dream so much, 'they agreed passionately out of the depths of their tormented private lives', and he is amazed by their response. Only the intelligence of Piggy is not tempted by the tribal dances, and his character is presented with great compassion. His fat, asthmatic body is a natural butt for children, and continual mockery has taught him to be humble and to enjoy being noticed even only as a joke. But he has a powerful belief in the importance of civilised order, and gradually Ralph learns to appreciate his value. His death is a poignant reminder of the unjust and cruel treatment given by society to so many good men.

Simon is perhaps the one weakness in the book. We see his friendship for Ralph, when he touches his hand as they explore the island, and his love of all people when he ministers to the dead body of the parachutist, but alone among the characters his actions at times appear to be motivated, not by the dramatic action, but by the symbolic implications of the story. At the beginning, when he withdraws at night from the other children, his motives are left uncertain. But the scene where he confronts the lord of the flies is most convincing. In this pig's head covered with flies, he sees 'the infinite cynicism of adult life'. He has the courage to face the power of evil, and, knowing that the beast is in all of them, he climbs the hill to find out the truth about the dead parachutist.

The whole story moves towards Simon's view of reality. The growth of savagery forces Ralph to make strange speculations about the meaning of human identity. When they hold an assembly at nightfall, he is surprised at the different effect made by the darkness:

> Again he fell into that strange mood of speculation that was so foreign to him. If faces were different when lit from above or below—what was a face? What was anything?

He faces the possibility that there is no absolute perspective to human life, and that all experience may be meaningless. He longs to return to the world of adults, and the irony of this illusion is shown when, after a battle in the skies, the dead parachutist comes down 'as a sign from the world of grown-ups'. At certain stages of the story, Golding deliberately makes us forget that these are only young children. Their drama and conflict typify the inevitable overthrow of all attempts to impose a permanent civilisation on the instincts of man. The surprising twist of events at the end of the novel is a highly original device to force upon us a new viewpoint. The crazy, sadistic chase to kill Ralph is suddenly revealed to be the work of a semi-circle of little boys, their bodies streaked with coloured clay. But the irony is also directed at the naval officer, who comes to rescue them. His trim cruiser, the sub-machine gun, his white drill, epaulettes, revolver and row of gilt buttons, are only more sophisticated substitutes for the war-paint and sticks of Jack and his followers. He too is chasing men in order to kill, and the dirty children mock the absurd civilised attempt to hide the power of evil. And so when Ralph weeps for the end of innocence, the darkness of man's heart, and the death of his true, wise friend, Piggy, he weeps for all the human race.

Bernard S. Oldsey and Stanley Weintraub (essay date 1965)

SOURCE: Oldsey, Bernard S., and Stanley Weintraub. "Beelzebub Revisited: *Lord of the Flies*." In *The Art of William Golding,* pp. 15-40. New York: Harcourt, Brace, and World, Inc., 1965.

[*In the following essay, Oldsey and Weintraub approach* Lord of the Flies *as an allegory about good and evil.*]

Lord of the Flies (1954), Golding's first novel and the one that established his reputation, is still most widely acclaimed as his major work. Not only has it captured a large segment of the popular and academic imagination (having the effect there of replacing J. D. Salinger's *The Catcher in the Rye*), but it has also attracted the greatest amount of critical attention directed toward Golding.

To date, that critical attention has proven various, specialized, and spotty. A remarkable "first novel" on any terms, ***Lord of the Flies*** has been praised on literary grounds much less often than as sociological, psychological, or religious tract, as "pure parable," fable, or myth.[1] The terminology of Frazer and Freud are more often brought to bear upon the novel than the yardsticks of literary criticism. As literature, however, it has been—even while praised—called unoriginal and derivative, filled with "gimmickry," devoid of characterization, and lacking in logic.[2] Only twice has it been blasted as insignificant art encased in bad writing.[3]

Certainly ***Lord of the Flies*** is derivative, in the sense that it falls well within the main stream of several English literary traditions. It is a "boys' book," as are *Treasure Island, The Wind in the Willows, High Wind in Jamaica,* and other books primarily about juvenile characters which transcend juvenile appeal; it is in the tradition of the survival narrative, along with *Robinson Crusoe, The Swiss Family Robinson,* and even Barrie's *Admirable Crichton;* it is in the tradition—best exemplified by Conrad, Cary, and Greene in our century—that examines our culture by transplanting it harshly to an exotic locale where it prospers or withers depending upon its intrinsic value and strength; it is in the long tradition of anti-science writing in England, where authors for centuries have equated scientific progress with dehumanization; and it at least appears to be in the Nonconformist English religious tradition, which assumes mankind's fall from grace.

If all these traditions lead back to one key source of inspiration, it may be no accident. The traditions embodied in ***Lord of the Flies*** can be discovered in *Gulliver's Travels*—Swift's version of the primeval savagery and greed which civilization only masks in modern man. It seems no coincidence that we also find in Golding a Swiftian obsession with physical ugliness, meanness, and nastiness (sometimes bordering on the scatological), and with the sense of how tenuous is the hold of intelligence, reason, and humaneness as a brake upon man's regression into barbarism.

Eventually, of course, Golding must be judged according to his individual talent rather than tradition or polemical appeal. Other critical visits to his minor devil's island have been accomplished mainly at a distance, through special field glasses. Here we revisit the island armed only with the knowledge that Golding is essentially a literary man who uses scene, character, and symbol (not to mention an exceedingly fine style and some admittedly tricky plot methods) to achieve imaginative literary effects.

The scenic qualities of ***Lord of the Flies*** help make it an imaginative work for the reader as well as the author. Although Golding occasionally provides consolidating detail, he more commonly requires the reader to pull narrative and descriptive elements into focus. For example, he provides no end-paper map or block description of his fictional island. The reader must explore it along with the participants in the story and piece together a usable concept of time and place. What we learn in this way is just enough to keep the work within the realm of fiction, but not enough to remove it from the realm of allegory. *And the essence of Golding's art resides exactly within the area of overlap.*

Fable-like, time and place are vague. The Queen (Elizabeth?) still reigns, and "Reds" are apparently the vague enemy. It is the postcatastrophic near-future, in which nuclear war has laid waste much of the West. ("They're all dead," Piggy thinks. And "civilization," corroborates Golding, is "in ruins.") The fiery crash of the boys' plane upon a tropical island has been the final stage of their evacuation from England. The island seems to lie somewhere in the Indian or Pacific Ocean, probably on a line extending from England to Australia, which could well have been the planned terminus of their evacuation. Jack provides the clue for such geographical extrapolation when he speaks of Simon's seizures at "Gib." (Gibraltar) and "Addis" (Addis Ababa), as well as "at matins over the precentor."[4]

Shaped roughly like an outrigged boat, the boys' haven is a tropical island with a coral base. A mile out along one side runs a barrier reef, between which and the island lies a lagoon, on whose inward shore the boys hold their assemblies. At one end of the island there appears to be another, smaller island; but upon close inspection this is found to be attached by a rocky isthmus. Topographically, the island rises from low jungle and orchard land to a mountaintop, or ridge, with few or no trees. By way of food, it provides the boys with bananas, coconuts, an "olive-grey, jelly-like fruit," and wild pig, as well as crab and fish taken from the sea. At midday the island gets hot enough to produce mirage effects.

If there were an end-paper map for Golding's island, it would no doubt be marked to indicate these major points of interest: (1) the beach along the lagoon, where Piggy and Ralph find the conch, and where assemblies are held near a natural platform of fallen trees; (2) the mountaintop, from which the island is surveyed, where the signal fire is placed, and where eventually the dead parachutist is trapped by wind and rock; (3) the burned-out quarter mile, where the mulberry-faced boy dies in the first fire; (4) Simon's leafy bower, to which he makes mystic retreats and from which he views the ceremony of impaling the pig's head upon a stake; (5) the orchard, where the fruit is picked and where some of the "littluns" are "taken short," leaving behind their fecal trail; (6) the "castle" at the tail end of the island, rising a hundred feet from the sea, where the first search for the "beast" is made, and where Piggy is killed after Jack has made this bastion his headquarters; and (7) the jungle, with its hanging vines that recall snakes and "beasties," with its pig trails where Jack hunts and where Ralph is finally hunted.

When the details are extracted and given order under an analytical light, Golding's island looks naturalistic in specification. But matters are not at all that clear in the book. The location of the island, for example, is kept deliberately vague: it is sufficiently remote to draw only two ships in a month or so, yet close enough to "civilization" to be the floor above which deadly, and old-fashioned, air battles are fought miles high (the boys' plane itself has been shot down). The nearby air and naval war in progress, with conventional weapons, is somewhat out of keeping with earlier reports of utter catastrophe. Equally incongruous is the smartly attired naval officer and savior of the closing pages, whose jaunty mien is incompatible with catastrophe. Yet he is as important to the machinery of the allegory as the earlier crash, which is equally difficult to explain on rational grounds. During the crash the fuselage of the evacuation plane has apparently broken in two: the forward half (holding pilot and others, including more boys) has been cleanly washed out to sea by a conveniently concomitant storm; and the after-section (which makes a long fiery scar as it cuts through the jungle) tumbles unscathed children onto the island. As incompatible, obscure, askew, and unrealistic as these elements may be, they are no more so than Gulliver's adventures. And Golding's graphically novelistic character and topographic details, both poetic and naturalistic, tend to blur the fabulous qualities of the narrative's use of time and setting in its opening and close. Although it is enough to say that the fabulist must be permitted pegs upon which to hang his fable, it is Golding's richly novelistic elements of the telling that call attention to the subtle dissonance. Paradoxically—yet artistically—this very tension between realistic novel and allegorical fable imparts to ***Lord of the Flies*** some of its unique power.

Golding's characters, like his setting, represent neither fictional reality nor fabulistic unreality, but, rather, partake of the naturalistic and the allegorical at the same time. As a result, they emerge more full bodied than Kafka's ethereal forms, more subtly shaded than Orwell's animal-farm types, and more comprehensibly motivated than Bunyan's religious ciphers. Bit by bit we can piece together fairly solid pictures of the major figures in ***Lord of the Flies.*** And since a number of commentators have fallen into interpretative error by precipitously trying to state what these characters "mean," perhaps it would be best here to start by trying to state what they "are."

Ralph, the protagonist, is a boy twelve years and a "few months" old. He enters naïvely, turning handsprings of joy upon finding himself in an exciting place free of adult supervision. But his role turns responsible as leadership is thrust upon him—partly because of his size, partly because of his attractive appearance, and partly because of the conch with which, like some miniature Roland, he has blown the first assembly. Ralph is probably the largest boy on the island (built like a boxer, he nevertheless has a "mildness about his mouth and eyes that proclaimed no devil"). But he is not so intellectual and logical as Piggy ("he would never be a very good chess player," Golding assures us), not so intuitively right as Simon, nor even so aggressively able to take advantage of opportunity as Jack. For these reasons there has been some reader tendency to play down Ralph as a rather befuddled Everyman, a straw boy of democracy tossed about by forces he cannot cope with. Yet he should emerge from this rites-of-passage *bildungsroman* with the reader's respect. He is as much a hero as we are allowed: he has courage, he has good intelligence, he is diplomatic (in assuaging Piggy's feelings and dividing authority with Jack), and he elicits perhaps our greatest sympathy (when hounded across the island). Although he tries to live by the rules, Ralph is no monster of goodness. He himself becomes disillusioned with democratic procedure; he unthinkingly gives away Piggy's embarrassing nickname; and, much more importantly, he takes part in Simon's murder! But the true measure of Ralph's character is that he despairs of democracy because of its hollowness ("talk, talk, talk"), and that he apologizes to Piggy for the minor betrayal, and that—while Piggy tries to escape his share of the guilt for Simon's death—Ralph cannot be the hypocrite (this reversal, incidentally, spoils the picture often given of Piggy as superego or conscience). Ralph accepts his share of guilt in the mass action against Simon, just as he accepts leadership and dedication to the idea of seeking rescue. He too, as he confesses, would like to go hunting and swimming, but he builds shelters, tries to keep the island clean (thus combating the flies), and concentrates vainly on keeping a signal fire going. At the novel's end Ralph has emerged from his age of innocence; he sheds tears of experience, after having proven himself a "man" of humanistic faith and action. We can admire his insistence upon individual responsibility—a major Golding preoccupation—upon doing what must be done rather than what one would rather do.

Ralph's antagonist, Jack (the choir leader who becomes the text's Esau), is approximately the same age. He is a tall, thin, bony boy with light blue eyes and indicative red hair; he is quick to anger, prideful, aggressive, physically tough, and courageous. But although he shows traces of the demagogue from the beginning, he must undergo a metamorphosis from a timidity-shielding arrogance to conscienceless cruelty. At first he is even less able to wound a pig than is Ralph, but he is altered much in the manner of the transformation of the twentieth-century dictator from his first tentative stirrings of power lust to eventual bestiality. Although Golding is careful to show little of the devil in Ralph, he nicely depicts Jack as being directly in league with the lord of flies and dung.[5] Jack trails the pigs by their olive-green, smooth, and steaming droppings. In one place we are shown him deep in animalistic regression, casting this way and that until he finds what he wants: "The ground was turned over near the pig-run and there were droppings that steamed. Jack bent down to them as though he loved them." His fate determined, Jack is a compelled being; he is swallowed by the beast—as it were—even before Simon: "He tried to convey the compulsion to track down and kill that was swallowing him up." Jack's Faustian reward is power through perception. He perceives almost intuitively the use of mask, dance, ritual, and propitiation to ward off—and yet encourage simultaneously—fear of the unknown. Propitiation is a recognition not only of the need to pacify but also of something to be pacified. In this instance it is the recognition of evil. "The devil must have his due," we say. Here the "beast" must be mollified, given its due. Jack recognizes this fact, even if he and his group of hunters do not understand it. Politically and anthropologically he is more instinctive than Ralph. Jack does not symbolize chaos, as sometimes claimed, but, rather, a stronger, more primitive order than Ralph provides.

Jack's chief henchman, Roger, is not so subtly or complexly characterized, and seems to belong more to Orwellian political fable. Slightly younger and physically weaker, he possesses from the beginning all the sadistic attributes of the demagogue's hangman underling. In his treatment of the sow he proves deserving of his appellation in English slang. Through his intense, furtive, silent qualities, he acts as a sinister foil to Simon. By the end of the novel Golding has revealed Roger; we hardly need to be told that "the hangman's horror clung round him."

Simon is perhaps the most effectively—and certainly the most poignantly—characterized of all. A "skinny, vivid little boy, with a glance coming up from under a hut of straight hair that hung down, black and coarse," he is (at nine or ten) the lonely visionary, the clear-sighted realist, logical,[6] sensitive, and mature beyond his years. We learn that he has a history of epileptic seizures—a dubious endowment sometimes credited to great men of the past, particularly those with a touch of the mystic. We see the unusual grace and sensitivity of his personality crop up here and there as the story unfolds until he becomes the central figure of the "Lord of the Flies" scene—one of Golding's most powerful and poetic. We see Simon's instinctive compassion and intelligence as he approaches the rotting corpse of the parachutist, which, imprisoned in the rocks on the hill in flying suit and parachute harness, is the only palpable "monster" on the island. Although Simon's senses force him to vomit with revulsion, he nevertheless frees it "from the wind's indignity." When he returns to tell his frightened, blood-crazed companions that, in effect, they have nothing to fear but fear itself, his murder becomes the martyrdom of a saint and prophet, a point in human degeneration next to which the wanton killing of Piggy is but an anticlimax. In some of the novel's richest, most sensitive prose, the body of Simon (the boys' "beast" from the jungle) is taken out to sea by the tide, Golding here reaching close to tragic exaltation as Simon is literally transfigured in death:[7]

> . . . The beast lay huddled on the pale beach and the stains spread, inch by inch.
>
> The edge of the lagoon became a streak of phosphorescence which advanced minutely, as the great wave of the tide flowed. The clear water mirrored the clear sky and the angular bright constellations. The line of phosphorescence bulged about the sand grains and little pebbles; it held them each in a dimple of tension, then suddenly accepted them with an inaudible syllable and moved on.
>
> Along the shoreward edge of the shallows the advancing clearness was full of strange, moonbeam-bodied creatures with fiery eyes. Here and there a larger pebble clung to its own air and was covered with a coat of pearls. The tide swelled in over the rainpitted sand and smoothed everything with a layer of silver. Now it touched the first of the stains that seeped from the broken body and the creatures made a moving patch of light as they gathered at the edge. The water rose farther and dressed Simon's coarse hair with brightness. The line of his cheek silvered and the turn of his shoulder became sculptured marble. The strange attendant creatures, with their fiery eyes and trailing vapors, busied themselves round his head. The body lifted a fraction of an inch from the sand and a bubble of air escaped from the mouth with a wet plop. Then it turned gently in the water.
>
> Somewhere over the darkened curve of the world the sun and moon were pulling, and the film of water on the earth planet was held, bulging slightly on one side while the solid core turned. The great wave of the tide moved farther along the island and the water lifted. Softly, surrounded by a fringe of inquisitive bright creatures, itself a silver shape beneath the steadfast constellations, Simon's dead body moved out toward the open sea.

With his mysterious touch of greatness Simon comes closest to foreshadowing the kind of hero Golding himself has seen as representing man's greatest need if he is to advance in his humanity—the Saint Augustines, Shakespeares, and Mozarts, "inexplicable, miraculous."[8] Piggy, on the other hand, who, just before his own violent death, clutches at a rationalization for Simon's murder, has all the good and bad attributes of the weaker sort of intellectual. Despised by Jack and protected by Ralph, he is set off from the others by his spectacles, asthma, accent, and very fat, short body. Freudian analysts would have Piggy stand as superego, but he is extremely id-directed toward food: it is Ralph who must try to hold him back from accepting Jack's pig meat, and Ralph who acts as strong conscience in making Piggy accept partial responsibility for Simon's death.[9] Although ranked as one of the "biguns," Piggy is physically incapable and emotionally immature. The logic of his mind is insufficient to cope with the human problems of their coral-island situation. But this insight into him is fictionally denied to the Ralphs of this world, who (as on the last page of the novel) weep not for Simon, but for "the true, wise friend called Piggy."

How many children originally landed on the island alive we never learn; however, we do know that there were more than the eighteen boys whose names are actually mentioned in the course of the novel. Census matters are not helped by the first signal fire, for it goes out of control and scatters the boys in fright. Ralph, worried about the littluns, accuses Piggy of dereliction of duty in not making a list of names. Piggy is exaggeratedly indignant: "How could I . . . all by myself? They waited for two minutes, then they fell in the sea; they went into the forest; they just scattered everywhere. How was I to know which was which?" But only one child known to any of the survivors has clearly disappeared—a small unnamed boy with a mulberry-marked face. This fact lends little credence to Piggy's tale of decimation.

Of those who remain, at least a dozen of whom are littluns, a significant number come alive through Golding's ability to characterize memorably with a few deft lines. Only two have surnames as well as Christian names: Jack Merridew, already mentioned as Ralph's rival, and the littlun Percival Wemys Madison. Jack at first demands to be called, as at school, "Merridew," the surname his mark of superior age and authority. Percival Wemys Madison ("The Vicarage, Harcourt St. Anthony, Hants, telephone, telephone, tele—") clutches vainly at the civilized incantation, learned by rote—in case he should get lost. And he is. His distant past has so completely receded by the end of the novel that he can get no farther in self-identification than "I'm, I'm—" for he "sought in his head for an incantation that had faded clean away." We learn little more about him, and hardly need to. Here again, in characterization, Golding's straddling the boundary line between allegory and naturalism demonstrates either the paradoxical power of his weakness as novelist or his ability to make the most of his shortcomings.

Whatever the case, Percival Wemys Madison epitomizes the novel and underlines its theme, in his regression to the point of reduced existence. In fact, most of Golding's characters suggest more than themselves, contributing to critical controversy as well as the total significance of the novel. In the years of exegesis since publication of ***Lord of the Flies,*** critical analysis has been hardening into dogmatic opinion, much of it allegoristic, as evidenced by such titles as "Allegories of Innocence," "Secret Parables," and "The Fables of William Golding."[10] And even where the titles are not indicative (as with E. L. Epstein's Capricorn edition afterword, and the equally Freudian analysis of Claire Rosenfield),[11] critical literature has generally forced the book into a neat allegorical novel. The temptation is strong, since the novel is evocative and the characters seem to beg for placement within handy categories of meaning—political, sociological, religious, and psychological categories. Yet Golding is a simply complicated writer; and, so much the better for the novel as novel, none of the boxes fits precisely.

Oversimplifying, Frederick Karl writes that "When the boys on the island struggle for supremacy, they re-enact a ritual of the adult world, as much as the college Fellows in Snow's *The Masters* work out the ritual of a power struggle in the larger world."[12] Jack may appear to be the demagogic dictator and Roger his sadistic henchman; Ralph may be a confused democrat, with Piggy his "brain trust"; but the neatness of the political allegory is complicated by the clear importance of the mystical, generalization-defying Simon. Although Simon, who alone among the boys has gone up to the mountaintop and discovered the truth, is sacrificed in a subhuman orgy, those who have seen a religious allegory in the novel find it more in the fall of man from paradise, as the island Eden turns into a fiery hell, and the Satanic Jack into the fallen archangel. But Ralph makes only a tenuous Adam; the sow is a sorry Eve; and Piggy, the sightless sage, has no comfortable place in Christian myth. Further, it is an ironic commentary upon religious interpretations of ***Lord of the Flies*** that of an island full of choirboys, not one ever resorts—even automatically—to prayer or to appeals to a deity, not even before they begin backsliding. And the Edenic quality of the island paradise is compromised from the beginning, for, although the essentials of life are abundant, so are the essentials of pain, terror, and death: the fruit which makes them ill, the animals which awaken their bloodthirstiness and greed, the cruel war in the air above them, the darkness and the unknown which beget their fears.

As a social allegory of human regression the novel is more easily (perhaps too neatly) explainable as "the way in which, when the civilized restraints which we impose on ourselves are abandoned, the passions of anger, lust and fear wash across the mind, obliterating commonsense and care, and life once again becomes nasty, brutish and short."[13] The island itself is shaped like a boat, and takes on symbolic proportions, not simply in the microcosmic-macrocosmic sense, but as subtle foreshadowing of the regression about to take place among the boys: "It was roughly boat-shaped. . . . The tide was running so that long streaks of foam tailed away from the reef and for a moment they felt that the boat was moving steadily astern." This sternward movement not only conjures up the regressive backsliding away from civilization that constitutes the theme of the novel, but is imagistically associated with Piggy's "ass-mar" and the general note of scatology—as with the littluns being "taken short" in the orchard—which prevails in this book on Beelzebub, lord of the flies *and* dung. Later, when Simon asks the assembly to think of the dirtiest thing imaginable, Jack answers with the monosyllable for excrement. This is not what Simon means at all: he is thinking of the evil in man. But the two concepts merge in Golding's imagination—covertly in ***Lord of the Flies*** and manifestly in ***Free Fall,*** which is a literary cloaca, full of that revulsion psychologists try to explain in terms of the proximity and ambiguity of the apertures utilized for birth and excreta.

Some critics who see the allegory of evil as just the surface meaning of the novel have been led into psychological labyrinths, where Jack appears as the Freudian id personified; Ralph the ego; and Piggy the superego, conscience of the grown-up world. But William Wasserstrom has dealt severely with Miss Rosenfield in this kind of interpretation; the experts have fallen out;[14] and, besides, the Freudian *ménage à trois* fails to accommodate the vital Simon. Indeed, the problem in all attempts to explain ***Lord of the Flies*** as some kind of parable is that the novel is not a parable: it is too long, and lacks the point-by-point parallelism necessary to meet the definition. Nor, in the precise sense, is it a fable, since it deals primarily with human beings, since it does not rely upon folkloristic or fantastic materials, and since it does not provide the convenience of an explicit moral. It *is* allegoristic, rich in variant suggestions, and best taken at the level of suggestive analysis.

This novel has been taken, too, as a straight tale of initiation, with Ralph as hero—an interpretation to which the book's ending is particularly susceptible. Yet there is more to it than Ralph's facing a brutal adult world with a lament for his lost childhood and for the innocence he thinks has been stripped from him. What Ralph dimly fathoms, the naval-officer "rescuer" cannot possibly understand—that the world, in the words of Shaw's Saint Joan, is not yet ready to receive its saints, neither its Simons nor even its Piggys and Ralphs. Whether he means it or not Golding provides a hopeful note, for even at mankind's present stage of development Piggy and Ralph, the latter with shame, relapse only slightly toward the barbarism of their contemporaries (and that of the officer, who is engaged in a no less barbaric war "outside"); while Simon withstands the powerful regressive pressures completely. That these three represent three-quarters of the novel's major characters defeats any explanation of the novel in totally pessimistic terms.

Almost endlessly, the four major characters are thematically suggestive, and are usually identified in the book with certain imagery and talismanic objects: Jack with blood and dung, with the mask of primitive tribalism (imagistically he is in league with the Lord of the Flies); Piggy with pigs' meat (his physical sloth and appetite and eventual sacrifice), with his glasses, which represent intellect and science (though they could hardly coax the sun into making fire); Ralph with the conch and signal fire, with comeliness and the call to duty, with communal hope (all shattered when the conch dwindles in power and is finally shattered, and the signal fire dies out). Again, however, it may be Simon—not so thematically suggestive as the others—who provides the best clues to the un-Swiftian side of Golding's intentions, for we recall not only his mysticism, his intelligence, his fragility, but also his association with the bees and butterflies that hover sweetly and innocently (by comparison with the flies) about the island, and the tragic beauty of his transfiguration. Perhaps it is Simon who best suggests Golding's optimism in the face of his apparent allegory of regression. "The human spirit," writes Golding, "is wider and more complex than the whole of the physical evolutionary system. . . . We shall have . . . to conform more and more closely to categories or go under. But the change in politics, in religion, in art, in literature will come, because it *will* come; because the human spirit is limitless and inexhaustible." Just around the corner, he promises, are the Saint Augustines, Shakespeares, and Mozarts: "Perhaps they are growing up now."[15]

What can be said of ***Lord of the Flies*** eventually is that, in structure and narrative method, it is Golding's simplest novel. It lacks the ironic mystification of ***The Inheritors,*** which results from the necessity of working through primitive brains making simple and often erroneous "pictures" of situations. It escapes the often cryptic involvement, the sudden wrench of context, that come from the stream of consciousness and recall methods of ***Pincher Martin*** and

Free Fall. But it is not an obvious novel, as sometimes claimed. It shares with his other books an ending technique that constitutes a reversal—a sudden shift of viewpoint. Here the timely arrival of the naval officer acts as no concession to readers demanding a happy ending. What we get instead of "gimmick" or conventional *deus ex machina* is a necessary change of focus: the boys, who have grown almost titanic in their struggle, are suddenly seen again as boys, some merely tots, dirty-nosed and bedraggled. And then a retrospective irony results, since the boys deserve to be thought of as titanic: if they have been fighting our battle, we realize—with both hope and dismay—that mankind is still in something of a prepuberty stage. Thus ***Lord of the Flies*** ends as no act of hope or charity or even contrition. It is an act of recognition. The tone is peculiarly calm: Golding keeps his distance from his materials; he does not interfere or preach; and the material is made to speak for itself through a simplicity of prose style and a naturalistic-allegorical form. The vision of Golding is through both ends of the telescope.

Kenneth Burke has said that any novel is but the expansion of a single sentence, perhaps simply the expansion of a single gesture. In the same way, criticism of any writer is but the expansion of a single sentence definition. We place the author within a *genus* and then describe the *differentia.* We may eventually conclude that his work is *sui generis,* but the defining method helps us to this conclusion. Much the same thing is true if we try to place him by tracing his origins and the influences exerted on his work; and any analysis or evaluation of Golding's fiction must revolve around the compound question of originality and derivation, for although Golding has been called the most original English novelist of the last twenty or thirty years, it is becoming increasingly clear that his originality in prose is much like that of T. S. Eliot's in verse. Golding, in fact, stands as a remarkable example of how the individual talent operates within a strong tradition. Tradition (the English novelistic tradition primarily, but with elements derived from American, French, and Classical sources) leaves its mark on his work, but his work leaves its individual mark, and sometimes excoriatingly, on tradition. What has become apparent is that Golding is a literary counterpuncher. Put another way, *he is a reactionary in the most basic sense of the word.* Reacting strongly to certain disagreeable aspects of life and literature as he sees them, he writes with a revolutionary heat that is contained rather than exploded within his compressed style. Restoration rather than preservation is his aim: he would restore concepts of Belief, Free Will, Individual Responsibility, Sin, Forgiveness (or Atonement, anyway), Vision, and Divine Grace. He would restore principles in an unprincipled world; he would restore belief to a world of willful unbelievers.

From the outset of his career, Golding received critical recognition on the basis of his providing something new, something original (most early commentators put it down to his renovation of parable and fable as literary modes of serious expression). One early reaction to his work was that here at last the Home Counties had succeeded in bringing forth a voice capable of contending with the universal wilderness and the everlasting whirlwind. It might not be the voice of a Dostoevsky or Melville or Conrad or Camus, but certainly it was not the voice of still another angry young man. With each successive novel Golding seemed to be marking an end to all that—the novel of manners, the novel of social commentary—and thus to the great tradition as well. It was as though he were pointing at *Howards End* as a literary cul-de-sac.

Aside from his novels, which did their own attesting, Golding himself lent credence to the idea that he was indeed original, something of an experimenter in the making of modern myths.[16] In a Third Programme radio discussion, for example, he expressed a wish to make each book say something different, and in a different way each time:

> It seems to me that there's really very little point in writing a novel unless you do something that either you suspected you couldn't do, or which you are pretty certain nobody else has tried before. I don't think there's any point in writing two books that are like each other. . . .
>
> I see, or I bring myself to see, a certain set of circumstances in a particular way. If it is the way everybody else sees them, then there is no point in writing a book.[17]

This self-portrait of Golding as literary experimenter is fairly accurate, but it needs expansion. In this connection, we should remember that he spent his first years at Oxford as a student of science before he switched emphasis to English literature. And there remains in his literary efforts something of the scientific stance—that of a white-coated experimenter working in the isolation of a laboratory, isolating in turn his literary elements on islands, promontories, and rocks, in closets, asylums, and prison camps. But in doing his experiments Golding inevitably has a finger stuck in someone else's lab book, along with a marginal note indicating what is wrong or at least what remains to be done. If we were allowed to expand Golding's statement about himself, we would have to—on the basis of what proves to be his practice—add this presumptuous comment: "I often see what others have been getting at, and disagree strongly. So I conduct counter-experiments with results that state: 'Not that way, but this.'"

All Golding's novels, products of his peculiar literary temperament and habit, are reactive experiments. The wonder is how habitual a process this has been. Piecemeal, several critics have nicely documented certain influences or stimuli affecting his work. Yet important instances have been left undiscovered, overlooked, underestimated. What remains to be said is that this reactive method of composition has become the *modus operandi.* It provides a key as to what Golding has derived from others and what he has provided that is original. Yet Golding has insisted, "But one book never comes out of another, and *The Coral Island* is not ***Lord of the Flies.***" And, adamantly, that *"one work does not come from another unless it is stillborn."*[18] Nevertheless, with Golding the process may be, if he has created counter-experiments which are original fiction, not stillbirth but birth.

The process begins with ***Lord of the Flies,*** and here the critical documentation has been fairly solid. In separate essays Frank Kermode and Carl Niemeyer make it quite apparent that a strong connection exists between Golding's novel and one published almost exactly a century earlier, R. M. Ballantyne's *The Coral Island* (1857).[19] Golding reworks Ballantyne's basic situation, setting, and narrative episodes. Like Ballantyne in each respect, he isolates a group of English boys on a coral island that seems an earthly paradise, with a plentitude of fruit and coconuts. He introduces pig killings, cannibalistic tendencies, and the question of ghosts. He names three of his major characters Jack, Ralph, and Piggy in honor of Ballantyne's Jack, Ralph, and Peterkin Gay (the last might just as well be called Piggy, because in one instance, when he is off hunting pigs, Jack alludes to him with the phrase "When Greek meets Greek," the implication being, of course, when pig meets pig).

If Golding works closely to Ballantyne's outline, it is mainly to show by contrast to his own findings how inane the nineteenth-century experiment in youthful isolation was. Eventually the contrast shows through strongly. While Ballantyne's characters, for instance, are stout English lads who overcome evil introduced into their worldly paradise by natives and pirates, Golding's characters find evil within themselves and almost go under, until finally extricated by a *deus ex machina.* The officer who is the long arm of that godly machine underscores the difference between Golding's novel and Ballantyne's when he says with Old Boy naïveté: "Jolly good show. Like the Coral Island." Ralph looks at the officer dumbly, uncomprehendingly, and his look measures the distance between generations as well as the distance between the fictional visions of 1857 and 1954.

Knowing about Ballantyne's contribution to ***Lord of the Flies*** makes for a fuller and richer reading of the novel than might otherwise be obtained. To see how hollow a reading can result when the necessary connection is not made, one need simply read the French version, in which the English naval officer is made to speak for the benefit of an uninitiated audience: "L'officier l'encouragea du menton.—Oui, je comprends. La belle aventure. Les Robinsons . . ." *The Swiss Family Robinson* (and even *Robinson Crusoe,* if it is intended in the pluralization) will not do. (See *Sa Majesté des Mouches,* translated by Lola Tranec, Gallimard, Paris, 1956.) In ironic contrast to ***Lord of the Flies,*** Golding has written of *The Swiss Family Robinson,* "This is how children live when they are happy. . . . The days are endless and time has no meaning. . . . In the text, as ever, the children take a child's place. There is simply no possibility of juvenile delinquency. The [parental] guiding hand is gentle but adamant. . . ."[20]

As Kermode perceptively declares, the related books of Ballantyne and Golding can be used as documents in the history of ideas, Ballantyne's contribution belonging "inseparably to the period when boys were sent out of Arnoldian schools certified free of Original Sin,"[21] ready to keep the Empire shipshape. Golding writes with a vivid sense of paradox, with the eyes of someone who has seen the Empire crumble and witnessed twentieth-century manifestations of Original Sin.

Although it has gone unnoticed or unmentioned in comparisons of Golding and Ballantyne, both authors use similar conclusions involving the technical assistance of the *deus ex machina.* Jack, Ralph, and Peterkin are in the clutches of savages near the conclusion of *Coral Island;* they believe they will never more see home, and await death, only to find their bonds severed, and themselves set free. A "teacher," who stands in the place of the naval officer in ***Lord of the Flies,*** acquaints them with the miraculous fact that their captor, chief Tararo, "has embraced the Christian religion." This is no less a miracle in its way than the appearance of the naval officer who arrives just in the nick of time to save Golding's Ralph. Religion also appears in ***Lord of the Flies*** in truncated form: as already mentioned, some of the boys are choir members, but no prayer is ever heard. Religion enters only by way of hindsight and moralistic impingement from the outside, as the reader considers a hidden theme. In *The Coral Island,* as we can see by the quite Christian ending, it plays a central, well-advertised part. Not only are Ballantyne's youths invincible Britons, as they often call themselves, but they have faith, in the usual sense of the word. The Ralph of that group could be speaking for them all when under difficult pressures he remembers his mother's parting homily: "Ralph, my dearest child, always remember in the hour of danger to look to your Lord and Saviour Jesus Christ. He alone is both able and willing to save your body and soul." This is exactly what Golding's children do not do. Golding made clear why in an interview in which he explained his approach to the efficacy of *Coral Island* morality:

> What I'm saying to myself is "don't be such a fool, you remember when you were a boy, a small boy, how you lived on that island with Ralph and Jack and Peterkin." . . . I said to myself finally, "Now you are grown up, you are adult; it's taken you a long time to become adult, but now you've got there you can see that people are not like that." There savagery would not be found in natives on an island. As like as not they would find savages who were kindly and uncomplicated and that the devil would rise out of the intellectual complications of the three white men in the island itself.[22]

Although Golding does not provide easy answers to all the questions he raises in ***Lord of the Flies,*** it is clear that his religious answer is not Ballantyne's. The real savior in ***Lord of the Flies*** is not the naval officer, but Simon—and his voice goes unheeded, as once again the crucifixion takes place, this time without redemption or resurrection.

Notes

1. See, for example, John Peter, "The Fables of William Golding," *Kenyon Review,* XIX (Fall, 1957), 577-92; Claire Rosenfield, "'Men of Smaller Growth': A Psychological Analysis of William Golding's *Lord of the Flies,*" *Literature and Psychology,* XI (Autumn, 1961), 93-101; and Edmund Fuller, "The Compelling Lure of William Golding," *New York Herald Tribune Books,* November 4, 1962, pp. 1, 3.

2. Carl Niemeyer, in "The Coral Island Revisited," *College English,* XXII (January, 1961), 241-45, makes explicit Golding's use of R. M. Ballantyne's *The Coral Island,* a boys' book published in 1857; and James Gindin, in "'Gimmick' and Metaphor in the Novels of William Golding," *Modern Fiction Studies,* VI (Summer, 1960), 145-52, tries to indicate how much of Golding's work is marred by "clever tricks."

3. There is some adverse criticism of Golding, on the grounds of "gimmick" or philosophy, but Martin Green's "Distaste for the Contemporary," *The Nation,* May 21, 1960, pp. 451-54, seems egregiously harsh and willful, and R. C. Townsend's "Lord of the Flies: Fool's Gold?," *Journal of General Education,* XVI (July, 1964), 153-60, is a specious denigration of *Lord of the Flies* through a working out of proposed parallels with *A High Wind in Jamaica,* Golding coming off second best philosophically and stylistically each time. Kenneth Rexroth ("William Golding," *The Atlantic,* 215 [May, 1965], 96-98), like the French translator of *Lord of the Flies,* shows his failure to comprehend the book in his calling it merely a "carelessly documented" *Swiss Family Robinson.* All Golding's novels are "rigged," he adds.

4. *Lord of the Flies* (New York: Capricorn Books, 1959). All subsequent references to the novel are to this edition.

5. The Lord of the Flies is not only Beelzebub and the endless variations upon him, but, in Greco-Roman tradition, the all-mighty Zeus, described (for example, in Sartre's play *The Flies*) as "god of flie and death. The image has white eyes and blood-smeared cheeks." To the naïve Orestes, Sartre's Zeus explains that the carrion-attracted flies are "a symbol," representative of a need in "all those creeping, half-human creatures" called men: "They have guilty consciences, they're afraid—and fear and guilty consciences have a good savor in the nostrils of the gods. Yes, the gods take pleasure in such poor souls. . . . What, moreover, could you give them in exchange? Good digestions, the gray monotony of provincial life, and the boredom—ah, the soul-destroying boredom—of long days of mild content. Go your way, my lad, go your way. The repose of cities and men's souls hangs on a thread. . . ."

6. Simon is usually thought of as being mystical or prophetic, but he is also as logical as any of the others, even Piggy.
7. Any attack that concentrates on Golding's style should come to grips with the kind of writing used to depict this scene. Martin Green's article does not. Nor does Kenneth Rexroth's attempt at deflation (*The Atlantic, op. cit.*). Golding not only writes about Neanderthals, according to Rexroth, "he writes for them. His message is not unlike that of Jack London. . . . Golding's prose is almost as bad. In some ways it is worse, because it lacks specificity. In London there is a degree of sensual immediacy and passionate rhetoric unknown to Golding." Clearly, Rexroth has scanned Golding rather cursorily.
8. William Golding, "On the Crest of the Wave," *The Writer's Dilemma* (London, 1961), pp. 42-51.
9. Psychoanalytical articles thus far published fail to account for such behavior.
10. John Peter's perceptive article has already been noted; see also Millar Maclure, "Allegories of Innocence," *Dalhousie Review,* XL (Summer, 1960), 145-56; and V. S. Pritchett, "Secret Parables," *New Statesman,* August 2, 1958, p. 146.
11. Both Epstein and Rosenfield concentrate on the Freudian concept of id, ego, superego; but Epstein makes his most original analytical point with the Oedipal wedding night aspect of the sow's death. Golding has commented to an interviewer: "Yes, what is all this talk about Oedipal wedding nights, ids and egos? *And to think I've never read Freud in my life.* Someone wrote a terribly erudite article showing that Ralph was an id and Piggy an ego. Or was it the other way around? I was quite impressed, but the whole thing was simply untrue. I suppose I'm doing the same thing as Freud did—investigating this complex phenomenon called man. Perhaps our results are similar, but there is no influence." Bernard F. Dick, in "The Novelist Is a Displaced Person," *College English,* XXVI, 481.
12. *The Contemporary English Novel* (New York, 1962), p. 258.
13. J. Bowen, "One Man's Meat: The Idea of Individual Responsibility in Golding's Fiction," London *Times Literary Supplement,* August 7, 1959, p. xii.
14. William Wasserstrom and Claire Rosenfield, "An Exchange of Opinion concerning William Golding's *Lord of the Flies,*" *Literature and Psychology,* XII (Winter, 1962), 2-3, 11-12.
15. "On the Crest of the Wave," p. 51.
16. See Frank Kermode's "The Novels of William Golding," *International Literary Annual,* III (1961), 13-14.
17. As quoted by John Bowen, "Bending Over Backwards," *Times Literary Supplement,* October 23, 1959, p. 608.
18. Dick, "The Novelist Is a Displaced Person," *College English,* XXVI, 481.
19. See Niemeyer, *op. cit.,* and Kermode, *op. cit.*
20. "Islands," review of reprint editions of *Swiss Family Robinson* and *Treasure Island, The Spectator,* June 10, 1960, p. 844.
21. Kermode, *op. cit.*
22. As quoted in *William Golding,* by Samuel Hynes (New York, 1964), pp. 7-8.

F. C. Bufkin (essay date spring 1965)

SOURCE: Bufkin, F. C. "*Lord of the Flies:* An Analysis." *The Georgia Review* 19, no. 1 (spring 1965): 40-57.

[*In the following essay, Bufkin envisions* Lord of the Flies *as reflective of the Christian myth of the fall of man with a plea for order to combat evil.*]

William Golding's ***Lord of the Flies*** is about evil; and it recounts a quest for order amidst the disorder that evil causes. Golding has said that the theme of the novel "is an attempt to trace the defects of society back to the defects of human nature. The moral is that the shape of a society must depend on the ethical nature of the individual and not on any political system however apparently logical or respectable." Theme and moral are worked out through an adaptation of the Christian myth of the Fall of Man, which has been overlaid with what may be termed the myth of the desert island. Since Golding is a serious student of Greek, and has stated that Euripides is one of his literary influences, it is not surprising that in ***Lord of the Flies*** the principal technical device he uses is irony. It, like the myth of fallen man, permeates the novel. The presence of the myth has been duly noted by critics but, though commentators have perceived and incidentally remarked on a wide variety of ironies in the novel, almost none, with the notable exception of John Peter, has so far recognized that ***Lord of the Flies,*** piercing through illusion and appearance to truth and reality, is essentially an ironical novel. Recognition of this is basic to any analysis of the work, providing as it does the key to both the author's development of theme and his handling of his subject-matter.

Indeed, of two of the major literary influences on ***Lord of the Flies,*** one, R. M. Ballantyne's adventure story *The Coral Island,* serves a chiefly ironical purpose. The exact nature of that influence has been established by Golding himself in an interview with Frank Kermode. Asked whether his novel is not a "kind of black mass version of Ballantyne," Golding replied that it is not: "I think," he said, "it is, in fact, a realistic view of the Ballantyne situation." When further asked "just how far and how ironically we ought to treat" the connection between the two books, Golding gave an illuminating reply about the origin of his novel:

> Well, I think, fairly deeply, but again, not ironically in the bad sense, but in almost a compassionate sense. You see, really, I'm getting at myself in this. What I'm saying to myself is "don't be such a fool, you remember when you were a boy, a small boy, how you lived on that island with Ralph and Jack and Peterkin" (who is Simon, by the way, Simon called Peter, you see. It was worked out very carefully in every possible way[,] this novel). I said to myself finally, "Now you are grown up, you are adult, it's taken you a long time to become adult, but now you've got there you can see that people are not like that; they would not behave like that if they were God-fearing English gentlemen, and they went to an island like that." Their savagery would not be found in natives on an island. As like as not they would find savages who were kindly and uncomplicated and that the devil would rise out of the intellectual complications of the three white men on the island itself.

Ballantyne's book, to which Golding refers in this comment, is about an "agreeable triumvirate" of boys who are marooned on a coral reef in the South Seas: Ralph, the narrator of the story; Jack, their "king"; and Peterkin. Survivors of a "frightful" shipwreck during a "dreadful" storm, they explore the island, which they think must be "the ancient paradise," and, making the best of their situation, lead a happy and orderly life there, hunting hogs, eating fruit, and exploring. "There was, indeed," says Ralph, "no note of discord whatever in the symphony we played together on that sweet Coral Island; and I am now persuaded that this was owing to our having been all tuned to the same key, namely, that of *love!* Yes, we loved one another with much fervency, while we lived on that island; and, for the matter of that, we love each other still." This much of the plot is what Golding used; he neglected the later episodes that deal with pirates and cannibals. But it was just this much of the plot that must have seemed false, or unrealistic, to Golding.

Although neither appreciation nor understanding of ***Lord of the Flies*** is dependent upon familiarity with *The Coral Island,* the reader acquainted with Ballantyne's work can better see what Golding has done in his own novel. The person who knows both stories is aware of the contrast between them, and knows that the contrast is, in effect and purpose, ironical. It resides in the discrepancy between the falseness, or unreality, of his source, as Golding sees it, and the truth, or reality, of ***Lord of the Flies.*** Golding must surely have had this juxtaposition in mind, else he would not have so carefully duplicated in his own novel details from Ballantyne's.

A second major literary influence on ***Lord of the Flies,*** an influence that no critic has noted before, despite its almost glaring presence, is *Paradise Lost.* The epic and the novel have a common theme, the Fall of Man; and it is altogether feasible that Golding, in paralleling in ***Lord of the Flies*** situations highly similar to those in *Paradise Lost,* meant to enrich and to enlarge, by associative suggestion, the scope of his narrative.

The first of these parallels is the setting. Golding's island, like Milton's Eden, represents the original earthly paradise where occurs the Fall of Man. That the island is meant to represent this paradise is easily deduced from the following sentence: "The forest re-echoed; and birds lifted, crying out of the tree-tops, as on that first morning ages ago." And it is quite possible also that the killing of the sow, to which the boys are "wedded in lust," may itself, since the passage is presented in terms of sexual intercourse, function as a symbolic, parodic re-enactment of the Original Sin:

> . . . the sow fell and the hunters hurled themselves at her. This dreadful eruption from an unknown world made her frantic; she squealed and bucked and the air was full of sweat and noise and blood and terror. Roger ran round the heap, prodding with his spear whenever pigflesh appeared. Jack was on top of the sow, stabbing downward with his knife. Roger found a lodgment for his point and began to push till he was leaning with his whole weight. The spear moved forward inch by inch and the terrified squealing became a high-pitched scream. Then Jack found

> the throat and the hot blood spouted over his hands. The sow collapsed under them and they were heavy and fulfilled upon her.

These two passages may be said to deal with the natural aspects of the Fall—the natural world and, in it, man. Other passages paralleling incidents in *Paradise Lost* may be said, in contrast, to be based on the supernatural. In the one, Golding's boys represent the earliest man and his Fall in Eden; in the second, they represent the fallen angels, or devils, and the island is Hell. Golding makes clear that Jack and the choirboys are devils—fallen angels. Curiously, no critic has commented on why they are choirboys and not just ordinary schoolboys. Golding, having "worked out very carefully in every possible way this novel," certainly had a definite purpose in making them so. Even though the concept of angels as singers is both traditional and common, Golding points out the connection between the boys and angels explicitly. He says that "ages ago"—a repeated phrase connecting the singing boys and the singing birds of "that first morning"—the boys "had stood in two demure rows and their voices had been the song of angels." A double irony is at work here. The phrase means that the boys, who are devils, sang *like* angels and also that they sang songs *of* angels; that is, liturgic chants which, on the island, undergo pagan and savage metamorphosis into "*Kill the pig! Cut his throat! Kill the pig! Bash him in!*" (which Golding terms a "chant" rising "ritually").

In *Paradise Lost* the angels fall from Heaven while war is raging there, and Golding has duplicated this situation, too; for the plane carrying the boys is attacked and shot down during a war. In fact, war is the very cause of their being there, just as it is the cause of the angels' fall from Heaven. Thus while the island the boys land on is an emblem of Paradise, it is ironically also an emblem of Hell, complete with the traditional fire (watching which, Piggy "glanced nervously into hell"). And there is also a presiding demoniac god, the Lord of the Flies—Beelzebub, the Prince of Devils.

Finally, in ***Lord of the Flies*** the boys, all of them, assemble, exchange names (perhaps a parallel to the roll-call of the infernal host), hold a council, elect a leader, and explore the island. These are the same acts, and they occur in the same order, that the fallen angels perform in Milton's Hell. Ironically, not Jack, who is "the most obvious leader," but Ralph, who is "no devil," is chosen. But since the movement of the plot is toward the emergence of evil in the boys and its gradual domination of them, it is, fittingly, not long before Ralph's position is usurped by Jack, who finally leads the now savage tribe of boys with their "anonymous devils' faces" and sits in the midst of them "like an idol." (This movement may be viewed, further, as a correspondence to Satan's securing of power in the world.)

The story of ***Lord of the Flies*** is told from the omniscient point of view. Golding as narrator shifts from one boy to another, among the major characters, telling each one's thoughts and decisions, explaining his motivations and reactions, or seeing a situation with his perspective; and at the very end he shifts away from the boys to their adult rescuer. Occasionally, at certain crucial times when the context of the novel calls for an objective, uninvolved voice to be heard as the voice of truth, Golding stands back from the action and comments unobtrusively on the situation. For the most part, however, the story develops through dramatic action and dialogue, not through authorial exposition and comment; and this method contrasts with the moralizing first-person narration of *The Coral Island,* which Golding is "correcting." He perhaps felt that readers familiar with the Ballantyne story would be aware of this contrast. Instead of telling, then, Golding is showing; and the difference in this technique is as significant as the contrast between the two writers' attitudes toward their material.

The omniscient point of view is another device for widening the scope of the novel, for obviously a part of the whole plan of the narrative is that the attitudes of each of the four principal characters—Ralph, Jack, Piggy, Simon—be included. This particular point of view—the omniscient—is, furthermore, appropriate and important to the novel in that it can control and unify both what happens on the island and what is happening in the world surrounding it. This fictional device is capable of producing an over-all irony that another device could hardly so economically and directly create. The identification of the dead parachutist, for instance, and the information about where he comes from and why, would be impossible without the omniscient point of view; and the kind of irony that derives from the contrast between the reader's knowledge of the true situation and the characters' ignorance of it would have been otherwise unobtainable.

One of the most arresting features of the structure of ***Lord of the Flies*** is that, though it develops as a chronologically straight narrative, it is actually bipartite, Chapters I-IX forming one part, the last three chapters (X-XII) forming the other. Thematically, an important point is subtly made by this division. The first part shows the boys in a state of innocence, and the second shows them in a primitive state of evil. What is not immediately perceived is that in the second part the boys are placed in situations almost identical to situations in the first part (notably those created by storm and by fire). In their changed state, however, the boys react to the situations entirely differently; and the second part thus functions as a concentrated, contrasting restatement of much of the material of the first part of the novel.

This contrast points directly to the theme of the novel: the loss of innocence is the acquisition of the knowledge of evil, which corrupts man and darkens his heart. Movement of plot from innocence to evil is thus thematically vertical, not horizontal; it is a reenactment of the Fall and its consequences. In support of the theme Golding continually uses words of downward motion. The opening sentence itself sets in motion this running verbal motif: "The boy with fair hair lowered himself down the last few feet of rock. . . ." The boys are "dropped" from the sky. The parachutist is a sign come "down from the world of grown-ups," and later his corpse "swayed down through a vastness of wet air . . . ; falling, still falling, it sank towards the beach. . . ." Simon, after his hallucinatory conversation with the Lord of the Flies, "fell down and lost consciousness" and, when killed, he "fell over the steep edge of the rock" and the orgiastically excited boys surged after him and "poured down the rock," whereupon "the clouds opened and let down the rain like a waterfall." Piggy, hit by the rock, "fell forty feet," and Ralph weeps for "the fall through the air of the true, wise friend called Piggy." In the last episode of the novel the naval officer is introduced while "looking down at Ralph in wary astonishment." These are but a few of the many examples that run through the novel, suggesting the spiritual fall through words of physical action and direction.

This motif might actually be considered imagistic, one of the intricate network of interrelated symbols and images that, composing the texture of ***Lord of the Flies,*** enlarge and universalize its meaning. At least four such systems are prominent: cosmic symbols that transform the island into an emblem of the world, or universe, in miniature; symbols pertaining to order and reason and their opposites, supplemented by an ancillary group of head images; animal images that connote the degradation of the boys from the human to the bestial level; and "play" images that trace the ironical change from childhood games to deadly reality.

The cosmic symbolism is established at the beginning when the boys are dropped on an island in the Pacific Ocean. Golding draws on a long-established tradition by making the island "roughly boat-shaped"; and thus, as C. B. Cox has stated in elaborating on this fact, "the children typify all mankind on their journey through life." The island as a ship is, then, a symbol of the world in microcosm; it is to the boys, as first man, the Garden of Paradise or, as fallen angels, Hell. Thus boys are not only boys but men, Man, and angels.

Golding draws upon another traditional cosmic symbol, the storm, to reflect in the realm of nature the evil or chaotic doings in the world of man. A storm accompanies the confused landing of the boys on the island; and later another storm develops in gradual stages that parallel those leading up to the boys' feast and slaughter of Simon. On the day of these climactic actions "the sky, as if in sympathy with the great changes among them [the boys], was different . . . and so misty that in some places the hot air seemed white." After the slaughter of the sow, "high up among the bulging clouds thunder went off like a gun," and later "the thunder boomed again." In the next chapter, "over the island the build-up of clouds" continues, and when the boys eat their kill they do so "beneath a sky of thunderous brass that rang with the storm-coming." After Jack's sneering declaration that the conch no longer counts, "all at once the thunder struck. Instead of the dull boom there was a point of impact in the explosion." The thunder becomes more violent as the boys become more violent and wild in their dance; and the dark sky, also, becomes "shattered" by "blue-white scar[s]." Then at last, after Simon has been killed, "the clouds opened and let down the rain. . . ."

The island is further represented as microcosm through the presence of all the four elements—earth, air, fire, water. The storm itself represents a warring interplay of them all. The island—earth—is of course surrounded by the other three. But in addition earth is present as the clay with which the boys paint their faces. Fire is present as signal, hearth and comfort, and destructive force. And water and air are the elements from which the boys believe the beast comes. The dead airman, whom they finally think to be the beast, comes from the air but is carried away, by the wind, to the sea.

The three central symbols, in addition to fire (which is related to them), refer to concepts of order-and-reason and disorder-and-unreason. These, primary symbols pertaining to the quest for order that is necessary for life, are the conch and Piggy's glasses, and the pig's head. The conch, Golding makes clear, is a symbol of order and reason; it represents the voice of authority, at first heeded then flouted. Furthermore, it is an object of great beauty (a traditional attribute of order), having a "delicate, embossed pattern." (Ominously, the breakdown of order is foreshadowed by the remark made when the conch is first discovered: "Careful! You'll break it—") The conch is sounded for meetings, and at them only the holder of the conch has the right to speak. Toward the end of the novel Piggy and Ralph confront the others and make a final attempt to re-establish some form of order. Piggy, holding the conch, tries to appeal to the others' sense of reason; but he is greeted by booing. Then, "with a sense of delirious abandonment," Roger causes a great rock to crash down upon Piggy and, when it hits him, "the conch exploded into a thousand white fragments and ceased to exist." In other words, order, rational behavior, and benevolent authority have been completely smashed on the island: the quest has failed.

Piggy's glasses, functioning similarly as the conch, are a symbol of reason, fittingly worn by the thinker of the group. One side of them is eventually broken in a scuffle following the failure of the passing ship to see any smoke on the island; later the remaining lens is stolen in a night raid led by Jack. The breaking and losing of the glasses indicates, symbolically, the breakdown of visionary reason. Piggy's resulting blindness corresponds to the darkness of eclipsing unreason. He is led, finally, by Ralph to the "fort" to try to recover from Jack the stolen lens, in a symbolic episode. But Piggy does not regain even his half-sight; instead he is thrown into the great final darkness of death, since during this scene he is killed.

The fates of the conch and of the glasses, like their functions, are thus related to each other—and to Piggy: all are ultimately broken. Both conch and glasses serve practical purposes (as Piggy does also) on the island; the conch preserves order and the glasses serve as the means for lighting the fire necessary to rescue. After order, concretized in the conch, is finally shattered, the remaining lens yet serves a further purpose: Jack and his cohorts use it to make the fire in their pursuit of Ralph. The fire not only smokes out Ralph but also attracts the attention of the passing cruiser. The misapplication—or iniquitous application—of reason is thus made, ironically, to serve the ends that right reason itself was unable to bring about.

The spiked pig's head is, of course, the symbol of paramount interest. The head is stuck on a stick as a placatory offering to the beast, which the boys mistakenly believe in their fear to be the dead parachutist; it is termed by Golding a gift for darkness. This object is the Lord of the Flies, and it is a repulsive sight: "dim-eyed, grinning faintly, blood blackening between the teeth." Its half-shut eyes are "dim with the infinite cynicism of adult life," and they assure Simon that everything is "a bad business." The butterflies desert the open place where "the obscene thing grinned and dripped," but the flies, "black and iridescent green and without number," swarm buzzingly around it. To Simon the object declares, ". . . I'm the Beast," and then continues:

> "Fancy thinking the Beast was something you could hunt and kill! . . . You knew, didn't you? I'm part of you? . . . I'm the reason why it's no go? Why things are what they are?

The beast appeals to fear, not reason, and promises the disorder of pleasure. To Simon it says:

> "I'm warning you. I'm going to get angry. D'you see? You're not wanted. Understand? We are going to have fun on this island. Understand? We are going to have fun on this island! So don't try it on, my poor misguided boy, or else—"

The Lord of the Flies, then, is darkness—the embodiment and voice of evil and the demoniac. It is Beelzebub, lord of the flies and dung, the Prince of Devils. And it is the beast—the beast that is part of all men. The materialization of this devil coincides with the emergence of savage evil in the boys, revealed in the acts that they commit.

Cephalic imagery supports the theme of irrationality as evil and, importantly, the head, the center of reason, of each of the four major characters figures conspicuously in the plot. Through this imagery Golding depicts the breakdown of rational processes and rational control indirectly. Ralph stands on his head in moments of happiness or elation (which are few). This antic act he performs in the opening scene; as evil emerges and happiness disappears, Ralph significantly discontinues the act. Along with Piggy he is the main upholder of order on the island, and this inverted position of his is an anticipation of the routing of authority and the degradation of reason. Piggy's bespectacled head, the source of reasonable planning, breaks open after his fall—"His head opened and stuff came out and turned red." After this event right reason no longer exists; for this fall destroys the conch and, by splitting his head, kills Piggy. Jack's easy descent to savagery is indicated by his decoration of his face with colored clay; and when he smudges blood over his forehead the gesture is, as Claire Rosenfield has pointed out, a kind of pagan initiation "in which the hunter's face is smeared with the blood of his first kill." Thus Jack progresses, in descent, through the stages outlined by Piggy in his inquiry, "What are we? Humans? Or animals? Or savages?" The human Jack, disguising his head, tends to appear, and then to act, like an animal; and then, after wiping blood on his head, he becomes, through the releasing of the animal urges within, totally savage. His painted face becomes a mask behind which he hides, "liberated from shame and self-consciousness." Simon's head undergoes pain and illusion during the episode of his colloquy with the Lord of the Flies. The change begins with a throb: "In Simon's right temple, a pulse began to beat on the brain." His head, having been tilted slightly up, now begins to wobble, and it seems to him that the Lord of the Flies "was expanding like a balloon." Through this experience Simon, the mystic and saint, arrives at the truth about the beast; and that his reason is intuitive, not really rational, is signalized by the fainting fit that affects his head. Moreover, Simon, as saint, is an obvious contrast to the Lord of the Flies as Prince of Devils. Just as the shiny filth-loving flies circle the dead pig's head, so the "strange, moonbeamed-bodied creatures with fiery eyes" in the sea—their effectiveness heightened by the lack of more specific identification—busy themselves halo-like around Simon's head. Finally, Golding indicates the disorder through head imagery by describing the unkempt, ever-growing hair on all the boys' heads but Piggy's:

> He was the only boy on the island whose hair never seemed to grow. The rest were shock-headed, but Piggy's hair still lay in wisps over his head as though baldness were his natural state, and this imperfect covering would soon go. . . .

The pig's head is, of course, the principal symbol in this category. It is the ironic antithesis of reason, since (being a head, the seat of reason) it appeals, through fear, to the emotions or passions. It speaks "in the voice of a schoolmaster" and teaches a diabolically perverted lesson. It has promised fun; but the fun of darkness leads to death. In the last chapter the pig's head has actually become the traditional symbol of death—a skull. The ingenuity of Golding's handling of both symbolism and irony is evidenced in his linking the opposites, conch and pig's skull, in this passage:

> At length he [Ralph] came to a clearing in the forest where rock prevented vegetation from growing. Now it was a pool of shadows and Ralph nearly flung himself behind a tree when he saw something standing in the centre; but then he saw that the white face was bone and that the pig's skull grinned at him from the top of a stick. He walked slowly into the middle of the clearing and looked steadily at the skull that gleamed as white as ever the conch had done and seemed to jeer at him cynically. An inquisitive ant was busy in one of the eye sockets but otherwise the thing was lifeless.

The animal imagery is thus related to the symbolism of reasonunreason by means of the pig's head. The animal is, of course, distinguished from the human by the reasoning faculty, which it lacks; and a human's loss of this faculty reduces him to the bestial level. Through the use of animal imagery Golding is able to keep constantly before the reader the motif of degeneration, the changing from the reasoning human to the unreasoning animal state. Ralph explicitly tells the other boys, by way of warning, that "we'll soon be animals" and the prediction becomes a reality. (The animal imagery thus acts also as a foreshadowing device.) The boys are associated as agents of evil with flies through the use of the words *buzz* and *hum,* for they buzz and hum at meetings. And, as if to prefigure their change, the children are depicted by animal images. They cast "bat-like" shadows, sit like "black birds," and run round "like insects." They howl and pant "like dogs," point like setters, and steam like seals. Even Ralph eats "like a wolf" and terms himself, Piggy, and Simon "three blind mice." Jack in particular is described with such imagery. As hunter, he becomes doglike, "down like a sprinter, his nose only a few inches from the humid earth," "on all fours." He is swallowed up by the animal "compulsion to track down and kill," and his laughter as a "bloodthirsty snarling." He is "ape-like," and Ralph terms him a "swine." Ironically, Piggy himself is compared to pigs, besides being mocked by a pig nickname. When struck and killed by the rock, he has "no time for even a grunt" and his "arms and legs twitched a bit, like a pig's after it has been killed." In the last chapter the animal imagery is climaxed. The chased Ralph thinks as a chased pig must think and, significantly, the boys hunting him become a pack of animals. (To the naval officer they are "a pack of British boys.") Golding makes this identification through the repetitive use of the word, in its several forms, *ululate,* which means to howl like a dog or a wolf. The angels' chant has now become the cacophonous cry of the hunters. The emergence of the animal is now universal.

The fourth system of imagery traces the transition from the "fun" of the boys' games to horrible reality—the "fun" predicted by the Lord of the Flies. These games are childish amusements at first—"a time when play was good and life so full that hope was not necessary and therefore forgotten"—but gradually they become tinged with cruelty and violence. Moreover, the majority of the boys cannot grasp the seriousness of such matters as maintaining the fire; building it is to them merely an opportunity for a "good time" and they fancy themselves re-enacting *Treasure Island, Swallows and Amazons,* and *The Coral Island.*

Soon they play at pig-hunting, and Robert, who gets hurt acting the role of pig, appreciates the difference between pretending and reality. "Oh, my bum!" he moans with "frightened snivels," and tells the others, while "still caressing his rump," "You want a real pig . . . because you've got to kill him." But to Jack this is "a good game." The episode is a foreshadowing of the killing of the sow and also of the murder of Simon, each episode of the sequence being more savage and more evil than the one preceding it.

Finally Jack declares an end to the good games after the others will not agree to his replacing Ralph as leader: "I'm not going to play any longer." Soon afterward Ralph too puts an end to play, for he has realized that "being rescued isn't a game"—although he has long before realized that the councils should "not be fun, but business."

After the murder of Piggy the innocent games have become a seriously evil reality. When Ralph is pursued, the boys only pretend to pretend; their avowed intention is to kill him. And they would have succeeded had the naval officer not appeared. He speaks as authority; yet what he says is one of the most tragically ironic lines in the novel: "'Fun and games,' said the officer." The imagery has run its course and has done so in a circle. Adult authority with its rules has restored order and ended the reality-game of the children. The situation has accordingly been returned to "normal"; but the purpose of ***Lord of the Flies*** is to show that boys are not so innocently "normal" as, when restricted by authority, they appear to be.

The balance of structure of ***Lord of the Flies*** is reflected in the balance of the four principal boys, and the imagery is employed as a means of characterization. Ralph and Jack, conflicting contrasts, represent the principles of good and evil; and Piggy and Simon, also contrasts but not conflicting, represent the principles of reason, logical and intuitive. The personalities of these boys are worked out carefully along these sharply marked lines.

Ralph has the requirements to be the hero and the representative of good. He has the traditionally fair hair of the good man, the attractive appearance, and the ability of genuine leadership. He is the largest as well as the oldest of the boys; and he "might make a boxer, as far as width and heaviness of shoulders went." In addition, and importantly, he has a mildness about his mouth and eyes that proclaims him "no devil."

Yet Ralph, it should be noted, can possess only a limited goodness, since he is "ordinary bestial man," tainted with Original Sin. Like all the other boys he participates in the killing of Simon; but unlike them he is aware—and deeply bothered by the fact—that "that was murder." Nonetheless, Ralph is a boy of high standards and noble purpose, and he is the most forceful link with the authority of the adult world.

For this reason Ralph is the principal quester for order. He is not a thinker, but he possesses a practical intelligence, imagination, and reverence for order (he feels "a kind of affectionate reverence for the conch"). His great natural gift is to lead. And, though he must execute the plans that the more intelligent person (usually Piggy) might conceive, Ralph appreciates that "thought was a valuable thing, that got results."

Golding has developed Ralph more fully than any of the other boys. The reader learns that, when pleased, Ralph stands on his head; when agitated or worried, he bites his nails. His past is sketched: he remembers a cottage on the edge of the moors and, at the bottom of the garden, the wild ponies that came to the stone wall where he fed them sugar. His father is a commander in the Royal Navy. And Ralph is given to daydreaming.

Jack is his opposite. He is "the brilliant world of hunting, tactics, fierce exhilaration, skill"; Ralph, "the world of longing and baffled common-sense." They are "two continents of experience and feeling, unable to communicate." Jack is tall, thin, bony: in a word, ugly. He is the evil man, the boy devil. He is associated with Satan through his red hair; his anger, rage, and cursing; and the snake and swine images applied to him. Of all the boys he is the most obvious leader, having been chapter chorister and head boy. He is arrogant and knows his own mind; and his forceful personality exerts itself through proud jealousy of Ralph's position as leader. Jack is the principal culprit in consciously disobeying, ignoring, and finally abrogating the rules that have been established for the benefit, and possible rescue, of all. The most feral, as well as the leading savage (the "Chief"), of the boys, he sets up his own laws. Demonic order thus replaces good order.

Piggy is, perhaps, the most visually vivid of the boys. He is fat, clumsy, wears heavy spectacles, and is asthmatic. He does not like to work. He is the thinker on the island; to him life is "scientific." The function of sticks, he believes, should be to make a clock (a sundial), not spears. He possesses, as Ralph says, intellectual daring and can discount certain matters "learnedly." Ralph recognizes, like a wise leader, this quality: "Piggy could think. He could go step by step inside that fat head of his, only Piggy was no chief. But Piggy, for all his ludicrous body, had brains." Thus Piggy and Ralph are complements, as Jack and Ralph are contrasts.

Piggy (along with Ralph and Simon) has much respect for decorum, that observance of proprieties established by social authority and reason. When he becomes "a-bubble" with excitement, the excitement is "decorous"; but even he can on occasion be "shocked out of decorum" and say "Nuts!" He warns the others that they cannot expect to be rescued if they "don't put first things first and act proper." Both his first appearance in the novel and his last are breaches of decorum. The first is humorous. Just after appearing and meeting Ralph, Piggy reveals that he is suffering from diarrhea ("Them fruit," he says) and must leave his new-found companion to crouch "down among the tangled foliage." His last appearance is pathetic. Knocked roughly to his death over a cliff, he twitches like a pig, the fat boy who disliked his name, Piggy.

Simon, according to Golding, is a saint. Small and skinny, with a pointed chin and very bright eyes, he is subject to epileptic fits. He is filled with compassion. He finds Piggy's glasses when they are, the first time, knocked off, and he is the littluns' favorite bigun. To the critics who find Simon the weakest aspect of the novel, an unconvincing portrait, Golding has answered:

> What so many intelligent people and particularly, if I may say so, so many literary people find, is that Simon is incomprehensible. But, he *is* comprehensible to the illiterate person. The illiterate person knows about saints and sanctity, and Simon is a saint.

And then he continues:

> You see, a saint isn't just a scapegoat, a saint is somebody who in the last analysis voluntarily embraces his fate, which is a pretty sticky one, and he is for the illiterate a proof of the existence of God because the illiterate person who is not brought up on logic and not brought up always to hope for the worst, says, "Well, a person like this cannot exist without a good God." Therefore the illiterate person finds Simon extremely easy to understand, someone who voluntarily embraces this beast[,] goes . . . and tries to get rid of him and goes to give the good news to the ordinary bestial man on the beach, and gets killed for it.

With an amazing exactness Ralph, Jack, Piggy, and Simon all fit into Jung's classification of psychological types, set forth in *Modern Man in Search of a Soul.* These are sensation and intuition, which Jung terms essentially non-rational, and thinking and feeling, which he terms rational. He characterizes these types in this way: "When we think, it is in order to judge or to reach a conclusion, and when we feel it is in order to attach a proper value to something; sensation and intuition, on the other hand, are perceptive—they make us aware of what is happening, but do not interpret or evaluate it. They do not act selectively according to principles, but are simply receptive of what happens."

According to this scheme, Simon represents the intuition-type since intuition is "perception by way of unconscious contents and connections" and "points to the possibilities of the whence and whither that lie within the immediate facts." This definition helps clarify Simon's perception that the beast is "only us"; and it also helps explain Simon's conversation in delirium with the Lord of the Flies, his discovery of the true identity of the parachute-entwined "beast" on the mountain, and his going to the other boys to tell them about that discovery.

Jack represents the sensation-type, sensation being "perception through conscious sensory processes," that which "establishes what is actually given." Thus he sees pigs and wants to hunt them. When the littluns become afraid of the beast, Jack reassures them by declaring that, if one does exist, they will hunt it down and kill it.

Piggy is the thinking-type, the man of thought, not action. Ralph is the feeling-type: for "thinking enables us to recognize" the meaning of what is actually given, and "feeling tells us its value." These two, then, are both rational, according to Jung's scheme, and so are complementary. Ralph, for instance, has affection for the conch, but it is Piggy who first perceives its meaning: "We can use this to call the others. Have a meeting. They'll come when they hear us—" he says.

The effect of this comprehensive representation of the four psychological types of men is the creation of the impression that ***Lord of the Flies*** concerns not four principal boys in a cruel, violent, bloody story, but rather that the four are merely aspects of one, who is Man himself. Thus all four boys' points of view have been presented and combined by the omniscient narrator. And the devices of point of view and characterization integrate to turn the story of the novel into the Fall of Man and his experiences as he journeys, on the island-ship, through life in this world.

In ***Lord of the Flies*** Golding has thus created a picture of man's universal situation, "mankind's essential illness," and has traced the emergence of evil, the result of Original Sin, as man's common mortal inheritance. Like the first man, the boys land on the island in a state of innocence; but, like him, they gradually ignore the voice of authority and violate the rules that have been previously created—by state (king), church (God), family (father)—for order, mutual benefit, and happiness. Thus they enact, paradoxically, their "liberation into savagery": paradoxically, because their freeing is into a state of bondage to evil and undiscipline. Man, whether acting on the psychological, social, political, or Christian level, is most truly free when he is most truly disciplined. When law and rules, simultaneously the accouterments and the guardians of order, are discarded and the private, individual good takes control and precedence over the public, common good, things begin to fall apart, reason and common sense become baffled, and chaos ensues. Man, defying prescripted authority, whether divine or mundane, becomes corrupt; and the "understandable, lawful world," as a result of "intellectual complication," ceases to be a reality. It can only retreat into the memory, whence occasionally in some form—perhaps a daydream of feeding ponies over a wall in the bottom of a garden—it can be recalled.

Lord of the Flies depicts universal evil as a beast concept: the boys represent "ordinary bestial man." At first this concept exists in the littluns' subconscious, disturbing their dreams and begetting fear. They believe that the beast is a "snake-thing" and imagine that it goes abroad at night to eat them, turning, in the morning, "into them things like ropes in the trees." Thus the beast is a man-made, man-eating product of general superstition, ignorance, and darkness—out of which it comes and in which it operates. Gradually, however, this beast evinces more tangible proof of its existence; it appears to the children as "a dead man on a hill." But Simon discovers that they are mistaken. To him, the mystic whose knowledge is intuitive, the *real* beast is "only us"; and the Lord of the Flies, a true demonic and comminatory beast, confirms that this identity is correct. Evil, the beast, exists within men, and it is kept within by the authoritative restraints of laws, rules, and knowledge. This internal beast is the beast that cannot be hunted and killed; and this internal beast is the "reason why it's no go" and "things are what they are."

When released, the beast turns man into a savage, and reason is destroyed, both the intuitive type represented by Simon and the logical type represented by Piggy. Simon sees man as "at once heroic and sick." All men are sick because they are tainted with the universal disease of Original Sin, first contracted by Adam and passed to all his posterity. But men, though tragically not all, are also heroic in their struggle with this disease. Such men are Ralph, Piggy, and Simon. Simon, like the nursing sow, becomes in his death a sacrificial object to the beast, and the victim of the wanton evil and savagery unleashed in man. Men reject the common sense and reason that a few individuals like Ralph and Piggy try to force beneficially upon them. They also reject the divine truth that saints like Simon, if permitted to be heard, would disclose to them—the divine truth that would really free them from the illusive state of savage liberation. Simon, like his namesake Simon called Peter, seeks to bring truth (the "good news"—the gospel) about a "dead man on a hill" and, also like him, is martyred for the undertaking.

Yet man has the power to choose; he has free control and free exercise of his will. He can accept the real freedom of truth or he can accept the false freedom of savagery. But ironically, as Peter Green suggests, man "cherishes his guilt, his fears, his taboos, and will crucify any saint or redeemer who offers to relieve him of his burden by telling the simple truth." Thus, as Green has shown, ***Lord of the Flies*** states that "it is man who creates his own hell, his own devils; the evil is in him." Such is the message of the Lord of the Flies, echoing its own lord of darkness in *Paradise Lost:*

> The mind is its own place, and in itself
> Can make a Heav'n of Hell, a Hell of Heav'n.

Golding has commented:

> "The whole book is symbolic in nature except for the rescue in the end where adult life appears, dignified and capable, but in reality enmeshed in the same evil as the symbolic life of the children on the island. The officer, having interrupted a man-hunt, prepares to take the children off the island in a cruiser which will presently be hunting its enemy in the same implacable way. And who will rescue the adult and his cruiser?"

At the end of ***Lord of the Flies*** Golding employs a technical gimmick by a sudden shift in perspective to make this implicative point. The gimmick shifts the reader's identity from boys to rescuer, and then, in the same way but taking the procedure one step further, the gimmick serves to identify the rescuer with the boys and so to sever the reader's identity with any character. Thus the reader is left, at the end, to look at the novel from the outside. The boys' rescuer, heroic and sick like them and all men, is himself now ironically but a boy, decorated with his official insignia just as the children are decorated with clay and charcoal; and he too is engaged in a war. The ending, therefore, is merely another beginning of this mythic story. The final view is then that of the author, the cosmic ironist: not of just an island of boys but of the world of men who pursue the beast and turn paradise into pandemonium.

J. D. O'Hara (essay date winter 1966)

SOURCE: O'Hara, J. D. "Mute Choirboys and Angelic Pigs: The Fable in *Lord of the Flies*." *Texas Studies in Literature and Language* 7, no. 4 (winter 1966): 411-20.

[*In the following essay, O'Hara tries to clarify his idea of what the novel means and examines its validity.*]

Lord of the Flies has been around now for twelve years—time enough, one would think, for its significances to be common knowledge. Critical articles on the novel are disappointing, however; in their haste to get to Golding's later works or to his sources, most critics skimp on their analysis of the novel itself. I propose, therefore, to clarify the fable's meaning and then to examine its validity. Along the way I will offer answers to some of the most obvious unanswered questions generated by the fable: What does Simon know about the Beast that the other boys do not? Why do the children divide the work so awkwardly that hunting and firetending fall to one group? Why is the story's unbrutish intellectual named Piggy? Why is Beelzebub's symbol a pig's head? Most readers of ***Lord of the Flies*** will agree that it is a fable about the impossibility of a utopian society, a social fable that deals largely in psychological rather than political, economic, or social ideas. They will also agree that through the fable Golding expands Hobbes to read, "Life in nature or in society is nasty, brutish, and short."

Golding begins by assembling what seem to be the ideal ingredients of Utopia. The island is isolated, fertile, healthy, and comfortable. The humans are young, homogeneous, and remarkably innocent; not a Teddy boy in the lot. Sex is no problem ("Two Paradises 'twere in one / To live in Paradise alone"). But Golding sees no hope for any Earthly Paradise. *Et in Arcadia ego*—and id and libido, Golding adds, but precious little superego. The fierce demands of the mind and the contradictions of human society make peace on the island impossible.

Society's contradictions are acted out in Golding's fable when the children divide themselves up to carry on the daily routine of life. To one group, headed by Ralph, falls the task of building the community. The other group, composed of Jack and his choirboys, takes on the duties of tending the signal fire and providing meat. The implications of these tasks seem clear enough. The moral leaders of society must build and guide; their leadership requires that they shelter their followers and inspire them. Ralph's moral leadership is essentially religious: the purpose of his life is to get home, and *home* acquires in the course of the fable the connotation of Heaven, while the signal fire, their means of salvation, increasingly suggests an altar tended by priests. Here, of course, complications enter.

We might naturally assume that Ralph's group would tend to the fire as well as the hut building, since piety and domesticity go hand in hand. But Golding gives the fire tending job to those who must also do the hunting, in order to make his fable point a moral. Society, he argues, tries to serve both God and Mammon; they cannot both be served. The altar fire therefore goes out, significantly, when the hunters kill their first pig. That is, the strength of present appetites and impulses overcomes the necessarily vague and otherworldly serving of God in hope of salvation. Since killing and meat can pervert even the choirboys, we are expected to conclude that anyone may be lured away from piety. Even Ralph and Piggy crave meat, and in a later hunt Ralph also tastes the stronger meat of the desire to kill.[1] (Simon, though a choirboy, does not turn hunter but inexplicably joins

Ralph's group—which rather weakens the force of Golding's moral, since Simon is the only "typical" choirboy.)

Having made his point about warrior-priests, Golding rearranges his characters into two opposed societies. Ralph, the fair-haired boy, heads a pastoral, peaceful, vegetarian, and religious group intent upon tending the fire and going home. Jack, ugly, red-haired, and knife-wielding, leads a much larger group made up of materialists who live for the moment, for meat, and for the hunt. Ralph rules his group by emphasizing their hopes for salvation; Jack preys upon his followers' fear of the Beast and promises protection and food. As time passes—and human history, the fable implies—the clouds of glory trailed from home fade into the light of common day. The half-remembered morality of home soon can induce a momentary hesitation and no more; the attractiveness of home fades into dreams that soon become nightmares.

For the religious group, the dominant image is the conch shell. Its authority rests on the shaky foundation of the boys' *contrat social:* since that has no force behind it, the conch becomes increasingly less effective and fittingly perishes with Piggy. Moral suasion, lacking punitive force, is impotent, Golding tells us. The other group is differently imperfect. It is held together by "irresponsible authority" (p. 197), by force without moral guidance. The group's dominant image is, appropriately enough, Jack's knife and its offspring, the sharpened sticks used for hunting and torture.[2] By the end of the story, Golding has made it clear that the absolute power suggested by the knife tends to corrupt. Even Jack seems a little unhappy about the excesses to which his reliance on force and fear has led him, and the sadistic Roger is clearly preparing himself to challenge Jack's authority and institute an even nastier regime (pp. 224, 233 ff.). Hunting brutalizes the hunters, Golding tells us, and the Gresham's Law of human existence makes the survivors Hobbesian wolves to men. Historically, Golding implies, this happened long ago (see ***The Inheritors***); we live now at the fag end of the process. There is no possibility of escape.

Golding's descriptions of society are psychological rather than sociological; in other words, the boys create certain social conditions by being certain types of boy. Ralph's health and good looks are apparently the decisive facts for him; typecast as a prefect, he merely plays his part. Piggy's asthma, poor eyesight, obesity, and lack of vitality have forced him to rely upon his mind; Jack's unattractive appearance has generated in him a resentment against winners like Ralph, a resentment that his physical strength and skill allow him to express in the form of intense competitiveness. ("Ralph sighed, sensing the rising antagonism, understanding that this was how Jack felt as soon as he ceased to lead" [p. 146].) Roger's sadism and Simon's mysticism (with a touch of epilepsy, like Dostoevski's Idiot) also appear to be inherent or inadvertently acquired attributes, rather than earned attainments. Although several of the children unmask their true selves on the island, none of the leaders can be said to change his basic character. That, it would seem, is determined not by society but by the innate cast of their minds. Since defects of character are not, in Golding's view, caused by society, we may conclude that social pressure has served to control the bad boys, but that they cannot be cured, no matter what social conditions are imposed upon them. (Ralph's society only antagonizes Jack.) On the other hand, since Ralph's mildness proclaims no devil he will always be basically good, like Simon and Piggy. On the island, if not in the real world left behind, these qualities and defects of character in the leading boys become the qualities and defects of their separate societies.

Golding describes several kinds of goodness. It is spiritual for Simon, common sense for Piggy; for Ralph it seems to be primarily obedience to the dictates of duty. Even after his dreams of home and a better world have faded, duty drives him to insist almost mindlessly on the need for smoke and shelter. These kinds of goodness, especially Ralph's, determine the social characteristics of his culture, Golding believes (pp. 250 ff.). Significantly, that society is a drab one, dominated by the dull and uncongenial toil of shelter building, coconut cup filling, and (later) fire tending. The only form of entertainment offered is the political sociability of the assemblies. If we generalize, as of course we must, from the specific situation of the fable to the real world, we must conclude that the moral and religious life is to Golding a remarkably unattractive one. We see no sign of ritual religion (except in Jack's demonic pig dance), no glorifying of God or his works, no hopefulness. The only message from Heaven is the dead parachutist; and the "strange, attendant creatures, with their fiery eyes and trailing vapours," that accompany Simon's body out to sea are not angels but ocean creatures (p. 190).

Heaven's existence itself is dubious, especially insofar as England stands for Heaven. At one point Simon significantly assures Ralph, "you'll get back all right" to "where you came from" (p. 137). Does he mean Heaven or England? Golding's references to the world outside the island are contradictory, but it seems clear that the English are at war with "the reds" (p. 200) and that the war is world-wide. The calm, self-assured *miles ex machina* at the end of the story certainly implies that England is winning. On the other hand, the airport from which the boys took off has been destroyed by an atom bomb (p. 20), and Golding explicitly tells us that the boys' "civilization was in ruins" (p. 78). The earthly equivalent of Heaven is evidently in a bad way, and we must think of the rescuing naval officer as no more than a grown-up Jack. Ralph's secular and religious salvation is surely dubious—although literary convention assures us that portentous utterances by such as Simon are always true. (See Salinger's story "Teddy" for a more eloquent example of the species.)

In contrast to Ralph's dully dutiful society and its dubious promises, Jack's world offers the immediate pleasures of feasting and hunting. Curiously, however, most of the boys seem to find little joy in the feasting—although they "dribble" at the mouth as predictably as Pavlov's dogs—and even less joy in the hunting. Only Jack and Roger take much pleasure in the chase; the other boys are generally scared. Many boys do no hunting; they join Jack's group only for food and for protection against the Beast. The reader may well sympathize with their choice. Since the hope of home, happiness, and Heaven is apparently a deluded one, man might as well make the best of a bad bargain. Jack's objection to Ralph—"He just gives orders and expects people to obey for nothing" (p. 157)—seems unanswerable.

What lesson are we to learn from Golding's two opposed societies, Ralph's and Jack's? Golding is quoted as saying that "the theme is an attempt to trace the defects of society back to the defects of human nature. The moral is that the shape of a society must depend on the ethical nature of the individual and not on any political system however apparently logical or respectable" (pp. 250 ff.). *Must* here apparently means *does,* not *ought to,* since the novel does not seem to offer any prescription for social, political, or moral reform. Society's basis is "the ethical nature of the individual," then; but society is composed of many individuals, whose average ethical nature, Golding demonstrates in ***Lord of the Flies,*** is evilly inclined, morally sick. It is true that Simon's vision of the Beast is "the picture of a human at once heroic and sick" (p. 128). In the novel, however, humans are generally one or the other. Ralph might possibly be both heroic and sick, but his illness—his pleasure in hunting (pp. 140 ff.) and his participation in the killing of Simon—is relatively mild.

Humans as Golding characterizes them have a strong eighteenth-century flavor. Each person takes his character from a ruling passion that expresses itself in physical as well as psychological traits. Ralph must be handsome, Jack ugly. Like Henry Fielding, Golding separates mankind into sheep and goats in deterministic fashion. The majority of men are goats, whose defective ethical natures inevitably misshape society.

In ***Lord of the Flies*** two characters stand outside this irremediably defective society and comment on it. Piggy's comments, as well as the comment made by his death, seem clear enough to most readers; Simon's role is less well understood. Of the two boys, Simon is the more perceptive. Golding has stated that Simon represents the Apostle Peter—a representation that surely escapes the average reader, but that indicates Simon's importance to Golding as a purveyor of religious truth. Simon's interview with the Lord of the Flies, especially, allows Golding—at the expense of substantial improbability—to ram his lesson home: it's no go because evil is internal and ineradicable.

Golding has apparently given a great deal of thought to the specific nature of this evil, but his presentation of it has not been widely understood. There is considerable emphasis in the novel on killing, eating, and defecating. Simon, for example, trying to express man's sickness, asks the boys what the dirtiest thing is; the answer they give is excrement. This emphasis leads many readers to the obvious conclusion that Golding, like Hamlet, thinks of man as a combination of angel and animal and sees in his animal nature the source of his corruption. Such an interpretation is logical under the circumstances and seems to be given force by the novel's dominant images of evil—the Beast, the Lord of the Flies, and the pig's head. Here the obvious sensual and unpleasant connotations of *beast, pig, hog,* and *flies* seem to reinforce the philosophical idea of nasty animality.

A substantial barrier to this interpretation is raised by the character Piggy, however. His name obviously forces us to connect him with the pigs, a connection reinforced especially at the time of his death. The pigs having been called "bloated bags of fat" (p. 166), Golding describes Piggy as "a bag of fat" (p. 221) and says that when he died "Piggy's arms and legs twitched a bit, like a pig's after it has been killed" (p. 223). This enforced correspondence between the story's intellectual and its animals may seem pointless. Piggy is obviously not animalistic; his hair doesn't even grow (p. 81). But Golding forces us to revise our conventional attitude toward pigs—whose hair, of course, doesn't grow beyond a certain length either. Like Piggy, Golding's pigs are harmless and lazy. Both provide necessities of life; the pigs provide meat as Piggy provides fire, unwillingly. Both pigs and Piggy fall victim to the hunters' bloodlust. (Pigs are also quite intelligent animals.)

We must conclude that the pigs, like Piggy and Simon, are characterized chiefly as innocent victims, inhabitants of an Eden in which the boys are snakes (the Beast is first thought of as a snake). Evil in this world, says Golding, is not sensual or animal. The Lord of the Flies is not a pig, not an animal; as Simon points out, it is a "pig's head on a stick" (p. 177), the emblem of man's sadistic cruelty to natural things and of his ignorant attempts to placate a falsely externalized evil. The flies preying on the head and on Simon are the boys, worshipers of a revolting demon and devourers of innocence.[3]

That Simon understands the symbol in this way is demonstrated when he finds the dead parachutist and untangles his shrouds. Golding emphasizes "the poor body," "the poor broken thing"; and Simon realizes that "the beast was harmless and horrible" (p. 181). The beast in man, what unites him with the other animals, is not evil. (Simon never objects to meat eating.) Evil is specifically human, says Golding, and it inhabits the mind, not the body. He gives no sign of thinking that this tendency toward evil is fostered by life in society, despite his views on society, nor does he suggest that it is accepted deliberately by man's free will. On the contrary, the Lord of the Flies deterministically assures Simon that "I'm part of you" (p. 177). Not part of Simon himself, surely, nor of Piggy, but part of most people. Fielding reached much the same deterministic conclusion two hundred years earlier when he said that "there is in some minds a sensation directly opposite to that of benevolence, and which delights and feeds itself with acts of cruelty and inhumanity" ("A Clear State of the Case of Elizabeth Canning"). Against this innate delight in savagery, shown especially by Jack and Roger but shared in the dances by everyone except Piggy and Simon, all of man's ideals, principles, and distant goals are useless. At one point Ralph, dismayed at the growing anarchy on the island, insists that "the rules are the only thing we've got!" (p. 114). But the exclamation is made to seem as futile as Piggy's later insistence that "what's right's right" (p. 211). Jack has all the weight of force behind him when he answers, "Bollocks to the rules! . . . We're strong—we hunt!" (p. 114).

In a world where evil is so pervasive, the only way to be good is to be born good; but Golding suggests that early social training is of some value in restraining the vile impulses of those born bad. The inhibitions imposed upon innate savagery by civilization stop Jack from killing the piglet (p. 40) and make even Roger aim his stones to miss the littlun (p. 78). These inhibitions fade quickly, to be sure, but they are more effective than any means of coercion shown by Golding except physical fear. (Though society also used fear, probably, to develop the inhibitions.)

Fear controls most of man's actions in ***Lord of the Flies.*** As a deterrent from action, it is seen especially at the end of the story, when Jack's police state controls its citizens with threats of hunger, torture, and the Beast. Fear as an activating force is the basis for violence and cruelty. We see it in action especially during the storm, when the boys begin their dance out of terror and then turn savage because of the fear: "out of the terror," Golding says, "rose another desire, thick, urgent, and uncontrollable" (p. 188). All men would be cowards if they durst, Golding implies, but because fear is shameful, men transmute it into a compound of murderousness and sexual lust—the latter shown most explicitly in the killing of the sow (p. 168). Perhaps with maturity the boys will find lust as basic an impulse as fear, and will become that much more dangerous.

Fear as a motivating force is everywhere, but we look in vain for love. Even saintly Simon displays no more than disinterested charity. Piggy's attachment to Ralph is compounded of hero-worship and fear of Jack, while Ralph's lament at the story's end for the "true, wise friend called Piggy" is sentimental rather than factual; we are shown no sign of friendship between them. No one much likes anyone, in short. No friendships spring up on the island (although Golding apparently believes in the Ralph-Piggy friendship); no one laments his absence from parents or sisters or brothers; no one's memories of home include memories of friends.

We may conclude that Golding's view of our present civilization, conveyed primarily through his description of Jack's society, is a gloomy one. Men have banded together out of fear of the Beast, but necessarily have brought the Beast along with them. The resultant civilization offers a specious but reassuring protection against the Beast by inaccurately identifying it and setting up defenses like the pig's head on a stick. Such a civilization is aptly described by Golding as a "demented but partly secure society" (p. 187). Since the Beast is really within us, civilization cannot be purged of its discontents.

Furthermore, the battle between good and evil is an unequal one. On the island, existence is to good malignant, to bad men benign, and no day of reparation for the just is at hand. In a curious scene Henry (the littlun) bullies minute ocean creatures, Roger throws stones at Henry, and a palm tree drops coconuts on Roger (pp. 77 ff.). This chain of hostilities is probably a joke; we are not to conclude that nature is antagonistic to evil. Nature—human nature, especially—seems to favor the wicked. Jack and Roger are more than equal to their evil tasks, but Ralph is not good at goodness. He learns painfully to think in public as if playing chess, Golding tells us, but "the trouble was that he would never be a very good chess player" (p. 145). The good boys are all inadequate. Simon cannot communicate his ideas, and his insights into mankind's essential illness bring him only martyrdom. Piggy is perceptive but poorly educated and not much better at persuasive communication than Simon. He suffers also from another disadvantage; he is socially different. He is apparently the only lower-class boy on the island; he is physically unpleasant, incompetent, lazy, and cowardly; and his grammar is worse than the littluns'. In short, Golding sees to it that we are presented with a more than Manichean heresy and a world partial to the devil's party. In this world's idyllic youth, people may have lived simply and thought primarily of salvation, guided by philosopher kings, but now we are driven by fear and ruled by savage tyrants, our only desire the appeasing of our passions. The few good men, like Auden's Just, are no more than ironic points of light in an overwhelming darkness. Such, at least, is the message of ***Lord of the Flies.***

The ordinary work of fiction can be defensibly judged only by its own laws; if a novel's world is consistent with itself, its divergence from a reader's own understanding of reality is irrelevant. But fables are different. They claim to describe our objective world, not their own. Such works can and must be judged by the accuracy with which they reflect our world and the perceptivity with which they interpret it. So judged, ***Lord of the Flies*** is open to several objections.

Perhaps the basic objection is that its subject is irrelevant. It claims to demonstrate that man cannot begin anew and create Utopia. But the human race cannot start from scratch; whatever we do, think, say, and assume is deeply conditioned by our past, rooted even in the structure of our languages. Nor could we isolate one generation. So when Golding tells us what happens when a generation is isolated, we may be academically interested, but we cannot—or should not—see in the children's situation any image of our own. They come to a bad end, and we may come to a bad end; but there is more coincidence here than prediction. Mankind has always been partial to the opinion that things aren't what they used to be, and in a time of crisis the opinion seems especially valid. But we cannot agree with every expression of this opinion simply because it flatters our own predilection.

In its description of human existence, the fable's lesser assumptions also seem open to criticism. Golding tells us that benevolent, paternal societies are overcome by warlike hunting tribes. Our historians find more warrior kings in the past, more paternal rulers in the present. Golding tells us that individual goodness cannot survive the attack of evil; we can only point out that it has done so for thousands of years. Golding tells us that man savagely craves meat and becomes evil in killing for it; we eat meat mildly, ourselves, and find that butchers are not ordinarily dangers to society. Golding tells us that the Lord of the Flies is inside us; agreeing, we add that the means of restraining him are also there. Golding says that the most angelic men (the choirboys) are most prone to become hunters and soldiers. What we know about hunters and soldiers does not confirm this assertion.

In addition, we may argue that Golding tries to eat his cake and have it too. He shows us Jack's society as an image of ours, yet he criticizes and condemns it by our standards. He tells us that civilization reflects man's dominant qualities and that those qualities are evil; yet in the novel the influence of society is almost always a good one. Thanks to society the boys find bullying a cause for shame and killing so distasteful that they must drive themselves to it. They have acquired rudimentary moral codes and have learned to control their impulses—within limits, of course, but after all they are only boys. And that fact is also awakward.

Golding's choice of children, rather than adults, for his utopian experiment suggests that he considers them better and more likely to succeed in establishing an ideal society. (Or perhaps he only thinks that *we* believe this.) Yet time and again he shows that he really thinks children worse than adults. The littluns are useless, but even the older boys cannot cope with abstractions like duty and salvation, nor can they organize a society whose morality is both acceptable (i. e., Ralph's, not Jack's) and supported by force. More practically, the boys never think to plant gardens or make tools and utensils; they never try to educate the littluns; and, confusing shopping trips with warfare, they hunt pigs with spears when nets, traps, and pigsties would be more sensible and less passionate. In short, the reader repeatedly sees the children going wrong where he himself would not. Necessarily, then, he must conclude that this utopian experiment failed because of childish weaknesses and ignorance, not because of man's essential illness.

When he has concluded this, the reader has reversed what seems to be part of Golding's moral: the fable has become willy-nilly a defense of society rather than an attack on it. So potent a force is society, the reader finds, that even hunters like the naval officer can be kind, sadists can be kept from bullying children, and a hunter's son (Ralph's father is a naval officer) can become a moral leader. When we perceive the value of society, we must decide that Golding's images of society are erroneous. Our society, though bad, is not as corrupt as Jack's; our society's morality is not as impotent as that of Ralph's society. Even a skeptic must admit that society restrains barbarity more often than it licenses it.

But perhaps a milder criticism would conclude more fittingly. English newspapers tell us that juvenile delinquency has almost disappeared in Liverpool, the Beatles' home city, because the hoodlums are all busy playing musical instruments and singing in imitation of their heroes. Is it credible, realistically or fabulously, that the choirboys on the island never sing? Not even the *Dies irae?*

Notes

1. William Golding, *Lord of the Flies* (New York, 1959), pp. 140 ff.
2. There seems to be only one knife, Jack's, on the island, but the matter is not clear. Notice this curious passage: "'I cut the pig's throat,' said Jack. . . . 'Can I borrow yours, Ralph, to make a nick in the hilt?'" (p. 87). "Yours" has no antecedent, but surely refers to a knife. Later, after the spectacular killing of the sow, this dialogue takes place (p. 169):

   > [Jack] knelt down and was busy with his knife. . . . He spoke over his shoulder to Roger.
   >
   > "Sharpen a stick at both ends."
   >
   > Presently [Jack] stood up, holding the dripping sow's head in his hands.
   >
   > "Where's that stick?"
   >
   > "Here."

   What did Roger sharpen the stick with?
3. The flies surely suggest this on page 171, when they cover Simon, but eight pages later Golding has changed his mind and tells us that "even when the vessel broke in Simon's nose and the blood gushed out they left him alone, preferring the pig's high flavour." The contradiction is one of several signs of haste in the writing. We have already noted the ghost knives. A similar confusion is generated by the characters. On page 75 Henry is a littlun; on page 169 he's a bigun. On page 169 Bill is one of five hunters selected by Jack to steal Piggy's glasses. On page 175 Robert has replaced Bill; on page 176 Bill is a member of *Ralph's* group and explicitly not a hunter. The disparity between the ruin of civilization on page 78 and the calm officer of the ending is probably another example of muddle rather than a symbolic matter. The O. Henry ending was irresistible, or at least unresisted.

Samuel Hynes (essay date 1968)

SOURCE: Hynes, Samuel. "William Golding's *Lord of the Flies.*" In *Critical Essays on William Golding,* edited by James R. Baker, pp. 13-21. Boston: G. K. Hall and Co., 1988.

[*In the following essay, originally published in 1968, Hynes discusses* Lord of the Flies *in light of Golding's influence on post-war literature.*]

> I am very serious. I believe that man suffers from an appalling ignorance of his own nature. I produce my own view, in the belief that it may be something like the truth. I am fully engaged to the human dilemma but see it as far more fundamental than a complex of taxes and astronomy.

William Golding wrote these words in reply to a literary magazine's questionnaire, "The Writer in His Age." The questionnaire raised the question of "engagement": should the writer concern himself with the political and social questions of his time? Golding's answer is unequivocal: the job of the writer is to show man his image *sub specie aeternitatis.* It is in this sense of engagement, not to the concerns of the moment but to what is basic in the human condition, and in the forms that this engagement has led Golding to create, that his uniqueness lies: he is *the* novelist of our time for whom the novel matters because of what it can mean, and what it can do.

In the note from which I quoted above, Golding described himself as "a citizen, a novelist and a schoolmaster." The latter term is no longer literally applicable, but there is still a good deal of both the citizen and the schoolmaster in the novelist. The citizen is concerned with "the defects of society"; the schoolmaster is concerned to correct them by proper instruction; the novelist finds the appropriate forms in which man's own nature may be embodied, that he may learn to know it. One consequence of this will-to-instruct is that Golding is an unusually disciplined, schematic writer; he thinks his novels out very slowly, and in careful detail (he wrote ***Lord of the Flies,*** he said, "as if tracing over words already on the page"), and he is willing, even eager, to discuss what they mean. Another consequence is his desire to have his works read with the same kind of conscious intelligence, and his distrust of irrational and intuitive views of literary creation. He clearly thinks of his novels as the expressions of conscious intentions that existed before the writing began. Indeed he has twice spelled out what those intentions were. This does not, of course, imply that they took the form of abstract moral propositions which were then clothed in plot; but it does suggest that for Golding the entire plan of the work, *and* the meaning of that plan, were worked out first—that he started with meaning rather than with character or situation. Golding's own glosses of the meanings of ***Lord of the Flies*** and ***Pincher Martin*** have not seemed satisfactory to most readers—the teller in fact supports Lawrence's view of the creative process, and not Golding's; nevertheless, the fact that Golding thinks of his books as he does tells us something useful about the forms that they have taken.

There is no adequate critical term for that form. Golding himself has called his books both *myths* and *fables,* and both terms do point to a quality in the novels that it is necessary to recognize—that they are unusually tight, conceptualized, analogical expressions of moral ideas. Still, neither term is quite satisfactory, because both imply a degree of abstraction and an element of the legendary that Golding's novels simply do not have, and it seems better to be content with calling them simply *novels,* while recognizing that they have certain formal properties that distinguish them from most current fiction.

The most striking of these properties is that Golding so patterns his narrative actions as to make them the images of ideas, the imaginative forms of generalizations; the form itself, that is to say, carries meaning apart from the meanings implied by character or those stated more or less didactically by the author. "In all my books," Golding has said, "I have suggested a shape in the universe that may, as it were, account for things." To direct the attentions of his readers to that shape, Golding has chosen situations that isolate what is basic, and avoid both the merely topical and the subjective existence of the author. All but two of his novels employ a situation that is remote in time or space, characters who are radically unlike the author, and a narrative tone that is removed, analytical, and judicial. Consequently we must look for human relevance to the patterned action itself; if we "identify," it must be with the moral—with the conception of man and the shape of the universe—and not with this character or that one.

The forms that Golding uses carry implications both for the kind of action selected and for the kind of characters involved in it. Since Golding proposes to embody general truths in his novels, he is committed, one would think, to select those human experiences that can be viewed as *exemplary,* not merely as *typical;* it is not enough to propose that a fictional event might happen. To be justifiable in a Golding novel an event must also bear its shape of the patterned meaning. Consequently the novels tend on the whole to be short and densely textured, and the characters, while they are usually convincingly three-dimensional human beings, may also function as exemplars of facets of man's nature—of common sense, or greed, or will (one of Golding's most impressive gifts is his ability to make characters exemplify abstractions without *becoming* abstractions).

What we acknowledge if we choose to call Golding a fabulist is not that the total story is reducible to a moral proposition—this is obviously not true—but rather that he writes from clear and strong moral assumptions, and that those assumptions give form and direction to his fictions. But if Aesop and La Fontaine wrote fables, we need another term for Golding. We might borrow one from scholastic aesthetics, and call them *tropological,* meaning by this that the novels individually "suggest a shape in the universe," and are constructed as models of such moral shapes. Or if tropological seems too rarefied, *moral models* will do. The point, in any case, is to suggest the patterned quality of Golding's work, and to recognize the assumptions which that quality implies. Golding accepts certain traditional ideas about man and his place in the world: that mind, by meditation and speculation, may arrive at truth; that it may find in the past, meanings which are relevant to the present, and available through memory; that it may appropriately concern itself with metaphysics and with morals. Not all of these ideas are current now, certainly not in the avant-garde, and consequently Golding's work may seem, in the context of his time, more didactic and moralizing than in fact it is. For though Golding is a moralist, he is not a moral-maker, and his novels belong, not with Aesop's fables, but with the important symbolic novels of our century—with Camus's and Kafka's.

Golding has founded ***Lord of the Flies*** on a number of more or less current conventions. First of all, he has used the science-fiction convention of setting his action in the future, thus substituting the eventually probable for the immediately actual, and protecting his fable from literalistic judgments of details or of credibility. A planeload of boys has been evacuated from an England engaged in some future war fought against "the reds"; after their departure an atomic bomb has fallen on England, and civilization is in ruins. The plane flies south and east, stopping at Gibraltar and Addis Ababa; still farther east—over the Indian Ocean, or perhaps the Pacific, the plane is attacked by an enemy aircraft, the "passenger tube" containing the boys is jettisoned, and the rest of the plane crashes in flames. The boys land unharmed on a desert island.

At this point, a second literary convention enters. The desert island tale shares certain literary qualities with science fiction. Both offer a "what-would-happen-if" situation, in which real experience is simplified in order that certain values and problems may be regarded in isolation. Both tend to simplify human moral issues by externalizing good and evil; both offer occasions for Utopian fantasies. Golding's most immediate source is R. M. Ballantyne's *Coral Island,* a Victorian boys' book of South Sea adventure, but Ballantyne didn't invent the island dream; that dream began when man first felt the pressures of his civilization enough to think that a life without civilization might be a life without problems.

The relation of Golding's novel to Ballantyne's is nevertheless important enough to pause over. In *Coral Island,* three English boys called Ralph, Jack, and Peterkin are shipwrecked on a tropical island, meet pirates and cannibals, and conquer all adversities with English fortitude and Christian virtue. We may say that *Coral Island* is a clumsy moral tale, in which good is defined as being English and Christian and jolly, and especially an English Christian *boy,* and in which evil is unchristian, savage, and adult. The three boys are rational, self-reliant, inventive, and virtuous—in short, they are like no boys that anyone has ever known.

Golding regards *Coral Island* morality as unrealistic, and therefore not truly moral, and he has used it ironically in his own novel, as a foil for his own version of man's moral nature. In an interview Golding described his use of Ballantyne's book in this way:

> What I'm saying to myself is "don't be such a fool, you remember when you were a boy, a small boy, how you lived on that island with Ralph and Jack and Peterkin.". . . . I said to myself finally, "Now you are grown up, you are adult; it's taken you a long time to become adult, but now you've got there you can see that people are not like that; they would not behave like that if they were God-fearing English gentlemen, and they went to an island like that." There savagery would not be found in natives on an island. As like as not they would find savages who were kindly and uncomplicated and that the devil would rise out of the intellectual complications of the three white men on the island itself.

One might say that ***Lord of the Flies*** is a refutation of *Coral Island,* and that Golding sets about to show us that the devil rises, not out of pirates and cannibals and such alien creatures, but out of the darkness of man's heart. The *Coral Island* attitude exists in the novel—Jack sounds very like Ballantyne's Jack when he says: "After all, we're not savages. We're English; and the English are best at everything." And the naval commander who rescues the boys at the end of the book speaks in the same vein: "I should have thought that a pack of British boys—you're all British aren't you?—would have been able to put up a better show than that—I mean—" But Jack and the commander are wrong; the pack of British boys are in fact cruel and murderous savages who reduce the island to a burning wreckage and destroy the dream of innocence.

The fable of the novel is a fairly simple one. The boys first set out to create a rational society modeled on what "grown-ups" would do. They establish a government and laws, they provide for food and shelter, and they light a signal fire. But this rational society begins to break down almost at once, under two instinctual pressures—fear and blood lust. The dark unknown that surrounds the children gradually assumes a monstrous identity, and becomes "the beast," to be feared and propitiated; and hunting for food becomes killing. The hunters break away from the society, and create their own primitive, savage, orgiastic tribal society. They kill two of the three rational boys, and are hunting down the third when the adult world intervenes.

This fable, as sketched, is susceptible of several interpretations, and Golding's critics have found it coherent on a number of levels, according to their own preoccupations. Freudians have found in the novel a conscious dramatization of psychological theory: "denied the sustaining and repressing authority of parents, church and state, [the children] form a new culture the development of which reflects that of genuine primitive society, evolving its gods and demons (its myths), its rituals and taboos (its social norms)." The political-minded have been able to read it as "the modern political nightmare," in which rational democracy is destroyed by irrational authoritarianism ("I hope," said V. S. Pritchett, "this book is being read in Germany"). The social-minded have found in it a social allegory, in which life, without civilized restraints, becomes nasty, brutish, and short. And the religious have simply said, in a complacent tone, "Original Sin, of course."

It is, of course, entirely possible that Golding has managed to construct a fable that does express all these ideas of evil, and that what we are dealing with is not alternative interpretations, but simply levels of meaning. The idea of Original Sin, for example, does have political, social, and psychological implications; if it is true that man is inherently prone to evil, then certain conclusions about the structure of his relations to other men would seem to follow. The idea of Original Sin seems, indeed, to be one of the "great commonplaces," one of those ideas which are so central to man's conception of himself that they turn up, in one form or another, in almost any systematic account of human nature. It describes one of perhaps two possible accounts of the nature of human behavior (*Coral Island* assumes the other one).

Since the novel is symbolic, the best approach would seem to be to examine first the "meaning" of each of the major characters, and then to proceed to consider the significance of their interactions. Ralph—in *Coral Island* the first-person narrator—here provides the most consistent point of view, because he most nearly speaks for us, rational, fallible humankind; Ralph is the man who accepts responsibility that he is not particularly fitted for because he sees that the alternative to responsibility is savagery and moral chaos. He tries to establish and preserve an orderly, rational society; he takes as his totem the conch, making it the symbol of rational, orderly discussion.

Ralph's antagonist is Jack, who represents "the brilliant world of hunting, tactics, fierce exhilaration, skill," as Ralph represents "the world of longing and baffled common-sense." Between them there is an "indefinable connection"; like Cain and Abel, they are antithetical, but intimately linked together—man-the-destroyer confronting man-the-preserver. Jack is the hunter, the boy who becomes a beast of prey (and who uses *kill* as an intransitive verb, an act which is for him an end in itself). He is also the dictator, the authoritarian man-of-power who enters the scene like a drill sergeant, who despises assemblies and the conch, and who becomes in the end an absolute ruler of his tribe. He devises the painted mask of the hunter, behind which a boy may hide, "liberated from shame and self-consciousness," and by painting the boys he turns them into an anonymous mob of murderous savages, "a demented but partly secure society." Jack is the first of the bigger boys to accept "the beast" as possible, and the one who offers the propitiatory sacrifice to it; he is the High Priest of Beelzebub, the Lord of the Flies.

Associated with each of these antagonists is a follower who represents in a more nearly allegorical form the principal value of his leader. Piggy, Ralph's "true, wise friend," is a scientific-minded rationalist, who models his behavior on what he thinks grownups would do, and scorns the other children for "acting like a crowd of kids." He can think better than Ralph, and in a society in which thought was enough he would be supremely valuable; but on the island he is ineffectual; he is incapable of action, and is a physical coward. His totem is his spectacles, and with them he is the fire-bringer; but when Jack first breaks one lens and then steals the other, Piggy becomes blind and helpless, a bag of fat. His trust in the power and wisdom of grownups is itself a sign of his inadequacy; for if the novel makes one point clearly, it is that adults have no special wisdom, and are engaged in a larger scale, but equally destructive, version of the savage game that the hunters play. (When Ralph wishes that the outer world might "send us something grown-up . . . a sign or something," the adult world obliges with the dead parachutist, an image of terror that destroys Ralph's rational society.)

Beside or slightly behind Jack stands Roger, around whom clings "the hangman's horror." Roger's lust is the lust for power over living things, the power to destroy life. In the beginning he is restrained by "the taboo of the old life . . . the protection of parents and school and policemen and the law." Jack and the paint of savagery liberate Roger from these taboos, and "with a sense of delirious abandonment" he rolls the rock down the cliff, killing Piggy, his opposite.

One character, the most difficult to treat, remains. Simon, the shy visionary, perceptive but inarticulate, occupies a central position in the symbolic scheme of the book. It is Simon who first stammers that perhaps the beast is "only us," who sees the beast in terms of "mankind's essential illness," and who goes alone to confront *both* beasts, the grinning pig's head and the rotting airman, because, as he says, "What else is there to do?" Golding has described Simon as a saint, "someone who voluntarily embraces this beast, goes . . . and tries to get rid of him and goes to give the good news to the ordinary bestial man on the beach, and gets killed for it." He would appear to be, then, at least in Golding's intentions, the embodiment of moral understanding. If this is so, those symbolic scenes in which he appears will be crucial to an understanding of the novel.

I have said that one distinction between Golding's novels and allegory is that the novels are meaning-in-action, general truth given narrative or dramatic form by the creative imagination. In considering the meaning of ***Lord of the Flies,*** one cannot therefore stop at an examination of character—meaning must emerge from character-in-action. In the narrative action certain scenes stand out as crucial, and most of these announce their importance by being overtly symbolic. There is, for example, a series of scenes in which Jack's hunters evolve a ritual dance. On the first occasion, in Chapter 4, a child *pretends* to be the pig, and the hunters *pretend* to beat him. A chapter later the dance has become crueler, "and littluns that had had enough were staggering away, howling." After the next hunt Robert, acting the pig in the dance, squeals with real pain, and the hunters cry "Kill him! Kill him!" After the dance the boys discuss ways of improving the ritual: "'You want a real pig,' said Robert, still caressing his rump, 'because you've got to kill him.'

"'Use a littlun,' said Jack, and everybody laughed." In the final ritual dance, the sacrificial function is acknowledged; the boys' chant is no longer "Kill the pig," but "Kill the *beast!*" and when Simon crawls from the forest, the boys fulfill their ritual sacrifice, and by killing a human being, make themselves beasts ("there were no words, and no movements but the tearing of teeth and claws"). Ironically, they have killed the one person who could have saved them from bestiality, for Simon has seen the figure on the mountaintop, and knows that the beast is "harmless and horrible."

Simon's lonely, voluntary quest for the beast is certainly the symbolic core of the book. The meaning of the book depends on the meaning of the beast, and it is that meaning that Simon sets out to determine. His first act is to withdraw to a place of contemplation, a sunlit space in the midst of the forest. It is to the same place that Jack and his hunters bring the pig's head, and leave it impaled on a stick as a sacrifice to the beast they fear. When they have gone, Simon holds hallucinatory conversation with the Lord of the Flies, Beelzebub, the Lord of Filth and Dung. The head, "with the infinite cynicism of adult life," assures Simon that "everything was a bad business," and advises him to run away, back to the other children, and to abandon his quest. "I'm part of you," it tells him (in words that echo Simon's own "maybe it's only us"), "I'm the reason why it's no go." Simon, apparently epileptic, falls in a fit. But when he wakes, he turns upward, toward the top of the mountain, where the truth lies. He finds the airman, rotting and fly-blown, and tenderly frees the figure from the wind's indignity. Then he sets off, weak and staggering, to tell the other boys that the beast is human, and is murdered by them.

How are we to interpret this sequence? We may say, first of all, that the beast symbolizes the source of evil in human life. Either it is something terrifying and external, which cannot be understood but must simply be lived with (this is Jack's version), or it is a part of man's nature, "only us," in which case it may be understood, and perhaps controlled by reason and rule. Simon understands that man must seek out the meaning of evil ("what else is there to do?"). By seeking, he comes to know it, "harmless and horrible." Thus far the moral point seems orthodox enough. But when he tries to tell his understanding to others, they take *him* for the beast, and destroy him in terror. Another common idea, though a more somber one—men fear the bearers of truth, and will destroy them. This has both political and psychological implications. A "demented but partly secure society" (read: Nazi Germany, or any authoritarian nation) will resist and attempt to destroy anyone who offers to substitute reason and responsible individual action for the irresponsible, unreasoning, *secure* action of the mass. And in psychological terms, the members of a "demented society" may create an irrational, external evil, and in its name commit deeds that as rational men they could not tolerate (the history of modern persecutions offers examples enough); such a society *has* to destroy the man who says, "The evil is in yourselves."

At this point, I should like to return to the argument that this novel is a symbolic form but not an allegory. One aspect of this distinction is that Golding has written a book that has a dense and often poetic verbal texture, in which metaphor and image work as they do in poetry, and enrich and modify the bare significances of the moral form. Golding's treatment of Simon's death is a particularly good case in point. At this instant, a storm breaks, the wind fills the parachute on the mountain, and the figure, freed by Simon, floats and falls toward the beach, scattering the boys in terror before passing out to sea. The storm ends, stars appear, the tide rises. Stars above and phosphorescent sea below fill the scene with brightness and quiet.

> Along the shoreward edge of the shallows the advancing clearness was full of strange, moonbeam-bodied creatures with fiery eyes. Here and there a larger pebble clung to its own air and was covered with a coat of pearls. The tide swelled in over the rain-pitted sand and smoothed everything with a layer of silver. Now it touched the first of the stains that seeped from the broken body and the creatures made a moving patch of light as they gathered at the edge. The water rose farther and dressed Simon's coarse hair with brightness. The line of his cheek silvered and the turn of his shoulder became sculptured marble. The strange attendant creatures, with their fiery eyes and trailing vapors, busied themselves round his head. The body lifted a fraction of an inch from the sand and a bubble of air escaped from the mouth with a wet plop. Then it turned gently in the water.
>
> Somewhere over the darkened curve of the world the sun and moon were pulling, and the film of water on the earth planet was held, bulging slightly on one side while the solid core turned. The great wave of the tide moved farther along the island and the water lifted. Softly, surrounded by a fringe of inquisitive bright creatures, itself a silver shape beneath the steadfast constellations, Simon's dead body moved out toward the open sea.

This is Golding's rhetoric at its richest, but it works. The imagery of light and value—*moonbeam, pearls, silver, brightness, marble*—effect a transfiguration, by which the dead child is made worthy, his death an elevation. In terms of allegory, this sort of metaphorical weighting would perhaps be imprecise and deceptive; in terms of a symbolic novel, it seems to me a legitimate application of a skillful writer's art.

In discussing the actions of ***Lord of the Flies*** I have again and again slipped from talking about boys to describing the characters as men, or simply as human beings. It is true that as the action rises to its crises—to the *agon* of Chapter 5, Simon's confrontation with the beast, the murders, the final hunt—we cease to respond to the story as a story about children, and see them simply as *people,* engaged in desperate, destructive actions. Consequently, Golding can achieve a highly dramatic effect at the end of the book by bringing our eyes down, with Ralph's, to a beach-level view of an adult, and then swinging round, to show us Ralph from the adult's point of view. The result is an irony that makes two points. First, we see with sudden clarity that these murderous savages were civilized children; the point is not, I take it, that children are more horrid than we thought (though they are), but rather that the human propensity for evil knows no limits, not even limits of age, and that there is no Age of Innocence (Ralph weeps for the end of innocence, but when did it exist, except as an illusion made of his own ignorance?). Second, there is the adult, large, efficient, confident—the "grown-up" that the children have wished for all along. But his words show at once that he is a large, stupid *Coral Island* mentality in a peaked cap, entirely blind to the moral realities of the situation. He may save Ralph's life, but he will not understand. And once he has gathered up the castaways, he will return to his ship, and the grown-up business of hunting men (just as the boys have been hunting Ralph). "And who," asks Golding, "will rescue the adult and his cruiser?"

To return briefly to the question of levels of interpretation: it seems clear that ***Lord of the Flies*** should be read as a moral novel embodying a conception of human depravity which is compatible with, but not limited to, thc Christian doctrine of Original Sin. To call the novel religious is to suggest that its values are more developed, and more affirmative, than in fact they are; Golding makes no reference to Grace, or to Divinity, but only to the darkness of men's hearts, and to the God of Dung and Filth who rules there. Simon is perhaps a saint, and sainthood is a valuable human condition, but there is no sign in the novel that Simon's sainthood has touched any soul but his own. The novel tells us a good deal about evil; but about salvation it is silent.

Jerome Martin (essay date March 1969)

SOURCE: Martin, Jerome. "Symbol Hunting Golding's *Lord of the Flies.*" *English Journal* 58, no. 3 (March 1969): 408-13.

[*In the following essay, Martin examines the symbolic content of* Lord of the Flies.]

Here's a wild exercise for the readers of William Golding's ***Lord of the Flies.*** No high school novel tempts students to read *into* a work instead of *out from* as does this. So, if you want to cure your symbol hunters, once and for all, involve them in the following exercise.

Duplicate for your students the following list of names, events, and items mentioned in the novel. Leave sufficient space next to each for the meaning of each symbol. Names: Ralph, Piggy, Johnny, Sam 'n Eric or Samneric, Jack, The Choir (Maurice, Simon, Roger, Robert, Henry, Harold, etc.), Percival Wemys Madison, Mulberry-color-birthmark boy, The Officer, Littluns. Events: Taking names, Standing on his head, Betraying Ralph, Blowing into the conch, Hunting pigs, Being saved. Items: Piggy's glasses, Black cloaks, Candle bushes, Knife, Original Sin, The conch, The Island, The Creepers, Spears and logs, Pigs, Fire, Castle Rock, The dead flyer, The Lord of the flies, Butterflies, Smoke, The Sea.

To establish an atmosphere of authenticity for what you will be saying later, announce to your students that William Golding is known to use the stylistic device of having the action of the surface story take place in a short span of time or in suspended time. (This is valid, for in ***Pincher Martin*** the flashbacks of Christopher Martin's experiences take place within seconds or less before his death. Also, in ***Free Fall,*** Samuel Mountjoy reflects on and establishes his reoriented world in a closet, again through flashbacks.)

Next, direct the attention of the class to what Golding says is the theme of the novel: "The theme is an attempt to trace the defects of society back to the defects of human nature." If Golding is describing human nature, it is natural to ask, "When is human nature best studied?" The answer is, "Under a crisis or a trauma." Ralph is the main character, so he must be experiencing the crisis or trauma. We read that Ralph is "old enough, twelve years and a few months, to have lost the prominent tummy of childhood."[1] If your students can discover that this is the beginning of the puberty crisis, that is good. If they can't, you can tell them.

They should then be ready for the next leap. Announce that there is only one total character in the novel, Ralph. The others are facets of his total personality. Hopefully, your students will begin writing on the duplicated sheet of items. The young mind likes to have "answers" that he can write down.

One of the main tenets of current criticism is to look at the structure of a work and to see the interrelating parts. A symbol cannot represent one thing in a certain section of a work and then be changed later to stand for something else. With this in mind, you are ready to let your students discover what happens when literary works are read *into.* The reader creates a most elaborate and complex system of symbolic meanings. What follows may be read to the students or drawn from them through questions. As the meaning of each symbol is "revealed," the students are to jot it down.

Introducing the names in the ***Lord of the Flies*** is very significant. The boy experiencing puberty is Ralph who is physically mature for his twelve years and a few months: "You could see now that he might make a boxer, as far as width and heaviness of shoulders went, but there was a mildness about his mouth and eyes that proclaimed no devil" (p. 8). Remembering that Golding wishes to establish human nature, we see that Piggy is next introduced. His words and actions reflect man's intellect and reasoning powers. He communicates in a way of imitating adults but with grammatically poor English, representing those who have read some truths about reality but have not made these their own through insight and/or experience. It is the job of the intellect to name things and to put labels on everything. This is exactly what Ralph tells Piggy to do, "Now go back, Piggy, and take names. That's your job. So long" (p. 21). This labeling is done in light of tradition and the wisdom of the ages, represented by Piggy's glasses. He rubs his glasses during crises and when making decisions. Piggy has asthma and can do no work, indicating that notional and conceptual knowledge is crippled without the experiential. It is for this reason that Piggy must be killed and washed out into the vastness and openness of the sea to become truly a meaningful facet of the whole person, Ralph. Even the dead flyer is washed out into the sea, the only hope of empty men.

Before puberty a child experiences relatively little conflict with the world or within himself. When Piggy questions, "Aren't there any grownups at all?" (p. 6), Ralph responds by standing on his head. This act, significantly, is done a few times at the beginning of the novel only, as Ralph sees the world through his youthful eyes.

Next on the scene is little innocent Johnny who is boyhood imagination, somewhat stilted, and for the time being satisfied by putting a pink thumb in his mouth. Later in the story Johnny cries over the images of the beastie.

With the intellect and the imagination established, Golding next presents Sam and Eric. Often written as one word, "Samneric" stand for Ralph's will. More than once they are locked in a struggling embrace because Ralph cannot always determine good from evil. They have hair like tow and are chunky and vital, but they are not completely developed as yet (p. 16). One of them reveals Ralph's hiding place and betrays him. Evil does betray the man.

Another important facet of the total personality to be established after intellect, imagination, and will is emotion. Coming down the beach, "marching approximately in step in two parallel lines" (p. 16) are the choristers. They are wearing black cloaks "from throat to ankle" denoting the subdued state of the emotions in the boy before puberty. When they are given permission to uncover, they emerge as powerful drives. This is seen when they begin to run wild to fetch wood for the fire and "their black caps of maintenance were slid over one ear like berets" (p. 34). Jack Merridew (Merry Andrew) depicts pride as the leader of the emotions. Maurice, next in size, "broad and grinning all the time" is joy. Roger is hate, often acting as lust, "a furtive boy whom no one knew, who kept to himself with an inner intensity of avoidance and secrecy" (p. 18). Everyone gets to know Roger since he later shows the others how to use their spears. It is Roger who kills Piggy. Bill, Robert, Harold, and Henry represent other emotions with an astonishing consistency of action and word.

There is one special member of this group whom Jack dislikes intensely because he is shy and "always throwing a faint." This is Simon, pure and simple love. On one of the first adventures, Ralph picks Simon to go with Jack and himself to investigate the island. Ralph remarks, "If Simon walks in the middle of us, then we could talk over his head." It is Simon who discovers at this time the candle bushes which symbolize church rituals. Jack slashes at one of them with his knife, and an aromatic scent spills over the three boys. Jack then remarks, "Green candles. . . . We can't eat them. Come on" (p. 27). Pride rebels here against the immaterial. If it isn't useful, it is valueless.

A little later we become aware of a boy with a mulberry-colored birthmark "warped out of the perpendicular by the fierce light of publicity, and he bored into the grass with one toe" (p. 31). In all his novels, Golding seems to be preoccupied with the idea of original sin. The blemished-one is Ralph's knowledge of original sin, since Piggy is very concerned about the stained boy. This boy is the first one who wants to know what Ralph is going to do about the snake-thing. With one hand on the shell, Piggy interprets what the boy with the mulberry-colored birthmark whispers, "He says the beastie came in the dark" (p. 31).

Another facet of Ralph's personality is Percival Wemys Madison, The Vicarage, Harcourt St. Anthony, Hants, telephone, telephone. . . . He is memory. Percival and Phil, the emotion of fear, are the two who tell the others about the beast from the sea. At the end of the novel, Percival is greatly changed:

"I'm, I'm—"

"But there was no more to come. Percival Wemys Madison sought in his head for an incantation that had faded clean away" (p. 247). Ralph's memory has a different hierarchy of values after the experience of puberty.

The others in the novel, not given labels, are known by the generic title of "littluns." Human nature is too complicated to be able to label all its facets.

Early in the story Ralph points out and Piggy grabs a conch which becomes the symbol of order and authority. Ralph is the only one who is supposed to blow into the shell to create a loud blast calling all facets of the personality to attention. These assemblies, resulting from the call, are times of decision. "That's why Ralph made a meeting. So we can decide what to do" (p. 18), echoes Piggy. At another assembly, Jack remarks, "We'll have rules! . . . Lots of rules! Then when anyone breaks 'em—." Since there is a close connection between authority and tradition, Piggy (intellect) shrieks in terror as Jack (pride) snatches the glasses from his face, "Mind out! Give 'em back! I can hardly see! You'll break the conch!" (p. 36), meaning that without tradition the mind is darkened, and one would have to start all over again investigating everything. Without tradition and authority, control and direction are impossible. Paradoxically, Piggy "sees" more after losing his glasses.

Later in the novel, Ralph asks Piggy what makes things break up. To this, Piggy, rubbing his glasses, replies, "I suppose it's Jack." Piggy tells Ralph that

Jack hates reason (Piggy) but respects the person (Ralph), and if Ralph were to stand out of the way, Jack would hurt the next thing and that is reason (p. 129).

Your students are now ready to accept Golding's special stylistic feature: suspending time. Human nature is established, and the crisis is puberty. Consider that Golding is speaking of Ralph's experience as happening during one night while the boy is in a semi-dream world existence. The island would be the boy's bed. The mountain where the vision is clear would be his head, the bridge over to Castle Rock would be his neck, and the fortress of Castle Rock itself would be his body. The creepers would be his blankets.

When his father, the naval officer, enters Ralph's bedroom at the end of the novel and sees the blankets ajar and Ralph's "filthy body, matted hair, and unwiped nose" (p. 186), he asks Ralph, "Who's boss here?" Ralph, replies loudly, "I am." That statement then becomes the most important one in the entire novel. Ralph had experienced his first nocturnal emission. The bulk of the novel expresses the conflict one must go through before the total personality can emerge, with a certain loss of innocence, but still be boss.

Throughout the story, spears, logs, and sticks are the phallic symbol, and they become Jack's preoccupation as the leader of the hunters. These hunters, the emotions, are searching for pigs, material goods. Wanting to possess and to dominate, to kill and yet to have, the hunters allow the goods to become the end. While others concern themselves about rescue, Jack and his hunters have fun hunting for pigs with their spears. Jack dismisses the thought of a snake-thing because pride could merely destroy it. "There isn't a snake-thing. But if there was a snake we'd hunt it and kill it. We're going to hunt pigs to get meat for everybody. And we'll look for the snake too—" (p. 32).

It is fitting that Sam and Eric are the first to find a large log which can be used for the fire. Fire throughout the novel represents the drives of man toward good and evil. "The twins, Sam 'n Eric, were the first to get a likely log but they could do nothing till Ralph, Jack, Simon, Roger, and Maurice found room for a hand-hold. Then they inched the grotesque dead thing up the rock and toppled it over on top" (p. 35). Golding has chosen carefully the names of those who help in this experience: Samneric (good and evil), Ralph (the person), Jack (pride), Simon (love), Roger (lust), and Maurice (joy). The author concluded this paragraph: "Once more, amid the breeze, the shouting, the slanting sunlight on the high mountain, was shed that glamour, that strange invisible light of friendship, adventure, and content" (p. 35).

When Jack breaks away from Ralph, Piggy, Samneric, and Simon, he and the passions find security in Castle Rock. It is from this strong fort that Jack runs his activities and seeks the pleasure of pursuit for apparent goods. There was sufficient fruit on the island to satisfy all, but this wasn't enough for Jack. He continues the destructive hunt. Even Ralph is tempted to give up the idea of rescue and go hunting, but Piggy keeps reminding him about salvation.

Simon, who remains faithful to Ralph, plays a very important part in the novel. It is he who feeds the "littluns" the choicest fruit which they cannot reach. And after the children have followed him and have had their fill, Simon suffers the arrow of the sun until the sweat runs from his pores (p. 123). He goes down on his knees three times in saving decaying man from his entanglements to tell the truth (of the dead flyer who has fallen from the sky) to the others (p. 136). But Simon is killed by those whom he wished to save, and he too is washed out into the openness of the sea. Whereas Simon is sacrificed for the group (society), Piggy is sacrificed to make Ralph whole. Of course, then we ask if the following passage is not the symbol of the resurrection of the body: "Somewhere over the darkened curve of the world the sun and moon were pulling, and the film of water on the earth planet was held, bulging slightly on one side while the solid core turned. The great wave of the tide moved farther along the island and the water lifted. Softly, surrounded by a fringe of inquisitive bright creatures, itself a silver shape beneath the steadfast constellation, Simon's dead body moved out toward the open sea" (p. 142).

Before he is killed, however, Simon has his bout with the devil, the lord of the flies, the one who would like to lie about what Ralph is experiencing in puberty. Through his deceit, Beelzebub (god of insects) tries to take control. He does not want Ralph to be master of himself. Simon knows what it could be, but it is the devil who colors all red, not green. In this light, the statement, "Passions beat about Simon on the mountaintop with awful wings," makes sense. Butterflies (the symbol of beauty; in Greek: life, spirit, and breath) have frequently been present when Simon has communicated with nature, but they desert the place where the head of the pig is forced onto the stick sharpened at both ends. One end is jammed into a crack of *mother earth;* the other holds the head of the lord of lies. The mouth of the beast is dark, a blackness that Simon experiences spreading (p. 133). The heart of darkness wants no part of love or true meaning. So the Lord of the Flies says, "I'm warning you. I'm going to get angry. D'you see? You're not wanted. Understand? We are going to have fun on this island! So don't try it on, my poor misguided boy, or else—" (p. 133). The way that the devil is to get ultimate control is through man's total pursuit of pleasure through materialism. Jack tries to make Simon eat of the meat of materialism, but Simon gives of his portion to Piggy, helping him experience both good and the sharing of things. "Simon, sitting between the twins and Piggy, wiped his mouth and shoved his piece of meat over the rocks to Piggy, who grabbed it. The twins giggled and Simon lowered his face in shame" (p. 68). Also, when Piggy loses his glasses, Simon finds them. Thus does love try to help reason.

Several other symbols have been well worked into the story. When the boys are investigating the "beast" on the mountain, they see a creature which moves as the wind blows it—the dead, hollow, decaying flyer. It is fallen man in a state of helplessness, moving as if alive. This figure has to be cleansed and washed by the rains of baptism before moving out to the sea.

Another symbol is Ralph's "shutter coming down," a flickering in his brain when he momentarily wonders about going with the others to hunt with spears. Should he go with the others to have fun, or should he be concerned about being saved? The symbol of salvation is smoke.

As the novel progresses, the forces divide, and decisions are to be made. Simon tells Ralph that things will be all right no matter what Ralph has to go through. Simon says, "You'll get back to where you came from" (p. 103). Ralph is discovering himself and asks Simon, "How do you know?" Simon replies, "I just think you'll get back all right."

Towards the end of the story, Ralph is hunted by all the forces which Jack controls. In his escape from the hunters, Ralph comes upon the skull of the pig which is mounted on the stick. He knocks off the head and wrenches the stick from the earth. "Ralph drew his feet up and crouched. The stake was in his hands, the stake sharpened at both ends, the stake that vibrated so wildly, that grew long, short, light, heavy, light again" (p. 183).

Piggy had been killed, and the conch smashed into a thousand pieces. Samneric had been tied up and then made to join the tribe. Bill (hope) is changed, Robert (desire) is satisfied with meat, and Ralph himself is hungry. Sam gives Ralph some meat. "If there were light—" remarks Ralph.

Roger is carrying death in his hands, so Ralph tries to think. He had never gone against reason (Piggy); made fun of, yes, but never violated. And yet, "he was beginning to dread the curtain that might waver in his brain, blacking out the sense of danger making a simpleton of him" (p. 181).

Finally, Ralph experiences what he doesn't totally understand or want. The security of boyhood is gone, and he tries to cry for mercy while warding off what comes. Through the entire semi-dreamworld state, Ralph has experienced his first nocturnal emission. He is no longer a boy. His experience has been one of awesome mystery. He now sees the power of the passions of man and realizes how all drives must be directed if one is to emerge as a full personality.

Now your students see what reading *into* a novel leads to. If the above exercise doesn't cure your symbol hunters, you may wish to have them play the game further by seeing Golding's first novel, ***The Inheritors*** as man's first crisis, birth (man becoming conscious of his consciousness); the ***Lord of the Flies*** as the puberty crisis; ***Pincher Martin*** as the adolescent crisis; ***Free Fall*** as the adulthood crisis; and ***The Spire*** as the spiritual crisis. It's all great fun, but your students are sure to get to the point. Or maybe both you and your students might find it all fits. Who knows?

Notes

1. William Golding, *Lord of the Flies* (New York City: G. P. Putnam's Sons, 1959), p. 8. Subsequent references to the novel will be to this paperback edition and will be incorporated into the text.

Arnold Johnston (essay date 1980)

SOURCE: Johnston, Arnold. "*Lord of the Flies:* Fable, Myth, and Fiction." In *Of Earth and Darkness: The Novels of William Golding,* pp. 8-20.

[*In the following essay, Johnston discusses the merits of* Lord of the Flies *as a modern myth.*]

Lord of the Flies deals, ostensibly, with a group of English schoolboys who, in the process of being evacuated by airplane from the dangers of a nuclear war, find themselves alone on a tropical island after their plane crashes. The boys, ranging in age from about six to thirteen, are faced with the problem of survival on the uninhabited island while attempting to attract the attention of passing ships and planes.

The problem of physical existence solves itself—the island is rich in fruit and game and the climate is favorable. The real problem that arises among the boys involves their own inner nature, and emerges most directly from a clash between those who wish to keep a fire burning on the island's mountain to attract rescuers and those who wish to hunt and indulge in what at first seems to be the natural inclination of children toward unrestrained play. The conflict begins in apparent childish innocence, and reaches its climax in acts of shocking brutality that carry far-reaching implications of guilt.

Golding has summed up the theme of ***Lord of the Flies*** as follows:

> The theme is an attempt to trace the defects of society back to the defects of human nature. The moral is that the shape of society must depend on the ethical nature of the individual and not on any political system however apparently logical or respectable. The whole book is symbolic in nature.[1]

As I have mentioned, Golding feels that evil arises from man's essential being, and he attempts to demonstrate his thesis in this self-consciously symbolic work which shows civilization totally unable to contend with man's apparently natural and voracious propensity for savagery. A systematic probing into the question of man's inherent good or evil is, without doubt, one of Golding's major concerns; and in the course of this study I shall attempt to show that his apparent preoccupation with the problems of survival (***Lord of the Flies, The Inheritors, Pincher Martin***) is an important key to understanding both his philosophy and his techniques.

Lord of the Flies falls into that hardy genre of accounts of shipwreck and survival on tropical islands: *Robinson Crusoe, The Swiss Family Robinson, The Coral Island,* and so forth. Golding particularly wishes the reader to associate his novel with Ballantyne's *The Coral Island.* The two main characters in both books are named Ralph and Jack, and the relationship between the names of Ballantyne's Peterkin and Golding's Simon needs little elaboration. Then, too, there are two direct references to *The Coral Island* in Golding's book, one near the beginning—

> "It's like in a book."
>
> At once there was a clamour.
>
> "Treasure Island—"
>
> "Swallows and Amazons—"
>
> "Coral Island—"

and one near the end—

> The officer nodded helpfully.
>
> "I know. Jolly good show. Like the Coral Island."[2]

Frank Kermode and Carl Niemeyer, in separate essays, discuss at some length Golding's use of *The Coral Island* as an ironic parallel to his own novel, pointing out the difference between Golding's vision of human nature and what Niemeyer calls the "cheerful unrealities" of Ballantyne.[3] And Golding himself, in the interview with Kermode, had this to say of his book's connection with *The Coral Island:*

> What I'm saying to myself is, "Don't be such a fool, you remember when you were a boy, a small boy, how you lived on that island with Ralph and Jack and Peterkin. . . . Now you are grown up, . . . you can see people are not like that; they would not behave like that if they were God-fearing English gentlemen, and they went to an island like that." Their savagery would not be found in natives on an island. As like as not they would find savages who were kindly and uncomplicated and that the devil would rise out of the intellectual complications of the three white men on the island itself.[4]

Golding's remark about kindly, uncomplicated savages stacks the anthropological cards a bit heavily against civilized man, and ignores a number of basic facts about primitive cultures. Of course, ***Lord of the Flies*** doesn't allow the reader any "real" savages with whom to compare the boys, as Golding's artistic sense evidently told him to avoid confusing the central human issue with such anthropological quibbles. However, the aforementioned remark does underline Golding's moralistic bias, and points toward a more serious charge that might be leveled against the novel: that his authorial presence is often overly obtrusive, either in didactic interpositions or, more seriously, in unconvincing manipulation of his characters.

In this connection Lionel Trilling says that Golding succeeds in persuading the reader that the boys' actions result from the fact that they "are not finally under the control of previous social habit or convention," but adds that he "should not have credited this quite so readily of American boys who would not . . . have been so quick to forget their social and moral pasts."[5] For my part, I am unable to see why Mr. Trilling is unwilling to carry his pertinent critical comment to its logical conclusion, without involving himself in speculations about the relative acculturation processes in Britain and the United States. Had he pursued his doubts to an expression of dissatisfaction with the credibility of the boys, he would have been on firmer ground, since there are several points at which Golding's manipulations of narrative and dialogue do ring false.

Two interrelated but discernibly distinct threads are evident in ***Lord of the Flies.*** One is the actual narrative, detailing meticulously the boys' descent into savagery; the other is the gradually developed symbol of the "Beast" that is first suggested by the wholly natural night fears of the "littluns" and that eventually becomes the object of worship by the boys-turned-savages. The Beast is an externalization of the inner darkness in the children's (man's) nature, and its ascendancy is steady, inexorable, as is the path to savagery, increasing in intensity with each new regression on the part of the boys. But despite his often brilliant handling of this apposite motivating symbol of the book, it is especially during scenes involving the Beast that Golding becomes particularly intrusive.

At one point, for instance, when the assembled boys are discussing the problem of the Beast, Piggy (the pragmatic rationalist) explains: "''Course there isn't a beast in the forest. How could there be? What would a beast eat?'" (p. 77). And the answer, supplied by the chorus of boys, is "'Pig!'"—to which the unmistakable voice of Golding (by way of reminding the reader just what his symbol represents) can be heard to add, "'We eat pig'" (p. 77). And a few pages later Simon, the convulsion-afflicted mystic, says of the Beast: "'What I mean is . . . maybe it's only us'" (p. 82). This rather subtle interpretation of human nature from a small boy demonstrates further that Golding is so intent on his moral message that he will not hesitate to make the youngsters dance to his tune.

This assembly scene is central to the novel's development in that it marks the last point at which "civilized" rules and procedures can be said to dominate the boys' words and actions. Grounds for the breakdown of the rules are furnished by dissent among the representatives of order (Ralph, Piggy, and Simon), as Piggy, with his unimaginative rationalist's intelligence, answers Simon's observation with a resounding "'Nuts!'" Even among the "civilized," communication is lacking, and when Jack—leader of the forces of disorder—shouts "'Bollocks to the rules!'" chaos and darkness are ushered in (p. 84).

However, Golding cannot let the matter of the Beast rest here, and after the assembly has dispersed, Ralph, shaken, turns to Piggy and asks, "'Are there ghosts, Piggy? Or Beasts?'" And here the ventriloquist's lips can be seen to move, as Piggy answers: "''Course there aren't. . . . 'Cos things wouldn't make sense. Houses an' streets, an'—TV—they wouldn't work'" (p. 85). Although beautifully camouflaged in boyish diction, the implication that a boy of about ten can reason that the existence of supernatural phenomena challenges the validity of natural law is simply too much to swallow.

A major objectification of man's inner Beast appears in the shape of a pig's head on a stick that Jack and his "hunters" leave as an offering for the Beast. Unknown to the hunters, Simon has been nearby during the killing of the pig, having hidden himself in some bushes at the onset of one of his fits. He is then left alone with the head, thus setting the scene for the most self-consciously symbolic incident in the book. At this point the significance of the book's title becomes evident, as the head, swarming with flies, enters into an imaginary conversation with Simon, a conversation in which Golding, speaking through this grotesque agent, removes any doubts that might still have lingered in the reader's mind with respect to the novel's theme or the source of the evil described therein:

> The Lord of the Flies spoke in the voice of a schoolmaster.
>
> "This has gone quite far enough. My poor, misguided child, do you think you know better than I do?"
>
> There was a pause.
>
> "I'm warning you. I'm going to get waxy. D'you see. You're not wanted. Understand? We are going to have fun on this island! So don't try it on, my poor misguided boy, or else—"
>
> Simon found he was looking into a vast mouth. There was blackness within, a blackness that spread.
>
> "—Or else," said the Lord of the Flies, "we shall do you. See? Jack and Roger and Maurice and Robert and Bill and Piggy and Ralph. Do you. See?"
>
> (p. 133)

The above scene, which places perhaps the greatest strain on the reader's credulity, may be defended as the book's clearest indication that human guilt is pervasive, including even the "good" characters, Ralph and Piggy. However, by comparing this strained encounter between Simon and the head with the scenes immediately preceding and following it, one may see that Golding makes his point there just as clearly and much more effectively.[6]

The killing of the pig by Jack's hunters is a case in point. The pig-hunting of former days has been relatively innocent, but to fully dramatize the deep inner evil that takes possession of the boys after they accept the Beast as their god, Golding depicts more than a mere killing. Conjuring up the most shocking imagery he could use to show the degeneration of these preadolescents, he describes the slaughter of a mother sow in terms of a sexual assault.[7] How better to portray the children's loss of innocence (since children are no strangers to killing) than by picturing them as perpetrators of an Oedipal violation?

> . . . the sow staggered her way ahead of them, bleeding and mad, and the hunters followed, wedded to her in lust, excited by the long chase and the dropped blood. . . .
>
> Here, struck down by the heat, the sow fell and the hunters hurled themselves at her. This dreadful eruption from an unknown world made her frantic; she squealed and bucked and the air was full of sweat and noise and blood and terror. Roger ran round the heap, prodding with his spear wherever pigflesh appeared. Jack was on top of the sow, stabbing downward with his knife. Roger found a lodgment for his spear and began to push till he was leaning with his whole weight. The spear moved forward inch by inch and the terrified squealing became a high-pitched scream. Then Jack found the throat and the hot blood spouted over his hands. The sow collapsed under them and they were heavy and fulfilled upon her.
>
> (p. 125)

The vividness of this scene makes it both a powerfully realistic component of the essential story and a major contribution to the novel's symbolic scheme. The episode involving Simon and the head, however—especially the "conversation"—is difficult to view in other than symbolic terms, marking it as another nagging flaw in a book that—whatever its thematic concerns—seems committed from the outset to creating believable boys on a believable island. Actually, the mere physical presence of the pig's head, the Lord of the Flies, would have served well without the didactic pronouncements, since "lord of the flies" is a translation of the Hebrew *Ba'al zevuv* (Beelzebub in Greek), implying quite effectively that the head is representative of man's "inner devil."

In any event, the most successful symbolic portrayal of the Beast as man appears earlier in the novel in the form of a dead airman whose parachute carries him in the night to the top of the mountain, where, tangled in the complication of strings, he becomes lodged in a sitting position, the upper half of his body alternately rising and falling as the breeze tightens and slackens the lines. Sam and Eric, the twins, are horrified by this grisly figure when they come to tend the fire, and when a subsequent expedition (headed by Ralph and Jack, but notably excluding Simon and Piggy) climbs the mountain to confirm the twins' garbled report, the following powerful passage shows the Beast impressed forever on the minds and hearts of the boys:

> Behind them the sliver of moon had drawn clear of the horizon. Before them, something like a great ape was sitting asleep with its head between its knees. Then the wind roared in the forest, there was confusion in the darkness and the creature lifted its head, holding toward them the ruin of a face.
>
> (p. 114)

This is the experience that accelerates the deterioration of civilized procedures, bringing confusion to the final assembly and committing Jack fully—in a parody of his initial appearance as leader of the choir, or perhaps an oblique commentary on the ritualistic mind—to high priesthood in the dark new religion. And it is to determine the truth of this experience and the nature of the so-called Beast from Air that Simon, after his ghastly interview with the head, courageously ascends the mountain, where he frees the wasted body "from the wind's indignity" (p. 135).

Simon, whom Golding has called quite explicitly a "Christfigure," comes down from the mountain to carry the truth to the others, but—still weak from his recent attack—he stumbles instead into a ritual reenactment of the pig-killing and is killed by the frenzied and fear-maddened boys, who ironically mistake him for the Beast.[8] And here Golding's sweeping indictment of humanity becomes most nearly complete, for Ralph and Piggy, lured by the prospect of food, have temporarily joined with the hunters and take part, albeit unwittingly, in the murder of Simon. And here, too, at the moment of Simon's death, in the midst of a storm that thunders within as well as around them, the boys are visited by the spectre of human history, embodied in the form of the dead airman. Dislodged from atop the mountain and carried again into the air by the winds, the grotesque figure of the decaying parachutist plummets to the sands, scattering the terror-stricken boys, and sweeps far out to sea. The beach is left desolate save for the small broken body of Simon, which follows the parachutist into the sea:

> Along the shoreward edge of the shallows the advancing clearness was full of strange, moonbeam-bodied creatures with fiery eyes. Here and there a larger pebble clung to its own air and was covered with a coat of pearls. The tide swelled in and over the rain-pitted sand and smoothed everything with a layer of silver. Now it touched the first of the stains that seeped from the broken body and the creatures made a moving patch of light as they gathered at the edge. The water rose farther and dressed Simon's coarse hair with brightness. The line of his cheek silvered and the turn of his shoulder became sculptured marble. The strange attendant creatures, with their fiery eyes and trailing vapors, busied themselves round his head. The body lifted a fraction of an inch from the sand and a bubble of air escaped from the mouth with a wet plop. Then it turned gently in the water.
>
> Somewhere over the darkened curve of the world the sun and moon were pulling, and the film of water on the earth planet was held, bulging slightly on one side while the solid core turned. The great wave of the tide moved farther along the island and the water lifted. Softly, surrounded by a fringe of inquisitive bright creatures, itself a silver shape beneath the steadfast constellations, Simon's dead body moved out toward the open sea.
>
> (p. 142)

The amount and kind of description devoted to Simon's death is ample indication of his saintly role even without Golding's identification of him as a Christ-figure.

All of the obvious parallels to Christ are there—from Gethsemane to Golgotha—and one may easily identify Simon's story with that of many a martyred mystic.[9] But why are they there? Why is Simon there? Is Golding merely speaking with the voice of moral and religious orthodoxy? As his subsequent novels have shown, Golding is not to be labeled so easily. But in those novels one sees a consistent preoccupation with the artist or artist-figure, someone actively engaged in interpreting the human condition: Tuami, the tribal artist in ***The Inheritors;*** Christopher "Pincher" Martin, the penultimate actor in ***Pincher Martin;*** Sammy Mountjoy, the guilt-torn painter in ***Free Fall;*** Dean Jocelin and Roger Mason, creative force behind, and architect of, ***The Spire;*** Oliver, the confused would-be musician in ***The Pyramid;*** and Matty Windrove, the naive prophet of ***Darkness Visible.***

Viewed in this light, Simon's habitual isolation from the other boys, his obvious inability to communicate to them the "truths" that he grasps intuitively, and finally his death at their hands, reflect the all-too-frequent fate of the artist in society. Of course, all that can be said of the artist's role may be applied to that of the religious or mystic; but again and again in his later works, Golding demonstrates that the nature of his unorthodoxy is its basis in that highly eclectic form of mysticism called art. Like many artists before him, he sees the artist as priest, as interpreter of life's mysteries and possible savior of mankind. Unlike many of his predecessors, though, Golding faces squarely the historical fact that the artist—like other saviors—has met with little success. And in this first novel, Simon should be recognized as the first of Golding's "portraits of the artist," embodying both his pride in the high calling and his frustration at the artist's inability to defend himself against the weaknesses of others, or to transcend his own human frailties. Even more important to a reading of his works as a whole is the realization that, for Golding, the artist is representative of humanity at large, and that Golding finds in creativity the source of man's strength and weakness, his good and evil.

In any case, the aftermath of Simon's death is the last point at which ***Lord of the Flies*** can be said to picture the existence of a calm and ordering vision. Total disintegration of the civilized forces follows swiftly, beginning with the theft of Piggy's glasses—the source of fire and symbol of intellectual power—by Jack and his hunters, and proceeding through Piggy's murder by the brutal Roger to the final hunt for Ralph, who is to be decapitated and sacrificed like a pig to the Beast.

The description of Piggy's death provides an informing contrast to that of Simon's, showing quite clearly, though subtly, Golding's antirationalist bias:

> The rock struck Piggy a glancing blow from chin to knee; the conch exploded into a thousand white fragments and ceased to exist. Piggy, saying nothing, with no time for even a grunt, traveled through the air sideways from the rock, turning over as he went. The rock bounded twice and was lost in the forest. Piggy fell forty feet and landed

> on his back across that square red rock in the sea. His head opened and stuff came out and turned red. Piggy's arms and legs twitched a bit, like a pig's after it has been killed. Then the sea breathed again in a long, slow sigh, the water boiled white and pink over the rock; and when it went, sucking back again, the body of Piggy was gone.
>
> (p. 167)

One notes here the same studious reportage of physical fact as in the passage quoted earlier. But this time Golding concentrates on matter-of-fact particulars, eschewing the angle of vision that might place Piggy's death in universal perspective: whereas Simon is described in language befitting a dead saint, Piggy is pictured as a dead animal. Of course, Piggy's actions immediately before his murder are brave in conventional terms; but his rationalist's faith in order and human perfectibility, ironically undercut throughout the book, seems nowhere more misguided than in this scene (p. 166). The mystic's intuitive recognition that good and evil coexist within man is the spark of his divinity; but the rationalist's denial of such intangible forces chains him forever to the material world of earth and organism.

After Piggy's death, Ralph finds himself being hunted by the other boys. But at the book's climactic moment, just as the "savages" are about to descend on Ralph, a "rescuer" appears in the person of a British naval officer. And at once, in a passage laden with irony, the shrieking painted savages become "a semicircle of little boys, their bodies streaked with colored clay, sharp sticks in their hands . . . standing on the beach making no noise at all" (p. 185). The officer, confronted with this scene of filth and disorder, rebukes the boys lamely (as Lionel Trilling might have noted): "'I should have thought that a pack of British boys—you're all British, aren't you?—would have been able to put up a better show than that—'" (p. 186). And Ralph, the book's Everyman, representative of the world of "longing and baffled commonsense" (p. 65), is left to weep "for the end of innocence, the darkness of man's heart, and the fall through the air of the true, wise friend called Piggy" (pp. 186-87).

Several early critics and reviewers of ***Lord of the Flies*** assailed the book's ending as too neat, if not actually as a question-begging compromise with lovers of happy endings.[10] However, a reflective reading shows that the "rescue" is no rescue at all: throughout the novel Golding is at pains to point out that the major human predicament is internal; the officer solves Ralph's immediate problem, but "the darkness of man's heart" persists. Practically, of course, as Golding says, in a book "originally conceived . . . as the change from innocence—which is the ignorance of self—to a tragic knowledge . . . If I'd gone on to the death of Ralph, Ralph would never have had time to understand what had happened to him."[11] And on a more sophisticated thematic level he observes, "The officer, having interrupted a manhunt, prepares to take the children off the island in a cruiser which will presently be hunting its enemy in the same implacable way. And who will rescue the adult and his cruiser?"[12]

Returning to the Simon-Piggy contrast discussed earlier, one might also note that it is Piggy, the misguided rationalist, for whom Ralph sorrows, not Simon, the "saint." Besides subtly underscoring Golding's concern for the fate of the artist-mystic, this fact seems to indicate that Ralph's tragic experience has not finally brought him to the sort of self-knowledge that can save him as a man.[13] The implications for humanity at large are clear and unencouraging. Thus, although the officer seems to suggest a deus ex machina, one will be hard pressed to find a happy ending here.

On a broader front, the plot of ***Lord of the Flies*** has been attacked as both eccentric and specious, either too far removed from the real world or too neatly microcosmic to be true.[14] The first of these charges, that of eccentricity, may be put aside for the time being. After all, removing one's setting and characters from the larger sphere of civilization has long been an acceptable, if not honorable, practice in almost every literary genre and tradition, as witness the success of Melville and Conrad, whose isolated fictional worlds remain real in both their concrete details and their human significance. The source of the objection seems to be predisposed literary tastes, rather than more rigorous aesthetic standards—preference for the novel as typical history, rather than symbolic vision. However, the related charge—that Golding oversimplifies complex truth through manipulation of his microcosmic world—is on firmer ground. And in speaking to this point, one must necessarily return to John Peter's identification of Golding as a fabulist, as well as to Golding's own wish to be seen as a "myth-maker."

The main concern, then, of both opponents and supporters of ***Lord of the Flies*** is whether or not it functions adequately on its primary, or "fictional," level; or more simply, is the story told convincingly? Peter, in "The Fables of William Golding," assails the novel for its "incomplete translation of its thesis into its story so that much remains external and extrinsic, the teller's assertion rather than the tale's enactment before our eyes." And indeed, I have detailed several instances of such didactic obtrusions, including some aspects of character and action that seem more concerned with theme than credibility. However, I would qualify Peter's observation rather strongly, noting that such instances seem more vulnerable to the charge of being extraneous than of betraying Golding's "incomplete translation" of his thesis, which is more than adequately communicated by the rest of the novel.

And what of the rest of the novel? Is it merely a skeleton of thesis incompletely fleshed by concrete detail? Kinkead-Weekes and Gregor are highly emphatic in answering this question: "Physical realities come first for Golding and should stay first for his readers."[15] They devote a long first chapter in their study to a demonstration of the "complex physical truth" of ***Lord of the Flies,*** concentrating heavily on the naturalistic clarity and inclusiveness of Golding's description, and arguing that his symbolic representations are often so reflective of life's complexities as to be actually ambiguous, perhaps even too ambiguous to be seen symbolically at all. This latter point is a bit extreme: Golding's main symbolic intentions are clear enough in the novel, even without the many explicit comments he has made since its publication. However, Kinkead-Weekes and Gregor may be excused their overstatement, since so much attention has been paid to the novel's symbolism that its objective vehicles have been too often deemphasized, if not forgotten.

And here, Golding's style becomes a major concern. As Kinkead-Weekes and Gregor demonstrate, Golding's descriptive prose carries the burden of his meaning and—coupled with the inexorable narrative of the boys' descent into chaos—provides the reader with a naturalistically concrete and complex surface world against which to view the symbolic drama. One need only note passages already quoted—the killing of the sow, the deaths of Simon and Piggy—to be convinced that the realities of ***Lord of the Flies*** live in the flesh, as well as in the abstract, comprising a universe not oversimplified, but paradoxically diverse, in which beauty and ugliness, good and evil, precariously coexist. The main features of Golding's best description are scientific accuracy and objectivity, combined with a felicitous use of simple adjectives and verbs that can transform his tersely pictured scenes into powerful evocations of transcendent beauty or obsessive ugliness. One thinks here of the extremes of such effects before the sow-killing, when "she staggered into an open space where bright flowers grew and butterflies danced round each other and the air was hot and still" (p. 125), and after, when "the pile of guts was a black blob of flies that buzzed like a saw" (p. 128). Without doubt, Golding's world exists compellingly on its primary level: its strained moments seem more like surface blemishes than structural defects, blemishes that catch the eye because of their dissimilarity to the skillfully woven fabric of the whole.

As for Golding's stature as a maker of myth, one must grant him a considerable measure of success. Certainly, if myth "comes out from the roots of things" and evokes age-old and recurrent human patterns, ***Lord of the Flies*** is much closer to myth than to simple fable. One may trace its literary roots alone back through the more immediate past (*The Coral Island*), to the ancient past (*The Bacchae*), and on a broader plane one may easily see in the story echoes and parallels from both the political and social dynamics of contemporary civilization (the rise of Fascism, anti-intellectualism) and the religious and philosophical foundations of Western culture (the Old Testament, the Fall, the New Testament, the Crucifixion, as well as nineteenth-century rationalism). Indeed, the very profusion of suggestive patterns in the novel should demonstrate that here is no simple allegorical reworking of the materials of *The Coral Island,* and that irrespective of Golding's initial plans, Frank Kermode properly observes: "In writing of this kind all depends upon the author's mythopoeic power to transcend the 'programme.'"[16] And in this first novel, William Golding displays "mythopoeic power" of an impressively high order. The flaws, the didactic interjections and manipulations remain. But, all in all, one may compare Golding to a puppet master who has wrought his marionettes meticulously and beautifully and led them skillfully through a captivating and frightening drama, while only occasionally distracting the audience by the movement of his strings.

Leah Hadomi (essay date spring 1981)

SOURCE: Hadomi, Leah. "Imagery as a Source of Irony in Golding's *Lord of the Flies.*" *The Hebrew University Studies in Literature* 9, no. 1 (spring 1981): 126-138.

[*In the following essay, Hadomi examines Golding's use of images for the purpose of irony in* Lord of the Flies.]

Irony, the constant evasion of generally accepted cultural assumptions and expectations, is a major principle of structure in ***Lord of the Flies.*** In this novel expectations are deliberately aroused in order to be undermined, so that the reader has constantly to readjust his choices in order to construct an appropriate reading.

In the process of reconstructing meaning Allemann's[1] terms may prove to be useful. He uses the term "Spieletemente" (play elements) within the "Ironische Spielraum" (ironic playground). The ironic playground lies between the foreground of visible reality and its background. The play elements shifting between the background and the foreground negate the previous meaning of the utterances or situations of the foreground.

The ironic playground in ***Lord of the Flies*** works on two levels. First, the level of "Circumstantial Irony", where the ironic playground consists of general cultural and literary expectations, from which an ironic light is thrown on the work as a whole. Second the level of "Internal Irony", mediated mainly by metaphor.[2]

Circumstantial Irony is based on the tension between outward cultural presumptions and the rhetorical effect of the novel. As critics have amply observed, there are several allusions in the text to R.M. Ballantyne's romance *The Coral Island.*[3] Beyond this specific literary reference lies the broader area of Utopia in the general sense of the word; the shift from reality into nowhere, the attempt to create a desirably way of life, a harmonious carefree existence.[4] Utopia in the sense developed by Northrop Frye, namely the idea of a social organization based on rituals rationally explained, is also undermined in the novel.[5] There are other wishful ways of existence pertaining to Utopia such as the pastoral *locus amoenas* and the Land of Cockaigne dream which are hinted at.

All these specifically literary and generally Utopian expectations are aroused in ***Lord of the Flies,*** then negated. The world of the novel is an observe Coral Island. The famous English democratic liberalism which the Choir boys bring to the island, is completely destroyed when aggressive instinctive forces are released. The pastoral element evoked by being close to harmonious nature during the first phase is also negated when nature turns out to be treacherous. The Cocknay Land's total satisfaction of sensual hedonistic needs is feasible on the island since there is an abundance of fruit, water and shelter, but, it turns out, what was expected to guarantee ultimate satisfaction of needs proves to be insufficient as aggressive and erotic drives demand their satisfaction.

To sum up, the ironic playground which creates circumstantial irony consists of general cultural beliefs or myths which are aroused and implied in the text at the outset, then prove to be incompatible with the narrative events as they develop. The social-rational Utopian notion, the pastoral world and the Cocknay Land dream are all denied. All expectations of Innocent Childhood in nature, including the myth of the Noble Savage, are exposed, unmasking the Wild Man who "has come to stand as a symbol not only for what we have lost in becoming civilized, but mainly for what we have repressed".[6] Finally, the Utopian dream is turned totally upside down—the desired social organization turns into a totalitarian state and the rational approach to human problems crumbles before irrational human desires. *Utopia* has become *Dystopia.*

Internal Irony is the playground where metaphors serve as play elements. I propose to examine the metaphors in ***Lord of the Flies*** in the light of Wayne Booth's analysis in the *Rhetoric of Irony.* According to Booth, both modes, the metaphoric and the ironic, share a dynamic, volatile, unstable character. The difference between them, however, is that "the powerful shock of recognition essential to irony is secondary or muted or perhaps sometimes even non-existent in metaphor".[7] Moreover, images used metaphorically evoke additional meaning; but when used ironically they create a continuum of subtraction and reversal. In ***Lord of the Flies*** the ironic potential in metaphor is released and realised in peculiarly effective ways.

Three familiar figurative clusters recur in the novel: the clothing-nakedness cluster, the cluster centered around firesight and the dominant man-animal cluster.[8] These figurative clusters, being structurally related among themselves as well as to other formal elements of the novel, are theme carriers with ironic overtones. The clothing imagery is a commentary on the validity of cultural coverage; the sight imagery reflects man's attempt to comprehend the covert and concealed truth under the coverage; and the man-animal cluster relates to the problem of human nature fluctuating between animality and spirituality. The complexity inbuilt in these figurative paradigms enriches the irony of ***Lord of the Flies,***[9] through symphonic variations and interrelations.

The clothing-nakedness cluster carries the truth-appearance theme. Clothing suggests false disguise and trickery which must be penetrated in order to disclose inner authenticity; Nakedness implies man unprotected against cosmic and human enemies, but revealed in his inner truth. In ***Lord of the Flies*** clothing is only one form of disguise, others being masks, names and attitudes towards norms and institutions. These different types of disguise serve both as protective physical measures against nature and as psychological measures to conceal man's unscrupulous drives from others and even from himself.

Each of the clusters has a covert thematic meaning, yet as a result of compositional placement this meaning is questioned, doubted and even negated. This instability produces an ironic effect. The relation of the clothing-nakedness cluster to the overall structure of the novel does not present a clear dichotomy between naked truth and false appearances; ironically, it points at the moral paradox whereby naked truth asks for covering by cultural robes because human existence is impossible in a state of total exposure. The boys stranded on the island adapt themselves to the physical conditions of the island and start shedding their clothes. They become more and more naked—stripped not only of clothes but of names, duties, rights and even memories of the adult world. By stripping down to essentials, their inner "truth" is supposed to be revealed, yet they immediately start anew the process of self covering. Here unstable irony eventuates as naked truth retreats again into false appearance.

In the first chapters of the book there is constant emphasis and elaboration concerning clothing: school-sweaters, shirts and trousers, pullovers, windbreakers, belts and badges. Parallel to the exposure of their naked bodies, and the tearing off of both actual and mental clothes, they lay themselves more and more open to their savage drives.[10] Indeed the more clothed they are, the more they turn out to be vulnerable to latent, undisciplined desires. The choir boys are rather overdressed when arriving on the island. They wear robes, caps, badges and even silver crosses, and with it the "different garments they carried in their hands". When they approach, their observers "saw that the darkness was not all shadow but mostly clothing" (p. 20). It is they, the dressed-up choir boys, who discard their clothes the most rapidly and equally rapidly approach savagery. The cultural appearance turns out indeed to be a sheer screen for their true inner nature; but the latter is hardly cheering.

Moreover, the shedding of their garments does not in fact lead to the revelation of their true nature; each stage reached calls for a further retreat, and the putting on of another type of disguise: the masks which they paint on their faces which still retain the features of humanity. It is this new disguise which helps release a brutal aggression and egotism in the process of "liberation into savagery" (p. 191).

To become truly "stripped and inimical creatures" (p. 206) they have to put on masks. In order to become "liberated from shame and self consciousness" (p. 69) they must cover their nakedness. The shedding of clothes, then, calls for further covering, and one type of disguise is, ironically, exchanged for another.

Another variation on the notion that nakedness needs coverage may be noted with regard to the Sameric twins. The twins represent the average person who conforms to existing conditions and goes along with the majority. They cling to external, socially conceived morality in whatever form it takes. Their lack of inner individual integrity is suggested by their mechanical, repetitive way of speech, as well as by their frightened, wavering behaviour. The twins do not wear masks to the very end of the story. Even when they join Jack's masked majority, Ralph observes "you two are not painted" (p. 207). Yet we know that their naked faces have certain peculiarities; their profiles are blurred and seem "to be provided with not quite enough skin" (p. 20). In this case lack of coverage appears to be a sign of incomplete individuality or identity.

Naming (identity) enters the clothing-nakedness cluster as a further element. Percival's mechanical, compulsive chanting of "name-address-telephone" which he later abandons indicates that naming has no function in the new conditions, it is merely a socially determined habit, like clothing. Jack, the only boy whose family name is mentioned and who tries to hold on to it, wondering "Why should I be Jack? I am Merridew" (p. 22), is the very one who leads the others into becoming a nameless crowd of savages. Roger, who does not disguise his sadism, is described as exercising "a nameless authority" (p. 201). Names, like clothing, enter the dialectic of disguise, concealing and revealing a naked and anonymous savage truth.

Since without names social relations are impossible, names prove to be a necessary cultural emblem both of individuality and of moral responsibility. To be nameless is to be exposed to alienation and hostility. The boys killed in the crash of the airplane are anonymous, thus their death is easily ignored; the death of the little "strawberry marked" boy, although nameless, individually "marked", draws more attention and has to be "flinched away from memory" (p. 94); the death of the boy Simon, individualized by a name, causes a constant feeling of guilt. Ralph, reporting to the officer on the number of deaths, mentions "Only two"—those named Piggy and Simon—and ignores the nameless ones. The importance of naming as a mark of personal human responsibility is part of Ralph's and Piggy's attempt to organize the children into a community. The failure of this effort at naming is part of the deterioration into savagery.

The clothing-nakedness cluster is moreover linked not only to social norms and institutions, but also to the technical and scientific achievements of the adult world outside the island. When children pray for a "sign" (p. 103) from the adult world, the message comes in the form of the dead parachutist: man wrapped up in mechanical devices aimed to save him, but ironically strangling him in his own technical inventions. Simon understands this and sees in the figure "the mechanics of this parody" (p. 161), the parody of technical achievements disguising moral nakedness. The supposedly rational and institutionalized world is in reality a "civilization that was in ruins" (p. 68), in the throes of deadly warfare. Even "rescue", in the final episode of the book, appears in the form of an overdressed and amply uniformed naval officer who represents simultaneously the accepted norms of cultural order and the insignia of the war that looms in the background.

Ralph seems to be aware of the ironic contradiction involved in the nakedness-clothing antinomy. He realizes that humanity preys on itself while disguising its cannibalism in different ways, and yet he continuously longs for clothes, names and norms. He hopes at least for a temporary "pax" as a compromise. In the process of learning "to adjust his values" (p. 85), though carefully keeping his and his followers' "faces" clean, Ralph wonders about the problem of appearance and reality: "If faces were differentlit from above or below—what was a face? What was anything?" (p. 85).

The fastest reach of this cluster is the ironic or mimetic disguise of the narrative itself. The fabula as a whole sets out wearing a mask, pretending to be a novel that will describe the good life of children on an island as a microcosm of a possible human existence. In the first episode the boys express their hope to relive a literary world on their island: "Here at last was the imagined but never fully realized place leaping into real life" (p. 16). In the last episode the officer tries to convince himself that what he witnesses is "Like the Coral Island" (p. 223). The truth revealed under the literary disguise of the Ballantyne-like child Utopia is that of a sceptical, disillusioned, dystopian reality. The literary convention of the Utopian dream is exploded by a dystopian nightmare.

The second image cluster to be discussed is the sight-fire group. This cluster carries the theme of man's way of looking at the world. It seems that here, too, there is an equivocal message; on the one hand, man has the inclination and ability to bring catastrophe upon himself. On the other hand he has the potential capacity to "see" and assert the endurance of values by which the catastrophe can be understood, defined and, perhaps, confined.

The three "seeing" heroes in the novel possess different but complementary aspects of the ability to see. Piggy possesses mainly knowledge, Simon understanding, and Ralph wisdom. But each one of the above is incomplete.

Piggy, with his "flashing glasses", has a stereotyped rational approach to reality. For him "Life is scientific, that's what it is" (p. 92); he "sees" in the progressive-scientific-technical-democracy of the adult world a way of life to be imitated. His rationalistic approach to life is rigid. He does not observe changing conditions around him, but adheres stubbornly to dogmatic solutions not applicable in the here and now. Piggy's rationality is based on defective vision, on being "spectacled"—and without these "specs" he becomes completely helpless, relying solely on Ralph's more pragmatic wisdom. The theft of Piggy's glasses to kindle the fire is, ironically, reminiscent of the Promethean theft of fire (p. 161).

Simon is the boy with "eyes so bright" (p. 60); he possesses visionary insight and empathy, as his "gaze was held by that ancient, inescapable recognition" (p. 152). He is the one who sees and understands the essence of the ***Lord of the Flies,*** but his message is not recognized or accepted by others. He is considered "queer" and "funny" and, ironically, is himself mistaken twice for a beast and eventually serves as a scapegoat for others' inner fears. Simon, who understands the meaningful undercurrent of human activity, has neither the ability to communicate his understanding nor the power to bring about change.

Ralph can neither "see" like Simon nor is his vision as rational as Piggy's. He is aware of his cognitive limitations, knowing that he "can't think, not like Piggy" (p. 85). Yet his way of seeing is intelligent, observant and flexible. Seeing teaches him that man is capable of losing his essential humanity and may revert to his beastlike nature.

All three "seers" blunder when the complexity of experience becomes too overwhelming. Piggy loses his life when the reality of the hunters destroys his "specs" as well as himself. Simon is wrongly taken for a beast and killed while trying to transmit his vision about the nature of the beast. Ralph, being a leader, confronts the divergence between seeing and doing. He constantly tries to apply his value system to circumstances but he finds "himself understanding the wearisomeness of this life, where every path was an improvisation and a considerable part of one's waking life was spent watching one's feet" (p. 83). His effort to close the gap between values and the demands of survival causes a growing fear of insanity.[11] Ralph "dreads the curtain" (p. 217) that foils his ability to comprehend the difference between good and bad. Thus the three "seeing" figures are all restricted in their vision and in their ability to interpret the phenomena of human existence. They are, as Ralph ironically summarizes: "Three blind mice" (p. 101).

The sight image is complexly clustered with the fire image. Fire, in its Promethean dimension, is the symbol of culture and rationality; it is also a natural and pragmatic source of light and heat; but here it also symbolises, dialectically, the volcanic animalism in human nature. Piggy and Ralph constantly urge that the fire be watched and preserved for their eventual "rescue" to civilization, even if this means giving up immediate gratification. Jack and the hunters, on the other hand, use the fire for hedonistic, morally myopic purposes.

The covert contradiction inherent in the image of fire as both a spiritual and poetical value creates irony. Ralph acknowledges the benefits of the material use of fire and is aware of its "double function" (p. 179), but the short range pleasure derived from fire almost makes him abandon its long range spiritual value for "rescue" and forget that there is "Something overwhelmingly good about it" (p. 180). But fire becomes simply an instrument of destruction when used by Jack and his followers.

The unstable many-sidedness and ambivalence of the sight-fire cluster becomes clear in the episodes when the "fire-smoke-rescue" sign gets out of bounds. In the first episodes the guards of the fire are diverted from their task by their hunting impulses and the fire either gets out of control, devouring the fruits of the island, or they let the fire die out, so that the passing ship does not see the rescue sign. In the last episode they indulge in the man-hunt and set fire to the island but, ironically, this is the way that leads to the rescue. This places man's ability to "see" the way to being rescued in doubt, just as the clothing-nakedness cluster threw doubt upon the regenerate nature of man.

The major theme carrier in the novel is the third, the beast-man cluster. The imagery concretizes and focuses the problem "What are we? Humans? Or animals? Or savages?" (p. 99). The cluster progresses from the perception of similarity between man and animals, to a projection of animal qualities onto himself, to a process of increasing identification between man and beast, till the final human-beast equation.

In the first part of the novel, in which the boys still make an effort to comply with their cultural inheritance, the bestial side of human nature only lurks below the surface. Recurrent animal similes are used to signify mainly some outward physical similarity between beast and man: human shadows are "bat like" (p. 20), the boys are moving "insect-like" (p. 31) or "ape-like" (p. 53), panting "like dogs" (p. 46) and resting "like cows" (p. 58). As the boys reel into bestiality these types of simile almost disappear and the beast is recognized to be within. Animality is what emerges from under the surface, behind the coverings and disguises.

This process develops by stages. At first the slogan "We want meat" expresses simply a desire to satisfy human hunger and even the Lotus eaters are not immune to this craving. The animal is still related to as a means of physical gratification. The next stage already involves a calling forth of the inner "Beastie". This emerges when they indulge in the memories and the knowledge "that had come to them when they closed in on the struggling pig, knowledge that they had outwitted a living thing, imposed their will upon it, taken away its life like a long satisfying drink" (p. 76). The hunting and killing of animals becomes much more effectively intensified as aggressive and erotic emotions are projected on the animal: "the sow collapsed under them and they were heavy and fulfilled upon her" (p. 149). When they offer the sow's head as a gift for the "Beastie" the animal has ceased to be an instrument, and animality has become an end in itself. The climax of identification with bestiality is Simon's scapegoatlike sacrifice. Here their regressive drives, unconscious fears and subdued guilt feelings find an outlet on a human being whom they consider as "the beast disguised" (p. 177). Piggy's seemingly contradictory statement that "I know there isn't no beast—not with claws and all that, I mean, but I know there isn't no fear either" (p. 92) is ironically contradicted and affirmed at once as in the ritual killing of Simon, the illusory Beast, as he ". . . leaped on the beast, screamed, struck, bit, tore. There were no words, and no movements but the tearing of teeth and claws" (p. 168).

The inquiry the novel conducts into the nature of man is symbolically revealed in the image-progress which leads finally to that equation of man-beast which is epitomized in the paradigmatic ***Lord of the Flies.*** It is when their vision has penetrated beyond its veils that the direction is reversed. The supposed "Beastie" turns toward the boys and as "the creature lifted its head holding towards them the ruin of a face" (p. 136) they realize, ironically, that the beast is really a man. The equation seems to be complete: it now encompasses both the man-animal and animal-man relationship. As they succumb to their primitivism, the feared animal turns out to be themselves. The supposedly hierarchic moral order which differentiates between man and animal is catastrophically collapsed.

But the equation is not complete. Man's nature is subject to violation and apparently conquerable by chaos, yet ultimately able to understand and reassert itself. Behind the ritual scapegoating there is the figure of Simon, the compassionate "seer", the one who releases the body of the parachutist from its pathetic bondage. Simon "sees" the truth about the beast and heroically tries to deliver his message to the others. "What else is there to do?" (p. 160). The two heroic human figures, the parachutist and Simon, are those that are, ironically, constantly seen by the others as beasts. Both are unable to communicate their identity, but by their unsuccessful effort, reveal the human situation as at once "sick" and "heroic".

The three main image clusters of the novel thus reflect the irony that evolves from man's limited capacity to see through disguises and to fully recognize the ambivalence of the human situation. Ironic transformations in all three imagery clusters intimate the limitations of man's vision and the instability of his moral nature.

There are obviously many links between the internal metaphoric sources of irony and the external or circumstantial sources. Yet, it may perhaps be added that Booth's variable of "covertness" (p. 6) on which the clothing-nakedness cluster is based, is an ironic play-factor mainly referring to *The Coral Island.* The variable of "instability" (pp. 240-241) to be found in the sight-fire cluster shares its playground mainly with the rational-social Utopia, while the variable of "infiniteness" (pp. 253-277) exemplified in the man-animal cluster, the scope of which is no less than the coexistence in nature of good and evil, ironically plays with the hedonistic land of Cockaigne or Fools' Paradise notion.

In spite of its epistemological scepticism and its powerful realization of human depravity, the novel seems nevertheless to offer an affirmation of values. Although "the rescue" is dubious, return to adult culture is the only possibility for man who may become mature enough to grasp and use it, as Ralph hopefully will. Ralph, after his arduous experience, learns and expresses this message. Though rescued, Ralph knows that the tension between the human and the bestial cannot be resolved—and so he "wept for the end of innocence, the darkness of man's heart" (p. 223). Ralph's reflection echoes a typical twentieth century existentialist irony, which views moral problems as indeterminate if not insoluble and yet amenable to nothing other than this recognition itself.

Notes

1. Beda Allemann, *Ironie und Dichtung* (Stuttgart: Neske, 1956), pp. 1-35.
2. Görar Hermenen, "Intention and Interpretation in Literary Criticism", *New Literary History,* 7 (1975), p. 75.
3. For a comparison between the two works see Stephen Medcalf, *William Golding* (London: Longmans, 1975) and Carl Niemeyer, "The Coral Island Revisited", *College English,* XXII (1961), pp. 241-245.
4. Darko Suvin, "Defining the Literary Genre of Utopia: Some Historical Semantics, Some Genology, A Proposal and a Plea", *Studies in the Literary Imagination,* 6 (1973), pp. 121-145.
5. Northrop Frye, "Varieties of Literary Utopias" *Daedalus* 94 (1965), p. 223-247.
6. For the development of the "Wild Man" image in western civilization and literature see Hayden White, "The Forms of Wildness: Archaeology of an Idea" *The Wild Man Within,* eds. E. Dudley and M.E. Novak (Pittsburgh; University of Pittsburgh Press, 1972), p. 298 (passim).

7. Wayne C. Booth, *A Rhetoric of Irony* (Chicago and London: University of Chicago Press, 1974), p. 22.

8. For archetypal aspects of these symbols see Carl G. Jung, *Symbols der Wandlung* (Zürich: Rascher, 1952), pp. 297, 567 ("pig"); pp. 300, 452, 728-729 ("animal"); pp. 40-41, 182, 222, 737 ("fire") and *Man and his Symbols* (London: Aldus Books, 1964), pp. 45, 236-238 ("masks"); p. 207 ("Animals" as symbol of self); pp. 282-283 ("pig"); p. 78 ("fire"). See also: J.E. Cirlot, *A Dictionary of Symbols* (London: Routledge & Kegan Paul, 1971) and Roy Willis, *Man and Beast* (New York: Basic Books, 1974).

9. A discussion of the symbolism in *Lord of the Flies* from a philosophical point of view can be found in Ralph Freedman, "The New Realism: The Fancy of William Golding", *Perspective* 10 (1958), pp. 118-128.

10. For the mimetic aspect of "clothing" see Mark Kinkead—Weekes and Jan Gregor, *William Golding* (London: Faber, 1967), pp. 15-67.

11. This probing of the limits of Human endurance facing moral disintegration is reminiscent of *King Lear.* The three discussed image clusters of fire/sight, clothing and man/animal also appear in *King Lear.* The range and depth of the poetic vision of the two works is very different, yet the recurrent imagery shows some similarity between the two works. John Peter, "The Fables of William Golding", *Kenyon Review,* Vol. XIX (1957), pp. 577-592. mentions Golding's references to *King Lear,* both explicit and implicit, in his novel *Pincher Martin.*

Bernard F. Dick (essay date 1987)

SOURCE: Dick, Bernard F. "The Anarchy Within." In *William Golding,* pp. 6-29. Boston: Twayne Publishers, 1987.

[*In the following essay, Dick provides a analysis of the novel including its place in Golding's body of work, the influence of on him of Euripides* Bacchae *and R. M. Ballantyne's* The Coral Island, *and status of* Lord of the Flies *as a modern classic.*]

Barefoot Boys

In 1857 Ballantyne published *The Coral Island,* something of a children's classic in England, in which three boys are shipwrecked on an unidentified Pacific island—Ralph Rover, the fifteen-year-old narrator; Jack Martin, "a tall, strapping broad-shouldered youth of eighteen, with a handsome, good-humoured, firm face"; and Peterkin Gay, "little, quick, funny, decidedly mischievous, and about fourteen years old."[1] The lads live in "uninterrupted harmony and happiness," presumably without the aftereffects of original sin, although faint, post-lapsarian rumblings can be heard in some of their activities, especially in Peterkin's butchery of an old sow to get leather for "future" shoes. These intimations of mortality are muted, however, since Victorian schoolboys do not kill for pleasure. Cannibals are also encountered, but heathen bloodletting can be overlooked. At the end of the novel, just as the boys think they will be devoured by savages, they are released into the hands of their deus-ex-machina teacher who announces that "through the great goodness of God you are free!" (310). The natives embrace Christianity, and all is well.

To a generation that has witnessed two world wars, Ballantyne's resolution is laughable. One is tempted to repeat Judge Brack's feeble reaction to Hedda Gabbler's suicide, "People don't do things like that," and to consign *The Coral Island* to the bedtime reading of the very young, the very old, or historians of ideas.

Golding clearly intended ***Lord of the Flies*** (1954) as a realist's answer to *The Coral Island:* "You see, really, I'm getting at myself in this [novel]. What I'm saying to myself is, 'Don't be such a fool, you remember when you were a boy, a small boy, how you lived on that island with Ralph and Jack and Peterkin. . . . Now you are grown up, you are adult; it's taken you a long time to become adult, but now you've got there you can see that people are not like that; they would not behave like that if . . . they went to an island like that."[2]

Golding's protagonists are also named Ralph and Jack; Peterkin becomes the overweight Piggy. Simon is an independent creation, although Golding for some unknown reason has claimed that Simon was inspired by Peterkin, perhaps meaning that the name of Peterkin evoked that of Simon Peter of the New Testament—two names deriving from one. Along with an indeterminate number of other boys ranging in age from six to twelve, they are abandoned on a South Sea island after being evacuated from Britain during a nuclear war. Like the Ballantyne trio, they also hunt pigs; but none of the Victorian boys would ever have sodomized the animal with a spear, since sexual defilement is apparently a vice peculiar to the post-Ballantyne age. Moreover, there is no "uninterrupted harmony and happiness" on Golding's coral island; the rules that Ralph thought would transform the motley group into a model utopia are irrevocably broken when the desire to hunt supersedes the need for a continually burning fire, shelter, and sanitation. The hunters don war paint, killing or absorbing all the others except Ralph who, in his refusal to revert to savagery, becomes a pariah, and is hunted down and smoked out of hiding. Fortunately, a navy cruiser spots the smoke, and Ralph and the remnants of the group are rescued after their initiation into adulthood.

Lord of the Flies introduces a structural principle that has become Golding's hallmark—a polarity expressed in terms of a moral tension: the rational (fire-watchers) pitted against the irrational (hunters) in ***Lord of the Flies***; one species destroyed and supplanted by another that is supposedly fitter (***The Inheritors***); fallen humanity defying God (***Pincher Martin***); science at odds with humanism (***Free Fall***); the vision versus the reality (***The Spire***); the mystic juxtaposed with the nihilist (***Darkness Visible***); the classical sensibility giving way to the romantic (***Rites of Passage***); the creative writer pursued by the academic hack (***The Paper Men***).

Although the polarity is moral, the resolution is literary. Golding expresses his moral vision through traditional literary themes (odyssey, quest, journey to self-knowledge) and characters (castaways, overreachers, repressed clergymen, writer-celebrities), incorporating them into a narrative that ends conventionally (rescue, fulfillment, death, *anagnorisis*), if disturbingly. In ***Lord of the Flies*** Golding starts from what might be called the "island premise." All island literature is essentially similar in the sense that castaways can live either in harmony or anarchy. And like all drama, island literature is potentially tragic or comic, depending upon the author's vision. The "abandoned child" theme can produce Sophocles' *Oedipus the King* or Oscar Wilde's *Importance of Being Earnest;* the theme of the individual challenging authority can result in Sophocles' *Antigone* or Garson Kanin's *Born Yesterday;* each, whether tragedy or comedy, is a valid elaboration of an archetypal situation. Since there is tragic potential in the comic, and seeds of comedy in the tragic, it is the author who determines the outcome. Ballantyne chose order; Golding chaos.

Island literature usually depicts three types of characters—children (*The Coral Island*), adults (*Robinson Crusoe*), or a combination (*The Swiss Family Robinson*). Following his source, Golding adheres to the first. As a novelist, he must offer some explanation for the absence of adults: "He [the pilot] must have flown off after he dropped us."[3] Thus far there is nothing unique about the situation except for the peculiarly modern use of a nuclear war to account for the evacuation.

The next events follow directly from the island premise. Piggy discovers a seashell ("the conch"), which Ralph uses as a trumpet to summon the others who are dispersed throughout the island. Last to appear is "something dark"; the amorphous blackness becomes an "it," then a "creature," and finally a party of boys—Jack Merridew and his choir. Jack immediately reveals his impatience with talk, asserting his claim to be chief because he was chapter chorister. It is Ralph, however, who wins, and the society splits into two halves: the fire-watchers and the choir turned hunters. From this point on, the plot can take only one course. Golding has imposed his own template on *The Coral Island,* and the lines zigzag, refusing to coincide with Ballantyne's.

The factionalized society in ***Lord of the Flies*** is not so much a case of antithesis as of polarization. Ralph seems to be the hero, although a close reading can prove otherwise. At the beginning, however, he has heroic potential. Ralph is fair-haired, with "a mildness . . . that proclaimed no devil." Jack, on the other hand, is satanic; his hair is red (a color often associated with Old Nick), he is dressed in black, and his eyes stare ahead. Furthermore, he is ugly and prone to anger. Jack is hardly the "handsome, good-humoured" lad he was in his Victorian incarnation.

An unspoken animosity stemming from their opposite natures arises between the two boys; it manifests itself in impatience, angry outbursts followed by sullen silence, and occasional attempts at coalescence. But these are only temporary solutions to an antagonism so ancient that neither Ralph nor Jack can fathom it. Later, Ralph asks the inevitable question "Why do you hate me?" There is no answer; there can be none with adolescents who do not realize they are embodiments of forces they do not understand, much less can name. Having read neither the Greeks nor Nietzsche, they do not know they are the embodiments of the Apollonian and the Dionysian, respectively.

Two Worlds, Two Wisdoms

During his self-imposed exile from contemporary life, Golding immersed himself in Greek literature, devoting a considerable amount of time to studying

E. R. Dodds's edition of Euripides' *Bacchae*.[4] The *Bacchae* is a landmark of Greek tragedy; to paraphrase Pope, to know the *Bacchae* is to know the Greeks; and to know it in Dodds's edition with its detailed introduction and exhaustive notes is to know it as thoroughly as any contemporary can.

The *Bacchae,* probably Euripides' last play and the most complex of the Greek tragedies, dramatizes the impact of the worship of Dionysus on the city of Thebes. To the ancient Greeks, Dionysus was the god of animal potency, the mythological incarnation of the life principle; it was Dionysus who gave life to plant, animal, and human. He could inspire his votaries to frenzy, perhaps even to human sacrifice. Dionysus symbolizes the elemental in animal and human nature; as such, he cannot be ignored, for to inhibit emotional expression is to deny humankind a natural form of worship. Dionysus can be gentle when he is propitiated, but when he is rejected, he exacts a terrible vengeance. His opposite is Apollo, who personifies the civilizing arts—healing, poetry, music, law, and order. Identified with light, he illuminates rather than beclouds the mind.

In *The Birth of Tragedy out of the Spirit of Music,* Friedrich Nietzsche made his famous distinction between the Apollonian and the Dionysian, attributing all art to the tension and interplay between these forces. Initially, Apollo and Dionysus are at odds with each other; Apollo represents the god in humankind, Dionysus the brute. Apollo favors the individual; Dionysus appeals to the group. Apollo invites us to enter a dream world, like Homer's Olympus, where we can find refuge from reality. Dionysus, on the other hand, pulls away the veil of illusion, revealing the world as it is in all its savagery. Ultimately, the Apollonian manages to master the Dionysian so that art is able to assume some form and order; yet at the center of all great art is Dionysian wisdom, knowledge bred of suffering. At the beginning of *The Birth of Tragedy,* Nietzsche tries to be impartial, yet it is obvious that he favors the Dionysian; without the Dionysian, real art, tragic art (to Nietzsche, the highest form) is impossible. While no art form is exclusively Apollonian or Dionysian, Nietzsche considers some predominately Apollonian (epic, painting, sculpture, pre-Wagnerian opera) and others largely Dionysian (music, lyric poetry, tragedy, Wagnerian opera). He concedes that in tragedy Apollo provides the form, but it is Dionysus who provides the content.

Lord of the Flies can be read in the light of the Apollonian-Dionysian dichotomy. In fact, this interpretation has been standard ever since Golding declared his debt to Greek tragedy, especially to the *Bacchae,* in which Euripides immortalized the age-old conflict between mind and heart, reason and emotion, showing that the way up and down is not the same, as Heraclitus believed, but rather that both paths must continually cross without superseding each other.[5] In the *Bacchae,* Pentheus, king of Thebes, is rooted in a frigid intellectualism that does not allow for the irrational. When the worship of Dionysus sweeps through the country, claiming Pentheus's mother, Agave, and the high priest Teiresias as followers (not to mention Cadmus, the city's founder), Pentheus is still unyielding; he refuses to acknowledge the new religion, even though Cadmus and Teiresias caution him that he must at least give it a hearing. Dionysus himself warns Pentheus; in a startling scene the god appears before him as a bull, one of the animal forms in which Dionysus was worshiped. Pentheus can only gape at the metamorphosis, unaware that he is in the presence of the god he is persecuting. When Dionysus induces Pentheus to observe the Bacchants at worship, he suggests that Pentheus wear women's clothes to escape detection. It is a logical suggestion; Dionysus's chief votaries are women, and male worshipers are expected to wear the fawnskin and carry the ivy-garlanded *thyrsus.* At the height of the ritual, Dionysus reveals the presence of Pentheus, who is observing from high up in a fir tree. Goaded by a frenzy that makes them oblivious to moral laws, the women hunt him down and dismember him. Triumphant, Agave, still under the Dionysian influence and thinking that she holds the head of a lion (another of Dionysus's sacred animals), appears with her son's head on a *thyrsus.* Although there is a break in the text at verse 1329, it is clear from the plot summary attached to certain manuscripts and from the final scene, that Dionysus appeared at the end of the play and banished Agave from her native Thebes.

Both ***Lord of the Flies*** and the *Bacchae* portray a bipolar society in which the Apollonian refuses or is unable to assimilate the Dionysian. Just as Pentheus's refusal to admit Dionysian worship polarizes Thebes, Ralph's inability to understand the hunters, whose Dionysian character is underscored by their being black-clad choristers, polarizes the island. Both drama and novel contain three interrelated ritual themes: the cult of a beast-god, a hunt as prefiguration of the death of a scapegoat-figure, and the dismemberment of the scapegoat. Golding deviates from Euripides in only one respect. Logically, Ralph, the Pentheus figure, should be the scapegoat; but Golding assigns this role to Simon, one of the choristers, who has clairvoyant powers. Ralph is allowed to live with his newfound knowledge of "the darkness of man's heart." Otherwise Golding has adhered to the ritual pattern of *agon* or struggle between king and rival (Pentheus and Dionysus, Ralph and Jack), *pathos* or suffering (Pentheus, Ralph), and *sparagmos* or dismemberment (Pentheus, Simon, replacing Ralph, as scapegoat).

The Boy Bacchants

Euripides depicts a Dionysus who retains the original characteristics of a beast deity incarnate in the form of bulls, lions, wild goats, and fawns. Since these animals were regarded as habitations of the god, they were often torn apart by the Bacchants, who would eat their flesh to achieve communion with Dionysus. As human and animal, Dionysus is both hunter and hunted. Thus beast-hunt imagery pervades the *Bacchae* (verses 101, 137, 436, 920, 1017, 1188 ff.). In ***Lord of the Flies*** the obsession with the hunt transforms the hunters into a group that functions conjointly but without personal identity; they had "the throb and stamp of a single organism." Their choral refrain "*Kill the beast! Cut his throat! Spill his blood!*" suggests the "hunt, kill, prey" of the *Bacchae.* In the drama, Pentheus's death is prefigured by the Bacchants' attack on a herd of cattle that they dismember. In ***Lord of the Flies*** the wanton killing of a sow prefigures the death of Simon. The sow's head is impaled on a stick (a reminiscence of Pentheus's head on the *thyrsus*) and is offered as a trophy to the imaginary beast the boys believe is lurking on the island. When Simon accidentally interrupts the reenactment of the pig hunt, he is mistaken for the beast and killed; when the Bacchants spot Pentheus in the fir tree, they drag him down under the delusion that he is the beast and then dismember him.

Both Pentheus and Simon are pitted against elemental forces that are their direct opposites. Pentheus alone sees Dionysus in animal shape, but he can neither recognize the god nor understand that his own intellectualism must be complemented by irrational yet necessary passions. Only Simon hears the cynical message of the "Lord of the Flies," the spirit of evil personified by the pig's head, assuring Simon that "everything was a bad business." Although Simon is an epileptic whom even Ralph considers "cracked" and whose seizures annoy Jack, he could have explained to the group—had he lived—about a natural proclivity to evil that can subvert harmony and order. Pentheus dies ignorant of his nature and that of humankind; Simon dies with a knowledge that he can never articulate.

Another point of similarity between Euripides and Golding is the deus-ex-machina ending of both works. At the end of the *Bacchae,* Dionysus appears to foretell the fortunes of all. A more human epiphany occurs at the end of the novel when a naval officer comes to the rescue, thereby resolving the action. In view of the previous bloodshed, however, Golding's ending is as ironic as Euripides'; it is also less obvious. Euripides' ending is a deus ex machina in the literal sense of the god's descending from a crane, but not in the conventional sense of outside intervention in order to resolve the plot. In the *Poetics,* Aristotle allowed for such an ending if the action could not be resolved in any other way. The *Bacchae,* however, does not involve outside intervention because Dionysus is not outside the action; he is very much a part of it. In fact, he is a character in his own play. The naval officer is external to the action; he is a deus ex machina like Heracles in Sophocles' *Philoctetes* or Apollo in Euripides' *Orestes,* neither of whom appears until the end.

In *Philoctetes* and *Orestes,* mortals have allowed the action to get so out of hand that divine intervention is necessary. But so have the boys in ***Lord of the Flies;*** hence the "god from the machine." Although Golding called his own ending a "gimmick,"[6] thus introducing a word that would plague him, his "gimmick" is certainly as legitimate as the one in Bertolt Brecht's *Three Penny Opera,* in which the Victorious Messenger arrives just in time to save Macheath from the gallows, although in Brecht's play the audience is warned that real-life messengers are rare.

Like Brecht, Golding has a reason for using an ex-machina ending. First, he wishes to parody Ballantyne's ending of *The Coral Island,* which is true gimmickry; second, he wishes to capture the uneasiness the Greeks must have felt in watching the *Bacchae* when that play, which was unfolding logically, suddenly took its irrational turn. Readers disturbed by Golding's ending might find comfort in knowing that the Greeks found Euripides' sense of denouement equally discomfiting: "I have always felt that the Athenians must have been deeply shocked by the *deus ex machina.* Here they had been watching a play with a beginning, a middle, and instead of an ending, one has a god coming down resolving everything."[7]

A Dionysian Is Made As Well As Born

Among the many instances of Golding's debt to Euripides is his reproduction of the Dionysian-Apollonian *agon* which, like that in the *Bacchae,* is depicted as a clash not so much of wills as of extremes. The *Bacchae* is an account of a Dionysian worship whose excesses are seen not as the result of ecstasy or orgiastic ritual but as a reaction to Apollonian intolerance. In the prologue, Dionysus makes it clear that he is punishing Thebes for growing so enlightened (no doubt because of Pentheus's rationalism) that it has denied his divinity by refusing to recognize his mother, Semele, as Zeus's consort. To vindicate his godhead as well as his mother's honor, Dionysus adopts a course of action—mass conversion—that will leave no doubt as to his parentage.

Although Dionysus is an alien god whose worship began in Asia Minor before spreading to Greece, he insists on his due. So does Jack Merridew in ***Lord of the Flies,*** and precisely because he comes from an alien tradition. What sets Jack apart from the others is his educational background: Jack comes from a cathedral school where he was a prefect and probably a scholarship student, which his being chapter chorister seems to suggest. Just as the Bacchants had their distinctive attire (fawnskin, *thyrsus*), Jack and his choristers wear black caps with silver badges and black cloaks emblazoned with silver crosses. Since Jack considers himself unique, he demands to be chief, claiming among his other attributes that he can sing C-sharp. Thus he appears to be a true son of Dionysus, who favored song over speech. Unlike the others who use first names, Jack introduces himself by his last name, thus disassociating himself from Apollonian individuation in favor of Dionysian group identity.

Like Euripides, Golding implies that a moderate Dionysianism can be beneficial to society while an immoderate Apollonianism can be fatal. Ralph is an incipient Pentheus, rational but immature. Pentheus ridicules Dionysus for his long hair, which he cuts to make the god conform to the Greek ideal of manhood. While Pentheus's immaturity is that of a book-burner and witch-hunter, Ralph's is that of an adolescent. Ralph squeals with glee and turns somersaults; he calls his friend, whose real name he never attempts to learn, "Piggy," although he knows how much the boy hates it. Both Pentheus and Ralph are obsessed with what is "good"; Ralph applies the term to almost everything including the island ("it's a good island"). Since Ralph claims to possess "the good," he can legislate for those who lack it. While both Pentheus and Ralph claim to be natural rulers, neither offers much proof of leadership. Dionysus does all but admit who he is to Pentheus, even causing an earthquake and staging a prison escape; still, Pentheus does not recognize him. Ralph thinks he is on an island; Piggy knows he is on one. Ralph has no idea what the conch is; he thinks it is a stone. Piggy corrects him and shows him how to use it. Had Piggy been slimmer and not afflicted with asthma and myopia, he might have been elected chief.

Initially, Jack seems far more qualified to govern than Ralph. First, he is more logical. He does not "think" he is on an island; he tries to determine whether the place on which he has landed is completely surrounded by water. When Ralph wonders if the tracks on the island were made by humans, Jack must tell him they were made by animals. Jack is just as concerned about being rescued as Ralph; he also agrees on the need for rules. When Ralph proposes they build a fire to attract any ships that might be in the vicinity, Jack shouts approval. Yet neither Ralph nor Jack knows how to make a fire; each is embarrassed at being unable to provide what the situation requires. At least Jack does not ask if anyone has a match, as Ralph does. Jack also knows how a fire can be started: by using Piggy's specs as a burning glass.

By having Jack discover how to create fire, Golding deepens the nature of the *agon:* it is not only a clash between the Apollonian and the Dionysian but between the true and the false Prometheus. Jack, not Ralph, is the real Prometheus, the true fire-bearer. The dark god becomes the culture hero. The mythic inversion is ingenious, especially if one remembers that "Prometheus" literally means "Forethought."

A similar inversion occurs in the case of Piggy's glasses. On one level, the glasses are a symbol of political insight. As an inadequate leader, Ralph depends on Piggy's judgment. Like the other relationships in the novel, theirs also is paradoxical. Ralph must "see" through eyes that themselves need corrective lenses. Although Piggy's vision is imperfect, even with glasses, it is all Ralph has. While the lenses remain intact, Ralph can at least go through the motions of statesmanship; but the smashing of one of the lenses diminishes Piggy's effectiveness, and the theft of the other by the hunters renders Piggy useless and Ralph helpless.

On another, equally complex level, the glasses are a means of creating fire to which Ralph assigns an Apollonian function: rescue/reason, in the sense that reason must prevail if rescue is to come. Jack takes a more pragmatic view of fire; while he is the first to agree that rules are necessary and is willing to have part of the choir act as fire-watchers, he also regards fire as a means of roasting meat. Ralph seems oblivious to the cooking properties of fire; he would have everyone eat fruit, with an occasional crab, even though fruit causes diarrhea. Yet even Ralph succumbs to the temptation: twice he eats the meat that the hunters have cooked. When Ralph castigates the others for defecting because they wanted meat, Jack must remind him that he has a bone in his hand. The Dionysian can be even more perceptive than the Apollonian.

In Golding's fiction, just when one meaning seems to have been established, another arises to compete with it; just as one paradox is resolved, another takes its place; just as the ultimate irony seems to have been reached, it is no longer ultimate. For example, if fire symbolizes civilization, as well as the means of returning to it, rescue is in vain because civilization is in the process of being destroyed. Moreover, fire may be an Apollonian symbol of rescue, but a Dionysian has made rescue possible by using fire to smoke Ralph out of hiding, thereby accomplishing what Ralph could not: to attract a passing ship. Perhaps the most ironic aspect of fire is that it is not a "small" Apollonian fire, the kind Piggy wanted, that effects the rescue; and it is not the fire on the mountain that Ralph wanted (and that, under the circumstances, would have been futile). It is a vast Dionysian fire, one that sets the jungle ablaze; only a fire raging out of control could generate enough smoke to attract attention.

Self-multiplying ambivalence is the way Golding has chosen to illustrate his theory of evil. Although evil is indigenous to the species and impervious even to the waters of baptism, it remains dormant until the right set of circumstances activates it. Just when one thinks reason will prevent evil from occurring, reason breaks down because those supposedly endowed with it either fail to exercise it or are not as rational as they seemed to be. Yet Golding is not really a fatalist, much less a Calvinist or an exponent of the Heidelberg Catechism. Fate and free will coexist in his universe. Evil is bound to erupt, but it requires, like T. S. Eliot's objective correlative, an event or a situation to precipitate it; a situation that humans cause themselves and for which there is a human explanation.

The crucial event in ***Lord of the Flies*** is not Jack's losing the election; that would be too easy. Jack's defeat did not turn him from a potential Apollonian into an incorrigible Dionysian. Jack lost the election because his manner alienated the others, who perceived him as a martinet or as a prefect who might bully them as their prefects had in school. They thought that Jack would also call them by their surnames as their teachers did. Ralph is less threatening; he can sound like an adult yet act like a child, insisting on rules as well as on having fun.

Interestingly, Jack is gracious in defeat; he is even cooperative. In a rare moment of magnanimity, Ralph asks Jack what role he wants to play in the newly formed society. Jack immediately chooses the role of hunter for himself and the choir; it is a wise decision since the boys need something to eat besides fruit. Jack sees an opportunity for himself and his choir to perform a meaningful function: they will kill pigs and provide the community with meat. What Jack does not know, however, is that Ralph regards the hunter as an inferior. Although Ralph has given Jack his choice of role, he determines how Jack will play it. By downgrading the hunter, Ralph exalts himself, thereby becoming a Pentheus and forcing the choir to become Dionysians.

Learning the Part

Becoming a Dionysian is a gradual process. There are times when the Dionysian seems so accommodating that coalescence appears possible. Ralph and Jack smile at each other when Ralph asks Jack his preference; they smile at each other again while gathering wood. But smiles are deceptive as well as evanescent. Ralph smiles at Simon when the latter predicts his rescue, but it is the smile of one whose spirits have been elevated. That the one who elevated them is "cracked" is irrelevant. There are also moments when some of the Dionysian rubs off on the Apollonian. After his encounter with a charging boar, Ralph participates in the reenactment of the incident, becoming so caught up in the drama that "the desire to squeeze and hurt was over-mastering" (142). Jack and Ralph are doubles, a favorite Golding device in which one character is the reverse of the other and the extreme opposite in terms of qualities. What they have in common is a plan for survival and an ability to take control of a situation, although in both respects Jack has an edge on Ralph. What causes the rift between them, and what widens the rift into an abyss, is Ralph's monolithic view of fire, which adumbrates his relationship with Jack. By limiting the function of fire to rescue and by regarding it as a panacea, Ralph excludes all other possibilities for its use. When Jack tries to tell Ralph about the dark urges he experiences while hunting, Ralph admonishes him not to forget the fire; "You and your fire!" is Jack's frustrated retort.

Gradually, ineluctably, Ralph is turning Jack into a Dionysian. Although Jack chooses the role of hunter, Ralph makes him live the part, not realizing that the myth requires the hunter also to be the hunted; just as the hunter stalks his prey, Dionysus stalks the hunter. Jack tries to explain this paradox to Ralph, who is too preoccupied with the fire to care: "'If you're hunting sometimes you catch yourself feeling as if—' He [Jack] flushed suddenly. 'There's nothing in it of course. Just a feeling. But you can feel as if you're not hunting, but—being hunted; as if something's behind you all the time in the jungle. . . . Ralph looked at him critically through his tangle of fair hair. 'So long as you and your hunters remember the fire—'" (67-68).

The hunter is a role Jack can play, although he must grow into it; he is not typecast. The first time Jack sees a pig, he is unable to kill it. Since Ralph is both director and writer of his utopian scenario, he criticizes Jack's performance: "You should stick a pig. . . . They always talk about sticking a pig." As the son of a naval commander, Ralph apparently heard about pig-sticking in colonial India. Pig-sticking was the equivalent of bear-baiting, if one is to believe Noel Coward, who, in one of his songs, told of the Briton who "took to pig-sticking / in quite the wrong way." Barry England dramatized the wrong way in his drama *Conduct Unbecoming,* in which a group of officers, for whom pig-sticking was sublimi-nated sodomy, attempted the same with a woman.

A pig is slain in ***Lord of the Flies;*** it is also sodomized with a pointed stick. Again, and this is something that can only be appreciated in retrospect, Golding is implying that anyone can take to pig-sticking in the wrong way. Even the British empire has its dark side, which is suddenly, and tragically, illuminated when one of the boys calls for the sow's degradation: "Right up her ass!" (168).

As repellent as the incident is, it is still a scene in a drama that originated with Ralph, except now the plot has gotten out of hand. None of the boys is a natural pig-sticker any more than a natural murderer. If there is a defect in the species, in the fullness of time and under the proper circumstances, it will be revealed. Golding is quite clear on this point; he is not caught on the horns of the nature-versus-nurture dilemma, because he believes that nature is defective, and therefore everything associated with it, including its institutions, is defective also. Within the child are the seeds of evil that will eventually flower.

In ***Lord of the Flies,*** however, it is a child who waters the dark bloom and brings another's evil to blossom. Although Jack chose the role of hunter, Ralph specifies how he will play it: as Dionysian hunter. That particular role is foreign to Jack; he must rehearse it. Jack goes down on all fours, "his nose only a few inches from the humid earth" (61). He practices crouching, slithering, crawling; yet still he has not learned the part. What forces him to master the role and then play it to the hilt is Ralph's refusal to forgive him and the hunters for letting the fire go out. Ralph, on the other hand, cannot master his role because it is beyond his capabilities; he might be the president of a school club but not the governor of an island. Ralph could possibly command a ship, like his father; but an island is not a ship, only a microcosmic ship of state, of which Ralph proves a poor captain.

Ralph also does not seem to like his role. In a telling moment, when both boys are on the verge of speaking openly, Ralph blurts out: "You want to hunt! While I—" (69). Ralph is insecure in his part, and the reason, Golding intimates, is that he is neither qualified for, nor suited to, it. It is also a role for which his class has not prepared him.

Class Consciousness on Coral Island

Golding has often remarked that, among other things, ***Lord of the Flies*** is about British society and particularly about class structure.[8] Like other interpretations, this one must be extricated from a narrative that has been skillfully woven. Although Golding tells the reader virtually nothing about most of the boys, he does provide—comparatively, at least—a good deal of background information about Ralph. We know, for instance, that he was a naval officer's son; Jack's parentage, on the other hand, is unknown. In a significant and usually ignored episode in chapter 7, Ralph dreams about the Dartmoor cottage where he lived with his parents. The cottage is especially meaningful to him because it was his last real home, after which his father's reassignments resulted in continual relocation. Even at twelve, Ralph can recall "a succession of homes." The Dartmoor cottage is doubly significant because "mummy had still been with them and Daddy had come home every day." Clearly, after Ralph had been packed off to school, Mummy was no longer with them, and Daddy did not come home every day since there was apparently no home to come to. Constant uprooting produced in Ralph a desire for stability and a need to stay in one place; hence he restricts the boys to the shore. His father instilled in him a sense of regimentation and a respect for order; hence he insists not on rules but on "more rules." More than what, one might ask, since Ralph has not yet formulated any rules. Ralph thinks in terms of excess: not rules, but more rules because one cannot get enough of them. His vaulting Apollonianism is even more evident when he calls for "more wood" for the fire which then proceeds to burn out of control. Ideally, Ralph should be a skipper where his sphere of influence would be limited to the confines of the vessel, and his penchant for assigning tasks and restricting activity might pass for maritime ability.

It is not coincidental that the island is boat-shaped: "it was roughly boat-shaped, humped near this end with behind them the humbled descent to the shore" (38). In a later and more intricate novel, ***Rites of Passage,*** Golding uses a ship, on which a white line separates the afterdeck from the quarterdeck, as a microcosm of British society. Even when he was writing ***Lord of the Flies,*** Golding was thinking of a ship as a metaphor of social stratification where the "class" in which one chooses to travel is dependent on one's social and economic background. Ralph behaves like a first-class passenger; because he feels superior to Piggy, whose parents are dead and whose aunt owns a candy store, he can order him about ("Get my clothes," he demands). Because Ralph attaches no importance to being a chorister or a prefect, he can be intolerant of Jack.

Ralph even extends his notions of class consciousness to the island which, topographically, lends itself to stratification. Ralph favors the shore; the hunters, the jungle. Once the boys discover that the peninsula is a natural fortress, they take possession of it and dub it Castle Rock. By the end of the novel, the entire island has been polarized, from the Apollonian shore to the Dionysian tip.

Although it may seem that Golding has grafted the class-consciousness theme onto the novel, it should be remembered that the same theme appeared in one of his sources. In the *Bacchae,* Euripides emphasizes that one of the most appealing features of Dionysian worship is its leveling of all distinctions. Dionysus is egalitarian; his appeal is to the masses. Apollo is elitist, and so is Ralph. Apollo was served by priests and priestesses. Similarly, Ralph requires a cabinet, yet it consists of one person—Piggy—whom he takes on as advisor. He ignores Jack who would have made a splendid defense minister. Simon could have been spiritual leader/high priest, but he is "batty" and "cracked." Furthermore, Simon cannot articulate his insights in the kind of direct speech Ralph requires.

Golding's island is a dystopia in which the classes do not cooperate for the common good. Instead of being chief of state, Ralph devolves into a minister of sanitation, preoccupied with shelter and exasperated by the boys' indifference to hygiene. Instead of being a defense minister, Jack reverts to a tribal warrior, emulating King Kong and Tarzan. Instead of being a peacemaker, Simon withdraws to a secluded part of the island inhabited by butterflies. It may be a fitting place for one so spiritual, since the Greek word for spirit, *psyche,* means both soul and butterfly. Ascetic withdrawal, however, accomplishes nothing when a world is in chaos. Yet this is Golding's point: evil is so endemic that its effects are everywhere, even in the actions of the good; we are on a good island, but it is an island where a leader cannot achieve the good by creating harmony among the classes. Thus Ralph, Piggy, Jack, and Simon go their own ways, along with what they symbolize. Piggy realizes Ralph's limitations as a leader and votes for him with reluctance. Piggy cannot function as a prime minister because he cannot help Ralph remove the one obstacle that stands in the way of unity: his antagonism toward Jack. But the main reason why Piggy cannot help Ralph is that Piggy himself is part of the problem. Jack loathes Piggy for his prissiness and for Ralph's reliance on him; from Jack's point of view, he is the one on whom Ralph should rely. Ideally, a dyarchy should have been established, but that would have been impossible since Ralph wanted to be chief. One would think Simon might have been able to help; as a chorister, he is part of Jack's world and should understand the sense of oneness that grows out of choral song. Simon, however, prefers solitude and Ralph's company to Jack's—understandably, since Jack has little patience with him and finds his fainting spells wearisome. There can therefore be no moral resolution, only a literary one—a deus ex machina; the situation has moved out of human bounds into the domain of the deity who alone can end the war between spirit and matter.

Beelzebub, Prince of Devils

Eventually, one must confront the meaning of the title which, like all of Golding's symbolism, derives from the narrative itself. "Lord of the Flies" is a translation of *Beelzebub,* the Greek transliteration of the Hebrew *Ba'alzevuv,* which in Judaism and Christianity denotes the principle of evil personified: the Devil, Satan, Mephistopheles. Golding equates the Lord of the Flies with the demonic force latent in humankind, a force so hideous, he notes, that fly-covered excrement would best represent it.

Evil is also an abstraction; it is a privation, the absence of the good. A novel, even an allegorical one, cannot portray abstraction. Thus Golding embodies evil in something concrete—in an animal's head swarming with flies. First the "littluns" insist a beast is lurking on the island. Ralph, Jack, and Simon consider their fears groundless, the product of their fitful imaginations. But when a dead paratrooper lands on the mountain top, bobbing up and down like a grotesque puppet, even Jack is forced to revise his opinion, thinking that the corpse is the beast, or rather a manifestation of the beast that, like Dionysus, can assume different forms. The boys can do nothing about the corpse-beast since they are afraid of approaching it; but they can try to appease it. Since they conceive of the beast as an animal, they make an animal offering to it; since pigs are plentiful on the island, their choice of offering has been made for them. This pig, however, is different from the first one that was slain: this pig is female. The attack has overtones of rape; the slaying culminates in defilement and decapitation.

In chapter 8, the hunters spot a sow and her young. The heat of the afternoon acts as an erotic stimulant; the animal's being female is an incentive for a rape-like assault; its being a mother is an invitation to perversity. The sow's screams intensify their desires the way the cries of a rape victim may excite a rapist instead of deterring him. The boys become "wedded to [the sow] in lust," with Jack becoming the chief bridegroom. While the others jab at the sow, Jack mounts her, "stabbing downward with his knife." Whether or not this is an oedipal wedding night, as one critic described it,[9] is debatable. It is, however, bestiality that stops short of intercourse—a stick driven into the sow's anus substituting for penetration. It is also scapegoating; an animal becomes an outlet for desires previously repressed but now unleashed upon a creature that cannot retaliate.

Dark of the Moon

As a classicist, Golding was familiar with Robert Graves's *White Goddess,* one of the most important studies of the mythmaking process ever written and one that is especially relevant to a discussion of ***Lord of the Flies.*** The White Goddess is the personification of the female in all her aspects, contradictory as they may be: maiden/crone, regenerator/destroyer, virgin/whore, human/animal. She was worshiped in a variety of forms, including the moon, and could even transform herself into animals such as the sow; hence the pig was sacred to the White Goddess. Understood as an avatar of the goddess, the sow in ***Lord of the Flies*** symbolizes both matriarchy and maternalism. Her presence has a negative effect on the boys who regard the sight of a mother with her young not as an image of domestic harmony but as a threat to their freedom. The sow suggests family, without which society, culture, and civilization are impossible. But family and all it represents is precisely what the boys have rejected, and anything that evokes the familial is repugnant to them, because they have chosen anarchy. They also associate family with Ralph, who tries to unite them, who imposes rules, and who preaches right and wrong. Ralph, then, is no different from the sow; everything he stands for—order, work, reprimands—has maternal overtones. Thus when the hunters declare Ralph an outlaw, Roger, Jack's sadistic lieutenant, sharpens a stick at both ends, planning to inflict the sow's fate on Ralph. And if the sow's death is paradigmatic, Ralph's death would also have included ritual sodomization as a fitting punishment for men who implement feminine values.

Since the stick had been sharpened at both ends, Ralph's head would have been impaled on one end like the sow's and offered to the beast. In the boys' Dionysian unconscious, the sow is both the beast (or a form of the beast) as well as an offering to the beast. Such duality, although it may seem contradictory, was consistent with the Dionysian religion in which both the god and his votaries were prey and predator, hunted and hunter. The Bacchants hunted Dionysus, who, in turn, hunted them. They hunted the god in his animal form; when they found his avatar, they often dismembered it and ate the raw flesh.

The slain animal was offered to Dionysus, as happens at the end of the *Bacchae* when Agave returns to Thebes, thinking she has killed a lion and planning to make a feast of its remains. Since gods die and are reborn, and since their animal forms are self-perpetuating, the paradox is resolvable: one can kill the god and then eat the god, thereby acquiring some of his power. The god lives on in his worshipers as well as in his animal incarnations. The pig in ***Lord of the Flies*** represents the same kind of Dionysian ambivalence: it is beast and beast-offering, sacramental meal and sacrificial victim.

That Golding intended the pig to be equated with the beast is evident from three incidents in the novel.

First, there is the slaying of the sow and the impaling of its head, both of which are witnessed by Simon. When the hunters leave, Simon looks up at the head whose eyes assure him that "everything was a bad business" (170). Although the head has not spoken, Simon construes its look as an expression of despair in humanity; hence, his reply "I know that." Endowed with prophetic insight, he also knows the meaning of what he has seen: the beast and its offering are synonymous. While the Bacchants make the same connection, there is a major difference between their killing of the Dionysian animal and the hunters' killing of the sow. The Dionysian animal is not evil because what the animal represents—the god—is good. The sow, however, is evil because, to the hunters, everything she represents is evil. Although the sow's head is offered to the beast, it is still part of the beast; if the beast is evil, the head is the apotheosis of evil—the Lord of the Flies.

When the boys reenact the slaying, they chant: "*Kill the beast! Cut his throat! Spill his blood!*" (187). They think of the pig as related to the beast in some way, but are too immature to understand how complete the identification is. Yet neither the slaying nor its reenactment has produced the desired effect of emotional liberation. The Bacchants experience release because they feel no guilt in slaying the sacred animal. The hunters, however, feel guilt but repress it. They enjoy only a temporary cessation of fear; the orgasm of violence has not assuaged their anxieties. If it did, the beast would be dead or at least appeased, and Simon would not have been mistaken for it. By ritualizing the slaying, the boys are acting out of guilt and fear, like the brothers in Freud's *Totem and Taboo* who kill the primal father and, to salve their conscience, establish a yearly ritual commemorating his death.

The final association of pig with beast occurs when Simon journeys to the mountain and discovers that the arch-beast is really a dead paratrooper. The paratrooper's body is also covered with flies. Just as the boys projected evil into the sow, with the result that its head became the Lord of the Flies, so too have they demonized the paratrooper, who was as unthreatening as the sow. Evil, then, is born in fear and nurtured by guilt. It exists within us; when it is unleashed, it breeds like flies, befouling whatever it alights on and swarming over what it has befouled. Just as humankind creates its ogres, so have the boys who made a pig's head emblematic of what was within them.

Evil is double-edged; it has a conscious and an unconscious dimension. History has made us conscious of its existence; yet evil can be ahistorical, originating in the unconscious as fear of the unknown. Simon realizes that the beast reflects humankind's ambivalence toward evil as a force both outside and within the self; he knows that the "beast was harmless and horrible" (181). Yet these are also the characteristics of irrational fear (harmless) and its effects (horrible). Simon senses that this "news must reach the others as soon as possible." When he descends the mountain to bring the others the good news, he recalls Moses coming down from Mount Sinai with the covenant. Moses found the Israelites worshiping a golden calf; Simon finds the hunters reliving the pig hunt. Simon becomes both the ritual intruder and the beast because, in their perversion of the Dionysian ceremony, the boys cannot make a distinction: each is evil, each must be destroyed. In the death of Simon, Golding makes a subtle but important change in his retelling of the *Bacchae.* While Pentheus was also intruder and beast, he was not both simultaneously. First, he was the unholy witness to the rites; later, in his mother's delirium, he was the beast of Dionysus. With a cast of children, Golding cannot stage a mad scene as Euripides did for Agave, nor can he have the boys come to a realization of what they have done. That would defeat his purpose; the boys will never know what they have done because, unlike the *Bacchae,* there is no god to come down and tell them. Only Ralph knows, and he must live with that knowledge for the rest of his life.

In the death of Simon, Golding has also made his definitive statement about the beast: the beast is *other.* Whatever one fears, whether it is mythic like ogres and bogeymen, or real like countries and ideologies, it is not-I, beast, and ultimately evil. First, it was the pig; then Simon; next Piggy; and if it were not for the Royal Navy, Ralph. All the deaths occur because the victims are perceived as *other;* all the deaths are variations on pig-slaying. Simon enters the hunters' circle while they are chanting, "*Kill the beast! Cut his throat! Spill his blood!*" Ralph was to suffer the sow's fate and by the same instrument. Piggy not only dies with limbs twitching "like a pig's after it has been killed" (223); Roger kills him the same way he speared the sow—by applying leverage to a rock which comes crashing down on Piggy.

Simon alone receives a requiem from the author, which may suggest Golding's fondness for his character or perhaps his fondness for *The White Goddess,* which helps to explain the novel's ambivalence. Both the fire-watchers and the hunters are, in some way, under the influence of the White Goddess: the hunters under her malefic form—Hecate, the moon in the underworld, the dark of the moon; the fire-watchers under her benign form—Diana, the moon goddess of the sky. When Simon is killed, the Moon officiates at his obsequies, wrapping him in a shroud of beams: "The line of his cheek silvered and the turn of his shoulder became sculptured marble" (190). That the most poetic part of ***Lord of the Flies*** follows a brutal murder is again evidence of Golding's debt to Graves, who also saw poetry coming out of ritual murder: "No poet can hope to understand the nature of poetry unless he has had a vision of the Naked King crucified to the lopped oak, and watched the dancers, red-eyed from the acrid smoke of the sacrificial fires, stamping out the measure of the dance, their bodies bent uncouthly forward, with a monotonous chant of: 'Kill! kill! kill!' and "Blood! blood! blood!'"[10]

The hunters' chant in ***Lord of the Flies*** is less monotonous, but the sentiments are the same; so is the source.

Flawed Classic or Classic Flaws?

Few first novels have been so powerfully conceived or so well written as ***Lord of the Flies;*** still, it is not without flaws. Its faults, however, are more attributable to the subject matter than to Golding's handling of it. Once Golding chose *The Coral Island* as his point of departure, he had no other choice but to use children as characters; once he merged *The Coral Island* with the *Bacchae,* he had no other choice but to make some of the children killers. Obviously, this was what Golding wanted. Children suited his moral purpose: as a potential adult, the child is as capable of anything—including evil—as the adult; if the child is shown to be naturally capable of evil, evil is endemic to the race.

Still, children have always posed a problem to the novelist, because they cannot disentangle cause and effect. The author must do it for them, explaining what would otherwise be dramatized or only inferable. In order to account for Simon's insight into the nature of evil, Golding makes him a visionary and a saint. Ballantyne did not have this problem since there was no Simon in *The Coral Island.* In creating Simon, Golding fell into a trap. Simon's realization of "mankind's essential illness" and his ability to visualize it as excrement are not characteristic of a child; nor are they necessarily characteristic of a saint. Traditionally, saints have been more attuned to God than to Satan; their knowledge of Satan was based on their knowledge of God: by understanding one, they understood the other. Simon, however, gives no evidence of understanding God, let alone His opposite.

At the end of the novel, Ralph weeps for "the darkness of man's heart." Yet Ralph is twelve, and what he knows about the darkness of the heart, despite what he has witnessed on the island, is minimal compared to what Anne Frank knew. In spite of everything, Anne believed people were essentially good. Ralph cannot even say they are intrinsically evil. In fact, he says nothing; he merely weeps.

Golding has given Ralph an adult's feelings and a hero's tragic awareness, while at the same time insisting Ralph is just a boy. But then, everyone on the island is a boy, including the savages. Just before their rescue, suddenly and cinematically, as in a dissolve, they revert to what they were when they landed on the island: kids. Golding, who often shifts point of view, presents them in the end from the perspective of the naval officer who knows nothing of their Dionysian behavior and sees Jack not as a Bacchant but as "a little boy with a black cap."

Ralph and Simon are by no means models of consistency. The last line of the novel has Ralph weeping for the darkness of the heart, the loss of innocence, and "the fall through the air of the true, wise friend called Piggy." Yet there was nothing about Ralph's behavior to indicate that he ever found Piggy wise or a friend. Piggy was an ally; to think of him as Ralph's friend is to ignore Ralph's early derision of him.

Simon's character is the novel's chief weakness. Simon is an amalgam of various types and strains. Like his namesake in the nursery rhyme, he is simple; he strikes others, including Ralph, as peculiar. He is also a Cassandra, whose prophecies are doomed to be ignored. To give him a spiritual aura, Golding inflicts him with what the ancients called the sacred disease—epilepsy. Simon is the classic case of one whose clairvoyance is compensation for physical suffering.

Simon has also been called a Christ-figure, not so much because he evokes Christ (his obviously Christian qualities are shared by saints) as because he is a sacrificial victim. Certainly no child in literature has been saddled with such a multimythic personality. Furthermore, he is also Golding's mouthpiece, for it is Simon who expresses, however inarticulately, the author's philosophy of evil. Simon alone confronts the Lord of the Flies, from whose gaze he intuits "an ancient, inescapable recognition"—namely, that "everything is a bad business." Simon knows that the reason for the dissolution of the island community, and for evil in general, is humankind's bedeviled nature. But that knowledge is itself destructive; once Simon admits it ("I know that"), there is no hope. The butterflies desert his covert, and the flies start swarming on him, as if he bears the mark of the beast—which he does, since he is later identified with it. To Golding, knowledge of evil brings evil on the knower, no matter how innocent that person may be.

In case anyone has missed the point, Golding adds another encounter between Simon and the pig's head in which the head speaks: "'You knew didn't you? I'm part of you? . . . I'm the reason why it's no go? Why things are what they are?'" (177) This time Simon faints because the "ancient, inescapable recognition" has been expressed so unequivocally.

The incident is gratuitous; it is as if Golding, uncertain that his readers would get the message, decided to enunciate it so there would be no misunderstanding. To do so, he uses a child; from a critical standpoint, he "uses" a character—a character who has already relayed the message to readers sensitive enough to comprehend it. It seems that Simon is Golding's scapegoat as well as the hunters'.

The incident is gratuitous for another reason. Simon's awareness of evil is made evident early in the novel. Like Ralph and Jack, Simon knows there is no beast; "maybe it's only us" (111) he suggests. To clarify his suggestion, he asks timidly, "What's the dirtiest thing there is?" Jack answers in a word of "one crude expressive syllable." The monosyllabic word is obviously "shit," which, at the time, Golding was too circumspect to use. In the context, periphrasis is out of place, but Golding later made up for his reticence, growing more explicit with the times.

The logic is elementary but depressing; if humans are the beast, then humans are shit—something Sweeney Todd, "the demon barber of Fleet Street" in Stephen Sondheim's eponymous musical drama, believes, for that is how he justifies avenging himself on the world.

The scene in which Simon made his suggestion, supplemented by the first encounter with the pig's head, would have been sufficient; together, they establish the two basic metaphors for evil: flies and excrement, so that the Lord of the Flies is the Lord of Dung, and what is true of the lord is true of his servants. Moreover, excrement is ubiquitous on the island. Eating fruit causes diarrhea, and the island is dotted with feces. The island, like everything in the novel, is a parody—a parody of the first garden, Eden, where the first sin was committed. The fruit is tainted by the first sin whose effects the boys, like all humanity, have inherited. The excrement they leave behind is a vestige of the primal sin.

It is precisely this kind of symbolism that has made ***Lord of the Flies*** such a teachable novel, to the extent that one can ignore Simon's unsatisfying characterization. The novel is a perfect illustration of the way the literal and metaphorical levels of a work complement each other since, in ***Lord of the Flies,*** the metaphorical level is a deepening of the literal. For those who find mythopoesis tough going, there are always the characters who are such identifiable types that, as one student observed, they could be found at camp.[11] For those capable of going beyond symbolism into irony and ambivalence, Golding facilitates the transition by using irony to underscore the symbolic action. The fire that was made by the reflection of light from Piggy's glasses goes out when Jack kills his first pig. When Jack prays for a sign from heaven, his prayer is answered in the form of the dead paratrooper. Finally, there are summary lines like "the dirtiest thing there is" and "I'm the reason why it's no go" which, as the novel moved into secondary school, were a godsend to students who had to locate the novel's central thought or the author's philosophy.

Lord of the Flies also affords an opportunity to test Golding's own interpretation of the novel and to decide whether one trusts the tale or the teller. In a 1962 lecture at the University of California at Los Angeles, Golding turned critic and interpreted the dead paratrooper as history that "won't lie down."[12] No doubt he meant that the paratrooper was another instance of humankind's irrational fears projected onto an object—a harmless object, at that. Golding apparently forgot that the paratrooper does lie down—literally—and can be laid down symbolically. Simon disentangles the parachute lines so the corpse does not jerk up and down; after Simon's death, the rain washes the corpse out to sea. Simon manages to get the corpse to "lie down," thus showing that the irrational can be put to rest; unfortunately, he never had the chance to announce his discovery to the others. Apparently even authors can misinterpret their work.

Finally, ***Lord of the Flies*** remains an excellent introduction to fable, myth, and allegory since it embodies features of each, although strictly speaking, it is none of them. It is a work whose foundation (or to use a favorite Golding word, cellar) is mythic; it has the moral purpose of fable and the symbolic linkings of allegory. It also has certain features in common with antiallegory, as defined by Northrop Frye in *Anatomy of Criticism.* Antiallegory is a peculiarly modern form that inverts the imagery of traditional allegory, so that instead of being exemplary and doctrinal, the imagery becomes ironic and paradoxical. Thus antiallegory is the reverse of classical allegory, which teaches that human nature is perfectible; antiallegory teaches the opposite, or, to use the words of the pig's head, that "it's no go." Antiallegory is merely another way of saying serious parody, which is perhaps the most accurate designation for the novel.

Notes

1. Robert Michael Ballantyne, *The Coral Island* (London: 1858), 25-26. Subsequent references in the text are to this edition.

2. "The Meaning of It All," *Books and Bookmen,* October, 1959, 10. For parallels between Ballantyne and Golding, see Carl Niemeyer, "The Coral Island Revisited," *College English,* 22 (January 1961): 241-45.

3. *Lord of the Flies* (New York: Capricorn Books, 1959), 12. Subsequent references in the text are to this edition.

4. Euripides, *Bacchae,* ed. with introduction and commentary by E. R. Dodds, 2d ed. (London: Oxford University Press, 1960). Golding knew this edition "better than [his] own hand."

5. For the Euripidean influence, see Bernard F. Dick, "*Lord of the Flies* and the *Bacchae,*" *Classical World,* 57 (January 1964): 145-46; Robert J. White, "Butterfly and Beast in *Lord of the Flies,*" *Modern Fiction Studies* 10 (Summer 1964): 163-70.

6. "The Meaning of It All," 10. Golding's explanation is, however, quite sensible: "Now, look, I have a view which you haven't got and I would like you to see this from my point of view. Therefore, I must first put it so graphically in my way of thinking that you identify with it, and then at the end I'm going to put you where you are, looking at it from the outside."

7. Dick, "'A Novelist Is a Displaced Person,'" 481.

8. James R. Baker, "An Interview with William Golding," *Twentieth Century Literature* 28 (Summer 1982): 136.

9. E.L. Epstein, "Notes on *Lord of the Flies,*" in *Lord of the Flies* (New York: Capricorn Books, 1959), 254.

10. Robert Graves, *The White Goddess: A Historical Grammar of Poetic Myth* (New York: Noonday Press, 1966), 448.

11. "Lord of the Campus," *Time,* 22 June 1962, 64.

12. "Fable," in *The Hot Gates,* 96.

S. J. Boyd (essay date 1988)

SOURCE: Boyd, S. J. "The Nature of the Beast: *Lord of the Flies* (1954)." In *The Novels of William Golding,* pp. 1-23. New York: St. Martin's Press, 1988.

[*In the following essay, Boyd gives an analysis of the novel as it he believes it to depict Golding's view of human nature and the nature of the world.*]

> And Jesus called a little child unto him, and set him in the midst of them,
>
> And said, Verily I say unto you, Except ye be converted,
>
> and become as little children, ye shall not enter the kingdom of heaven.
>
> St Matthew 18. 2-3

> As flies to wanton boys, are we to th' Gods;
> They kill us for their sport.
>
> *King Lear*

Lord of the Flies has become almost compulsory reading for those enduring the painful process of growing up. One has the impression that *everyone* has studied and been impressed by this novel in the latter part of schooldays. It is not difficult to give reasons for this popularity: its protagonists are schoolboys, drawn with a remarkable awareness of the realities of the playground world, its unhappy theme 'the end of innocence' (LF p. 223). The loss of innocence for which Ralph weeps at the novel's close is not, however, a matter of transformation from childish goodness to adolescent depravity, is not a growing into wickedness. It is rather the coming of an awareness of darkness, of the evil in man's heart that was present in the children all along. To acknowledge the presence of this darkness in one's own heart is a necessary but devastating condition of growing up, of becoming fully and yet flawedly human.

Golding's concern is to present us with a vision of human nature and also of the nature of the world which we inhabit through the experiences of a group of children cast away on a desert island. The two quotations above represent polar opposites of optimism and pessimism with regard to the nature of children (which we might take to be representative of essential or pristine human nature) and the nature of the universe in which we live. In the words of Jesus in St Matthew childhood is presented as a state of innocent goodness, a state which may be regarded as the kingdom of heaven on earth. As adults, fallen from this happy state, we may well hanker after a return to it and the possibility of such a conversion is held out to us in this passage by Jesus. There is room for optimism about human nature then, and there is considerable cause for optimism about the nature of our universe, for the speaker has traditionally been regarded as the creator and loving ruler of the universe, come down to earth to suffer and die so that we might be redeemed or rescued from our wickedness and restored to the original purity and happiness we see in children and remember, or think we remember, as our experience of childhood.

The tragic universe of *King Lear* is at its darkest in Gloucester's terrible words: we live in a cruel world which can only be governed by malevolent demons whose delight is to torture us; if we wish to see an image of these dark gods or devils we need look no further than children or our own childhood, need only examine 'the ghastly and ferocious play of children' (FF p. 150), where we see how little devils torture and kill insects for fun, playing god with flies. From within and without we are beset by evil, 'All dark and comfortless'.[1] *King Lear* is not everywhere so hopeless in outlook but it does seem to force us to accept that nature provides no evidence of beneficent paternal care for us and that in our human nature there is a terrifying propensity towards wanton cruelty which is evident even in children.

It scarcely needs to be said that the picture of childhood, of human nature, and of the nature of things, which emerges from ***Lord of the Flies*** is closer to that expressed by Gloucester than that in the passage from St Matthew, though in Golding's novel and in Shakespeare's play, as we shall see, some redeeming features are suggested which have much to do with the life of Jesus. The bleakness of the novel's vision has been eloquently encapsulated by Golding himself in a sentence which recalls the despair of Lear in its bludgeoning repetitions: 'The theme of ***Lord of the Flies*** is grief, sheer grief, grief, grief, grief' (MT p. 163). The grief which Golding expresses and powerfully elicits in the novel is grief at man's very nature and the nature of his world, grief that the boys, and we too, are 'suffering from the terrible disease of being human' (HG p. 87). Shakespeare's tragedy and Golding's novel both present us with a fearless and savage close-up of human nature, a stripping-down of man to what essentially he is. The effect is appalling and humiliating: we are, in Golding's words, a species that 'produces evil as a bee produces honey' (HG p. 87). As naturally as the humble insect produces sweetness, we produce the wickedness and violence which sour our lives. In *King Lear* the burgeoning evil of Lear's daughters and Cornwall finds extravagant expression in the blinding of Gloucester: in ***Lord of the Flies*** Jack and his gang with comparable callousness steal Piggy's glasses: '"That's them," said Piggy. "They blinded me. See? That's Jack Merridew."' (p. 187). Piggy has been blinded and his complaint indicates that this action of blinding was an expression of the essential nature of Jack Merridew and friends. The blinded Piggy has been granted insight. The darkness of Gloucester's experience leads to his despairing suicide attempt at the Dover cliff. He is, however, saved from death and despair by the loving care of his son: his heart, we are told, 'Twixt two extremes of passion, joy and grief,/Burst smilingly.'[2] Piggy too is led to the rocks at the island's tip—'"Is it safe? Ain't there a cliff? I can hear the sea."' (p. 193)[3]—but for him there is to be no comforting or consolation. The deathsman Roger wantonly knocks him over the cliff and his head bursts messily: 'His head opened and stuff came out and turned red' (p. 200). Piggy's experiences seem to recall those of Gloucester, but his end is more terrible. The crass prose that records his end matches the callousness of Cornwall in transforming Gloucester's eye to 'vile jelly',[4] which is exactly what Roger has done to Piggy's brain.

The evil of Cornwall and Roger transforms humanity into vileness. The compulsive viciousness of Roger might well provoke us to adapt Lear's exclamation concerning Cornwall's accomplice Regan: 'let them anatomise *Roger;* See what breeds about *his* heart.'[5] Roger's evil is inexplicable, in part because he is a shadowy character about whose background we know almost nothing, but Golding is determined, as was Shakespeare in *King Lear,* that we should confront the Roger or Regan within us, '"the reason why it's no go"' (LF p. 158). He has himself spoken of this characteristic determination to anatomise 'the darkness of man's heart' (LF p. 223):

> What man *is,* whatever man is under the eye of heaven, that I burn to know and that—I do not say this lightly—I would endure knowing. The themes closest to my purpose, to my imagination have stemmed from that preoccupation, have been of such a sort that they might move me a little nearer that knowledge. They have been themes of man at an extremity, man tested like a building material, taken into the laboratory and used to destruction; man isolated, man obsessed, man drowning in a literal sea or in the sea of his own ignorance.
>
> (MT p. 199)

In *King Lear* the trial by ordeal of human nature takes place on the inhospitable landscapes of a storm-blasted Dark Age Britain; the laboratory in which Golding's school-boys are used to destruction is the apparently more idyllic world of a tropical island. As we shall see, there are many islands, both real and metaphorical, in Golding's fiction: in ***The Inheritors*** the new people (i.e. we humans) are first discovered on an island and it is characteristic of them that they are isolated from each other in a way that the Neanderthal people are not; in ***Pincher Martin*** the central figure finds himself utterly alone and forgotten on a mere rock in the ocean; to Jocelyn in ***The Spire*** the great ship of the cathedral seems to offer insulation against the evils of the dangerous sea of the world; Wilfred Barclay in ***The Paper Men,*** despite his credit-card-given ability to travel anywhere at anytime, is isolated from his fellow man and from his own past by his alcoholism and his spiritual crisis occurs on one of the Lipari islands. Isolation is everywhere.

In confining the boys to a small island in ***Lord of the Flies*** Golding is using a long-established literary method of examining human nature and human polity in microcosm, as in Shakespeare's *The Tempest* or Thomas More's *Utopia,* in Defoe's *Robinson Crusoe* or Swift's *Gulliver's Travels.* These books provide a literary background to the boys' adventures on their island. In such works we find a tendency to present human nature at an extreme: in More's utopian fantasy and in Aldous Huxley's *Island* we see human nature and society at their best. In his introduction to the former Paul Turner remarks:

> The old-fashioned method of getting to Utopia is to be wrecked on an island, preferably in the South Seas, and Huxley's last essay in the genre [*Island*] is to this extent traditional. So is William Golding's ***Lord of the Flies*** . . . , which may, I think, be considered a rather individual form of Dystopia.[6]

The South-Sea island setting suggests everyone's fantasy of lotus-eating escape or refuge from troubles and cares. But for Golding this is the sheerest fantasy: there is no escape from the agony of being human, no possibility of erecting utopian political systems where all will go well. Man's inescapable depravity makes sure 'it's no go' on Golding's island just as it does on the various islands visited by Gulliver in Swift's excoriating examination of the realities of the human condition.

Robinson Crusoe belongs in part to the world of sheer escapist boys' adventure stories which also contribute to the literary background of ***Lord of the Flies.*** The castaway boys themselves are reminded of *Treasure Island, Swallows and Amazons* and Ballantyne's *The Coral Island:* prompted by the mention of these works, Ralph assures them: '"It's a good island. Until the grown-ups come to fetch us we'll have fun"' (p. 38). The boys imagine that they can have fun not only in swimming and hunting but in imposing decent, civilised English values upon their island, as Ralph, Jack and Peterkin Gay had done on Ballantyne's island and as Robinson Crusoe had done by converting his island to an English gentleman's country estate. But their efforts in this direction are a dismal failure. Things fall apart, or 'break up' in Ralph's phrase (p. 89), into atavism, savagery and bloodshed.[7] The boys regress to what might be called a state of nature, but the experience of this is not of an earthly paradise but a hell on earth.

Golding is determined to disabuse us not only of naive optimism about the nature of children but also of the sort of faith in the goodness of all things natural described by Aldous Huxley in his essay 'Wordsworth in the Tropics':

> In the neighbourhood of latitude fifty north, and for the last hundred years or thereabouts, it has been an axiom that Nature is divine and morally uplifting . . . To commune with the fields and waters, the woodlands and the hills, is to commune, according to our modern and northern ideas, with the visible manifestations of the 'Wisdom and Spirit of the Universe'.[8]

Such an optimistically Romantic view of the beneficence of the natural world is not confirmed by the visit of Golding's northern boys to the tropics. Golding has remarked of Huxley: 'I owe his writings much myself, I've had much enjoyment and some profit from them—in particular, release from a certain starry-eyed optimism' (MT p. 181). Huxley proposes in 'Wordsworth in the Tropics' that a visit to the tropics would cure any Wordsworthian of his faith in nature. The tropical island of Golding's novel, which seems to the boys paradisial in its unspoilt wildness, proves to be an inferno, a sort of pressure-cooker heated by a vertical sun which aims blows at the boys' heads in its violent intensity, which fires 'down invisible arrows' (p. 67) like an angry or malevolent god. It is just as Huxley describes: 'Nature, under a vertical sun, and nourished by the equatorial rains, is not at all like that chaste, mild deity who presides over . . . the prettiness, the cosy sublimities of the Lake District.'[9] Prettiness and cosiness are important elements in Ralph's memories of natural wildness back in England, but Ralph's experience of nature is hopelessly limited and naively comfortable: 'But the remembered cottage on the moors (where "wildness" was ponies, or the snowy moor seen through a window past a copper-kettle . . .) is utterly out of reach and unreal; a flimsy dream.'[10] The reality of nature in the tropics is profoundly sinister and threatening. From their experience of this natural environment the boys derive a sort of religion, but their theology is a demonology, their lord or god is a devil. In this they merely conform to the ways of indigenous jungle-dwellers as described by Huxley: 'The sparse inhabitants of the equatorial forest are all believers in devils.'[11]

The boys' physical surroundings are terrifying and encourage in them a belief in a malevolent god; the boys' own physical condition also is not improved by their stay on the island. Their return to a state of nature, insofar as it implies a lack of toilet facilities and wholesome food, has a very unpleasant effect on them. The 'littluns' in particular quickly become 'filthily dirty' and are affected by 'a sort of chronic diarrhoea' (p. 64). One of Ralph's problems as chief is that the boys fail to abide by the rule that only one clutch of tide-washed rocks should be used as a lavatory: 'Now people seem to use anywhere. Even near the shelters and the platform' (p. 87). Man seems to be a natural producer of filth as well as evil, and the one is a symbol of the other. Of this aspect of the boys' plight Leighton Hodson writes: 'the odour of decay pervades life from the diarrhoea of the littluns . . . to Jack hunting the pigs by following their steaming droppings; the association of the Beast, evil, excrement, and blood is both overpowering and purposeful.'[12] This physical degeneration is matched by an upsurge of cruelty, bloodlust and violent rapacity as the Beast, which they take to be a spirit or monster outside of themselves, rises up within them and takes over their lives. Overwhelmed by the horrors that have entered their lives, littluns will isolate themselves to wail, gibber and howl at the misery of their condition. Were Lemuel Gulliver to land on the island, he would instantly recognise that he had returned to a land inhabited by Yahoos.

In Book Four of *Gulliver's Travels* the hero lands on an island dominated by the Houyhnhnms, a nation of intelligent horses whose name signifies '*the perfection of nature*'[13] and whose generally very admirable way of life is lived in accordance with nature or, more precisely, with reason, which they take to be the supreme gift of nature. The peacefulness, cleanliness and reasonableness of their lives make their society an ideal towards which we humans might well wish to aspire. The humanoids of the island, however, have no such aspirations for they are, as Gulliver is mortified to discover, a disgusting race of passionate, violent, irrational, greedy and lustful creatures: these are the Yahoos. Their appearance and presence are rendered particularly offensive by 'their strange disposition to nastiness and dirt'.[14] They wallow in their filth, symbolising their propensity towards evil and the dark, perverse psychological forces which make them incapable of behaving reasonably or organising and maintaining a rational society. Swift thus gives us a painfully simple sketch of the human condition: we aspire to reasonableness and would like to construct and live in rational societies, but the nature of the beast within us, the innate propensity towards violence, cruelty and selfish and self-destructive wickedness, makes such optimistic schemes incapable of realisation. Swift rubs our noses mercilessly in our own filth. John S. Whitley has suggested that 'the Hebrew word "Beelzebub", though it means literally "Lord of flies", might be rendered in English as "lord of dung", that substance around which flies gather'.[15]

The Yahoo-nature inevitably brings about misery. It is not surprising that even the insensitive, brute Yahoo is driven at times 'to retire into a corner, to lie down and howl, and groan' like the half-demented littluns on Golding's island.[16] The transformation from schoolboys to Yahoos forces upon us the bitter truth of *Gulliver's Travels,* that we are creatures whose nature renders us incapable of maintaining rational, equable and peaceful societies such as that of the Houyhnhnms. Ralph and Piggy attempt to create such a society on the island. Piggy in particular has great faith in Houyhnhnm-like values, believing in government by persuasion, deciding issues by debate, above all in reason itself. For Piggy the world is reasonable: at one point he seems amusingly reminiscent of René Descartes: 'I been in bed so much I done some thinking' (p. 102). But Piggy's rationalism is as inadequate as his grammar. His reason cannot control the boys, his belief that science can explain everything makes him unable to comprehend the reality of the Beast, his democracy crumbles before the onslaught of the atavistic Jack, intuitively adept at using the Beast for his own ends. Piggy may be the brains of the outfit but the Beast in Roger, by smashing his skull, makes those brains useless. Piggy's body is quickly swallowed by the sea, which in the chapter 'Beast from Water' was suggested as a possible dwelling-place of the Beast. When Ralph first inspects the spot where Piggy dies, the sea's motion is described by the narrator as 'like the breathing of some stupendous creature', 'the sleeping leviathan' (p. 115). The sea is an insuperable obstacle to the boys' escape and one is tempted to detect a reference to Thomas Hobbes' *Leviathan,* wherein the life of man in a state of nature is characterised as being just as Yahoo-like as the boys discover it to be. It is, in Hobbes' famous phrase, 'solitary, poor, nasty, brutish, and short'.[17] ***Lord of the Flies*** insists that this is a truth, a grim reality, from which there is no escaping.[18]

The boys' return to nature, then, is not an idyll but a nightmare. It is tempting to see their misadventures as a regression from the Houyhnhnm-like values of our civilisation into the caveman world of the Yahoos. This is Piggy's view of the matter: if only they would behave like grown-ups all would be well; if only a ship carrying grown-ups would spot them they would be saved. This is a comforting view of the book since it seems to put us grown-ups on the side of the angels and endorse the view that our civilisation is rational, peaceful and even salvific. To take such a view is, however, to fall into what Golding suggests is one of the most dangerous of errors: to attempt to deny that the Beast is in us and to limit its existence or operancy to some other time, place, or group of people. Such a reading of the book is untenable. Piggy's faith in grown-ups is shown to be sadly misplaced. Here, displaying typical common sense and faith in the known laws of science, he tries to reassure Ralph: '"The trouble is: Are there ghosts, Piggy? Or beasts?" "Course there aren't." "Why not?" "'Cos things wouldn't make sense. Houses an' streets, an'—TV—they wouldn't work."' (p. 101). But the horrible truth is that man's organised civilisation and sophisticated systems of communication have failed to work, have been destroyed or have broken down in the nightmare of nuclear war.

Civilised values *are* endorsed by the novel—it is heartbreaking to see how friendship and fair-play are replaced by hostility and tyranny—but our actual civilisations are condemned as barbaric and monstrously destructive. Ralph and Jack, chiefs of rival gangs or tribes on the island, are 'two continents of experience and feeling, unable to communicate' (p. 60). They are thus an image of the tragic state of world politics in the mid-twentieth century and of the seemingly eternal need of civilisations to find rivals with whom to quarrel, the perennial argy-bargy of history which Joyce in *Finnegans Wake* sums up as 'wills gen wonts'.[19] When the Lord of the Flies himself, the focus of evil in the book, condescends to speak, it is with the voice of a schoolmaster, whose duty it is to instil the values of our civilisation into developing children. That these values are, to say the least, defective is made very clear by an outburst from Piggy just before his fatal fall: '"Which is better—to be a pack of painted niggers like you are, or to be sensible like Ralph is?"' (p. 199). Piggy *in extremis* lets slip that being 'sensible' may well involve adhering to tribal values and loyalties, regarding whomever is judged to be alien with contempt or loathing and treating them accordingly. But then Piggy knows what it is to be an alien, because he is made an outsider in part by his being physically unattractive but also as a function of that prominent feature of English civilisation, the class system.

Golding's later novels, especially ***The Pyramid*** and ***Rites of Passage,*** make abundantly clear his deep bitterness at and hatred of the evils of class. But even in this first novel, even on a desert island, this Golding obsession is in evidence. The novelist Ian McEwan has written of his adolescent reading of ***Lord of the Flies:*** 'As far as I was concerned, Golding's island was a thinly disguised boarding school.'[20] At one point the narrator seems to claim that class is of no importance in the alienation and persecution of Piggy: 'There had grown up tacitly among the biguns the opinion that Piggy was an outsider, not only by accent, which did not matter, but by fat, and ass-mar, and specs, and a certain disinclination for manual labour' (p. 70). But the narrator implicitly admits that accent, a mark of class, *is* an alienating factor ['not only'] and actually mocks, in passing, Piggy's way of speaking. The view that class does not matter in Piggy's misfortunes is scarcely borne out by events. From the very outset Piggy is isolated, stranded on an island within the island, by being lower-class. On the book's first page Ralph's 'automatic gesture' of pulling up his socks makes 'the jungle seem for a moment like the Home Counties' (p. 7) and unfortunately Piggy just does not fit into the middle-class ambience implied thereby. Ralph is a good-natured boy, but in this initial scene he seems very reluctant to accept the friendship of the one companion he has so far found on the desert island: '"What's your name?" "Ralph." The fat boy waited to be asked his name in turn but this proffer of acquaintance was not made' (p. 9). One has the uncomfortable feeling throughout this scene that Ralph has been conditioned to be unfriendly towards boys who talk like Piggy. Ralph is not slow to inform Piggy that his father is officer-class, but in response to the crucial question '"What's your father?"' Piggy can produce only the poignant reply: '"My dad's dead," he said quickly, "and my mum—"' (p. 14). The unseemly haste with which Piggy announces that his father is dead suggests a reluctance to reveal his place in life and the blank after the mention of his mum speaks unhappy volumes. Piggy has failed to produce satisfactory credentials. It is at least partly for this reason that Piggy is doomed to become 'the centre of social derision so that everyone felt cheerful and normal' (p. 164). Life seems cheery and normal provided there are the likes of Piggy around to be looked down on and derided.

Piggy's main persecutor is Jack, who from the first evinces contempt and hatred for Piggy, whom he seems to regard as an upstart. Jack's education appears to have instilled in him the belief that it is his right to give commands, to rule: '"I ought to be chief," said Jack with simple arrogance, "because I'm chapter chorister and head boy"' (p. 23). His privileged choir-school background has no doubt taught him much about the necessity of hierarchies, including the notion that head boy from such a school ought to be top man anywhere. Whitley comments: 'This assumption of leadership, bred by being part of a civilised élite, is maintained when he becomes a member of a primitive élite. The perfect prefect becomes the perfect savage.'[21] It would be difficult to imagine anything more suggestive of innocence than a group of cathedral choristers, but we first see the choir as 'something dark' in the haze, as 'the darkness' (p. 20): the choir is from the outset associated with evil. A cathedral choir connotes also a certain English middle-class cosiness, a social world 'assured of certain certainties'. Here is Jack at his most 'sensible', declaring some important certainties: '". . . We've got to have rules and obey them. After all, we're not savages. We're English; and the English are best at everything"' (p. 47). Golding has written that such cosy English chauvinism was something he particularly wished to attack in ***Lord of the Flies:***

> One of our faults is to believe that evil is somewhere else and inherent in another nation. My book was to say: you think that now the war is over and an evil thing destroyed, you are safe because you are naturally kind and decent.
>
> (HG p. 89).

The English error is to objectify and externalise the Devil, as the boys do, and this self-congratulatory attitude is dangerous because it allows the Devil to go to work, evils to be perpetrated, under cover of the belief that English people are good, decent and fair-minded. The classic jingoistic expression of such an attitude might be: 'Come off it! This is *England*! Something like that couldn't happen in England!' Whoever adopts such an attitude blinds himself to the evils which do exist in English life, prominent among which is the class system. Golding tries to expose the truth about this evil by translating it from England to a desert island: Jack's hatred of and violence towards Piggy is the raw naked truth about English social organisation. Classist attitudes not only ensure that under the motto of fair play a very unfair deal is given to most members of a society, they also bring about the reification of people. Thus a person may be treated not on the merits of his complex make-up as an individual but merely in accordance with his being recognised as a component of a mass class-group. The final blow dealt to Piggy transforms the extraordinary and miraculous complexity and beauty of his brain, the seat of consciousness and what makes him the particular and unique person he is, into mere 'stuff'.

The treatment meted out to Piggy makes the view that the boys' story is one of simple regression and degeneration a very difficult one to hold. But such a view is completely undermined by the adventitious arrival of the naval officer at the close. Every reader of the novel must have felt profoundly relieved when Ralph stumbles upon this white-clad saviour. All will be well now that the authority and values of civilisation have returned in the figure of this man, who might indeed almost be Ralph's father come to rescue them all. Critics have long recognised, however, that this warrior who stops the boys' war is anything but snowy-white morally. Virginia Tiger sums the matter up thus:

> There is no essential difference between the island world and the adult one and it is the burden

> of the fable's structure . . . to make it clear that the children's experiment on the island has its constant counterpart in the world outside.[22]

The officer is a warrior, a killer, and he is right to regard the boys' war as mere 'Fun and games', because compared to the massive death-dealing of the nuclear war in which he is involved it is very small-scale indeed. But the officer is nonetheless dismayed that a group of British boys should have degenerated into savages, should have failed 'to put up a better show than that'. Show, the keeping-up of a good appearance, is what this ultra-English officer is all about. The white uniform, the gold buttons, the 'trim cruiser' of the closing sentence are all signs of the officer's belief in orderliness, cleanliness, and of his and his nation's belief in their moral rectitude. The officer's first, and apparently kindly, thought about Ralph is that he 'needed a bath, a hair-cut, a nose-wipe and a good deal of ointment' (pp. 221-3). An advocate, no doubt, of the stiff upper lip, he is embarrassed by Ralph's heartbroken tears. The officer is no saviour at all. He is doubly guilty: of being a warrior on behalf of one of the world's two tribes and of sanitising the killing, the vast butchery, involved in such conflicts, of cleaning and dressing it up so that it seems sane and sensible. He is able to masquerade as a peacemaker, a bringer of light to the savages. He dislikes the blood and filth of the boys, he is embarrassed by Ralph's open display of emotion, but the blood and filth are the true symbols of war or warriors and Ralph's grief is an absolutely human and appropriate reaction to the revelations of the island.

The officer comes ashore like Lemuel Gulliver to discover a pack of Yahoos. Like Gulliver, he finds them distasteful. But Gulliver gradually comes to see that supposedly civilised humans are worse than Yahoos because they have all the filth and vices of the Yahoos, though they hide these under clothes and a clothing of pride in their own supposed moral rectitude, and have abused what reason they have by employing it in the invention of new ways in which to express their viciousness. It is a uniform-wearing Yahoo that has come to rescue the boys: there is even more reason than Ralph thinks to weep for 'the darkness of man's heart'. The phrase describes succinctly enough the central concern of Swift's writing but asks us specifically to think of Conrad. The overall picture of man's nature which emerges from ***Lord of the Flies*** is indeed similar to the one we find in *Heart of Darkness.* A return to the state of nature, an escape into primitivism such as that attempted by Conrad's Kurtz, leads only to the unleashing of brutality, greed for power, and sadism in the most naked and brutal forms, to the horror of orgiastic and murderous midnight dances and human heads stuck on poles. But the forces of civilisation, clad in shiny white to proclaim their moral excellence, are mere whited sepulchres, every bit as guilty as Kurtz and lacking even the honesty of open savagery. Both books offer this grim view of the human condition: there is no rescue, no way out, and the ending of ***Lord of the Flies*** is anything but happy. To regard it as such would be to ignore the prophetic voice of Simon.

In *The Coral Island* Ballantyne's three young adventurers had the names Ralph, Jack and Peterkin Gay. In Golding's novel we find a Ralph and a Jack but two boys seem to share the derivation of their names from the third member of Ballantyne's jolly-sounding trio: Piggy's name is an approximate and unpleasant contraction of Peterkin Gay, but the name Simon, we know from the Bible, was the original name of St Peter, so Simon has a claim too. Simon and Piggy are, indeed, alike in sharing a role in ***Lord of the Flies,*** the role of outsider, scapegoat and victim of murder. Though the two are alike in this way, however, they are otherwise very different from one another and represent, indeed, two mighty opposites, two warring ways of looking at the world, which occur again and again in Golding's fiction. Faith in science and rationality, with a marked disbelief in anything supernatural, is characteristic of Piggy. Simon, by contrast, is intuitive, introspective, other-worldly; his central insight is gained in a vision or trance; Simon represents and has access to a dimension of experience it is proper to call religious. Piggy cannot understand Simon and thinks him mad.

This conflict between the contrasting world-views of science or ratiocination and religious or visionary experience, between worldly commonsense and other-worldly mysticism, is dramatised time and again by Golding: in the figures of Nick Shales and Rowena Pringle in ***Free Fall,*** in Roger Mason and Jocelin in ***The Spire*** and in Edmund Talbot and Robert James Colley in ***Rites of Passage.*** This conflict is clearly of great importance to Golding and it would be true to say that, though he is at pains to be fair to and make a strong case for the scientific or worldly side, his sympathies ultimately lie with the Simons, Jocelins and Colleys. In an essay on education he writes: 'it cannot be said often enough or loudly enough that "Science" is not the most important thing' (HG p. 129). This too has a Swiftian air to it. In Book Three of *Gulliver's Travels* Swift demonstrates powerfully that the analytical intellect, alone and unaided by any higher insight, cannot even begin to offer solutions to the problems of being human. Golding has expressed admiration for Copernicus, whom he characterises as a man devoted to the quest for scientific truth but who nonetheless bears the signs of an inclination towards mysticism.[23] In ***Lord of the Flies*** Golding's bias in this matter is perhaps most clearly seen in the differing degrees of respect accorded to Piggy and Simon by the narrative in their deaths. Leighton Hodson describes this succinctly:

> Golding manages to deepen his meaning of what the boys' attitudes represent by providing them, in their common ends, with descriptions that correspond to the limited practical intelligence in the case of Piggy—dry in tone—and the intuitive depth of understanding in the case of Simon—eloquent and transfiguring.[24]

The limitations of Piggy's practical intelligence are, indeed, particularly highlighted by comparison with Simon. Piggy's clever and sensible schemes fail to bring about the rescue the boys desperately need; his rational approach is unable to sway the mass of boys in debate or preserve order among them; above all, he rejects Simon's suggestion that the Beast is a reality within the boys themselves. Piggy rightly condemns the notion that there is an external Beast that lives in the forest or the sea, but under great pressure comes to believe that Jack is the Beast or Devil, failing to see that this too is an externalisation, an avoidance of his own guilt. Piggy's scientific views dictate that there is no Devil in the world, but if he must allow that there is evil he is determined to 'believe that evil is somewhere else' and in someone else. He is himself, however, involved in the murder of Simon, for all his predictable attempts to exculpate himself and explain the killing away as an accident.

Simon is murdered by the boys when he emerges from the forest into the frenzy of their dance, supposedly a charm against the Beast. Their defence against an imagined external Beast allows the beast within them to gain absolute control and transform them into murderers. Simon had come to tell them that the creature on the mountain they thought to be the Beast was merely the horribly damaged body of a pilot, evidence of the effects of the beast within us in the world of warring adults. Simon had come to bring them confirmation of the truth that he had proposed earlier and for which he had been shouted down and derided, the dark truth that the Beast is within them, each and every one of them. The reception he is given proves his point once and for all. The truth which Simon offers is a grim one, but Simon himself is not at all a grim or dark figure. He is affectionate, gentle and kind, helping the littluns to find good fruit, for example, but also a loner, a 'queer' boy who isolates himself in a forest glade reminiscent of a church and goes into reveries. It is small wonder that the other boys regard this youthful mystic as mad or 'batty', a fool. We must take Simon a great deal more seriously. The traditional role of the prophet is to awaken men to the truth of their own sinfulness: this Simon does, and he also succeeds in fulfilling the popular view of the prophet's task by foretelling the future. He tells Ralph that he will get home safely and his voice comes back to Ralph just before he is in fact rescued. The boys are living in the dangerous error of believing that the Beast is an evil creature at the mountaintop, so Simon the prophet goes to the mountain to discover the truth. On his way he finds a forest glade desecrated by a sow's head on a stick, a gift for the Beast. Simon falls into a fit, or hallucination, or vision, in which the Lord of the Flies, the Devil, speaks to him through the foul mouthpiece of the head and tells him that he is '"part of you"'. He warns Simon to go back and fall into line or the boys will 'do' him (pp. 157-9). Simon defies the threat, climbs the mountain, finds the parachutist and descends to the beach to be slaughtered.

Amidst the bloody chaos of the storm and the demonic dance we are told that 'Simon was crying out something about a dead man on a hill' (p. 168) as he is being assaulted. He refers of course to the parachutist, but we must hear also a suggestion of the death of Christ on Calvary and realise that, in killing the true prophet who had come down to reveal to them their real nature, their sinfulness, and thus set them on the road towards saving themselves, the boys are re-enacting the crucifixion of Jesus Christ. Simon's life and death are an imitation of Christ. In ascending the mountain and returning to the boys, despite the warnings of the Lord of the Flies about what will happen to him, he takes up and shares the Cross like his namesake from Cyrene: '"Simon. He helps"', as Ralph earlier remarks (p. 59). His self-sacrifice does not, however, achieve an instant conversion of the boys to goodness. Nor did Christ's with regard to mankind as a whole. Piggy blames him for bringing his death on himself: '"Coming in the dark—he had no business crawling like that out of the dark. He was batty. He asked for it"' (p. 173). He walked right into his own death, so he must have been mad, a fool, a Simple Simon.

To suggest that a person or character is a fool would normally undermine any confidence we might have that the person or character concerned had wisdom to offer us. Here this is not the case. Simon imitates the folly of that supreme fool Christ, who allowed himself to be crucified and whose teachings must seem foolish to the worldly-wise. Christ the holy fool is admirably described by Erasmus in the *Praise of Folly:*

> Christ too, though he is the wisdom of the Father, was made something of a fool himself in order to help the folly of mankind, when he assumed the nature of man and was seen in man's form . . . Nor did he wish them to be redeemed in any other way save by the folly of the cross and through his simple, ignorant apostles, to whom he unfailingly preached folly.[25]

To those in darkness, to those under the sway of the Lord of This World who is the Lord of the Flies, the wisdom of Christ must indeed appear utter folly. Simon is the first of Golding's holy fools, characters who in many respects are holy or Christ-like and yet, almost by that very token, are ill-fitted for survival in the world of fallen man: two clear examples, whom we shall examine later, are Nathaniel in ***Pincher Martin*** and Matty in ***Darkness Visible.*** The holy or prophetic fool dares to challenge the cosy but delusive beliefs of the majority and so must be laughed at, dismissed, driven out or slaughtered by that majority.

The message or wisdom which Simon offers—that the Beast is in us, that we must acknowledge the 'thing of darkness'[26] as our own—is disturbing and negative. He does not appear to bring the good news of redemption or salvation. But his life and death offer some hope in the book's pervasive gloom inasmuch that among all the boys, so to say, at least one good man has been found, one person who is capable of imitating Christ's redemptive example. At the mountain top he is able to free the dead pilot, according to Golding a symbol of the nightmare of human history (HG p. 90), and allow him to fly off, just as Christ, from an orthodox point of view, changed the nature of history by freeing man from the bondage of sin, offering the *possibility* of escape from the endless backsliding and tribulations of human and personal history. There is, furthermore, the 'eloquent and transfiguring' description of the sea's disposal of Simon's body. Simon is carried 'towards the open sea' by the tide, attended by 'strange, moonbeam-bodied creatures with fiery eyes' who weave a halo of brightness around his head (pp. 169-70). These beautiful and seemingly magical little entities we have seen before in broad daylight:

> There were creatures that lived in this last fling of the sea, tiny transparencies that came questing in with the water over the hot, dry sand . . . Perhaps food had appeared where the last incursion there had been none; bird droppings, insects perhaps, any of the strewn detritus of landward life. Like a myriad of tiny teeth in a saw, the transparencies came scavenging on the beach.
>
> (p. 66)

But there is no beauty or magic or mystery. The creatures are simply the lowest point in the ugly world of living nature, vile scavengers as coldly destructive as sawteeth. It is Simon's self-sacrifice that transforms them to beauty, goes some way towards redeeming the world of nature and reestablishing its beauty and harmony.

What light there is in the book does, indeed, seem to be concentrated around Simon. There are, however, certain other aspects of the novel which may be seem as mitigating the generally excoriating treatment of human nature. 'I am by nature an optimist' Golding has remarked 'but a defective logic—or a logic which I sometimes hope desperately is defective—makes a pessimist of me' (HG p. 126). Though this is rather a dark utterance, it does make explicit that tension between optimism and pessimism, between hope and despair, which is characteristic of Golding's fiction. Indeed, from ***The Spire*** onwards it seems appropriate to characterise his fiction as broadly tragi-comic. Though comedy is a grotesquely inappropriate term to apply to ***Lord of the Flies,*** the outlook of the novel is not entirely pessimistic.

There is first the essential decency of Ralph, 'the fair boy' whose eyes proclaim 'no devil' and who tries to keep the other boys' eyes on the values of civilisation, tries 'to keep a clean flag of flame flying' (pp. 8, 11, 45). Though the book suggests that we should be sceptical about such an ocular proclamation and about 'Rally round the flag, boys!' sentiments, there is no doubt that Ralph does strive earnestly and sincerely to be fair and decent. There is also the goodness, the sheer vitality, of the twins Samneric, Ralph's most loyal supporters. Not only are they kind, loyal and generous, but their apparent blending into one another makes them seem representative of average everyday man, the 'man on the Clapham omnibus'. Moreover, we sympathise strongly with this group and abominate Jack and Roger. It seems that we can at least say of ourselves that we would *like to be* decent, fair and good. Our sympathy or even identification with Ralph is also very effective in intensifying the 'thriller' aspect of the novel: in the final chapter we have the very unpleasant feeling that *we* are being hunted by Jack and Roger. How we fear and loathe their extravagant and insatiable evil! There is some comfort to be taken in this, but we must remember that Ralph and Samneric, those models of decency, were involved in the murder of Simon and, like another decent man caught up in evil, they try to wash the innocent martyr's blood from their hands by their denial that they were present at the killing. Further, Samneric are coerced into joining Jack's tribe and in Ralph's final interview with them they have become, for all the kindness towards Ralph which they cannot quite fight down, guardians of a régime where all rules have disappeared except the rule of sadism. Samneric, like other ordinary men before them, have been transformed into concentration camp guards, porters at the Gate of Hell. Ralph's conversation with them at the Castle Rock is perhaps the most heartrending section of the entire book and there is every reason why that should be so.

Just as we sympathise with the nature of Ralph, Samneric and, indeed, even Piggy, so too we are attracted to the democratic system they create. The gentle, exhortatory paternalism of Ralph and Piggy seems both fair and sensible as a way of organising government. It is manifestly preferable to Jack's absolutist tyranny. Again our hearts seem to be in roughly the right place. And yet Jack's system has greater attraction for the boys, who desert Ralph's tribe in droves. In fairness to Jack it must be said that in certain important respects his reign of terror is a more effective form of government than Ralph's. He gives the boys meat and he is able to keep them in order, to put a stop to quarrels, fragmentation and even sheer laziness in a way which Ralph was not: '"See? They do what I want"' (p. 198), he pointedly remarks to Ralph, who has just become a one-man tribe. Once again the Leviathan raises its head: Hobbes' pessimistic view is that human fractiousness requires to be quelled and governed by an absolute monarch. ***Lord of the Flies*** could never be said to advocate Jack's monarchy however, since though in some ways it clearly 'works' it also panders to and is an expression of the worst aspects of human nature; greed, cruelty and lust. Like a vicious Roman emperor he provides food and entertainment for his mob, entertainment taking the form of beating littluns, murderous ritual dances, and the obscene and rapacious violence of the hunt: 'The sow collapsed under them and they were heavy and fulfilled upon her' (p. 149). Jack intuitively knows all about the lowest and vilest elements in our nature and how to exploit them:

> Simon became inarticulate in his effort to express mankind's essential illness. Inspiration came to him.
>
> "What's the dirtiest thing there is?"
>
> As an answer Jack dropped into the uncomprehending silence that followed it the crude expressive syllable. Release was like an orgasm . . . The hunters were screaming with delight.
>
> (p. 97)

Obscenity can be delightful: that is a symptom of our essential illness.

Jack may be successful in satisfying in the short-term certain basic and base human cravings, but his system offers no hope of rescue. Behaviour such as Jack indulges in and encourages seems to preclude redemption or salvation, even if salvation is no more than the imitation of Christ in *this* world which we see in Simon, whom Jack and his minions kill. The symbol of his terrible régime is the stick sharpened at both ends, the support of the totem Lord of the Flies, a weapon which seems to suggest that its killing-power may rebound against the user. It is a symbol which reminds us of the self-defeating nature of the weaponry deployed for nuclear war by those who build fortresses and bunkers against imagined external threats and evils in the world outside the island. The spear is sharpened by Roger and, for all that has been said about Jack's ability to command obedience, it is not difficult to imagine this sinister figure returning Jack's violent means to power upon him and completing his bloody and Macbeth-like career by sticking *his* head on a pole.

At the close the naval officer arrives to find the island paradise lost and burning, the scene 'with dreadful faces thronged and fiery arms'.[27] Coming from his warship, he is a veritable *deus ex machina* descending from the 'above' of the adult world to set things right and rescue the erring children. Despite the sinister associations of the naval officer, might he not still be seen as the caring and omnipotent God who finally intervenes in man's world to stop the course of the bloody history of fallen man and restore peace forever? Such a view would offer a glimmer of religious light at the end of the tunnel. Such a reading is perhaps allowable, but there is evidence in the novel which counts against it and which ought not to be ignored. There seems to be no haven for the boys to be rescued *to*. We are told much earlier that 'Roger's arm was conditioned by a civilisation that knew nothing of him and was in ruins' (p. 67). When the boys first spot a passing ship on the horizon the narrative speaks of 'the smoke of home' beckoning to them (p. 73), a touching phrase since it suggests both the homeliness the boys long for and the smoking ruins that are all that remain of home. Having been terrified by the dead parachutist that seems to be the Beast, Ralph complains that the 'thing squats by the fire as though it didn't want us to be rescued' (p. 138), and the corpse is, indeed, a sign that the civilisation which might rescue them has been destroyed by war. The naval officer has played a part in that war. Perhaps there is no comfort in seeing him as an image of God, because the image is of a flawed and irresponsible god, perhaps like the forgetful or lazy creator of the island's reef: 'The coral was scribbled in the sea as though a giant had bent down to reproduce the shape of the island in a flowing, chalk line but tired before he had finished' (p. 31). The creator's signature does not inspire confidence in his character and evidences from nature generally, as we have seen, from the 'enmity' of the sun, that traditional symbol of the Godhead, downwards, are not such as to encourage faith in absolute beneficence (pp. 13-15). The weight of evidence would seem to indicate that any creator must be a cruel selfish wielder of power, that the gods are indeed as Gloucester described them, swatting men like flies with an ease the naval officer might well envy or might even match, a source of no comfort or hope. What desperate hope the book offers is simply the example of Simon, the acknowledgement of our guilt, of the 'thing of darkness' within us, and the overcoming of this guilt and darkness in generous, if unsuccessful, self-sacrifice for the sake of others. Simon, like Cordelia, allows a little room for hope, but the book's abiding impression remains like that of *King Lear:* 'grief, sheer grief, grief, grief, grief'.

Notes

1. *King Lear,* III. 7. 81
2. Ibid., V. 3. 197
3. Compare *King Lear,* IV. 6. 4.
4. *King Lear,* III. 7. 81.
5. Ibid., III. 6. 74.
6. More, p. 20.
7. Alastair Niven suggests that 'Ralph's words are an uncomprehending child's expression of what W.B. Yeats wrote in his poem "The Second Coming"'. Niven, *William Golding,* p. 21.
8. Huxley, *Do What You Will,* p. 113.
9. Ibid.
10. Kinkead-Weekes and Gregor, *William Golding,* p. 40.
11. Huxley op.cit., p. 114.
12. Hodson, *William Golding,* p. 38.
13. Swift, *Gullivers Travels,* p. 190 (Book IV, Chapter 3).
14. Swift op.cit., p. 212 (Book IV, Chapter 6).
15. Whitley, *Golding* p. 43.
16. Swift op.cit., p. 213 (Book IV, Chapter 6).
17. Hobbes, *The Leviathan,* p. 186 (Book II, Chapter 13).
18. The importance of Hobbes as background-reading for *Lord of the Flies* is stressed by Alastair Niven. See Niven op.cit. p. 38.
19. Joyce, *Finnegans Wake,* p. 4.
20. Ian McEwan, 'Schoolboys', in Carey, *William Golding,* p. 158.
21. Whitley op.cit., p. 28.
22. Tiger, *William Golding,* p. 51.
23. See 'Copernicus' in *The Hot Gates.*
24. Hodson op.cit., p. 29.
25. Erasmus, *Praise of Folly,* pp. 198-9.
26. *The Tempest,* V.1. 275.
27. Milton, *Paradise Lost,* XII. 644.

L. L. Dickson (essay date 1990)

SOURCE: Dickson, L. L. "*Lord of the Flies.*" In *The Modern Allegories of William Golding,* pp. 12-26. Tampa: University of South Florida Press, 1990.

[*In the following essay, Dickson dissects the allegorical structure of* Lord of the Flies.]

Of Golding's nine novels, ***Lord of the Flies*** is most clearly an allegory. It has been criticized as both too explicit[1] and too ambiguous.[2] Walter Allen's skepticism is typical: "The difficulty begins when one smells allegory."[3] More accurately, Golding's ***Lord of the Flies*** combines the best features of realistic and allegorical fiction; the novel allows for "the simultaneous operation of the factual and the fabular."[4]

The tension between realistic novel and allegorical fable is established in the setting for the action in ***Lord of the Flies:*** the isolated island provides an appropriate stage for the survival story of the deserted boys, but also suggests a universal, timeless backdrop for symbolic action. Golding creates a microcosm, a procedure common "to the great allegorists and satirists," and then "examines the problem of how to maintain moderate liberal values and to pursue distant ends against pressure from extremists and against the lower instincts."[5] The protagonist's ironic "rescue" by a naval officer, who is himself engrossed in the savage business of international warfare, reveals that the chaotic island-world is but a small version of a war-torn adult world. The novel does not imply that children, without the disciplined control of adults, will turn into savages; on the contrary, it dramatizes the real nature of all humans. The nightmare world, which quickly develops on the island, parallels the destruction of the outside world through atomic warfare. The dead parachutist, whom the boys mistake for the Beast, is a symbolic reminder of the human history of self-destruction; the parachutist is literally and figuratively a "fallen man."

At first, the island world is compared to Eden: the boys "accepted the pleasure of morning, the bright sun, the whelming sea and sweet air, as a time when play was good and life so full that hope was not necessary and therefore forgotten."[6] But this setting is simultaneously sinister and hostile. The boys are scratched by thorns and entrapped by creepers. "The ground beneath them was a bank covered with coarse grass, torn everywhere by the upheavals of fallen trees, scattered with decaying coconuts and palm saplings. Behind this was the darkness of the forest proper and the open scar" (p. 6). Eventually the island becomes a burning hell: "Smoke was seeping through the branches in white and yellow wisps, the patch of blue sky overhead turned to the color of a storm cloud, and then the smoke bellowed around him" [Ralph, the protagonist] (p. 233). The island is a microcosm from the adult world; indeed, "you realize after a time that the book is nothing less than a history of mankind itself."[7]

The personified agents in ***Lord of the Flies*** are developed in all the four ways discussed in the first chapter. First, the analogy through nomenclature is the most obvious method by which the characters take on additional dimensions. Golding's novel represents an ironic treatment of R. M. Ballantyne's *The Coral Island,* a children's classic that presents the romantic adventures of a group of English schoolboys marooned on an Edenlike South Sea island. By mustering their wits and their British courage, the boys defeat the evil forces on the island: pirates and native savages. Not only is Golding's island literally a coral island (p. 12) where the boys "dream pleasantly" and romantically, but there are specific references to Ballantyne: "'It's like in a book.' At once there was a clamor. 'Treasure Island—' 'Swallows and Amazons—' 'Coral Island—'" (p. 37). At the conclusion of the novel, the dull-witted naval officer who comes to Ralph's rescue makes an explicit comparison: "Jolly good show. Like the Coral Island" (p. 242). Golding uses the same names for his main characters as Ballantyne did. Ralph, Jack, and Peterkin Gay of *The Coral Island* become Golding's Ralph, Jack, and Simon ("Simon called Peter, you see. It was worked out very carefully in every possible way, this novel"[8]). Golding's characters, however, represent ironic versions of the earlier literary work, and their very names, inviting comparison to Ballantyne, add ironic impact to the characterization.

The change of Peterkin's name to Simon better supports that character's function as a "saint" figure in Golding's novel. Obviously Piggy's name contributes to the symbolism: Piggy will become identified with a hunted pig, and eventually will be killed too, as the boys' savage hunt turns to human rather than animal victims. When Piggy falls to his death, his arms and legs twitch "like a pig's after it has been killed" (p. 217). Jack's name is a variant of John, the disciple of Christ, and indeed Jack is an ironic distortion of the religious connotations of his name, in the same manner as is Christopher Martin, the egocentric protagonist of Golding's third novel.

Second, the characters in ***Lord of the Flies*** become allegorical agents through the correspondence of a state of nature with a state of mind. The more the boys stay on the island, the more they become aware of its sinister and actively hostile elements. The description of the pleasant Coral Island fantasy world quickly dissolves into images of darkness, hostility, danger. The boys accept "the pleasures of morning, the bright sun" and the unrestricted play, but by afternoon the overpowering sunlight becomes "a blow that they ducked" (p. 65). Though dusk partly relieves the situation, the boys are then menaced by the dark: "When the sun sank, darkness dropped on the island like an extinguisher and soon the shelters were full of restlessness, under the remote stars" (p. 66).

The boys' attitude of childish abandon and romantic adventure changes to a much more sober one when the possibility of a beast is introduced. At that point the island is transformed into a dark haven for unspeakable terrors. The boys' increasing apprehension about their immediate physical safety parallels the gradual awareness that is taking shape in the minds of Simon, Piggy, and particularly Ralph, concerning the *real* evil of the island. The boys mistakenly project their own bestiality on an imaginary animal roaming the island, but Simon hesitantly speculates, "maybe it's only us" (p. 103). The others do not understand. They look into the blackened jungle for signs of the beast's movement. The darkness is "full of claws, full of the awful unknown and menace" (p. 116). Simon's inner vision, however, tells him that it is the human being who is "at once heroic and sick" (p. 121). When Simon confronts the Lord of the Flies, the pig's head on a stick, it tells him (but really he tells himself), "Fancy thinking the Beast was something you could hunt and kill! . . . You knew, didn't you? I'm part of you?" (p. 172). The hostile island and its dark mysteries are only a symbolic backdrop reinforcing the images of savagery, bestiality, and destruction that describe, and reveal, the boys themselves.

A third method by which the characters assume allegorical significance is through the implicit comparison of an action with an extrafictional event. James Baker was the first to point out similarities between Euripides' *The Bacchae* and Golding's novel. The mistaken slaying of Simon recalls Pentheus's murder at the hands of the crazed bacchantes of Dionysus. Pentheus's pride and his inability to recognize Dionysus's powers lead to his downfall: "This same lesson in humility is meted out to the schoolboys of ***Lord of the Flies.*** In their innocent pride they attempt to impose a rational order or pattern upon the vital chaos of their own nature. . . . The penalties (as in the play) are bloodshed, guilt, utter defeat of reason."[9]

Both the novel and the play contain a beast-god cult, a hunt sequence, and the dismemberment of the scapegoat figure.[10] Though Simon is the clearest equivalent for Pentheus, Piggy and finally Ralph are cast in similar roles. Piggy is destroyed, though not dismembered, by Jack's forces. Ralph is chased by frenzied hunters but is "saved" (by a deus ex machina process similar to that of the end of Euripides' play) from the prospect of beheading. Ralph fittingly becomes Golding's version of Agave. The boy, like Pentheus's mother, mistakenly takes part in a killing and then must live sorrowfully with the knowledge of his, and all humanity's, capacity for blind destruction.

The actions that help establish parallels to religious events emphasize biblical analogues. Ralph's first blowing of the conch, proclaiming survival after the crash on the island, recalls the angel Gabriel's announcing good news. Inasmuch as the boys' "survival" is quite tentative, however, the implied comparison to Gabriel is ironic. Simon's fasting, helping the little boys, meditating in the wilderness, going up on the mountain—all these actions solidify the Christ parallel. The recurring pattern of falls—the falling parachutist, Piggy's fall to his death, the destruction of the conch in the same fall, Ralph's tumbling panic at the end of the novel—emphasizes the fall of humankind motif.

The extrafictional events pertaining to classical mythology or to Christ's passion enlarge the surface action with additional symbolic meanings.

The fourth and final technique for intensifying allegorical agents concerns the manifestation in an action of a state of mind. In ***Lord of the Flies*** a series of hunts, for either pigs or humans, symbolically demonstrates the boys' gradual deterioration into savages. Moral order is corrupted and the end result is chaos. William Mueller has established convincingly that "the book is a carefully structured work of art whose organization—in terms of a series of hunts—serves to reveal with progressive clarity man's essential core."[11] Mueller identifies six "hunts," but there are at least nine separate instances where this symbolic act occurs: (1) the first piglet, "caught in a curtain of creepers," escapes when Jack is mentally unable to kill the helpless creature (p. 32); (2) a second pig eludes the hunters, much to Jack's disgust (p. 55); (3) Jack is successful the next time, and the hunters conceive the ritual chant of "Kill the Pig. Cut her throat. Spill her blood" (p. 78); later Maurice briefly pretends to be the pig (p. 86); (4) during a mock ceremony that gets out of hand, Robert plays the role of the pig, in a scene that sinisterly foreshadows the transition from nonhuman to human prey (pp. 135-36); (5) after another successful hunt, the boys smear themselves with animal blood, and Maurice plays the pig while Robert ritually pokes him with a spear, to the delight of Jacks's hunters (pp. 161-63); (6) Jack and Roger play hunter and pig respectively, as Piggy and Ralph "find themselves eager to take a place in this demented but partly secure society" (p. 181); (7) Simon is mistaken for the beast and is torn to pieces; (8) Piggy is killed by Roger, who acts "with a sense of delirious abandonment" (p. 216); (9) and finally Ralph is the object of the last murderous hunt.

The two fundamental patterns by which allegorical action is resolved are those of "progress" and "battle." The journey motif is first established by the plot circumstances of the opening chapter. A group of boys has been taken by airplane from a warthreatened England to a safer territory, but in the process their plane is attacked and they have been dropped to safety on a deserted island. Their thwarted flight is mentioned in the opening exposition. Though their physical, outer journey has ended, they soon begin a more recondite "journey." Through their quest for the beast, they (or at least Simon and Ralph) discover the real beast, humanity's own predilection for evil.

The structure of ***Lord of the Flies*** provides for a gradual revelation of insight, as Ralph sees his friends slowly turn into beasts themselves. The significance of the final scene, in which the naval officer reestablishes an adult perspective, is not what James Gindin once contended: "a means of cutting down or softening the implications built up within the structure of the boys' society on the island."[12] The officer's presence does not reaffirm that "adult sanity really exists," nor is it merely a gimmick that "palliates the force and the unity of the original metaphor."[13] On the contrary, it provides the final ironic comment: Ralph is "saved" by a soldier of war, a soldier who cannot see that the boys have symbolically reenacted the plight of all persons who call themselves civilized and yet continue to destroy their fellow humans in the same breath.

The irony of this last scene is consistent with Golding's sarcastic treatment of Ballantyne, and it also emphasizes the universality of Ralph's experience. There is no distinction between child and adult here. The boys' ordeal is a metaphor for the human predicament. Ralph's progress toward self-knowledge culminates in his tears: "Ralph wept for the end of innocence, the darkness of man's heart, and the fall through the air of the true, wise friend called Piggy" (p. 242). Because Piggy represents the failure of reason, the use of "wise" offers a further irony.

The battle motif is developed in both physical confrontations and rhetorical "combat." Initially, the pig hunts are ritualized tests of strength and manhood, but when the hunters eventually seek human prey (Simon, Piggy, and finally Ralph) the conflict is between the savage and the civilized; blind emotion and prudent rationality; inhumanity and humanity; evil and good. This conflict is further established in the chapter entitled "The Shell and the Glasses," when Jack's hunters attack Ralph's boys and steal Piggy's glasses. Jack carries the broken spectacles—which have become symbolic of intellect, rationality, and civilization—as ritual proof of his manhood and his power over his enemies: "He was a chief now in truth; and he made stabbing motions with his spear" (p. 201). In the "Castle Rock" chapter, Ralph opposes Jack in what is called a "crisis" situation: "They met with a jolt and bounced apart. Jack swung with his fist at Ralph and caught him on the ear. Ralph hit Jack in the stomach and made him grunt. Then they were facing each other again, panting and furious, but unnerved by each other's ferocity. They became aware of the noise that was the background to this fight, the steady shrill cheering of the tribe behind them" (p. 215).

More subtle forms of "battle"—debate and dialogue—are dramatized in the verbal exchanges between Jack and Ralph. Golding emphasizes their polarity: "They walked along, two continents of experience and feeling, unable to communicate" (p. 62). Later when Jack paints his face and flaunts his bloodied knife, the conflict is heightened: "The two boys faced each other. There was the brilliant world of hunting, tactics, fierce exhilaration, skill; and there was the world of longing and baffled commonsense" (p. 81). When Ralph does not move, Jack and the others have to build their fire in a less ideal place: "By the time the pile [of firewood] was built, they were on different sides of a high barrier" (p. 83). Different sides of the wood, different continents, different worlds—all these scenes intensify the symbolic as well as physical conflict. Here we encounter "a structural principle that becomes Golding's hallmark: a polarity expressed in terms of a moral tension. Thus, there is the rational (the firewatchers) pitted against the irrational (the hunters)."[14]

In both chapter 2, "Beast from Water," and chapter 8, "Gift for the Darkness," the exchange of views about whether there is a beast or not "becomes a blatant allegory in which each spokesman caricatures the position he defends."[15] Ralph and Piggy think that rules and organization can cure social ills, and that if things "break up," it is because individuals are not remembering that life "is scientific," rational, logical (p. 97). Jack hates rules, only wishes to hunt, and believes that evil is a mystical, living power that can be appeased by ritual sacrifice (p. 159). Simon feels that evil is not outside but rather within all human beings, though he is "inarticulate in his effort to express mankind's essential illness" (p. 103). He uses comparisons with excrement and filth to describe his notion of human inner evil.

Simon's confrontation with the pig's head on a stick, the Lord of the Flies, is another instance of allegorical dialogue. At first, Beelzebub seems to triumph:

Simon is mesmerized by the grinning face (p. 165); he is warned that he is "not wanted," for Simon is the only boy who possesses a true vision of the nature of evil; and finally he faints (p. 172). However, Simon recovers, asks himself, "What else is there to do?" (p. 174), discovers the dead parachutist, and then takes the news about the "beast" to the rest of the boys. The entire scene with the pig's head represents the conflict that is occurring within Simon's own consciousness. The Lord of the Flies is only an externalization of the inner evil in all humans. Later when Ralph comes upon the pig's head, "the skull [stares at] Ralph like one who knows all the answers and won't tell" (p. 22). Though Ralph does not understand the significance of the pig, he does feel a "sick fear." In desperation he hits the head, as if breaking it would destroy the evil on the island. However, the broken pig's head lies in two pieces, "its grin now six feet across" (p. 222). Rather than being destroyed, it ironically has grown. In the final pages of the novel, when Ralph is desperately fleeing from the hunters, he runs in circles and retraces his steps back to the broken pig's head, and this time its "fathom-wide grin" entirely dominates the burning island.

Four patterns of imagery reinforce the symbolism in ***Lord of the Flies.*** Images pertaining to excrement, darkness, falling, and animalism help define the human capacity for evil and savagery.

The many references to excrement, and also to dirt, underline thematically the vileness of human nature itself. As the boys' attempts at a sanitation program gradually break down, the inherent evil in human nature is symbolically manifested in the increasing images that refer to dung: "the two concepts merge in Golding's imagination—covertly in ***Lord of the Flies*** and manifestly in ***Free Fall,*** which is a literary cloaca, full of that revulsion psychologists try to explain in terms of the proximity and ambiguity of the apertures utilized for birth and excreta."[16]

Images associated with excrement (and more generally, dirt) are used in a negative sense, depicting human corruption. The conch makes "a low, farting noise" (p. 15). Johnny, the first "littlun" Ralph and Piggy meet, is in the act of defecating (p. 16). Pig droppings are closely examined by Jack's hunters to determine how recently the pig has left a particular place; the temperature of feces has become the central subject of interest (pp. 54 and 132). Ralph slowly loses his battle against filth: "With a convulsion of the mind, Ralph discovered dirt and decay, understood how much he disliked [his own long, dirty hair]" (p. 88). Even when Piggy tries to clean his glasses, the attempt is in vain (p. 11). He is appalled at the increasing filth on the island: "'We chose those rocks right along beyond the bathing pool as a lavatory. . . . Now people seem to use anywhere. Even near the shelters and the platform. You littluns, when you're getting fruit; if you're taken short—' The assembly roared. 'I said if you're taken short you keep away from the fruit. That's dirty'" (p. 92).

Weekes and Gregor recognize the realistic level of description here—eating nothing but fruit does indeed bring on diarrhea—but they add, "The diarrhea might seem to invite allegorical translation—the body of man is no longer fit for Eden."[17] At one significant point, the inarticulate Simon tries to think of "the dirtiest thing there is" (p. 103) in order to describe the fallen human condition, and Jack's answer, "one crude expressive syllable," reaffirms the metaphor of excrement, which prevails throughout the novel. The area near the decaying, fallen parachutist is "a rotten place" (p. 125). When the pig's head is mounted on the stick, it soon draws a "black blob of flies"; it is literally a lord of the flies, as well as figuratively Beelzebub, from the Hebrew *baalzebub,* "lord of flies." Sometimes this name is translated "lord of dung." By the end of the novel, Ralph himself has been reduced to a dirty, piglike animal.

Golding uses light-dark contrasts in a traditional way: the numerous images of darkness underline the moral blackness of the boys' crumbling society. The normal associations with the sinister, with death, with chaos, with evil are suggested by this imagery. Decaying coconuts lie "skull-like" amid green shadows (p. 7); Jack's choirboys are clothed in black; the beast is naturally associated with the coming of night (p. 39); the "unfriendly side of the mountain" is shrouded in hushed darkness (p. 48). Roger is described as a dark figure: "the shock of black hair, down his nape and low on his forehead, seemed to suit his gloomy face and make what had seemed at first an unsociable remoteness into something forbidding" (p. 68).

With a Hawthornesque touch, Golding describes the subtle change that has come over all the boys' faces, after the group has become largely a hunting society: "faces cleaned fairly well by the process of eating and sweating but marked in the less accessible angles with a kind of shadow" (p. 130). Jack is described as "a stain in the darkness" (p. 142). Generally, the coming of night turns common surroundings into a nightmare landscape of imaginary horrors: "The skirts of the forest and the scar were familiar, near the conch and the shelters and sufficiently friendly in daylight. What they might become in darkness nobody cared to think" (p. 155).

Images of light and brightness are identified with spirit, regeneration, life, goodness. The description of Simon's dead body as it is carried out to sea suggests transcendence: "Softly, surrounded by a fringe of inquisitive bright creatures, itself a silver shape beneath the steadfast constellations, Simon's dead body moved out toward the open sea" (p. 184). The contrast between the bright, gaudy butterflies and the black flies on the pig's head emphasizes the symbolic conflict between good and evil used throughout the novel. The bright butterflies are drawn to the sunlight and to open places (p. 64); they surround the saintly Simon (p. 158); they are oblivious to the brutal killing of the sow: "the butterflies still danced, preoccupied in the centre of the clearing" (p. 162). In this particular instance, they remind the reader of those indifferent seagulls in Stephen Crane's "The Open Boat"—simply a part of nature, not threatened by the environment, and a mocking contrast to the violent predicaments that human beings either perpetuate or suffer. But the butterflies represent a more positive force, and significantly they desert the open space dominated by the grinning pig's head.[18]

Golding's obsession with the fallen human state permeates the imagery of ***Lord of the Flies.*** The opening chapter is typical. Ralph appears amid a background of fallen trees. He trips over a branch and comes "down with a crash" (p. 5). He talks with Piggy about coming down in the capsule that was dropped from the plane. He falls down again when attempting to stand on his head (p. 25). He pretends to knock Simon down (p. 28). In addition to the descriptions of the fallen parachutist, Simon's fainting spells, Ralph's "nightmares of falling and death" (p. 229), and his final collapse at the feet of the naval officer, the act of falling is closely associated with the idea of lost innocence. Ralph weeps for "the end of innocence . . . and the fall through the air" of Piggy.

Animal imagery reinforces the boys' transformation into savages and subhumans. Predictably, evil is associated with the beast, the pig's head, or a snake, but as the story progresses, the boys themselves are described with an increasing number of animal images.

The boys' disrobing early in the novel at first suggests a return to innocence, but as the hunters become more and more savage, their nakedness merely underscores their animalism. Sam and Eric grin and pant at Ralph "like dogs" (pp. 17 and 46). Jack moves on all fours, "dog-like," when tracking the pig (p. 53); during the hunt he hisses like a snake, and is "less a hunter than a furtive thing, ape-like among the tangle of trees" (p. 54). Ralph calls him a "beast" (p. 214). Piggy, whose very name suggests an obvious comparison, sees that the boys are becoming animals; he says that if Ralph does not blow the conch for an assembly, "we'll soon be animals anyway" (p. 107). Without his glasses, Piggy laments that he will "have to be led like a dog" (p. 204). When he dies, his body twitches "like a pig's after it has been killed" (p. 217). Simon, hidden in the shadows of the forest, is transformed into a "thing," a "beast," when the narration shifts to the other boys' view (pp. 182-83).

Ralph's transformation is slower than the others, but it is clearly discernible. Early in the novel, he viciously accepts the hunters' raw pig meat and gnaws on it "like a wolf" (p. 84). He is caught up in the savage ritual when Roger plays the pig (p. 181); he is part of the unthinking gang that murders Simon. When Piggy is killed, Ralph runs for his life and obeys "an instinct that he did not know he possessed" (p. 217). In the last chapter, Ralph is little more than a cornered animal. Ironically he sharpens a stick in self-defense and becomes a murderous hunter himself: "Whoever tried [to harm him] would be stuck, squealing like a pig" (p. 231). We are told that he "raised his spear, snarled a little, and waited" (p. 233). Ralph's transformation is both shocking and saddening. Alone in the forest, he brutally attacks the first adversary he meets: "Ralph launched himself like a cat; stabbed, snarling, with the spear, and the savage doubled up" (p. 234). When Ralph is trapped in the underbrush, he wonders what a pig would do, for he is in the same position (p. 236).

Related to these animal images is the continual reference to the word *savage.* In ***Lord of the Flies*** the distinction between civilized human being and savage becomes increasingly cloudy and a source of further irony. Early in the novel Jack himself proclaims, "I agree with Ralph. We've got to have rules and obey them. After all, we're not savages" (p. 47). Piggy asks more than once, "What are we? Humans? Or animals? Or savages?" followed by the double irony, "What's grownups going to think?" (p. 105). The painted faces of the hunters provide "the liberation into savagery" (p. 206), an ironic freedom to destroy society; and the animal imagery contributes to this idea.

Several "levels" of meaning operate in ***Lord of the Flies,*** apart from the surface narrative. First, from a particular psychological viewpoint, the tripartite organization of the human psyche—ego, id, superego—is dramatized symbolically in the characters of Ralph, Jack, and Piggy, respectively. The conflict between Ralph, the level-headed elected leader of the boys' council, and Jack, the self-appointed head of the hunters, corresponds to an ego-id polarity. Ralph realistically confronts the problem of survival and works out a practical plan for rescue. Jack is quick to revert to savagery, dishonesty, violence. Piggy, the fat, bespectacled rationalist, reminds Ralph of his responsibilities, makes judgments about Jack's guilt, and generally represents the ethical voice on the island. Since Piggy does not acknowledge his own share of guilt for Simon's death, Oldsey and Weintraub conclude that this inconsistency "spoils the picture often given of Piggy as superego or conscience."[19] However, the many times Piggy reminds the weakening Ralph of what must be done far outweigh this one reversal.

A second level of symbolism emerges from the archetypal patterns in the novel. The quest motif is represented by Ralph's stumbling attempts at self-knowledge. His is literally an initiation by fire. Ironically the knowledge he acquires does not allow him to become an integrated member of adult society, but rather it causes him to recoil from the nightmare world he discovers. He is a scapegoat figure who must be sacrificed as atonement for the boys' evils. Simon and Piggy are also variants of the scapegoat symbol. Simon is most clearly the saint or Christ figure. The Dionysian myth is also reworked, as the boys' blindness to their own irrational natures leads to their destruction. As James Baker has observed, Euripides' *Bacchae* "is a bitter allegory" of not only the degeneration of society but also of essential human blindness: "the failure of rational man who invariably undertakes the blind ritual-hunt in which he seeks to kill the threatening 'beast' within his own being."[20]

On still another level, ***Lord of the Flies*** accommodates a political allegory in which Ralph represents democracy and Jack totalitarianism. Golding has often stressed the impact of World War II on his own life and his change from an idealist who believed in human perfectibility, to a more skeptical observer who had discovered a dark truth "about the given nature of man."[21] In his most explicit statement about the effect of the war on his estimation of humanity and its political systems, Golding says:

> It is bad enough to say that so many Jews were exterminated in this way and that, so many people liquidated—lovely, elegant word—but there were things done during that period from which I still have to avert my mind lest I should be physically sick. They were not done by the headhunters of New Guinea, or by some primitive tribe in the Amazon. They were done, skillfully, coldly, by educated men, doctors, lawyers, by men with a tradition of civilization behind them, to beings of their own kind. . . . When these destructive capacities emerged into action they were thought aberrant. Social systems, political systems were composed, detached from the real nature of man. They were what one might call political symphonies. They would perfect most men, and at the least, reduce aberrance.
>
> Why, then, have they never worked?[22]

Such statements not only define Golding's own social background but also illuminate his use of the microcosmic island society in ***Lord of the Flies.***

Golding's own comments about ***Lord of the Flies*** continually focus on the potentials and the limitations of the democratic ideal. Though he supports a democratic doctrine, he recognizes its weaknesses: "You can't give people freedom without weakening society as an implement of war, if you like, and so this is very much like sheep among wolves. It's not a question with me as to whether democracy is the right way so much, as to whether democracy can survive and remain what it is."[23] By giving up all its principles, the island society of ***Lord of the Flies*** demonstrates the inefficacy of political organizations that attempt to check human beings' worst destructive instincts. It is only by first recognizing these dark powers that democracy can hope to control them.

The fourth level of meaning is the moral allegory, which focuses on the conflicts between good and evil, and encourages philosophical or theological interpretations. Golding is defining the nature of evil. Whether it is embodied in a destructive, unconscious force, a mistaken sacrifice that unsuccessfully atones for the boys' collective guilt, or a dictatorial power opposing the democratic order (corresponding to the psychological, archetypal, and politico-sociological levels, respectively), the problems of moral choice, the inevitability of original sin and human fallibility, the blindness of self-deception create a fourth level of meaning in the novel.

The island is not only a stage on which characters must make crucial moral decisions but also a microcosm for the human mind, in which ethical conflicts similarly occur. Because Golding believes that "a fabulist is always a moralist," he assigns a significant pattern of imagery to Ralph, "the fair boy" (p. 5), who unties the "snake-clasp of his belt" (p. 7). Ralph possesses a "mildness about his mouth and eyes that proclaims no devil" (p. 7); he rallies the boys to the open, sunlit part of the island; his conch sounds a Gabriellike note unifying (if only temporarily) his followers. Jack, on the other hand, is identified with darkness and violence: when his band of choirboys first appears, it is described as "something dark," like a "creature" (p. 19); the black caps and cloaks hide their faces; Jack's red hair suggests a devilish element; his impulsive decision to be a hunter and kill pigs foreshadows his demonic monomania for destruction; when he first meets Ralph, Jack is sun-blinded after coming out of the dark jungle.

However, because Golding complicates the characterization and shows Ralph to be susceptible to evil forces and at times paradoxically sympathetic to Jack, the reader recognizes ambiguities not easily compatible with a neat but rigid system of symbols. If ***Lord of the Flies*** "teaches" through its moral allegory, it is the lesson of self-awareness: "The novel is the parable of fallen man. But it does not close the door on that man; it entreats him to know himself and his Adversary, for he cannot do combat against an unrecognized force, especially when it lies within him."[24]

Notes

1. See Douglas Hewitt, "New Novels"; Francis E. Kearns, "Salinger and Golding: Conflict on the Campus," p. 139; Howard S. Babb, *The Novels of William Golding,* p. 19.
2. Margaret Walters, "Two Fabulists: Golding and Camus," p. 23. Walters criticizes *Lord of the Flies* for its "deliberate mystifications" paradoxically combined with "crude explicitness."
3. Walter Allen, "New Novels."
4. Clive Pemberton, *William Golding,* p. 9. For a detailed study of the close relationship between fantasy and realism in the modern novel, see Patrick Merla, "'What Is Real?' Asked the Rabbit One Day." A similar view is expressed by James Stern, "English Schoolboys in the Jungle": "Fully to succeed, a fantasy must approach very close to reality."
5. Phillip Drew, "Second Reading," 79.
6. William Golding, *Lord of the Flies,* p. 65. Subsequent references are to this edition, and hereafter page numbers will be indicated in the text.
7. Wayland Young, "Letter from London," pp. 478-79.
8. Golding and Kermode, "Meaning," p. 10.
9. Baker, *Golding,* p. 9.
10. Bernard F. Dick, *William Golding,* p. 31.
11. William Mueller, "An Old Story Well Told: Commentary on William Golding's *Lord of the Flies,*" p. 1203.
12. James Gindin, *Postwar British Fiction,* p. 198.
13. Ibid., p. 204. For other adverse criticism of Golding's "gimmick endings," see Young, "Letter," p. 481, and Kenneth Rexroth, "William Golding."
14. Dick, *Golding,* p. 21.
15. Baker, *Golding,* p. 10.
16. Bernard S. Oldsey and Stanley Weintraub, *The Art of William Golding,* p. 30.
17. Mark Kinkcad-Weekes and Ian Gregor, *William Golding: A Critical Study,* p. 25.
18. Also see Robert J. White, "Butterfly and Beast in *Lord of the Flies,*" in which he identifies the butterflies with the Greek word for butterfly, *psyche,* meaning "soul."
19. Oldsey and Weintraub, *Art,* p. 22.
20. Baker, *Golding,* p. 7. Also see Dick, *Golding,* pp. 29-33: "*Lord of the Flies* can also be read in the light of the Dionysian-Apollonian dichotomy" (i.e., the conflict between the irrational and rational worlds).
21. Granville Hicks, "The Evil that Lurks in the Heart," p. 36.
22. Golding, *Hot Gates,* pp. 86-87.
23. Keating and Golding, "Purdue Interview," pp. 189-90. Also see Douglas M. Davis, "A Conversation with Golding," p. 28; Maurice Dolbier, "Running J. D. Salinger a Close Second," p. 6.
24. Mueller, "Old Story," p. 1206.

John F. Fitzgerald and John R. Kayser (essay date 1992)

SOURCE: Fitzgerald, John F., and John R. Kayser. "Golding's *Lord of the Flies:* Pride as Original Sin." *Studies in the Novel* 24, no. 1 (spring 1992): 78-85.

[*In the following essay, Fitzgerald and Kayser examine Egyptian influence on Golding's novel.*]

"Just as the mathematicians say the rainbow is an appearance of the sun embellished by its reflection into a cloud, so the present myth is the appearance of a reality which turns the mind back to other thoughts."

—Plutarch—*Isis et Osiris*

In **"Fable,"** William Golding avers that ***Lord of the Flies*** is a multilayered work and open to various interpretations.[1] The novel has been plausibly interpreted as a Christian parable[2] and Greek tragedy, and less plausibly with reference to neo-Freudian, Jungian, and Marxian concepts.[3] In what has become the authoritative interpretation of ***Lord of the Flies,*** James R. Baker and Bernard Dick, who base their respective arguments on textual evidence and Golding's professed admiration for Greek tragedy,[4] conclude that the form and substance of Golding's myth owes much to Euripides's *Bacchae.*[5] Both Baker and Dick argue that ***Lord of the Flies*** is an allegory on the disintegration of society due to a tragic flaw in human nature: man fails to recognize, and thereby appease, the irrational part of his soul.

Ralph at the end of the novel, on the precipice, stares uncomprehendingly into the irrational darkness of his soul. He cries for the loss of innocence. He cries for the loss of his rational friend Piggy, who also denied the irrational. The boys have committed the sin of Pentheus, according to Baker, by trying to impose "in their innocent pride" an order on the "vital chaos of their own nature."[6] Their attempt took the form of a parliamentary government, and it failed. They regress into barbarism. The plight of the boys becomes an allegory for the plight of modern man, who denies and fears the irrational. Mankind's essential illness is irrational fear.

But such a conclusion does not adequately account for Golding's emphasis on "off-campus history",[7] the concept through which he explores the meaning of ***Lord of the Flies.*** Indeed, Dick candidly admits that he is "vexed" by Golding's emphasis.[8] Off-campus history, which Golding distinguishes from academic history, is characterized by prejudice for and pride in one's own. The partisan and the sport-fan alike are moved by the fortunes of their heroes; their passion for their own agitates them and clouds their judgment, whereas the scholar's objectivity inures him to partisan passions. Fear, the dead parachutist, and the various other manifestations of the beast are symbols of off-campus history and point to the vital core of this fabulist's tale.

No interpretation of ***Lord of the Flies,*** however, has sought an Egyptian influence. Yet Golding's interest in ancient Egypt and the Osiris myth is well documented.[9] This myth apparently left an indelible impression upon Golding, and its influence reverberates in the symbolism of ***Lord of the Flies.*** But most importantly, an Osirian interpretation illuminates man's fallen nature, while explaining the importance attached by Golding to off-campus history. The "trite, obvious and familiar" moral lesson of Golding's novel[10] is that we are capable of the most heinous cruelties in the service of our pride.

The "beastie" appears to the reader in a variety of guises: as a "snake-thing," "beast from water," "beast from air," and, finally, as an aspect of human nature. The nature of the beast is also implied by the suggestive symbolism of the title, ***Lord of the Flies.***[11] The "lord of the flies," or Beelzebub, has been associated with the Christian devil.[12] Leaving aside the pregnant symbolism of the decaying pighead, the beastie as a snake-thing invites comparison to the serpent of the Garden of Eden.[13] However, in the Osiris myth the Egyptian daemon Set-Typhon is also represented by "snakes,"[14] and with the ascent of Christianity he was transfigured into Baal or Beelzebub.[15]

A biblical interpretation of the symbolism of the snake is not at variance with an Osirian interpretation. Golding imputes that the fallen nature of man is related to his temptation by the subtle serpent in mythical Eden. Mankind's fallen nature is his desire to be "wise" and "as gods."[16] This would reduce the fallen nature of man to pride. May we then attribute man's ills, including war, to his vanity?

Set-Typhon, intriguingly, is also associated with the sea. The "beast from the air" comes, as it were, from "a sudden bright explosion" carried by the changing winds to its resting place on the island. Typhon, who is also regarded as "fire,"(367C) later became the god of winds. The narrator also informs us that the boys arrived on the island by some "enchantment. Some act of God—a typhoon perhaps."[17] It strikes us as more than coincidental that typhoon is derived from Typhon. Moreover, this passage appears to refer to the arrival of the boys, or Ralph, on the island. Given the construction of this passage, "his" could refer to the arrival of a god.

The beast's manifestations as "from the sea," "from the air," and "in us" are all associated with war. Rescue, long awaited and desperately needed, comes in the form of a trim warship off-shore; that is, rescue comes from the sea. The dead parachutist bears a message from the adult world, to the boys, from a "battle fought at ten miles' height." This sign descends upon the boys just as their society is disintegrating, and just as Ralph cries out for a sign from the supposedly well-ordered adult world, a world which, the narrator informs us, is embroiled in a cataclysmic war.[18] Our diseased nature, the beast "in us," leads the boys to war and barbarism just as it does in the adult world.[19]

The Osiris myth accounts for the emergence of discord and, hence, war. It thereby demonstrates the precariousness of civilization. According to Plutarch, while reigning as king on earth, the god Osiris gave the Egyptians civilization by introducing laws, worship of the gods, marriage, and agriculture. Before Osiris gave them agriculture the Egyptians had been savages and cannibals. Osiris's brother, the daemon Set-Typhon, filled with envy and pride, sought to usurp his throne. Frustrated in his attempt to take his brother's place, Typhon tricked Osiris and drowned him. Isis, the wife of Osiris, searched for the body, regained it and concealed it in the woods. Typhon, while hunting pig during a full moon, discovered and mutilated it. A war, punctuated with "terrible deeds" and "confusion," ensued until Horus, son of Osiris, appears to have defeated Typhon. But as Plutarch notes, although "weakened and shattered [the] power of Typhon still gasps and struggles" (362E).

Plutarch informs us that the wise interpret the myth as an explanation of entirely natural phenomena: the Nile is Osiris, Isis the earth, and Typhon the sea. The yearly inundation of the Nile valley marks the victory of Osiris and Horus over Typhon. But Plutarch also makes it quite clear that a strict allegory is an insufficient guide to understanding. The "wisest," Plutarch continues, "think that nature must contain in itself the creation and origin of evil as well as good" (369D). Osiris, then, represents good in the universe and Typhon evil. The creative, fertilizing, and nourishing aspects of nature are represented by Osiris as is the order of the universe. Typhon symbolizes "everything harmful and destructive in nature" (369A).

Plutarch also states that this myth, "because it is inbred into the body and into the soul of the universe," reverberates with meaning for the soul of man. Osiris represents reason and mind (*nous kai logos*) in addition to creativity (371A). Moreover, Plutarch concludes that Osiris and Dionysus are the same deity (356). They either represent the same qualities within the soul or have the same origin and source. The identification of Osiris with both the reasonable and creative elements of the soul (373B) poses a problem, because Osiris as both the creative principle and dispassionate reason questions our modern disassociation of reason from creativity or reason from intuition.

Typhon represents "the element of soul which is passionate, akin to the Titans, without reason, and brutish" (371B). He personifies the overpowering, violent, and proud (371B). On account of these qualities, Typhon lusted after Osiris's preferred position. His desire to garner power was described by Plutarch as a "mad frenzy" (368D). The ritual slaughter of animals becomes identified with Typhon through this myth.

The dramatic movement of the Osiris myth flows from the character of the daemon Typhon. Typhon's desire to rule leads him to wage war against his brother. If this myth does speak to the soul of man, and man like nature contains both Osirian and Typhonic traits, then we can conclude that man is by nature proud.[20] Man can, therefore, be said to be a fallen creature because of his desire to be preferred. Pride leads some, in this myth Typhon, to heroic exertions, but also to harm others. Thus, Typhon may be said to be heroic and sick. Pride leads to war.

The Typhonic element of human nature, in ***Lord of the Flies,*** is represented by Jack. Jack is red-haired, freckled, hence ruddy, and prone to blush when angry and frustrated. Typhon, according to the tradition, is described as red and ruddy. Indeed, red-haired men were burned and abused in ancient Egypt because they represented Typhon.[21] When Jack's face "blushes with mortification," on the election of Ralph, he can be said to be red. And as Golding again describes, after the second vote, "Jack turned, red in face," because he had been outwitted (p. 115).[22] Jack desires to be preferred, and when his pride is offended he blushes. It should also be noted that when Ralph's moral superiority is in doubt he too blushes (p. 137). Thus, blushing appears as a manifestation of wounded pride. Golding's depiction of the character Jack, and blushing, accords well with Plutarch's description of Typhon as envious, proud, and red.

Jack's soul is also Typhonic. He evinces an overweening ambition and a burning desire to be chief, demonstrated by his competition with Ralph both when the boys first selected a chief and when Jack calls for a vote of "no confidence" in Ralph. After his second parliamentary defeat, Jack responds by creating his own society and waging war on Ralph's. Jack's successful society is dedicated to hunting, war, protection from the beast, but most importantly to placating Jack's ego. Jack's regime reverts to savagery, and the narrator describes it as "demented" (p. 92). It is the antithesis of the society he opposes, the society made possible by Piggy and his specs.

Ralph seems to be the civilized counterpart to Jack: Osiris to Jack's Typhon. Ralph blows the conch, articulates the idea for a rescue fire, and, according to Jack, "gives the orders." Ralph certainly looks the part of a leader and, unlike Piggy, he comes from the class expected to lead.[23] He insists that the boys must have and follow rules.

Yet after arriving on the island, Ralph does not know how he got there. The opening conversation makes it pellucid that Piggy does. Although Ralph discovers the conch, Piggy knows what it is and how to use it. But perhaps, most important of all, Piggy sees the need for a meeting. Once the boys are gathered, Piggy "moved among the crowd asking names and frowning to remember them" (p. 17). Not Ralph, but Piggy knows the importance of assemblies. Piggy can, for these reasons, be deemed the true founder of the parliamentarian society created by the assembly. At the start of the novel, the narrator states, "what intelligence had been shown was traceable to Piggy" (p. 21).

Damning to the interpretation that Ralph is the reasonable character is his attraction to the seductions of hunting, fierce exhilaration, and ambition. In the incident where Ralph almost maims Robert in the ecstacy of a pig killing ritual, he was "carried away by a sudden thick excitement" and overmastered by a "desire to squeeze and hurt" (p. 104). More damning is his participation in yet another pig killing ritual: the murder of Simon. His self-forgetting in the irrational, frenzy of the boy's orgiastic rituals conspires against the *Bacchae* interpretation, discussed above, for the authors of that interpretation concluded that Ralph was Pentheus who tried to repress irrationality causing his downfall.[24] He demonstrates that he too can be carried away by mad frenzy.

If Ralph does not represent the Osirian elements, what does he represent? Following Golding, we agree that Ralph is "the average rather more than average, man of goodwill and commonsense."[25] Ralph represents better than average humanity;[26] his tale is ours.

Golding represents the duality of Osiris's nature with Simon and Piggy. They together embody that mixture of reason and intuition, which is the root of creativity. It should be recalled that the distinction made in Plutarch's *Isis et Osiris* was between the destructive and passionate, on the one hand, and creative and rational, on the other. Again, unlike modern perceptions, the Osiris myth, does not disassociate reason and creativity. Golding insists that art and reason are connected. As he related: "this business that the artist as a sort of starry-eyed inspired creature, dancing along with his feet two or three feet above the surface of the earth, not really knowing what sort of prince he's leaving behind him, is nothing like the truth."[27]

Golding may have felt it necessary to bifurcate Osiris to make this myth accessible to a modern audience. Golding has supported this "reduction" of Simon and Piggy to the same root by stating that Simon is "Simon called Peter," and that this character was derived, in part, from the character Peterkin Gay of Ballantyne's *Coral Island.*[28] Piggy is also an odd contraction of Peterkin's name by combining the first initial and one vowel of each part of his name to form PiGy.

An Osirian interpretation also avoids the difficulty of explaining why Golding deviated from Euripides over the choice of "scapegoats." Golding, according to the authors of the "*Bacchae*" interpretation, assigned the scapegoat role to Simon, but from the logic of their analysis the scapegoat should have been Ralph, "the Pentheus in embryo."[29] Neither Dick nor Baker offer a satisfactory solution to this problem of Golding's choice. Golding also passionately denies that Simon is a scapegoat.[30]

From the moment we first see the boys on the island, Piggy appears as a knower. Piggy has an inkling of the chaos into which the adult world has fallen. He understands that their coming to be on the island is linked to the war raging outside. He attempts to dispel the irrational fear of the littluns by offering a rational account of fear and the beast. Speaking of "doctors . . . for the inside of your mind," Piggy concludes that fear is in the beholder; it does not result from a healthy apprehension of the unknown. The author has Piggy proclaim the credo of scientific humanism, "Life is scientific, that's what it is" (p. 76).

Piggy's knowledge is, however, quite limited.[31] Its roots are modern science and deductions from empirical observations. Only that which can be demonstrated in the light of day is real and rational. Piggy, moreover, lacks practical wisdom; he doesn't understand people. For example, he questions whether the island can sustain a beast. He asks, "What would a beast eat?" (p. 75). The obvious, and ironic, answer is that it would eat pig. He goes on to precipitate the debate that marks the boy's undoing by asking Phil to recount his experience of the beast. Phil's tortured rambling initiates a chain of events that would lead the narrator to relate, "That the world, that understandable and lawful world, was slipping away" (p. 82). Had Piggy been an acute observer of men, or boys, he would have realized how fragile the island society had become and foreseen the impact of Phil's tale.

Piggy's lack of prudence points to another fatal flaw in his understanding. He proves incapable of diagnosing the disease that afflicts the boys: he cannot see the beast for what it is. Piggy refuses to admit that Simon's death was murder. Calling it an accident, he refuses even to acknowledge his participation. He rationalizes the entire incident by arguing, "He hadn't no business crawling like that out of the dark. He was batty. He asked for it" (p. 143). Piggy denies the moral implication of their collective guilt. He coldly declares, "We never done nothing, we never seen nothing." Piggy's reason ill-equips him to understand the nature and origin of evil. Indeed, Piggy's scientific humanism precludes him from seeing the beast in us.

Scientific humanism, which is faith in the progressive and liberating power of science and man's ability to rationally posit values, has stripped man naked of the religious context which gave his life meaning. Confidence in mankind's ability to conquer nature and prejudice gave modern man the sensation that hitherto undreamed of possibilities were now opened to him. However, recent history and the myriad of variations on the philosophy of Friedrich Nietzsche indicate that scientific humanism precludes us from positing any value; that is, it precludes us from seeing evil for what it is.[32] The scientific humanist, the "model intellectual," is "literally in a state of free fall."[33]

However, there is one character who sees, but the status and nature of his understanding disturbs modern sensibilities. Golding's "saint" Simon knows the truth about the beast.[34] He arrives at the novel's truth about the fallen nature of man. As the lord of the flies asserts:

> "There isn't anyone to help you. Only me. And I'm the Beast."
>
> Simon's mouth labored, brought forth audible words.
>
> "Pig's head on a stick."
>
> "Fancy thinking that the beast was something you could hunt and kill!" said the head.
>
> For a moment or two the forest and all the other dimly appreciated places echoed with a parody of laughter. "You knew didn't you? I'm part of you? Close, close, close! I'm the reason why it's no go? Why things are what they are?"
>
> (p. 130)

This truth comes to Simon in the form of a revelation.[35] He had also intuited it earlier. In the disastrous assembly, which signaled the collapse of Ralph's regime, we learned that Simon knew the truth about the beast. But the boys, principally Piggy, shout him down.

Simon attempts to articulate his vision of the beast with, "What is the dirtiest thing there is?" Jack's crude, monosyllabic response literally ruins Simon's effort. The reader is left to wonder what the dirtiest thing is, Jack's response, and how they relate to the beast. From the vantage point of a young boy we may infer that excrement, which can be conveyed in one crude syllable, is the dirtiest thing.[36] "Shit" is in us, entirely natural, and yet invisible like the beast. Like the beast, it too evokes revulsion when it becomes manifest. Simon's inspired image and Jack's reply are altogether apt. Simon may not be able to articulate his message, because, by its very nature, it can not be rationally defended.[37] Simon would have been unable to persuade the other boys even if he could find the words. He is ridiculed, later mistaken for the beast, and eventually beaten to death for his insight and effort.

Simon's death symbolically marks the death of the god Osiris by the power of Typhon. Just as Simon's murder is prefigured by the pig-hunting ritual, by moonlight, so too is Osiris's body discovered by Typhon during a moonlit pig hunt. A similar fate befalls Piggy, the rational face of Osiris, in the mad, ego-driven frenzy that sweeps away the last vestiges of sanity. Again, on the surface, both the similarity of Pig to Piggy and that animal's association with Osiris support an Osirian interpretation. The sea claimed the battered bodies of Piggy and Simon just as the sea had claimed the body of Osiris.

We are not, however, offering up either Simon or Piggy as scapegoats.[38] A scapegoat unwillingly becomes a surrogate for the god; he appeases the god by being sacrificed to him. Given the situation on the island at the time of their deaths, we witness the stuff out of which new cults and their attendant rituals are made. We observe the death of the "gods," not their scapegoats who will come later. The return of "civilization" in the guise of the naval officer neither precludes the destruction of Western civilization, as we know it, nor that Ralph will pass on his new found knowledge in the form of a myth.

Golding appears to contradict the foregoing interpretation by insisting that Simon is a saint. His depiction of Simon as a "saint" carries definite Christian connotations. But a saint is, as Chesterton revealed, "a medicine because he is an antidote. Indeed that is why the saint is often a martyr; he is mistaken for a poison because he is an antidote."[39] Simon represents the antidote for a rationalism that cannot see. Simon's insight into the beast offers the boys the possibility of salvation on the island, not, insofar as we know, in heaven. Simon's knowledge, had it been believed, would have made up for the defects in Piggy's. Piggy's knowledge coupled with the ability to see beyond mere appearance would have made Ralph's regime resilient to the inroads of Jack's barbarism.

As Leo Strauss observed, "The very life of Western civilization is the life between two codes [the biblical and Greek philosophic], a fundamental tension."[40] The separation of rational and revelatory knowledge, from Golding's perspective,[41] is both the essence and the illness of the West. It "has begotten that lame giant we call civilization as Frankenstein created his monster."[42] The ascendancy of scientific humanism, its inability to see or to posit eternal verities, leaves modern man free falling in the abyss of nihilism. We confront, through our excavation of Golding's myth, the value problem. Until Simon and Piggy together comprise an Osiris, Western civilization cannot diagnose, let alone cure, its essential illness.

The narrator reveals mankind's essential illness with compelling clarity in the following scene:

> "This was fascinating to Henry. He poked about with a bit of stick, that itself was wave-torn and whitened and a vagrant, and tried to control the motions of the scavengers. He made little runnels that the tide filled and tried to crowd them with creatures. He became absorbed beyond mere happiness as he felt himself exercising control over living things. He talked to them, urging them, ordering them. Driven back by the tide, his footprints became bays in which they were trapped and gave him the illusion of mastery."
>
> (p. 56)

Henry, who is a child, the modern apotheosis of innocence, seeks mastery over other living things, and he too is marked by the beast. The root of his will to mastery is vanity. Henry may be distinguished from Jack, or Typhon, but only in power and magnitude. This is the terrible, dark truth that resides at the heart of ***Lord of the Flies.***

Pride has various manifestations, among them honor, prestige, fame, and wealth. Off-campus history, or nationalism, is but one manifestation of this deeper tragic flaw. But perhaps even more troubling for modern man, pride in our ideas has "thrust our world into a mental straitjacket from which we can escape only by the most anarchic violence."[43] The virulent, global atrocities of the twentieth century were caused by both ideological pride and nationalism. But these otherwise impressive edifices are merely projections out from the self, which seeks to have its views sanctified. They are mirrors, if you will, that reflect back to us our own petty prejudices. Modern man, who can explain everything in entirely antiseptic, sanitary ways cannot, no matter how often he cleanses himself, rid himself of the decay that comes from within.

Notes

1. See "Fable," in *The Hot Gates and Other Occasional Pieces* (New York: Harcourt, 1966), p. 98 (hereafter *HG*). Golding also invites speculation on the moral lesson by arguing that "the novelist ought not to preach overtly in a fable" (p. 94). See also "Belief and Creativity," in *A Moving Target* (New York: Farrar, 1982), p. 198 (hereafter *MT*). He indicates, however, that not all of these diverse interpretations are equally correct.

2. See for example Howard S. Babb, *The Novels of William Golding,* 2d ed. (New York: Columbia Univ. Press, 1986); Peter Bien, "Visions of a Latter-Day Modernist: William Golding's Nobel Prize," *World Literature Review* 58 (1982): 165-66; and Virginia Tiger, *William Golding: The Dark Fields of Discovery* (London: Calder and Boyars, 1974). In support of this view, Golding points out that Simon is a "Christ-figure" and a "saint." See "Fable," p. 96, and Golding's BBC interview with Frank Kermode, "The Meaning of It All," *Books and Bookman* 5 (1959):9-10.

3. James J. Whitley, *Golding: Lord of the Flies* (London: Edward Arnold, 1970); E. L. Epstein, "Notes on *Lord of the Flies,*" in Golding's *Lord*

of the Flies (New York: Perigree Books, 1954); Leighton Hodson, *William Golding* (Edinburgh: Oliver and Boyd, 1969), pp. 30-31. See also Golding's own comments on the over-interpretation of *Lord of the Flies* in *MT,* pp. 171, 198.

4. William Golding and James R. Baker, "An Interview with William Golding," *Twentieth Century Literature* 28 (1982):165-66.

5. Bernard Dick, *William Golding* (New York: Twayne, 1967), pp. 26-33, and James R. Baker, "Why It's No Go," in *Critical Essays on William Golding,* ed. James R. Baker (Boston: G. K. Hall, 1988).

6. Baker, pp. 25ff. We may impute to the boys pride in English superiority. As Jack says, "We're English, and the English are best at everything." Howard Babb, on the other hand, argues that the "innocent pride" attributed to the boys is pride in their own wisdom (p.33 n. 8).

7. "Fable," p. 90.

8. Dick, p. 36.

9. See William Golding, *An Egyptian Journal* (Boston: Faber and Faber, 1985), pp. 10-12, 161-62. Golding makes it clear that he is fond of Plutarch's account of the Osiris myth; indeed, he calls the absence of it on his voyage down the Nile a "disaster" (p. 12). See also Golding and Baker, "An Interview," pp. 157-58, 160, and "Egypt From My Inside," in *HG,* pp. 71-73. For additional examples of his interest in things Egyptian see William Golding, "Egypt From My Outside," in *MT,* and William Golding, *The Scorpion God: Three Short Novels* (New York: Harcourt, 1972).

10. "Fable," p. 88.

11. Whitley, p. 48.

12. Samuel Hynes, "William Golding's *Lord of the Flies,*" in *Critical Essays on William Golding,* ed. James R. Baker (Boston: G. K. Hall, 1988) and Epstein, p. 187.

13. See Stephen Metcalf, *William Golding* (Harlow, Essex: Longman, 1975), pp. 11-12.

14. John Gywnn Griffiths, "Commentary," in *De Isis et Osiris,* by Plutarch (Cambridge: Univ. of Wales Press, 1970), p. 388. All references to Plutarch will be from this edition by line number in text.

15. Epstein, pp. 418-19. Beelzebub is the Greek equivalent of the Hebrew *Ba'alzevuv.*

16. Genesis 3:3-7.

17. William Golding, *Lord of the Flies* (New York: Perigee Books, 1954), p. 12. All subsequent references will be from this edition by page number in text.

18. Had the boys seen the descending parachutist, whom Golding equates with "history that won't lie down" and off-campus history, their situation could have worsened. It was sufficiently difficult for Ralph to convince the boys to keep the fire going in the hope of being rescued. Had the boys known that the adult world was in flames, itself in need of rescue, their descent into barbarism would have been hastened. For Golding's connection between "history that won't lie down" and the dead parachutist see "The Meaning of It All," pp. 9-10.

19. "Fable," pp. 87-88.

20. The foregoing interpretation of the Osiris myth loosely resembles the view of man advanced by Thomas Hobbes in *Leviathan,* and obliquely attacked by Jean Jacques Rousseau in *Discours sur l'origine de l'inegalite.* Man is a fallen creature, destined to prey upon his kind, because he is vain.

21. James G. Frazer, *The Golden Bough: The Roots of Religion and Folklore* (New York: Avenel Books, 1981), vol. 2, p. 59.

22. There are numerous other examples where the narrator describes Jack as "red." See pp. 21, 37, and 127.

23. S. J. Boyd, *The Novels of William Golding* (New York: St. Martin's Press, 1988), p. 11.

24. See Baker, pp. 27-28, and Dick, p. 31. See pp. 2-4 above.

25. "Fable," p. 89.

26. Alternatively, the two boys whose last names are given by the author—Jack Meridew and Percival Weyms Madison—are the poles of the adult world. Jack is bullying, competitive, and aggressive, while Percival is frightened, overwhelmed, and diffident. Only a Hobbean theoretical framework divides man into two such starkly contrasting character types: the mad man of great vain glory and the common man of fear. See Thomas Hobbes, *Leviathan,* ch. 8 and ch. 13.

27. "The Meaning of It All," p. 9.
28. Ibid., p. 10.
29. Dick, p. 31.
30. "The Meaning of It All," p. 9.
31. Whitley, pp. 26-27; Babb, pp. 21-22; and Boyd, p. 8.
32. We live, for example, in an age that refuses to call young, brutal rapists, who leave their victim lying in a park bloody and comatose, evil. Instead we rationalize their behavior by finding socioeconomic factors to explain it.
33. Jack I. Biles, *Talk: Conversations with William Golding* (New York: Harcourt, 1970), pp. 79-80.
34. Roger too knows our natures, he knows what moves men. When Samneric are captured Roger stops Jack from seriously injuring them, not out of human kindness, but because he realizes they will prove useful. Roger tortures and apparently converts them. Roger does this to nab Ralph. He knows that Ralph will smell the meat, hunger for it, and this in addition to his isolation will draw him to Castle Rock. Roger posts the two recent converts on watch, but he watches them. Roger's manipulation of Ralph's hunger and isolation is all the more troubling because he is only a boy.
35. This is not, of course, Simon's only revelation. Simon also prophesized that Ralph would get rescued. As Simon put it, "You'll get back to where you came from" (p. 101).
36. Following a similar line of reasoning, Whitley argues that lord of the flies could be rendered in English as "lord of dung" (p. 43).
37. There are two ways of knowing: reason and revelation. Reason, by definition, is a logical demonstration based upon orderly deductions or inductions. Revelation is a mysterious way of knowing that is implanted in the receiver, who as a consequence becomes a knower. A revelation is neither speculation nor a chain a reasoning based upon observation. Moses, for example, faithfully accepts Yahweh's revelation that he will lead the Israelites from bondage in Egypt. Yahweh's message admits neither theoretical speculation nor logical demonstration. It is not that words cannot describe the prophetic vision, but rather the veracity of its claim is questionable. Scientific humanism, which is based upon empirical observation, has demoted revealed religion to the status of opinion.
38. The scapegoat is usually an unwilling participant in the ritual. Golding vigorously denies that Simon is a scapegoat. Simon willingly accepts his fate like a saint ("The Meaning of It All," p. 9).
39. G. K. Chesterton, *St. Thomas Aquinas: The Dumb Ox* (New York: Doubleday, 1956), p. 23.
40. Leo Strauss, "The Mutual Influence of Philosophy and Theology," *The Independent Journal of Philosophy* 3 (1979): 111.
41. Golding makes clear his opposition to scientific humanism in "A Moving Target," in *MT,* p. 163; "Belief and Creativity," pp. 186-87; and "On the Crest of the Wave," in *HG,* pp. 129-31. See also James R. Baker, "Three Decades of Criticism," in *Critical Essays on William Golding,* p. 2.
42. "Egypt from My Inside," p. 72.
43. "Belief and Creativity," p. 187.

Lawrence S. Friedman (essay date 1993)

SOURCE: Friedman, Lawrence S. "Grief, Grief, Grief: *Lord of the Flies.*" In *William Golding,* pp. 19-32. New York: Continuum, 1993.

[*In the following essay, Friedman explores the theme of grief.*]

Lord of the Flies opens in Eden. Ralph, fair-haired protagonist, and Piggy, faithful companion and resident intellectual, look about them and pronounce their island good. And so it is, for William Golding has set his young castaways down upon an uninhabited Pacific island as lush as it is remote. Fruit hangs ripe for the picking; fresh water flows abundantly from a convenient mountain; and the tropical climate soon prompts the boys to throw off their clothes. Ralph joyfully stands on his head, an action he will repeat at moments of high emotion. It is easy to forget that the world is at war, and that the plane that carried Ralph, Piggy, and the many other English boys stranded on the island, was shot down by the enemy.

As war and plane crash recede from memory, the visible world shrinks to the desert island and its populace of six-to twelve-year-old-boys. Because of the island's fecundity and mild climate the boys are largely exempt from the struggle for food and shelter; because of their youth they are exempt from sexual longing and deprivation; because of their isolation they are exempt from adult constraints. Free to live as they choose, they can act out every boy's dream of romantic adventure until their eventual rescue. ***Lord of the Flies*** begins, therefore, as a modern retelling of R. M. Ballantyne's Victorian children's classic, *Coral Island.* Indeed Golding traces his book's genesis to a night when he had finished reading just such an island adventure story to his eldest child.[1] Exasperated by the familiar cutout characters and smug optimism of the original, he conceived of breathing life into a moribund genre by isolating boys on a desert island and showing how they would *really* behave. Ballantyne's shipwrecked boys, somewhat older than Golding's, lead an idyllic life on their remote South Seas island. Tropical nature is benign, the boys' characters conventionally innocent. What evil exists on Coral Island enters in the form of such adult intruders as savage cannibals or pirates. Ballantyne's vision is doubly optimistic: man is inherently good; and good will win out in the end. Like most fairy tales, *Coral Island* is an amalgam of faith and hope.

On Golding's coral island, Piggy's allusions to atomic war, dead adults, and uncertainty of rescue barely ripple the surface of Ralph's pleasant daydreams. Soon the boys recover a conch from the lagoon. More than a plaything, the conch will become a means of communication, and ultimately a symbol of law and order. Instructed by the wise but ineffectual Piggy, Ralph blows on the conch, thereby summoning the scattered boys. Possession of the conch ensures Ralph's election as chief. Later the assembled boys agree that whoever wishes to speak must raise his hand and request the conch. Cradling the conch in one's hands not only confers instant personal authority but affirms the common desire for an orderly society.

Read as a social treatise, Golding's first chapter seems to posit notions of fair play and group solidarity familiar to readers of *Coral Island.* But the same chapter introduces us to Jack Merridew marching at the head of his uniformed column of choirboys. Clad in black and silver and led by an obviously authoritarian figure, the choirboys seem boy Nazis. Frustrated by Ralph's election as chief, Jack barely conceals his anger. The chapter ends with Jack, knife in hand, reflexively hesitating long enough on the downward stroke to allow a trapped piglet to escape. The civilized taboo against bloodletting remains shakily in place as the angry boy settles for slamming his knife into a tree trunk. "Next time," he cries.

It is the exploration of Jack's "next time" that will occupy much of the remainder of ***Lord of the Flies.*** By fixing incipient evil within Jack, Golding reverses the sanguine premise of nineteenth-century adventure stories that locate evil in the alien or mysterious forces of the outside world. According to Golding his generation's "liberal and naive belief in the perfectibility of man" was exploded by World War II. Hitler's gas chambers revealed man's inherent evil. His followers were not Ballantyne's savage cannibals or desperate pirates whose evil magically dissipated upon their conversion to Christianity. Rather they were products of that very Christian civilization that presumably guarantees their impossibility. Nor does it suffice to accept Ballantyne's implication that his boys' Englishness, like their Christianity, marks them as inevitably good. "We've got to have rules and obey them. After all, we're not savages. We're English, and the English are best at everything. So we've got to do the right things." Coming from Golding's Jack, these words effectively shatter Ballantyne's easy optimism. Conditioned no less by the theology of man's fall than by Nazi atrocities, ***Lord of the Flies*** traces the spreading stain of man's depravity from its first intimations in Jack to its near-total corruption of the boys and their social order. "I decided," explained Golding, "to take the literary convention of boys on an island, only make them real boys instead of paper cutouts with no life in them; and try to show how the shape of the society they evolved would be conditioned by their diseased, their fallen nature."[2]

Too immature to account for the enemy within, the boys project their irrational fears onto the outside world. The first of these projections takes the shape of a snakelike "beastie," the product of a small boy's nightmare. One side of the boy's face "was blotted out by a mulberry-colored birthmark," the visible sign of the dual nature of fallen man. More by force of personality than by reason, Ralph succeeds in exorcising the monster from the group consciousness. Now the boys struggle to drag logs up the mountain for a signal fire, Ralph and Jack bearing the heaviest log between them. Jack's momentary selflessness combined with the manipulation of the lenses of Piggy's spectacles to start their fire—as well as the very act of fire building itself—signal a resurgence of civilized values. But the fire soon rages out of control; exploding trees and rising creepers reinvoke cries of "Snakes!, Snakes"; and the small boy with the birthmark has mysteriously disappeared. The seed of fear has been planted. Reason has failed to explain the darkness within, and the island paradise begins its fatal transformation into hell.

Soon Ralph and Jack find communication impossible, the former talking of building shelters, the latter of killing pigs. Increasingly obsessed with his role as hunter, Jack neglects his more important role as keeper of the signal fire. Painting a fierce mask on his face he is "liberated from shame and self-consciousness." Shortly thereafter he and his frenzied followers march along swinging the gutted carcass of a pig from a stake to the incantory chant, "Kill the pig. Cut her throat. Spill her blood." Abandonment to blind ritual has displaced the reasoned discourse governed by the conch. Meanwhile the untended fire has gone out, and a ship has sailed past the island. Lost in blood lust, Jack's thoughts are far from rescue, and he at first barely comprehends Ralph's anger. When he does, he strikes out at the helpless Piggy, shattering one of his lenses. Reason henceforth is half-blind; the fragile link between Ralph and Jack snaps; and ritual singing and dancing resume as the boys gorge themselves on the slaughtered pig. That Ralph and Piggy join in the feast indicates the all-too-human failure to resist the blandishments of mass hysteria.

Killing marks the end of innocence. It is a wiser Ralph who "found himself understanding the wearisomeness of this life where every path was an improvisation and a considerable part of one's waking life was spent watching one's feet . . . and remembering that first enthusiastic exploration as though it were part of a brighter childhood, he smiled jeeringly." Here at the beginning of the important fifth chapter, "Beast from Water," the regression and initiation themes converge. On the basis of his newfound knowledge, Ralph assembles the boys to discuss such practical matters as sanitation, shelter, and, most crucially, the keeping of the fire. But the tension among the boys is palpable, and Ralph soon confesses, "Things are breaking up. I don't understand why. We began well, we were happy." And he concludes, "Then people started getting frightened." Piggy's theory that life is scientific is countered by new reports of a beast from the sea. Neither Piggy's logic nor Ralph's rules can hold the boys together, and the meeting scatters in confusion.

E. M. Forster pleads in his introduction to the 1962 American edition of ***Lord of the Flies*** for more respect for Piggy.[3] Of course he is correct. Faced with specters of water beasts and Jack's authoritarian violence, who could fail to opt for Piggy's rationalism? Yet unaided reason cannot tell Ralph why things go wrong; it can only deny the physical reality of the beast. It is left to Simon, the skinny, inarticulate seer to "express mankind's essential illness" by fixing the beast's location: "What I mean is . . . maybe it's only us." Golding's moral—that defects in human society can be traced back to defects in human nature—can be illustrated by the fable of the scorpion and the frog:

> "Let me ride across the pond on your back," pleads the scorpion.
>
> "No," replies the frog, "for if I let you on my back your sting will prove fatal."
>
> "Listen to reason," cries the scorpion. "If I sting you, you'll sink to the bottom of the pond, and I'll drown."
>
> So the frog takes the scorpion on his back and begins swimming. Midway across the pond, he feels the scorpion's fatal sting. "How could you," gasps the frog with his dying breath. "Now you'll drown."
>
> "I couldn't help it," sighs the scorpion. "It's my nature."[4]

Though his irrationality, like the scorpion's, may cost him his life, man is his own worst enemy. Undone by the beast within, man self-destructs no matter what form of social organization he adopts.

"Beast from the Air" opens with the sign from the world of grown-ups that answers Ralph's desperate cry for help after the breakup of the assembly. Dropping from the air battle high above the island, a dead parachutist settles on the mountaintop where fitful breezes cause him spasmodically to rise and fall. This grotesque "message" recalls the adult savagery that marooned the boys on the island. Moreover, the boys now take the faraway figure for the beast that haunts their dreams. Confronted by its apparent physical reality even Ralph succumbs to fear. The ironic appropriateness of the man-beast foreshadows Jack's growing power and the final unraveling of the social order. Now that the primary task is to kill the beast, Jack assumes command. Promising hunting and feasting he lures more and more boys into his camp. Man regresses from settler to roving hunter, society from democracy to dictatorship.

It is at this point, shortly after the collapse of social order under the pressures of inherent evil associated with Jack and irrational fear embodied in the beast from the air, that Golding paints his most startling and powerful scene. Simon, the only boy who feels the need for solitude, returns to his place of contemplation, a leafy shelter concealed by the dense growth of the forest. There he witnesses the butchering of a frantically screaming sow, its gutting and dismemberment, and the erection of its bleeding head on a pole. This head, abandoned by the hunters as a "gift" to the beast, presides over a pile of guts that attracts great swarms of buzzing flies. And the Lord of the Flies speaks: "Fancy thinking the Beast was something you could hunt and kill. You knew didn't you? I'm part of you? Close, close, close! I'm the reason why it's no go? Why things are what they are?" Looking into the vast mouth, Simon sees only a spreading blackness into which he falls in a faint.

As previously noted, Golding has called himself a fabulist and his novel a fable. All fables contain morals; and the moral of ***Lord of the Flies*** is stated most explicitly in the confrontation between Simon and the pig's head. "I included a Christ-figure in my fable. This is the little boy Simon, solitary, stammering, a lover of mankind, a visionary."[5] Since the Lord of the Flies is Beelzebub, the Judeo-Christian prince of devils, the scene dramatizes the clash between principles of good and evil. To accept the consequences of Golding's symbolism is to recognize the inequality of the struggle between Simon and the head. The Lord of the Flies has invaded Simon's forest sanctuary to preach an age-old sermon: evil lies within man whose nature is inherently depraved. Simon cannot counter this lesson. Engulfed by the spreading blackness of the vast mouth, he is overwhelmed by Beelzebub's power and loses consciousness. While it does not necessarily follow that Christ's message is similarly overpowered by Satan's, the forest scene strongly implies that innocence and good intentions are lost amidst the general ubiquity of evil. That evil cannot be isolated in Jack or in the beast; it is "close, close, close," a part of all of us.

The Simon who awakens from his faint trudges out of the forest "like an old man," stooping under the heavy burden of revelation. Immediately he comes face-to-face with a second awful symbol of human corruption—the rotting body of the downed parachutist. It, too, has been found by the flies; like the pig's head it too has been reduced to a corrupt and hideous parody of life. Releasing the broken figure from the tangled parachute lines that bind it to the rocks, Simon staggers back down the mountain with his news that the beast is harmless. But he stumbles into the frenzied mob of dancing and chanting boys who take him for the beast, fall upon him, and tear him apart.

The ritual murder of Simon is as ironic as it is inevitable. Ironically, he is killed as the beast before he can explain that the beast does not exist. His horrid death refutes his aborted revelation: the beast exists, all right, not where we thought to find it, but within ourselves. Inevitably, we kill our savior who "would set us free from the repetitious nightmare of history."[6] Unable to perceive his truth, we huddle together in the circle of our fear and reenact his ritual murder, as ancient as human history itself. Golding's murderous boys, the products of centuries of Christianity and Western civilization, explode the hope of Christ's sacrifice by repeating the pattern of his crucifixion. Simon's fate underlines the most awful truths about human nature: its blindness, its irrationality, its blood lust.

That the human condition is hopeless is revealed in the fact that even Ralph and Piggy felt the need to join in the "demented but partly secure society" of the hunters just prior to Simon's murder. Later, they console themselves with the excuse that they remained outside the dancing circle. When Ralph recalls the horror of the murder, Piggy first tries to deny its reality. And when Ralph refuses to drop the subject, Piggy shrills again and again that Simon's death was an accident. His desperate rationalizations point to the inability of human reason to cope with the dark reality of human nature. Piggy's excuses are mere frantic attempts to explain away our basest instincts and actions. Their transparent failure to do so marks the limits of the human intellect. Symbolic of the fall of reason is the loss of Piggy's sight. His broken glasses, the means of fire making, are stolen in a raid by Jack and his hunters. As Jack stalks triumphantly off with the glasses dangling from his hand, the reign of savagery is all but sealed.

Jack's victory comes swiftly in the following chapter, "Castle Rock." Again Golding sets up a contest between principles of good and evil. But this time the outcome is a foregone conclusion. The pack of painted savages who blindly murdered Simon has by now abandoned all restraints. Personified by Roger, Jack's fanatical self-appointed "executioner," the hunters turn viciously against Ralph and Piggy and the twins Sam and Eric, the last four remnants of an orderly society. From high atop a cliff Roger pushes a great rock that, gathering momentum, strikes Piggy, killing the fat boy and shattering the conch. Although the conch has long since lost the power to invoke order, its explosion signals the final triumph of lawlessness. Screaming wildly, "I'm chief," Jack hurls his spear at Ralph, inflicting a flesh wound, and forcing the former chief to run frantically for his life.

"Cry of the Hunters," the novel's concluding chapter, marks the final degenerative stage in Golding's fable of man's fall. Ralph's pursuers, freed by Piggy's murder from the faint restraint of reason, have reduced Ralph to their quarry. As the savage pack closes in, the sad lesson of the hunt is inescapable: not that the boys are dehumanized, but that they are all too human. Man's basic instinct is to kill; and the depth of his depravity is measured by the urge to kill his own species. Not only does the metaphor of the hunt complete Golding's definition of the human animal, but it forges a link to analogous hunts in Greek drama that loom in the background of ***Lord of the Flies.***

Golding has often acknowledged the formative influence of the ancients. Together with the biblical version of man's fate expressed in the doctrine of original sin, Greek drama fleshes out the myth of the fall. If it is true that a writer's forebears surface most apparently in his early work, then the final hunt of ***Lord of the Flies*** is second only to Simon's "passion" in fixing the origins of Golding's most cherished ideas. While it is true that Simon's confrontation with the pig's head and his subsequent martyrdom are couched primarily in Christian terms, the Greek influence is also apparent. The pig's head is at once the Judeo-Christian Beelzebub and the king of the Olympian gods. Thus Jean-Paul Sartre's modern reworking of Greek motifs in *The Flies* opens on a public square in Argos, "dominated by a statue of Zeus, god of flies and death. The image has white eyes and blood-smeared cheeks."[7] Zeus himself appears in the play to explain the great swarms of buzzing flies that plague the city. "They are," he says, "a symbol," sent by the gods to "a dead-and-alive city, a carrion city" still festering fifteen years after the original sin of Agamemnon's murder. The citizens of Argos are "working out their atonement." Their "fear and guilty consciences have a good savor in the nostrils of the gods." Zeus implies that man's blood lust is balanced by his reverence for the gods, a view shared by Golding: "As far back as we can go in history we find that the two signs of man are a capacity to kill and a belief in God."[8] Human fear and guilt are perverse affirmations of the gods' existence and therefore find favor with the gods. For Sartre, the existential philosopher, man's awful freedom, won at the expense of breaking his shackles to the gods, is all-important. But for Golding, the Christian believer, man is lost without God. The absence of prayer, even among fearful young choirboys, is one of the darkest aspects of ***Lord of the Flies.***

Although *The Flies* may have no direct bearing upon Golding's novel, its title as well as its identification of Zeus as god of flies and death reveal the same backdrop of Greek tradition. At the end of Sartre's play, the hero Orestes, drawn directly from Greek drama, is pursued by the shrieking Furies. No such deities hunt Ralph, only his fellow boys. Yet chase scenes of all kinds fill Greek drama, and Golding the classicist seems indebted not merely to the general metaphor of the hunt but specifically to its powerful treatment in two plays of Euripides: *The Bacchae* and *Iphigenia in Tauris.*

Euripides wrote *The Bacchae,* his greatest and most difficult play, in the wake of a disillusionment with the Peloponnesian War as profound as Golding's with World War II. As skeptical about human nature as Golding, Euripides had already written the most devastating antiwar play that survives from antiquity, *The Trojan Women.* Both ***Lord of the Flies*** and *The Bacchae* are anthropological passion plays in which individuals—children in Golding, adults in Euripides—revert to savagery and murder during a frenzied ritual.[9] At Thebes, where Dionysus (Bacchus) comes to introduce his worship to Greece, King Pentheus adamantly denies the new religion. To Dionysus's orgiastic revels Pentheus opposes the rule of reason. Yet he is tempted to disguise himself in the fawn skin of a Dionysian follower in order to watch the rites of the female devotees. Spied by the Bacchants, he is hunted down and torn to pieces by the frenzied women, led by his own mother, Agave. Maddened by the god, the hapless Agave bears Pentheus's head, which she imagines is a lion's, triumphantly back to Thebes. There she comes to her senses and awakens to the horrid proof of Dionysus's power. To deny Dionysus is to deny a fundamental force in human nature. That the destruction of Pentheus is so disproportionate to his offense constitutes poetic justice in *The Bacchae:* Pentheus denies the primitive power of unreason only to become its victim. Yet the orgiastic worship that transforms Agave into the unwitting murderess of her son is hardly preferable to Pentheus's denial. Euripides, in dramatizing the clash between emotionalism and rationalism, may be arguing the primacy of neither. However one interprets *The Bacchae,* its affinities with ***Lord of the Flies*** are striking:

> Specifically, both drama and novel contain three interrelated ritual themes: the cult of a beast-god,

> a hunt as prefiguration of the death of the scapegoat-figure, and the dismemberment of the scapegoat. Golding deviates in only one respect from Euripides: logically Ralph, the Pentheus in embryo, should be the scapegoat; but the author assigns this role to Simon, allowing Ralph to live instead with his new-found knowledge of "the darkness of man's heart."[10]

Dionysus is the true hero of *The Bacchae;* his merciless destruction of Pentheus is but the opening salvo in his campaign to establish his worship in Hellas. Golding is no less concerned with the primitive force that Dionysus represents; but his primary concern is the impact of that force upon his hero. Ralph, the latter-day Pentheus, must therefore survive the ordeal of the hunt and live with his hard-won knowledge. Against the backdrop of the flaming island, a hell that once was Eden, the savage tribe pursues Ralph until, stumbling over a root, the frantic boy sprawls helplessly in the sand. Staggering to his feet, flinching at the anticipated last onslaught, Ralph looks up into the astonished face of a British naval officer. Ralph's miraculous salvation completes the drama of his initiation as, in a shattering epiphany, he weeps "for the end of innocence, the darkness of man's heart, and the fall through the air of the true wise friend called Piggy."

Although Golding shifts the focus from God's power to man's knowledge he relies on a familiar Euripidian device for ending his novel. Golding calls the timely arrival of the naval officer a "gimmick," a term subsequently used by critics to plague him. Yet the officer is neither more nor less than the Greek deus ex machina in modern uniform. Employed most strikingly by Euripides, the "god" in the machine is hoisted high above the other actors to solve the problems of the preceding action and to supply a happy ending. Most often, when the deity imposes a happy ending, the normal consequences of the action would be disastrous. Neither *The Bacchae* nor Sartre's *The Flies* employs the device in its purest form. In the former, Dionysus resolves the action by heaping even more woe upon the Thebans who denied his godhead. In the latter, Sartre's Zeus absents himself from the ending, having already explained its significance. Moreover, both gods take major roles from the outset of their respective plays. Neither makes the single in-the-nick-of-time appearance to reverse the action that generally characterizes the deus ex machina.

In *Iphigenia in Tauris,* however, Euripides relies upon the deus ex machina for a resolution markedly similar to that of ***Lord of the Flies.*** Iphigenia, her brother Orestes, and his friend Pylades, pursued by the minions of the barbarian king Thoas, reach the seacoast where a Greek ship waits to carry them home. But Thoas's troops control the strait through which the ship must pass; and a strong gale drives the ship back toward the shore. Enter the goddess Athena, who warns Thoas to cease his pursuit. It seems that the fates of Iphigenia and her companions have been foreordained, and against this "necessity" even gods are powerless. Thoas wisely relents, the winds grow favorable, and the ship sails off under Athena's divine protection.

Barbarian pursuit, friendly ship, and miraculous rescue are no less present in Golding's conclusion. And when to these elements are added the hunt for sacrificial victims and the bloody rites of the Taurian religion, the resemblances between *Iphigenia in Tauris* and ***Lord of the Flies*** seem more than skin deep. Yet the lessons of the two works radically differ. Greek drama is ultimately conditioned by the proximity of the gods: omnipresent yet inscrutable they influence human action and determine human destiny. Since, as Sartre's Zeus admits, the gods need mortals for their worship as much as mortals need objects for their devotion, it follows that Greek drama chronicles this interdependence. In *The Flies,* Sartre's Zeus, the fading though still powerful king of the gods, owes his rule to human fear and superstition and relies upon man's willing servitude. When Orestes finally strides boldly into the sunlight, the spell of the gods is broken; henceforth he will blaze his own trail, acknowledging no law but his own. For Sartre, man's freedom begins with his denial of the gods and his full acceptance of responsibility for his actions and their consequences. And while existential freedom is as fearful as it is lonely, it is infinitely preferable to god-ridden bondage. Whether Dionysus stalking through *The Bacchae,* Athena watching over *Iphigenia in Tauris,* or Zeus brooding in *The Flies,* the gods play a role in the human drama. Note that all three deities carefully define their roles: Dionysus to punish the errant Thebans whose king denied him; Athena to ensure the proper worship of her sister, Artemis; and Zeus to warn the recalcitrant Orestes of the consequences of rebellion. So closely are the gods involved with mortals that their interventions, no matter how arbitrary, take on a certain inevitable logic.

What Golding calls the "gimmicked" ending of ***Lord of the Flies*** and the Greek deux ex machina used most conventionally in *Iphigenia in Tauris* are alike in their technical function: to reverse the course of impending disaster. Yet their effects are quite different. Athena's wisdom is incontrovertible, her morality unassailable. High above the awed mortals she dispels chaos and imposes ideal order. The very fact of her appearance underlines the role of the gods in shaping human destiny. Golding's spiffy naval officer is, however, no god. Nor does he represent a higher morality. Confronted by the ragtag melee, he can only wonder that English boys hadn't put up a better show, and mistakes their savage hunt for fun and games à la *Coral Island.* While he cannot know the events preceding his arrival, his comments betray the same ignorance of human nature that contributed to the boys' undoing. Commanding his cruiser, the officer will direct a maritime search-and-destroy mission identical to the island hunt. ***Lord of the Flies*** ends with the officer gazing at the cruiser, preparing to reenact the age-old saga of man's inhumanity to man.

Just as the naval officer cannot measure up to Euripides' Athena, so Ralph falls short of Sartre's Orestes. Orestes strides into the sunlight of his own morality to live Sartre's dictum that existence precedes essence. Creating himself anew with each action, he will become his own god. Ralph can only weep for the loss of innocence from the world; he shows no particular signs of coping with his newfound knowledge. To understand one's nature is not to alter it. Morally diseased, mired in original sin, fallen man can rise only by the apparently impossible means of transcending his very nature. In man's apparent inability to re-create himself lies the tragedy of ***Lord of the Flies.*** The futility of Simon's sacrificial death, the failure of adult morality, and the final absence of God create the spiritual vacuum of Golding's novel. For Sartre the denial of the gods is the necessary prelude to human freedom. But for Golding, God's absence leads only to despair and human freedom is but license. "The theme of ***Lord of the Flies*** is grief, sheer grief, grief, grief."[11]

Notes

1. William Golding, the title essay in *A Moving Target,* p. 163.
2. Golding, "Fable," p. 88.
3. E. M. Forster, introduction, in William Golding, *Lord of the Flies* (New York: Coward-McCann, 1962), p. xiii.
4. Orson Welles, *Mr. Arkadin,* 1955. Welles, in the title role of a wealthy and powerful tycoon, relates this story at one of his sophisticated soirees. Written and directed by Welles, the film depicts Arkadin hunting down and killing former friends who might expose his shady past.
5. Golding, "Fable," pp. 97-98.
6. James R. Baker, *William Golding* (New York: St. Martin's Press, 1965), p. 13.
7. Jean-Paul Sartre, *The Flies,* in *"No Exit" and Three Other Plays,* tr. Stuart Gilbert (New York: Vintage, 1955), p. 51.
8. Biles, *Talk: Conversations with William Golding,* p. 106.
9. Bernard F. Dick, *William Golding* (New York: Twayne, 1967), p. 30.
10. Ibid., p. 31.
11. Golding, "A Moving Target," p. 163.

Minnie Singh (essay date 1997)

SOURCE: Singh, Minnie. "The Government of Boys: Golding's *Lord of the Flies* and Ballantyne's *Coral Island.*" *Children's Literature* 25 (1997): 205-13.

[*In the following essay, Singh compares and contrasts* Lord of the Flies *and R. M. Ballantyne's novel* The Coral Island.]

> *government: . . . 2. The manner in which one's action is governed. a. In physical sense: Management of the limbs or body; movements, demeanor; also, habits of life, regimen. b. In moral sense: conduct, behaviour; be coming conduct, discretion.* Obs.
>
> *Oxford English Dictionary*

> *Perhaps in the twentieth century, the sort of fables we must construct are not for children on any level.*
>
> William Golding, 1962[1]

A memorable scene early in William Golding's 1954 ***Lord of the Flies*** eloquently suggests the ambition of Golding's fabulist intentions. On the island that at this point in the text is still an innocent playground, one of the younger boys, Henry, who is building castles in the sand, is covertly observed by an older boy, Roger:

> Roger stooped, picked up a stone, aimed, and threw it at Henry—threw it to miss. The stone—that token of preposterous time—bounced five yards to the right and fell in the water. Roger gathered a handful of stones and began to throw them. Yet there was a space round Henry, perhaps six yards in diameter, into which he dared not

> throw. Here, invisible yet strong, was the taboo of the old life. Round the squatting child was the protection of parents and school and policemen and the law. Roger's arm was conditioned by a civilization that knew nothing of him and was in ruins.
>
> (Golding, ***Lord,*** 62)

The "space round Henry, perhaps six yards in diameter," into which Roger dare not throw, is nothing other than the shrunken dimensions of civil society—the restraints taught by parents, school, policemen, and the law. What Roger is unable to disobey is not the express prohibition of civil society against violence, but an internalized restraint—that is, civility. Significantly, in the penultimate chapter of the book, it is Roger who hurls the mighty rock that sends Piggy crashing to his death (181): more starkly than any other character, he represents the erosion of restraint, the return to a sort of Stone Age. If the project of government may be understood macropolitically as civilization, then its micropolitical counterpart is education, with civility as its project. Golding's text is notable for making explicit this cluster of associations, which has long been the implicit staple of the literature of boyhood.

Lord of the Flies is an overseas adventure story, the self-conscious culmination of a long line of boys' adventure stories. "It's like in a book," Ralph announces after their initial exploration of the island:

> At once there was a clamour.
>
> "Treasure Island—"
>
> "Swallows and Amazons—"
>
> "Coral Island—"
>
> . . . . .
>
> "This is our island. It's a good island. Until the grownups come to fetch us we'll have fun."
>
> (34-35)

Golding's story seeks to dispel this intertextual glamor with grim realism; it both participates in and criticizes the history of the adventure story, whose originating canonical text is *Robinson Crusoe.* But the adventure story that was almost schematically Golding's pre-text was Robert Michael Ballantyne's 1858 *Coral Island,* one of the earliest such stories to have boys, in the absence of adults, for its main characters.

Children's literature has so naturalized this device that we forget how important a narrative innovation it must have been: we may be reminded of its innovative quality by the analogy of an exclusive dogs' club, where pampered pets may watch *101 Dalmatians* and other canine classics starring their own kind. *The Coral Island* is *for* boys and *about* boys, and it is even narrated *by* a boy, or, at least, by a former boy:

> I was a boy when I went through the wonderful adventures herein set down. With the memory of my boyish feelings strong upon me, I present my book specially to boys, in the earnest hope that they may derive valuable information, much pleasure, great profit, and unbounded amusement from its pages.
>
> (Ballantyne, xxx)

The Coral Island preserves the homiletic form of the educational tract, but it delivers the homily in user-friendly terms—and thus inaugurates a dominant tradition in the literature of boyhood. R. L. Stevenson gratefully acknowledged Ballantyne in the verses that preface *Treasure Island* (Stevenson iii); and G. A. Henty, the most prolific boys' writer of the late nineteenth century, is known to have been influenced by Ballantyne's methods (Carpenter and Pritchard 43).

More than a century after Ballantyne's daring and successful experiment in boys' literature, William Golding declared, in his 1962 lecture at Berkeley on the writing of ***Lord of the Flies:*** "Ballantyne's island was a nineteenth-century island inhabited by English boys; mine was to be a twentieth-century island inhabited by English boys" ("Fable" 89). Written out of the agonized consciousness of England's loss of global power, ***Lord of the Flies*** may be read with some accuracy as a parodic rewriting of Ballantyne's *Coral Island.* The three central characters of ***Lord of the Flies***—Ralph, Piggy, and Jack—are caricatures of Ballantyne's three boy heroes—Ralph, Peterkin, and Jack—who, shipwrecked on an island like Crusoe's (albeit in the South Seas), heroically survive violent encounters with cannibalistic natives and bloodthirsty pirates. The idyllic Coral Island is transformed by Golding into an infernal place: whereas Ballantyne's adventurers master nature, using and developing technology for the purpose, Golding's boy characters are helpless captives whose only hope is rescue.

Indeed, the first part of Ballantyne's text is a protracted meditation on a Rousseauistic education in which the boys learn to gather, hunt, cook, fight, save, and hide not through instruction but from necessity. We may remember that Rousseau suggests that Emile read and mime *Robinson Crusoe*

(Rousseau 147-48); in Ballantyne's book, the boys' forced sojourn on the island is both the occasion and the means for their education. They also learn science, or specialized knowledge, from the disinterested study of their surroundings and the inferences they draw from their observations. In this way, they discover that crabs shed their skins and that hydraulic pressure causes water to spout inland. This spirit of rational inquiry distinguishes Ballantyne's boys from Golding's, who forget more than they learn and unresistingly fall prey to their irrational terrors.

Moreover, Ballantyne's boys take a blithely utilitarian view of their material environment, which represents to them the availability of ready-made value. Upon discovering the milk of the coconut, which he takes to calling "lemonade," Peterkin, who is by common consent the jester (and as such is distinct from Golding's Piggy, the butt of all jokes), exclaims, "Meat and drink on the same tree! . . . washing in the sea, lodging on the ground—and all for nothing! My dear boys, we're set up for life; it must be the ancient paradise—hurrah!" (27-28) and, later, "So . . . we seem to have everything ready prepared to our hands in this wonderful island—lemonade ready bottled in nuts, and loaf-bread growing on the trees" (43). The boys' life on the island joyfully conjoins work and pleasure. By studied contrast, in ***Lord of the Flies*** work and play are absolutely and irrevocably divorced: work is conservative and constructive; play, liberating but destructive.

The thrills of the Coral Island are twofold: they alternate between delight in eating—literally sucking at the bountiful plenitude of the island—and terror of being eaten (if not devoured by cannibals, then swallowed up by the bloody jaws of a shark). ***Lord of the Flies*** effects a darkly Freudian conversion of this wholesome orality into analsadistic pleasure. Here even the consumption of tropical fruit, that richly suggestive marker of paradise regained, causes chronic diarrhea—producing not value but waste. Self-consciously representing a later phase of erotic development, ***Lord of the Flies*** counts on our willingness to see the pleasures of boyhood as immature and outmoded.

We could continue to list the ways in which ***Lord of the Flies*** deflates and diminishes the heroic occasion and mode of *The Coral Island.* Yet the two books are overwhelmingly similar in their thematic concern with legitimate authority, leadership, and government. Both texts equate good government with the containment and defeat of savagery (whether the savagery is shown to reside within us or without); and both characterize savagery as the absence of a restraining law. Late in *The Coral Island,* the narrator, Ralph, who is now separated from his comrades, appeals to the pirate Bill, his guide through the South Sea islands:

> "Have these wretched creatures [native islanders] no law among themselves," said I, "which can restrain such wickedness?"
>
> "None," replied Bill. "The chief's word is law. He might kill and eat a dozen of his own subjects any day for nothing more than his own pleasure, and nobody would take the least notice of it."
>
> (Ballantyne 242)

A cluster of associations equates the pirates with "white savages" (193); and their savagery, like that of the natives, manifests itself in "wanton slaughter" (216). If the restraint of pleasure is the defining characteristic of civilization, then boyhood, Ballantyne appears to suggest, is that state of grace where pleasure is harmless, appetite is healthy, and play is productive. Beyond boyhood, pleasure must be restrained, appetite curbed, and play governed.

Lord of the Flies proposes its own version of irresponsible authority in the terrifying figure of Jack, who "makes things break up like they do" (Golding, *Lord,* 139). The Jack of *The Coral Island* had been a natural leader who ruled by superior knowledge—he had read more adventure stories than had the others—and by playful violence. Golding's Jack, on the other hand, is clearly drawn from contemporary alarms about the totalitarian personality. It must be remembered that ***Lord of the Flies*** achieves its ominous generality of reference by glossing over the specificity of its Cold War context. The boys suspect that there has been a nuclear explosion (Golding, ***Lord,*** 14), and, at the end, Ralph's greatest remembered fear is of the "Reds" (162).[2] Golding himself uses the term "totalitarian"—a word that only took on its full negative import after World War II—in his remarks on ***Lord of the Flies:***

> Before the Second World War I believed in the perfectibility of social man; that a correct structure of society would produce goodwill; and that therefore you could remove all social ills by a reorganization of society. It is possible that today I believe something of the same, but after the war I did not because I was unable to. I had discovered what one man could do to another. . . . I am thinking of the vileness beyond all words that went on, year after year, in the totalitarian states . . . there were things done during that period from which I still have to avert my mind lest I

should be physically sick. They were not done by the head-hunters of New Guinea, or by some primitive tribe in the Amazon. They were done skilfully, coldly, by educated men, doctors, lawyers, by men with a tradition of civilization behind them, to beings of their own kind.

(Golding, **"Fable,"** 86-87)

Golding finally leaves us with the not entirely convincing position that totalitarianism is a form of savagery, and that not even boyhood is exempt from its encroachments. In Golding's own formulation,

> Man is a fallen being. He is gripped by original sin. His nature is sinful and his state perilous. . . . I looked round me for some convenient form in which this thesis might be worked out, and found it in the play of children. I was well situated for this, since at this time I was teaching them. Moreover, I am a son, brother, father. I have lived for many years with small boys, and understand and know them with awful precision. I decided to take the literary convention of boys on an island, only make them real boys instead of paper cutouts with no life in them; and try to show how the shape of the society they evolved would be conditioned by their diseased, their fallen nature.
>
> (Golding, **"Fable,"** 88)

Rhetorically and ideologically, the claim of ***Lord of the Flies*** over *The Coral Island* is the claim of experience over innocence, realism over romance, truth over illusion, maturity over naivete, and hardship over ease. At a crucial narrative moment in ***Lord of the Flies,*** before the reversion to savagery is properly under way, Ralph, the good leader, has an introspective realization: "He found himself understanding the weariness of this life, where every path was an improvisation and a considerable part of one's waking life was spent watching one's feet. He stopped, facing the strip; and remembering that first enthusiastic exploration as though it were part of a brighter childhood, he smiled jeeringly" (Golding, ***Lord,*** 76). ***Lord of the Flies*** encourages us to locate the possibility of good government in the irrecoverable brighter childhood of political thought. At the same time, it makes childhood itself as archaic as the colonial metaphor of enthusiastic exploration.

Steven Marcus wrote in an introduction to Kipling's *Stalky & Co.* in 1962 (the very year in which the increasing classroom use of ***Lord of the Flies*** led Golding to explain to college students how he had come to write it):

> In no other language does the word for boy have the kind of resonance that it does in English. . . . In what other language is there such an epithet as "Oh, boy!"—an expression of the very essence of spontaneous delight . . . boy is one of the sacred words of the English language; boyhood is—or for one hundred and fifty years was—a priestly state or condition; and the literature of boys and boyhood has had, for a secularized era, something of the aura of doctrinal or holy writ.
>
> (Marcus 152)

In part, at least, the doctrine of boyhood relies on the congruence of subject and implied reader; thus, *The Coral Island* is a founding text of the genre. ***Lord of the Flies*** violently debunks the mythic doctrine: it is a book *about* boys, but evidently is neither *for* boys nor *by* a boy. In disrupting the generic economy of boyhood, it opens its textual portals to *any* reader who is prepared to take pleasure in the sober triumph of modernist truth over heroic illusion. If pleasure is, indeed, a suitable criterion for making cultural and generic distinctions, then ***Lord of the Flies,*** by consistently and mysteriously pleasing young readers (even those who first encounter it as prescribed reading), has invented the genre of adolescent writing. For the innocent homosocial pleasures of boyhood it substitutes the potent but shameful solitude of adolescence; for the nostalgia of the literature of boyhood it inserts the alienation of the new literature of adolescence.

The substitution of adolescence for boyhood is, of course, a powerful historical phenomenon, not simply a textual one. One way of understanding the shift is by grasping the relation of boyhood to the maternal feminine. Underwriting the pleasure of boyhood is the absent yet authorizing figure of the mother—Ralph Rover's mother who stoically bids her adventurous son adieu in *The Coral Island:* "My mother gave me her blessing and a small Bible; and her last request was that I would never forget to read a chapter every day, and say my prayers; which I promised, with tears in my eyes, that I would certainly do" (Ballantyne 5). Boys will be, and can be, boys only with the complicity and permission of their mothers; an extreme instance of this narrative typology can be found in J. M. Barrie's Peter Pan, the eternal boy who kidnaps two generations of Wendys because he needs a mother.

From the barren emotional landscape of ***Lord of the Flies,*** the female parent is all but missing. Only once in Ralph's daydreams does she appear, and then she is associated with severe emotional loss: "Once . . . they had lived in a cottage on the edge of the moors. In the succession of houses that Ralph had known, this one stood out with particular clarity because after that house he had been sent away to school. Mummy had still been with them and Daddy had come home every day" (Golding, ***Lord,*** 112). Had Mummy not abandoned him, would Ralph's government of the island have succeeded? In fundamental ways ***Lord of the Flies*** remains tethered to the social discourse of family values. If boyhood is guaranteed by the familiar and forgiving figure of the mother, surely adolescence is betrayed by the unforgivable absence of the mother—an absence that represents simultaneously the terrible failure of civilization and the enabling condition of maturity.

In a recent Film Board of Canada production, a character laughingly recommends that the world be governed by postmenopausal women. The film is *Forbidden Love: The Unashamed Stories of Lesbian Lives;* the character is one of the aging women who were interviewed for the documentary. Men, she explains, are only boys, and, she adds, we know from ***Lord of the Flies*** what *boys* are like.

Oddly enough, her reading of William Golding's pessimistic fable is clever only in substituting the gendered "men" for the universal "man." In other respects it might well meet with the author's approbation, for ***Lord of the Flies*** takes considerable pains to establish that at the heart of civilization lurks a persistent savagery, and that men, once stripped of the veneer of adulthood, quickly revert to being wanton boys who kill one another for their sport. Indeed, the book's remarkable success has made the reversion to savagery a cultural byword, and a powerful one because it represents the transformation from the civilized to the savage as simultaneously regression and maturation. To become savage is to regress to the anthropological infancy of mankind, but to recognize one's essential savagery is to be psychologically mature: this is the intriguingly mixed message of Golding's book.

Notes

1. "Fable," 86.
2. Golding's parodic intent—to spoof "redskins," that cliché of boyhood culture—takes a tendentious form in the book, for Reds-as-native-Americans (an obsolete enemy) are made to share features of savagery with Reds-as-Communists (the real enemy). Thus, Jack and his troop, the enemies of civilization, appropriate Native American cultural practices (warpaint and ululation) to mark their association with bad government.

Works Cited

Ballantyne, R. M. *The Coral Island: A Tale of the Pacific Ocean.* Ed. J. S. Bratton. The World's Classics. Oxford: Oxford University Press, 1990.

Carpenter, Humphrey, and Mari Pritchard. *The Oxford Companion to Children's Literature.* Oxford: Oxford University Press, 1984.

Forbidden Love: The Unashamed Stories of Lesbian Lives. Dir. Aerlyn Weissman and Linne Fernie. Film Board of Canada English Programs, Studio D, 1992.

Golding, William. "Fable." In Golding, *The Hot Gates and Other Occasional Pieces.* New York: Harcourt, Brace, & World, 1965.

—. *Lord of the Flies.* New York: Perigee, 1954.

Locke, John. *Locke on Politics, Religion, and Education.* London: Collier Macmillan, 1965.

Marcus, Steven. "Stalky & Co." In *Kipling and the Critics,* ed. Elliot L. Gilbert. New York: New York University Press, 1965. 150-62.

Rousseau, Jean-Jacques. *Emile.* Trans. Barbara Foxley. Everyman's Library. London: J. M. Dent, 1911.

Stevenson, Robert Louis. *Treasure Island.* Medallion Edition. New York: Current Literature, 1909.

Kirstin Olsen (essay date 2000)

SOURCE: Olsen, Kirstin. "Literary Analysis." In *Understanding Lord of the Flies: a Student Casebook to Issues, Sources, and Historical Documents,* pp. 1-21. Westport, Conn.: Greenwood Press, 2000.

[*In the following essay, Olsen provides a thorough literary analysis of* Lord of the Flies.]

> Absurd and uninteresting fantasy about the explosion of an atomic bomb on the colonies and a group of children who land in jungle country near New Guinea. Rubbish and dull. Pointless.
>
> —Verdict of a manuscript reader on the first version of ***Lord of the Flies,*** then titled *Strangers from Within*

The very idea of putting ***Lord of the Flies*** into a social and historical context seems, at first, absurd. After all, it is a deliberately mythic novel, almost as abstract as it is possible for a work of fiction to be. The setting is never identified. It could be almost any small island in the tropics. The characters, except for Jack (and Percival Wemys Madison, whose last name exists solely as a symbol of lost civilization) have no surnames; many of them, including most of the littluns and choirboys, do not even merit first names. The war that brings them to the island in the first place is mentioned only briefly. An early draft of the novel contained additional chapters outlining the course of the nuclear war that occasions the boys' evacuation, but Golding's editor felt that the novel was stronger without this material,[1] and the chapters in question were cut. Thus stripped of unnecessary detail, the central conflicts come into sharper focus, and the story seems more nearly universal.

Yet ***Lord of the Flies,*** like all novels, comes from its author's experiences and interests. It is shaped by Western ideas about civilization and savagery and by the British colonial past. It reacts to the pervasive belief in the superiority of British culture and to the belief that to be British was in some sense the direct opposite of being a savage. It evolves from Christian, perhaps even Calvinist, theories about human nature and sin. It is influenced by debates about biological determinism, by the English school system that both produced and employed Golding, by the adventure stories that boys of Golding's time read, and by the events and aftermath of World War II. The remarkable thing is that, despite being very much a product of its place and time, full of dated schoolboy slang and cold war anxiety, ***Lord of the Flies*** remains an influential and powerful commentary on human evil.

In part this is because it explores some of the most intense urges and emotions in our repertoire: the desire for power, the fear of the unknown, fear of other people, anger, and jealousy. In short, this novel asks hard questions about what Golding, taking a cue from Conrad, calls "the darkness of man's heart" (202).

The Universal Fascination with Power

Anyone who has watched children at play for a significant length of time observes, over and over, the exercise of power. Children, powerless in so much of their daily lives, act our roles that they believe come accessorized with power: mother, father, teacher, police officer, king, queen, and hero. Even their animal play, once they become aware of the predator-prey relationship, is informed by a desire for power. Few children choose to be the brachiosaurus or zebra if they can be the *T. rex* or the lion. Similarly, when they play with dolls, blocks, and other toys, they see themselves as little gods, determining what happens to their tiny creatures much as their own fates are dictated by parents and others.

Golding recognizes this tendency in children and even includes an example of it in ***Lord of the Flies.*** One of the younger children, Henry, amuses himself on the beach by trapping, herding, collecting, and thereby controlling, small sea creatures (61). Significantly, Golding describes Henry's experience not as actual power but as an "illusion of mastery," a phrase that could describe many of the power relationships in the novel. Is Piggy master of himself or his fate? Clearly not. When put to the test, he cannot even retain control over his own eyeglasses. Is Ralph master of anything? He appears to be, but his political power proves, too, to be an illusion, as evanescent and as incapable of containing living beings as Henry's tiny footprints in the sand. Even Jack's power is illusory or at least temporary, vanishing the moment an adult authority arrives on the island.

Golding thus simultaneously taps into one of our greatest desires and one of our greatest fears: the desire to control ourselves and others and the fear that any sense of control we possess is ultimately false. He shows us the means by which power is ordinarily seized: physical force, knowledge, size, beauty, insight, currency (in the case of the island, the currency is pork), and friendship. Every reader has tried to gain the upper hand in some situation by at least one of these means. Yet, in the novel, every one of them proves to be a trap or a mirage. Small wonder that most readers feel a sense of horror at the disintegration of the island's small society. It is not only the fictional community that is dissolving, but also the readers' own sense of personal control.

The Universality of Fear

Another strength of ***Lord of the Flies*** is its attempt to explain one of our most fundamental emotions: fear. Fear is, in Darwinian terms, a good thing. It urges creatures in danger to flee, fight, or hide and thus allows them to live longer and to pass on their wariness to their offspring. Like power struggles, it can result in a stronger, fitter community and a more successful species.

However, like power struggles, fear can exceed useful limits and become a destructive force. A diurnal animal in the wild needs to be alert even at night, sleeping lightly and in a relatively safe place, and exercising special caution at times when its vision is impaired. Even so, it may fall prey to nocturnal predators better adapted to the dark. Fear, in this context, is rational and directed at a specific threat.

A child safe at home in bed may fear the dark for the same reasons but without the threat. Its ancient evolutionary instincts tell in that danger lurks in the unseen. It is primarily a visual creature, with faint powers of smell and hearing, and it relies on its eyes. When light is removed, it must assume, according to its evolutionary programming, that danger is eminently possible. The parents, with the benefit of years of experience of safe sleeping, know that there is no danger. The child, however, has only the instinctive alertness and fear that kept its ancestors alive. With no namable threat close by, it creates something to fill the place left empty by jaguars and lions and bears. Therefore, there are monsters under the bed, in the closet, outside the window, down the hall—in short, in all the unseen places that a wild creature would be reasonable to fear.

Early human societies had plenty to fear. Besides wild beasts and natural disasters, there were diseases, infections, accidents, enemy tribes, false allies, and food shortages. Their inventions, like the monster in the closet, gave tangibility and limits to intangible or uncontrollable fears. They named gods and demons, told stories about them, and gave them faces and attributes. A nine-headed hydra, a goat-footed devil, a many-breasted goddess, and a jackal-headed god were mysterious, yet easier to understand than bacteria, viruses, electromagnetic charges, cold fronts, and betrayal. If a child falls ill and dies without apparent cause, what does it mean? Whom does it help? Who might fall ill and die next? In the absence of the answers, humans make a demon. Something unseen ate the child, wanted it, hated it, or wanted something it possessed. Appease the demon, hunt it, drive it out of the village, oppose it, find it, trick it, destroy it, or bribe it, and the problem will be solved. Sometimes it actually worked. A frightened village might isolate itself, hoping to ward off evil spirits, and by quarantining itself escape a plague. A violent member of the community might do less damage if presumed to be possessed by evil spirits and driven away or subjected to public scrutiny or punishment. A fortunate coincidence might lead to the natural disappearance of a threat at about the time a purifying ritual was performed. Even when such tactics did not work, appeasing unseen dangers made the community feel that it had taken action.

But what if, as in the child's bedroom, there is no threat? The alertness and wariness do not vanish simply because no rational threat is present. This is the situation on the island, where there are no predatory animals, no enemy tribes, and no purely natural disasters. Still, the boys have two basic problems. The first, as Golding recognizes, is that the tendency to find and name enemies does not evaporate. In the absence of real danger, people—especially children, accustomed to sudden and apparently inexplicable changes imposed from above, and lacking the experience to judge the rationality of their fears—often create an imaginary danger to take its place.

The second problem is that there is one genuine cause for fear on the island, but it is the one thing that must remain unspoken. Despite their initial joy at being away from all adult authority, the boys are terrified that they will never be rescued. The importance of the fire to rescue is often stressed, but the natural consequences of failure are voiced only by Piggy, who states his fear that they could stay there until they die. Ralph, confronted with this horrible fate, pushes it away. He asserts that his father will come for them, and when Piggy asks how he will know the boys are there, Ralph cannot even give voice to his fear or to his denial of fear (14). These children come from a British schoolboy culture that valued stoicism and often separated boys from their parents at quite a young age. Boarding-school boys would see pining for parents and home as babyish, and the boys—the "biguns," at least—are old enough to want to seem like men. Unable to gaze into the dark corners of their worst fear, the boys are left with an empty closet and a willingness to put a monster into it.

Into this void steps the birthmarked boy with his tale of a "beastie," a "snake-thing, ever so big" (35). Just as he denied his fear of abandonment, Ralph denies the existence of the beast. As if to reinforce his point, he follows his last denial with a renewed statement of faith in rescue (37). However, this merely delays the hunt for a beast. It is an ineradicable part of human nature, Golding seems to be saying, to make a beast where none exists or to put a beast in the place of a more abstract threat. Soon the boys are enacting all the universal responses to demons—searching for the beast, opposing it, appeasing it. By this time, however, the fear of dying on the island has been joined by a new fear, a fear of each other. One could also argue, given that the actual "beast" is the decaying body of a paratrooper, that the beast also represents the boys' generalized fears of and about the war in which their country is engaged. The attempt to make their vague and terrifying fears concrete is mocked by the beast itself: "Fancy thinking the Beast was something you could hunt and kill!" (143) says the pig's head to Simon. The real horror, Golding seems to imply, is that our worst fears have no names—or the wrong names.

The Universality of the Characters

Much of the novel's strength also lies in its characters, who, despite all the "waccos" and "wizards," remain recognizable as the sort of people everyone has known in school, work, and society. Almost everyone has known a Piggy—a person set aside by some defect or difference who becomes the target of all sorts of teasing and torment. Plenty of people have known, or been, the littluns, the people on the fringe of the real action, motivated only by fear and hunger, victimized at random (60), seemingly unable to direct the course of events themselves, led by whomever promises the fastest end to fear and hunger.

Piggy

Of all the characters, the one who often makes the most lasting impression is Piggy. Partly it is his nickname that makes him memorable; partly it is the distinctiveness of his physical incapacities. Fat, asthmatic, nearsighted, unable to swim (13), and a whimpering mama's (or auntie's) boy, he is by no means suited to an adventure in the wild. Yet it is he who has most of the best ideas. He tries to make a sundial (64-65), names and organizes the boys, and insists on the rights of the littluns. He even, on one occasion, serves as the littluns' literal voice, repeating the words of the birthmarked boy so that the full group can hear (35). It is he who identifies the conch shell that becomes the symbol of parliamentary order on the island, and it is he who first gives it a purpose, changing it from a purely natural object into a tool of civilization (16). Furthermore, it is Piggy who provides, albeit somewhat unwillingly, the tool that bestows the power to create fire—his spectacles (40-41). It makes sense that he tries to re-create civilization in the wilderness, because he must know, at some level, that in civilization lies his best protection. Civilization protects the weak and different; the wilderness does not.

The wilderness, in fact, as symbolized by Jack, Roger, and their adherents, chooses the weak and different as its first prey. From this simple and brutal fact of predation comes Piggy's concern with fairness and his defense of the littluns. It is no coincidence that, in the wake of the fire, the boy who is called "Fatty" and told by Jack to "shut up" should be the first to notice the absence of "[t]hat little 'un . . . him with the mark on his face" (45-46). Piggy, a marked man in his own way, is good at spotting his own kind, and it does not take very long for the boys to identify the relationship between the boy Piggy and the animal piggies. In the debate over the existence of the beast, the subject of the predator-prey relationship is enlisted on the side of reason by Piggy, but the other boys ignore the logic and make a leap that the astute reader has already made, from the actual pigs on the island to the one boy named after a pig (83). In the wild, zebras survive by forming herds, confusing their enemies with numbers and movement. In politics, the disenfranchised, the weak, and the poor survive by forming parties or staging riots and demonstrations. Piggy, if he were able to form the littluns and other marginal boys into some kind of coalition, might be able to survive, but he is a poor leader. The minute he is left in charge, the littluns scatter (46). The herd is doomed.

In a happy version of the story, Piggy's good ideas and spectacles would compensate for his physical differences, his bad grammar, and his nagging insistence on behaving like grownups. It is possible that this could happen in real life as well. But it is equally plausible, perhaps more plausible, that things would work out as Golding envisions, with Piggy made into a favorite victim and someone, sooner or later, realizing that the spectacles can be possessed without the wearer. His good ideas, in the end, count for nothing. It is sad but true that a good idea can be torpedoed simply by being espoused by the wrong person. Piggy is not beautiful, popular, strong, or charismatic, and his only advantage is that he is, for the most part, right. It is not enough.

It is, in fact, in Piggy's hands, something of a disadvantage. No one likes Piggy, with the half-hearted exception of Ralph, and so no one really wants him to be right. When he is, they resent him for it. He sounds perpetually like Cassandra foretelling the fall of Troy, cursed with foreknowledge and bad timing. Over and over, he thrusts himself forward, strong in his convictions, but weak in presentation. He is too shrill, too repetitive, too disdainful of fun. He is too much like a parent, and few of the boys on the island seem to want their parents back in any form. He in fact chides them for acting like children, virtually guaranteeing that he will become an outcast. And, like Cassandra, he can see his own fate (14). He knows he is saying the right things in the wrong way and he knows how Jack feels about him. (93). Yet he cannot stop himself. He remains the voice of civilization, of parents and nannies and policemen and teachers, to the last: "Which is better—to have rules and agree, or to hunt and kill?" (180) As always, he misjudges the mood of his audience, or perhaps does not care enough about their mood. To mention hunting and killing at this juncture is no hollow piece of rhetoric, but practically an invitation.

Ralph

If Piggy is civilization's voice, Ralph is its public face. He is a profoundly average boy, better-looking than some, but of average capacities. He shares the average boy's desires, for rescue and fun, in that order or not as the whim takes him, and he has good, but not brilliant, oratorical skills. In a moment of stress, for example, he discovers that "his voice tend[s] either to disappear or to come out too loud" (104). Sometimes he finds the right words, but often he fails, as when Jack apologizes for letting the fire go out (72).

Ralph follows this misstep with another, an "ingracious mutter" (72) to relight the fire. He is, after all, a frightened and angry boy, not a master statesman. His initial election as the boys' chief is haphazard and nearly instinctive, and he is chosen for much the same reasons that many people select their leaders: "The most obvious leader was Jack. But there was a stillness about Ralph . . . there was his size, and attractive appearance, and most obscurely, yet most powerfully, there was the conch" (22). At first, Ralph is delighted to play leader. Like the conch or the vote, power itself is a toy. Later, like most elected officials, he worries both about his responsibilities and about maintaining power.

His responsibilities are few enough, and they constitute the basic set of duties of any leader, whether parent or president: feed his charges, shelter them, protect them from harm, work for their greater security or salvation. The boys constantly measure Ralph's success as a leader by his ability to perform these tasks, yet every one of these responsibilities is twisted by circumstances into a symbol of failure or futility. Feeding the boys is no trouble, since there are crabs and fruit on the island, but food, in the form of roast pork, becomes the boys' sole focus. Meat becomes the island's money. It is hard to obtain but can be gotten with hard work and skill, and the getting of meat interrupts all other work. Shelters go unbuilt, and Ralph is powerless to force the boys to build. The hunt plays havoc with the schedule for keeping the fire lit, making salvation difficult to obtain. Most of all, the idea of protection from danger is warped by the conditions on the island. There are no natural enemies on this small scrap of land, yet danger is such a part of the boys' notion of adventure that danger must be invented if it does not exist. Thus the beast is conjured from dreams and glimpses, while the real danger, the all-consuming desire for power and acceptance among the boys, goes unheeded by almost all. Ralph recognizes his essential failure to lead, even while the outward forms of leadership remain intact. Nevertheless, every time he loses power to Jack, he seems surprised by this latest turn of events and newly shocked by his incapacity to perform his duties.

He has options, of course, but fails to make use of them. He could yield power to Jack and ask to be placed in charge of a fire detail, sacrificing his own vanity and ambition to the greater good of rescue. He could challenge Jack physically and defeat him once and for all. He could lend Piggy more assistance in forming a coalition. Yet he lacks something—vision, urgency, a willingness to be unembarrassed by Piggy's friendship, or something else altogether—that would give him the courage to force the issue. Instead, he embarks on a campaign of appeasement and diplomacy.

Golding, of course, was writing within recent memory of one of history's great diplomatic failures: the policy of appeasement that preceded Britain's entry into World War II. The British prime minister, Neville Chamberlain, averted his eyes while Hitler's Germany armed for war and began invading its neighbors, and it was not until Chamberlain's replacement by Winston Churchill and Hitler's invasion of Poland that Germany's aggression was met with a significantly aggressive response. The world was fortunate to have a Churchill at the time and a Roosevelt who urged support for Britain despite an isolationist climate in the United States. However, there is not always a Churchill or a Roosevelt in the right place at the right time, a failure of political systems made all too clear in the 1990s by worldwide dithering over genocide in Rwanda and the Balkans. Political and moral cowardice, after all, are nothing new. Martin Luther King, Jr., derided it when he declared that evil triumphs in the absence of action by good people, and Susan Sontag, referring to the violence in Bosnia and to the defiant post-Holocaust slogan "Never again," reflected, "Never again doesn't . . . mean anything, does it. I mean, never again will Germans be allowed to kill Jews in the 1940s. That's . . . true. But do we have the will and the interest to prevent a genocide in Europe now?"[2]

Ralph is Chamberlain, and Clinton, and every other leader who fails to act at the perfect time, in the perfect way, to avoid a monumental tragedy. In other words, he is a good many of the world's leaders throughout history—flawed, uncertain, trapped by a multiplicity of possibilities in a web of inaction or wrong action, too tangled to find the way out.

All he knows for certain is that he is bound to be a better leader than Jack, whose desires are for pleasure and power and self-glorification, with no room left for the good of the community. Ralph at least has some sense of responsibility. So he blunders on, unwilling to yield to the bad boy. To retain his power, he even resorts to hunting, attempting to become more like Jack in order to steal back some of Jack's growing glory. Unfortunately, his attempt is all too successful. Flushed with a small success, he adopts, for the moment at least, Jack's value system: "'I hit him, all right. The spear stuck in. I wounded him!' He sunned himself in their new respect and felt that hunting was good after all" (113). The rest of this chapter details Ralph's descent into Jack's world. Instead of returning to Piggy and the island's small civilization, he remains with Jack, leaving Simon to carry out his responsibilities. He and Jack spar verbally, with Ralph mostly on the defensive. His one attempt to cut through the posturing to the "darkness of man's heart," his query to Jack on the reason for his hatred is an embarrassing failure (118). The chapter ends, significantly, with Ralph's direct encounter with the beast, the novel's supreme symbol of fear and evil. In the end, Ralph can only co-opt Jack's leadership qualities by living in the wilderness of predation, aggression, and fear, and he cannot tame Jack and absorb him into the civilized world.

Therefore, Ralph fails as a leader. He neither preserves his people nor retains his position as chief, mostly because he never understands the fragility of his power. Like most politicians, he has (or at least develops) a sense of the people's mood, and he has a talent for shifting responsibility (37). Eventually, he also learns a few basic principles of government, for example, that important things have to be repeated to be understood (78). In this sense, he understands that he is addressing an audience of children, but he never quite manages to be the leader, the parent, that they and Piggy want him to be. For, despite their resentment of control, the children simultaneously miss the safe boundaries and the freedom from decision making that their parents and teachers provided them. Ralph never gains real control of the household, or the state, since he has no rewards to offer for good behavior and no punishments to threaten for disobedience. Unlike a parent, he cannot offer food or playthings as rewards. Food is abundant on the island and can be taken at will, while playthings like sticks and crabs are everywhere and "civilized" playthings are entirely absent. Similarly, he cannot send the boys to their rooms or rescind their privileges. Unlike the state, he cannot offer tax breaks or incentive programs as rewards, nor can he jail the boys or impose corporal punishment for their laziness or mutiny. Just as the conch appears to be a symbol of power, but in fact is subverted whenever it suits the purpose of the moment, Ralph appears to be the chief but has no actual power, only a slight influence that ultimately dissipates. He cannot force the boys to build shelters (80) or to keep the fire lit, and even the eventual rescue is only indirectly caused by him.

Ralph is not a fool. He knows that everything is going wrong, and his responsibilities begin, literally, to devour him. He begins biting his nails beyond the quick, almost entirely unconsciously (131). Eating is never simple in ***Lord of the Flies;*** it always carries heavy symbolism. Eating fruit is synonymous with laziness, and eating meat is synonymous with violence. Ralph is doing neither. As the symbol of the civilized community that almost was, he is slowly consuming himself. It is the group's sin of self-cannibalism, a literally gnawing awareness of his failure, that torments him.

Jack

Ralph's most significant failure is his inability to control Jack. If he could make Jack his faithful servant or ally, as successful politicians make servants or allies of the military, he might actually have some leverage over the rest of the boys, because Jack has the one real reward on the island under his control. This reward is the knowledge of the hunt. Unlike the task of keeping the fire lit, which is tedious and apparently unending, Jack's hunt offers camaraderie, hard work, esoteric knowledge, a clear end to the task, and a tangible reward at its end. The hunt is also something that the boys cannot easily duplicate on their own. In Jack's case, it takes a great deal of study to learn to track and kill the wild pigs on the island; a good example of his efforts can be found at the beginning of Chapter 3. For the littluns, acquiring this knowledge on their own is impossible. Even for the older boys, it would be tiresome and difficult to repeat Jack's experience. Therefore, Jack has the only currency on the island, and he knows it.

It is Jack, not Ralph, who is the clear choice as leader on the island. Unlike Ralph, Jack is a grand master of manipulation and public image. Almost everything he does, whether by instinct or calculation, increases his power over the boys. He grants or withholds meat, grants or withholds the right to hunt, stages public recreations of the hunt to demonstrate his hunters' prowess (115), makes use of uniforms—first the choirboys' uniforms and then the hunting paint—to create a sense of belonging, and, cleverest of all, hints at the exclusivity of his band while intending to absorb the entire island population under his control:

"If you want to join my tribe come and see us. Perhaps I'll let you join. Perhaps not. . . . He was safe from shame or self-consciousness behind the mask of his paint" (140). It is the mention of "shame or self-consciousness" that makes Jack one of Golding's most ingenious creations. Jack is the Freudian id, the wild man, Hitler, the school bully, a smug and devious co-worker, a savage, a killer. Yet he is also a boy, frightened of the other boys' disapproval, frantic to be popular, and jealous of Ralph's friendship with Piggy (91). All of his evil, all of his machinations and displays, come from such basic human insecurities that it is possible, in our most honest moments, to see ourselves in Jack as well as in Ralph or Piggy.

It is thus possible to detest Jack's use of power and to admire the skill with which he obtains it. In the beginning of the novel, he has nothing but the leadership of his choir, a leadership that the elected leader, Ralph, bestows upon him. The conch, symbol of parliamentary discourse, is in Ralph's control. Jack cannot even manage to wound a pig, let alone kill it (31). Yet, with sheer political genius, he elevates the hunt while denigrating the conch until the former becomes the whole focus of the island and the latter is destroyed. He begins by speaking out of turn, without the conch (87), later shouting down those who hold the conch. Each encroachment on the conch's power as a symbol is either tolerated or ineffectively opposed. By the time Piggy asks to carry the conch (171), the conch is the one thing that Jack no longer needs.

Even as he undermines the conch's significance, Jack magnifies that of the hunt. From the time of his first kill in Chapter 4, he surrounds the hunt with the kind of ritual that humans seem to crave. There are processions, chants of *"Kill the pig. Cut her throat"* (69), and re-enactments of the kill, complete with sound effects and vivid narrative. Finally, there is the tangible reward of the hunt—roast pork—which exceeds anything offered by the fire or the shelters for sheer physical pleasure. Even the fact that the hunters neglect the fire, obtaining their first kill at the expense of a chance of rescue, becomes less important in the rapture of the feast.

From that point, the hunt becomes not only a hobby and a source of sustenance but a determinant of manhood and worth. After the first kill, Jack justifies withholding pork from Piggy because he did not hunt (74). Ralph, afraid of pursuing the beast, tries to get Jack to go after it by saying, "You're a hunter," and then hunts it himself because he realizes that it is his job as chief to hunt a threat to his tribe (104). Jack then follows him and joins this hunt (106). Is he unable to let Ralph hunt the beast alone because of their friendship, because of duty, or because of the personal glory attached to a perilous hunt? Given what we know about Jack at this point in the novel, the last explanation seems most likely. Then, when Jack is knocked down during a hunt, and it is Ralph who wounds the boar, Jack manages to turn events to his advantage once again, displaying his own wound to general admiration (114). Almost immediately, there is another hunt reenactment, with Robert unwillingly playing the role of the pig, and a new element is added to the ritual—a human stand-in for the prey, who will be subjected to increasing tortures and even murder as the novel progresses.

Eventually, Jack tries to make hunting a prerequisite for leadership. He calls Ralph a coward and attacks him for his failure to hunt, using this as a basis to challenge him for the chieftainship (126-27). Though the tactic fails in the short term and results in Jack becoming an outcast, he turns the situation to his advantage, withholding meat from those who will not support him and offering knowledge of the hunt to those who will. In Jack's society, meetings are not run according to the principles of equality and free discourse symbolized by the conch, but according to the fierce rituals of the hunt, with chants, violence, and displays of personal power dictating the outcome. By breaking the old rules and making his own, Jack comes to leadership at last, but he lacks Piggy's insight, and in the end, he has nowhere to lead the boys but into hell.

Roger

The logical product of Jack's society is Roger, a boy who is far harder to understand or appreciate than his nominal leader. If Ralph is Chamberlain and Jack Hitler, Roger is the Gestapo, an instrument of torture and terror released from conventional morality and thus capable of unspeakable cruelty. He and Simon are the two most inscrutable major characters and serve as foils for each other. Both seem to understand that the lack of real authority on the island creates a potential for great evil, but for Simon this represents a threat to be contested, while for Roger it represents an opportunity to be embraced. Little by little, Roger tests his lack of limits. At first he explores cruelty in secret, lobbing stones at an unwitting Henry. Then he throws himself wholeheartedly into the half-serious torment of the pig-Robert (114), a public and socially acceptable outlet for his violence. The hunt is his element, a glorified excuse for madness and killing, and he is particularly savage in this activity, spitting a live sow on the point of his spear by stabbing her in her rectum (135). Yet even the slaughter of animals cannot contain his mounting capacity for cruelty, and Jack's bid for power gives him the chance to display its full range. Robert informs Roger that Jack intends to beat the bound Wilfred for no stated reason; he has finally found the society that will impose no humane limits on behavior.

Now his aggression is directed at humans, publicly and with increasing viciousness. He feels powerful flinging stones at Sam and Eric (175). He dehumanizes Ralph and Piggy in his mind and murders Piggy "with a sense of delirious abandonment" (180). Jack imposes no penalties for this act, giving it his tacit approval, and Roger becomes imbued with "a nameless authority" (182). It is he, it seems, who hurts Samneric, and it is he, even more than Jack, whom they fear (188-89). The last specific reference to him in ***Lord of the Flies*** is a hint that he is torturing the twins during the hunt for Ralph (192), and the penultimate reference to Roger is the most chilling of all, an implication that he means not only to kill Ralph but to behead him and display the severed head (190). Roger's behavior is horrifying and seemingly incomprehensible, but not, unfortunately, unusual. Human sacrifice, medieval tortures, genocide, purges, and a host of other atrocities testify to the capacity of *Homo sapiens,* "wise man," for murder and terror and a host of unwise acts when authority approves or fails to resist.

Simon

If we find it hard to see anything of ourselves in Roger because identifying with him is distasteful, we find it equally hard to see ourselves in Simon, though for different reasons. Simon is so decent, so selflessly brave, so opaquely meditative, so unjustly executed, that it is as desirable yet difficult to identify with him as it is to identify with Christ, after whom he is modeled. In fact, in the first draft of ***Lord of the Flies,*** Simon was so obviously a Christ figure that Golding's editor suggested that the analogy be toned down a bit.[3] Simon is thus made less completely Christlike, but no less obscure and mysterious than before, as Golding explained. "Simon," he said in an interview, "is understood by nobody, naturally enough."[4] The other boys certainly do not understand him. They call him "queer," "funny" (55), and "batty" (157). Piggy, as the voice of science and reason, is especially unsympathetic to Simon's spiritual approach. Asked if Simon could be climbing the mountain in search of the beast, he replies, "He might be. . . . He's cracked" (132).

Simon, in the finished version of ***Lord of the Flies,*** has characteristics that are not pointedly Christlike. He faints (20, 22), he is shy (25) and uncomfortable speaking before groups (103), traits not shared by the Bible's carpenter-rabbi who always seemed to have a parable ready. Simon happily enters into the business of the world, symbolized by his willingness to accompany an exploratory expedition and his excitement about making a map of the island (24-30). His ascetic appearance, barefoot, barely clad, long-haired, and dark-skinned (55-56) is subverted by "eyes so bright they had deceived Ralph into thinking him delightfully gay and wicked" (55). Simon is thus no point-by-point counterpart to Christ.

Yet he is the most spiritual of the boys. Unlike Piggy, who follows the rules because it is in his own interest to enforce them, Simon is no automatic outcast. He appears to respect the rights of the disenfranchised not because he is, by extension, defending his own rights, but because he really believes in the virtue of the rules. Ralph and Piggy often insist on the rule of the conch, usually when they are trying to make themselves heard, but Simon actually follows the rule without self-interest, stifling his own comments deliberately on at least two occasions (34, 86) because someone else has the conch. Alone among the boys, he thinks about the welfare of others, not because he believes it is his duty or because he believes it will help him, but because it is his inescapable nature to do so.

Incident after incident demonstrates Simon's essential generosity and empathy. He defends Piggy's role in starting the fire to Jack by pointing out that Piggy's glasses were of help (42). He helps build shelters long after the others have yielded to the temptations of swimming and hunting (50). Like Christ, who fed the masses with loaves and fishes, Simon feeds those incapable of feeding themselves. He gives his own meat to Piggy when Jack refuses to give Piggy any (74) and picks fruit for the littluns (56). He also, in order to ease a littlun's fear of a beast, confesses that he has been going off by himself at night. He is, as perhaps he suspected he would be, rewarded with ridicule. All of these acts are humble, self-abnegating, and as anonymous as it is possible for any act to be in such a small community. Most people would probably like to have Simon's gift for quiet charity, but most people would probably also end up swimming, hunting, and trying to stay on Jack's good side. Nonetheless, Simon resembles a rare type of person who does exist. There are people who give of themselves because it is their nature or their sole ambition. They do consider their own needs from time to time, but they are principally concerned with the needs of others.

Therefore, it is likely that Golding's readers have known someone at least somewhat like Simon. The reader may have known someone poorly understood, someone who really believed in society's rules, or someone who was innately generous. It is even possible that the reader knows someone who shares all three of these characteristics. What makes Simon unique, and thus harder to comprehend than any of the other boys, is that to these three personality traits Golding adds a fourth, rarer than the other three: a yearning and an aptitude for seeing the truth. In the midst of the dark jungle, Simon finds a private pocket "of heat and light" (56), light here serving as a metaphor for knowledge in the midst of ignorance and superstition. Unfortunately for Simon, he lacks the words to express what he perceives. Like Piggy, he sees to the heart of the boys' animosities, but, unlike Piggy, he does not attempt to name the hatred he observes (68). He understands the essence of the beast even before his conversation with it, but he cannot communicate his vision (89). Undermined, ridiculed, belittled, Simon persists in his quest, even if he no longer attempts to explain it to his companions. He remains silent, with an awareness still more visual than verbal (103). Not until his direct conflict with the Lord of the Flies does Simon find adequate words, and then it is unclear whether the words are a true description or a weapon in a verbal battle. Succinctly, he calls the Lord of the Flies what, in the physical world at least, it really is: "Pig's head on a stick" (143). However, this is not a complete identification of the beast. The pig's head, beginning to rot and preyed on by scavenging flies, is only a symbol of the beast, not the beast itself, and Simon cannot fully express in words the nature of what he sees.

Small wonder, then, that the boys think him a little crazy. He prophesies. He speaks to visionary demons. He sees things and understands great issues but cannot explain well what he knows. He may indeed be ill, either physically or mentally. During his conversation with the pig's head, Simon's own head wobbles as he feels "one of his times" coming on (143). The phrase "one of his times," combined with Simon's fainting spell at his first appearance with the choirboys, implies epilepsy or a similar disease. Clearly, Simon has episodes of some kind with some frequency. He recognizes the state he is entering. Golding never explains what Simon's "times" are or whether they are to be perceived as a state of illness, madness, or awareness, but these distinctions are hardly relevant. Whether Simon is ill or not, he sees the truth, and to dismiss the truth because its messenger may be ill is itself a little crazy.

Simon behaves like a person with a mental illness, yet he is the only one on the island who fully comprehends what is going wrong and why. Is Golding saying that crazy people are crazy because they see more truth than the rest of us, or that seeing truth resembles insanity so closely that the one is bound to be mistaken for the other? The novel is lean enough not to give away the answer to that question, but it is true that in the modern world, a Simon, a Jesus, a Buddha, or a Mohammed is more likely to be institutionalized than revered. Who is really crazy, after all: The boy who talks to a pig's head, or the boys who murder him? The man who talks to the Devil in the desert, or the society that nails him to two boards and outlaws his teachings? These are among the provocative questions that ***Lord of the Flies*** raises.

Simon's perception is clearer than that of the other boys, and he is willing, despite his own fears and the probability of unpleasant consequences for himself, to stare unblinkingly into the face of ugly realities. He sees past superstition, past loyalty, even past the power of words to convey what he sees. To find this extraordinarily uncommon characteristic in harness with the previous three is beyond the personal experience of most readers. If they have known such a person, they have probably, like the boys on the island, misunderstood him or her. Simon is thus the least universal of the novel's characters.

Sam and Eric

It is hard to imagine oneself as Simon, but all too easy to imagine oneself as Samneric, the twins so lacking in individual identity that they have one voice, one work shift, and one merged name. In fact, Golding's readers are, in the act of reading, very much like Samneric, passive observers of events, swept along and approving or objecting as events dictate, but unable to alter the unfolding of the disaster. Samneric are the ordinary person's surrogates. They do not rule, or make rules, or have the best ideas, or stage coups, or invent horrible tortures, or see the essence of evil for its true self, or really change anything at all. Basically decent but ineffective, they act when acted upon. They react.

Samneric cannot act independently (96). This is true from quite early in the novel, when they find a log for the fire but can "do nothing" without the others

(39). The fire will test them again and again, and they fail each time. They fall asleep tending it. They question the good of keeping it alive, lacking the innate will to seek rescue (163). They are the least perceptive of the big boys, the least original thinkers, less imaginative even than some of the littluns. In Chapter 6, they are the first to spot the downed parachutist, but instead of investigating, they flee from it. The idea of a beast has been planted in their minds, and like the great mass of humans everywhere, they perceive things according to their preconceptions. They do not, like Simon, question what they have witnessed or attempt to formulate an alternative explanation.

In fact, their encounter with the parachutist is emblematic of their approach to everything. They run from conflict at every turn, sometimes aware of the right course of action but seldom strong enough to take it. When Jack hosts a feast, they yield, with most of the other boys, to the lure of meat. The twins are swayed by the proximity of an influence. When Jack is near, they drift toward him; when Ralph returns, they sidle his way and pretend that nothing has happened. In a similar vein, they willingly enter into the selective memory of Simon's murder (158), a revisionist-history scene that, coming as it does not quite ten years after the end of World War II, begs to be likened to the convenient forgetfulness of war criminals.

Samneric stay with Ralph longer than any of the biguns except Piggy, but to no avail. They simply lack enough moral strength and determination to do him much good as allies. Captured and tortured by Jack's tribe, they yield quickly (182). They make a feeble attempt to provide him with inside information, but what they offer is of little use. Jack means to hunt him; Ralph could probably have figured that out on his own, though it shows some good will on Sam's part to overthrow his "new and shameful loyalty" (187) for long enough to reveal Jack's plan. Still, they have not the brains or the imagination to figure out why Roger is sharpening a stick at both ends, and instead of trying to rebel against Jack, they can offer Ralph no better option than to run. Even this plan is ruined by their cowardice. Tortured again, they reveal Ralph's hiding place, betraying him once again (192). One wonders about the boys' lives after they are rescued from Golding's island. One suspects that many of them would be tormented by nightmares, guilt, and self-loathing. Samneric, however, might very well be able to convince themselves that they had behaved as well as humanly possible, and exonerate themselves in all but the deepest recesses of their consciences. It is, after all, how many people rationalize their own bad behavior or inertia. Golding's application of everyday cowardice to an extraordinary situation is one of the reasons that ***Lord of the Flies*** is so disturbing.

Conclusion

This analysis has frequently mentioned the behavior of children for the same reason that Golding chooses children as his subjects in ***Lord of the Flies.*** Children have spent fewer years absorbing the particular cultural quirks of their societies. Their behavior is, therefore, closer to "nature"—to the genetic programming with which each of us is born. In this novel, Golding explores some of the universal traits that define humanity: power hunger, fear, faith, betrayal, jealousy, curiosity, logic, cowardice, and violence, among others. His conclusions about people are deeply saddening. In at least one kind of situation, the novel says, politics (Ralph) fails, science (Piggy) and spirituality (Simon) are murdered, power (Jack) and cruelty (Roger) prevail, and the ordinary decent fellow (Samneric) cannot do anything to change the course of events. The use of children to illustrate these concepts strips away layers of social conditioning that would be found in adults and increases the novel's atmosphere of abstraction.

However, the use of children practically requires that Golding mention play, since children spend a good deal of their time playing. Play, in all species where it occurs, serves as training for adult activities. Baby wolves play at hunting, while baby humans play at talking on the phone and driving cars. In Golding's day, boys played sports, board games, and make-believe adventure games, and though games are never extraordinarily prominent in this novel, they are mentioned, subtly, throughout. There are references to rugby (115), chess (117), and other games from time to time. The boys play at controlling sea creatures and each other, and the naval officer who lands on the island to rescue the boys at first interprets their hunt for Ralph as an ordinary children's game. This introduces an entirely new level of complexity into an already many-layered novel. Is the whole thing a game or not, the natural behavior of humankind (including children) or an imitation of the adult world?

At first glance, it seems deadly serious. Even the officer is taken aback when the answer to his joking question, "Nobody killed, I hope? Any dead bodies?" is "Only two" (201). Furthermore, the presence of the very real warship off the island's coast is an ample reminder that war is no game. Yet the whole saga of these stranded schoolboys seems to be game and reality at once. The conch is not a symbol of authority but a boy's toy version of a symbol of authority, serving the same purpose as a toy telephone. Until the arrival of the navy, there is no voice at the other end of the line. By the same token, the voting for chief, Ralph's authority, the hunt, the kill, and the feast each follow the pattern of child's play, as the boys imitate what their elders might do in similar circumstances. Each chapter reveals a new game or a new stage of the game.

How many people get married, or take certain jobs, or have children, or join certain organizations simply because it seems to be the next step in the game? Perhaps the boys hunt Ralph simply because it seems to be the next step in the game and because there is no outside authority to call them in for dinner. There is a long, shaded continuum between the toddler with a toy soldier and a water pistol, the older boy hunting animals with a real gun or blasting aliens into bloody body parts on a computer screen, and the adult general moving markers on a map to represent real bodies dying somewhere in battle. We can all put ourselves somewhere on that continuum between play and earnest, between what we naturally wish and the patterns set by our predecessors. Golding thus touches another universal aspect of humanity. ***Lord of the Flies*** is a novel that encourages questions about the human condition, not the least of which is this: At what point do you put down your toys and decide not to play anymore?

Notes

1. Charles Monteith, "Strangers from Within," in *William Golding: The Man and His Books,* ed. John Carey (London: Faber and Faber, 1986), 58.
2. Susan Sontag, on *Charlie Rose,* August 2, 1995.
3. Monteith, "Strangers from Within," 59.
4. Jack I. Biles, *Talk: Conversations with William Golding* (New York: Harcourt Brace Jovanovich 1970), 14.

Paul Crawford (essay date 2002)

SOURCE: Crawford, Paul. "Literature of Atrocity: *Lord of the Flies* and *The Inheritors.* In *Politics and History in William Golding: The World Turned Upside Down,* pp. 50-68, 79-80.

[*In the following excerpt, Crawford defines "literature of atrocity" as the use of fantasy, demonization, and the grotesque to create a reactions and examines* Lord of the Flies *as a treatise about Nazism and the Holocaust.*]

> We are post-Auschwitz homo sapiens because the evidence, the photographs of the sea of bones and gold fillings, of children's shoes and hands leaving a black claw-mark on oven walls, have altered our sense of possible enactments.
>
> —George Steiner, *Language and Silence: Essays, 1958-1966*

> Never shall I forget that night, the first night in camp, which has turned my life into one long night. . . . Never shall I forget the little faces of the children, whose bodies I saw turned into wreaths of smoke beneath a silent blue sky. Never shall I forget those flames which consumed my faith forever.
>
> —Elie Wiesel, *Night*

In moving beyond the earlier critical recognition that Golding interrogates English "immunity" from totalitarian violence and the institutionalization of this brutality in its class structure, we need to show how this attack is achieved through the use of fantastic and carnivalesque modes, modes that amount to Juvenalian or noncelebratory satire in opposition to merely universal or ahistoricist readings. As such, the fantastic is a technique of "literature of atrocity," significant in terms of the Holocaust experience, and its theme of demonization joins the noncelebratory carnivalesque in foregrounding exclusionary gestures toward the Jews. Yet Golding's attack on English constructions of national identity in opposition to Nazism is obstructed by the fabular and hence indirect form of critique in both ***Lord of the Flies*** (1954) and ***The Inheritors*** (1955).

Contrary to those who claim the fantastic mode is escapist, Golding uses it in ***Lord of the Flies*** and ***The Inheritors*** to interrogate contemporary events and map out the violent superstition behind the exclusion and attempted extermination of the Jewish race that has been viewed historically as an outsider race.[1] In ***Lord of the Flies,*** fantastic hesitation breaks into the shocking natural explanation that the "Beast" is not an external, supernatural force of evil. The only "Beast" on the island is the fascist group of English adolescent males who kill or attempt to kill outsiders: Simon, Piggy, and Ralph. In their noncelebratory, violent, and fascistic carnivalesque behavior, we witness English schoolboys not only dressing but even acting like Nazis. Alan Sinfield, in his book *Society and Literature,* argues that "the British themselves (in spite of fighting against fascism in the war) were not immune from that very sickness [of regarding human beings as means rather than ends], diagnosed by the existentialists, which had given rise to fascist violence and totalitarianism. William Golding, in particular, challenged the notion that the British were, in some peculiar way, different or special." Sinfield asserts that "when Jack and Roger turn upon Piggy and Simon, they are, for Golding, simply making manifest the brutal and violent pattern of behaviour that underlies Britain's stratified and bullying social order." It is not insignificant that the boys who take up leadership roles, Ralph and Jack, appear to be from a privileged background, perhaps educated at public or boarding schools. In his essay "Schoolboys," Ian McEwan says: "As far as I was concerned, Golding's island was a thinly disguised boarding school." Certainly, as S. J. Boyd suggests, Golding's "deep bitterness at and hatred of the evils of class" are evident in ***Lord of the Flies,*** as in his later novels, ***The Pyramid*** and ***Rites of Passage.*** Boyd claims that there is a "middle-class ambience" to Ralph, who "is not slow to inform Piggy that his father is officer-class," and Jack, who has a "privileged choir-school background." He argues that Piggy himself is very much a "lower-class" outsider whose accent—a "mark of class"—is mocked. Indeed, Piggy's "main persecutor" is Jack who has strong notions of hierarchy because of his privileged education and previous status as head boy of his choir school. Sinfield's and Boyd's insights can be extended to reveal how Golding mixes his critique of the English class system with a critique of English fascism—a dual attack that is achieved through the deployment of fantastic and carnivalesque modes. If this is Golding's aim, we might wonder at the unfair nature of such a linkage, especially since being a member of the privileged classes does not necessarily make you right wing, as Auden, Spender, and Orwell can attest with their radicalism and Marxism during the 1920s and 1930s. In broad terms, however, Golding does seem to critique not just English complacency about being anti- or non-Nazi, but also the English class system that perpetuates so much division and exclusion of "outsiders." This suggests some link between Golding's work and what Blake Morrison calls the "token rebellion" against social privilege by "Movement" writers of the 1950s.[2]

In ***The Inheritors,*** the "shock tactic" of breaking fantastic hesitation brings a startling recognition that "civilized" human beings commit genocide against those they project as monstrous "ogres" or devils. The Cro-Magnon people, progenitors of Homo sapiens, exterminate a race that, Boyd argues, resembles the Jews. The fantastic tension between the real and unreal in all these novels is strongly evocative of the Holocaust experience and the kind of writing it provoked. This tension was not only a constituent of the Holocaust experience but also an aesthetic technique in "literature of atrocity" that portrayed horrors in a manner that went beyond documentary account.[3] ***Lord of the Flies*** and ***The Inheritors*** can be included in this tradition.

The carnivalesque in ***Lord of the Flies*** and ***The Inheritors*** is revealed in the suspension and shedding of the stable, ordered conformity of social life. Rules are forgotten for a period of time. In their place comes an enactment of desires and drives that have been repressed. But the carnivalesque behavior in these novels is presented as violently anti-Semitic. This noncelebratory aspect to carnival has been foregrounded by Peter Stallybrass and Allon White's argument that carnival "violently abuses and demonizes" outsiders such as the Jews, whose abjection is promoted by carnival practices such as the eating of pig flesh. The history of carnival's noncelebratory aspect was not lost on Golding in the light of the Jewish Holocaust. Indeed, ***Lord of the Flies*** is replete with violent carnival images of the pig. Thus, carnival is a site of violence against the weak, the marginalized. This was not missed in Golding's powerful evocation of English "Nazism." The carnivalesque, topsy-turvy world is widely represented in the violent, noncelebratory Dionysianism and scatology of ***Lord of the Flies*** and ***The Inheritors.*** This use of the carnivalesque cannot be understood within Mikhail Bakhtin's purely celebratory focus in *Rabelais and His World.*

Although ***Lord of the Flies*** is a strong attack on notions of English moral superiority vis-à-vis Nazism, such a critique is hampered somewhat by its fabular form. It subtilizes historical reference to Nazi-like group fascism. This obfuscation of historical reference continues in ***The Inheritors,*** which more generally attacks the notion of "civilization" rather than English moral superiority. However, we might see Golding's attack upon H. G. Wells's racial elitism and the comparison evoked between such views and Nazism as a general warning that the English have no grounds for complacency about their moral distance from atrocities carried out in the Holocaust. In ***The Inheritors,*** the Holocaust is strongly evoked in the racial extermination of Neanderthal Man but is again hampered by Golding's use of fable. As I will demonstrate in the following chapter, this reference to contemporary atrocity and fascism is strengthened in ***Pincher Martin*** and ***Free Fall,*** novels that shift progressively from fabular to historical form and delineate more closely the totalitarian personality.

In ***Lord of the Flies*** particularly, and perhaps more tenuously in ***The Inheritors,*** Golding's *Vergangenheitsbewältigung,* or "coming to terms with the past," concludes that the English and Nazis are not so different as one might expect. It is this painful evocation of similitude that has been overlooked in earlier critical readings. Both novels should certainly be included in the wider European tradition of "literature of atrocity." That we know Golding himself to have been deeply involved in the war, on intimate terms with its horror, and exercised by expressions not just of Allied moral superiority to Nazis, but of racial violence that broke out in England after the war as well, is significant for a full understanding of his early novels.

In ***A Moving Target,*** Golding tells of the impact this loss of belief in the "perfectibility of social man" had on ***Lord of the Flies:*** "The years of my life that went into the book were not years of thinking but of feeling, years of wordless brooding that brought me not so much to an opinion as a stance. It was like lamenting the lost childhood of the world. The theme of ***Lord of the Flies*** is grief, sheer grief, grief, grief, grief" ([***A Moving Target***], 163). Despite such commentary from Golding himself, the effect of the war and other social contexts such as racial violence on his writing has drawn scant attention from critics. This emphasis has tended to remain submerged.

Furthermore, there has been no consideration of how Golding, "punch drunk" on atrocity, uses fantastic and carnivalesque modes powerfully to register his grief about this context.[4] The following readings of ***Lord of the Flies*** and ***The Inheritors*** aim to redress this lack. These novels, which can be thought of as a pair, make an oblique response to the sociopolitical context of World War II and its aftermath. They provide an uneasy coexistence of the universal and historical.[5]

Lord of the Flies

In ***Lord of the Flies,*** fantastic and carnivalesque modes are used to subvert postwar English complacency about the deeds of Nazism, particularly the Holocaust. Although oblique, Golding effects an integration between literature and cultural context. This interpretation renegotiates previous critical paradigms that have, for the most part, centered on the timeless or perennial concerns of this novel about a group of English schoolboys, deserted on a South Pacific island following a nuclear third world war, and their descent into ritual savagery and violence.[6] As most critics attest, the characters replicate those in R. M. Ballantyne's *Coral Island* (1858), who in similar straits pull together and overcome external dangers from natives and pirates. Ballantyne's schoolboys exemplify cultural assumptions of imperial superiority and conversely the inferiority of the "fuzzy-wuzzies" or "savages," the indigenous race feared for its cannibalistic practices. For Ballantyne's boys, evil and degenerative nature is outside of them, and the suggestion is that imperial colonialism is beneficent, that the savage can be "saved" by the civilized, Christian Western man. Such inherent and dominant racial elitism is extended in Ballantyne's *Gorilla Hunters* (1861), in which older versions of the same schoolboys, on a scientific expedition in Africa, hardly differentiate between the gorillas and the natives.

Golding subverts these notions of racial and cultural superiority, of scientific progress, notions casting long shadows over atrocities against the Jews carried out in World War II.[7] He draws a parallel between the violent history of English imperialist adolescent masculine culture and the extermination of the Jews. He broaches the grim fact that English colonial warfare against "inferior" races, modeled on hunting and pig sticking, was not a million miles away from the extermination of the Jews. Pig sticking, of course, was at the heart of R. S. S. Baden-Powell's scouting repertoire. Indeed, in 1924 he published *Pig Sticking or Hog Hunting,* a guide for scouts on that very art. Given the whole setting of ***Lord of the Flies,*** with its reference to Ballantyne and empire boys, Golding appears to have the imperial scouting ethic in his sights. John M. MacKenzie alerts us to the greater reach of such an ethic:

> Africans swiftly became the human substitute for the usual animal prey. Baden-Powell constantly stressed that the scouting and stalking techniques of the Hunt could immediately be transferred to human quarry in times of war. Hunting was also . . . a preparation for the violence and brutalities of war. By brutalising themselves in the blood of the chase, the military prepared themselves for an easy adjustment to human warfare, particularly in an age so strongly conditioned by social Darwinian ideas on race.[8]

Golding's critique is not directed exclusively at Nazi war criminality but at the postwar complacency of the English who too readily distanced themselves from what the Nazis did. He reminds them of their long infatuation with social Darwinism. Graham Dawson maps the trajectory of the "soldier hero," an "idealized," militaristic masculinity at the symbolic heart of English national identity and British imperialism. He argues that this "imagining of masculinities" in terms of warfare and adventure pervades the national culture, swamps boyhood fantasies, and, in particular, promotes rigid gendering, xenophobia, and racial violence.[9] In ***Lord of the Flies,*** Golding's critique of British imperial, protofascist history is powerfully registered by the Nazification of English schoolboys: "Shorts, shirts, and different garments they carried in their hands: but each boy wore a square black cap with a silver badge in it. Their bodies, from throat to ankle, were hidden by black cloaks which bore a long silver cross on the left breast and each neck was finished off with a hambone frill" (***LF,*** 20-21).

James Gindin insists that Golding's description of Jack's gang—who are English—"deliberately suggests the Nazis." Despite a preference for the universal aspects of Golding's fiction, Leighton Hodson suggests Piggy might represent the "democrat and intellectual," Jack "Hitler," and Roger a "potential concentration camp guard." L. L. Dickson identifies the novel as political allegory, referring to World War II atrocities, particularly those inflicted upon the Jews. Suzie Mackenzie refers to Jack's gang as a "fascist coup" and sees the opposition between democracy and totalitarianism as one of the novel's themes. The "black" garments and caps are, indeed, highly suggestive of the Nazi *Schutzstaffeln,* or SS—the "Black Angels" responsible for the Final Solution. Certainly, Golding's candid comments to John Haffenden suggest this: "I think it's broadly true to say that in ***Lord of the Flies*** I was saying, 'had I been in Germany I would have been at most a member of the SS, because I would have liked the uniform and so on.'" They also suggest Oswald Mosley's Blackshirts. The silver cross may obliquely bring to mind both the Iron Cross *(Eisernen Kreuz)* and the anti-Semitic swastika. The reference to "hambone" may suggest the skull and crossbones or Death's Head *(Totenkopf)* insignia of the SS. Certainly, the "black cap with a silver badge in it" resembles the black ski caps decorated with the skull and crossbones worn by Hitler's early group of bodyguards, the *Stabswache.* Like Hitler's *Stabswache,* which was made up of twelve bodyguards, Jack's gang or squad is small in number. Nazification of Jack's gang is further amplified by its delight in parades and pageantry, which together with "the unshackling of primitive instincts" and "the denial of reason" is all part of what psychoanalytical theories categorize under the "style and methods of fascism," according to Ernst Nolte.[10] This mingling of Nazism and Englishness is not to be overlooked. Of course, it is the violence of Jack's gang that most powerfully suggests links between them and the Nazis.

The centrality of violence to fascism can be charted, for example, in the appeal that Georges Sorel's apparent valorization of direct violent action in *Reflections on Violence* had for fascist ideologues. Adolescent male aggression, like that of Baden-Powell's pig sticking, is central to Nazism and other versions of fascism or totalitarianism.[11] Silke Hesse contends that because adolescents are "unattached," "mobile," impressionable, physically strong, and easily "directed towards ideals and heroes" on account of unfocused sexuality, the adolescent gang is seen as "a most efficient tool in the hands of a dictator." She concludes: "Of course, Fascism cannot be exhaustively explained with reference to male adolescence. Yet most of the major theories of fascism emphasize the youthful nature of the movement and, even more, its masculinity, in terms both of participation and of traditionally masculine values." Hitler himself has been called "an eternal adolescent" by Saul Friedlander. We may see Jack's gang as an English version of the *Hitlerjugend,* or Hitler Youth, who grew into the jackboots of the SS, or, indeed, Mosley's New Party (NUPA) Youth Movement. Nicholas Mosley notes that Christopher Hobhouse, of Mosley's New Party, "said he saw the NUPA Youth Movement turning into something like the Nazi SS." Again, Robert Skidelsky argues that as with fascism in general, "the most striking thing about active blackshirts was their youth." In an early review, V. S. Pritchett links ***Lord of the Flies*** to "the modern political nightmare," and hoped that it was being read in Germany.[12] I would rather suggest that Golding hoped it was being read in Britain and other Allied nations.

For Golding, the dominant and prevalent cultural assumptions found in Ballantyne's stories support the projection of evil onto external objects or beings, such as savages, and in Nazi Germany's case the Jews.[13] But Golding maintains that the darkness or evil that humans fear, and consequently attempt to annihilate, is within the "civilized" English subject. Importantly, Golding appears to have a specific continuity in mind concerning an evil that is not overcome or displaced by English civilization, but is, in effect, a potential that comes hand in hand with it. He connects adolescent English schoolboys from privileged backgrounds, the imperial scouting ethos, and fascism. Thus, whereas in Germany fascism actually sprouted, while in England it did not, there is nonetheless the possibility that the English ethos could easily tip over into fascism (as it does on the island) since privileged education and scouting ideology have much in common with fascism. In order to rebut Ballantyne's projection of evil onto savages, and to draw attention to the ability of the English—with their schooling in fascistic behavior—to mirror Nazism, Golding uses the combined forces of fantastic and carnival modes.

In ***Lord of the Flies,*** the world of the island is apprehended from the viewpoint of the schoolboys. Initially, they appear to be all-around empire boys, characters in the island adventure tradition that stretches back to Daniel Defoe's *Robinson Crusoe* (1719), Robert Louis Stevenson's *Treasure Island* (1883), and Ballantyne's *Coral Island.* But their preoccupation with natural phenomena and survival rapidly changes to a preoccupation with the unknown and inexplicable. They face beasts and phantoms in a succession of apparently supernatural events. Uncertain and fearful, the boys are subjected to unexplained phenomena. Suspense and hesitation as to the nature of the "beast" follow, and their fear increases accordingly. Although at first it is only the "littluns" that appear affected by this fear, the circle widens until all the boys, including Ralph and Jack, believe in the "Beast." The term *beastie* (*LF,* 39) quickly matures into "beast" (*LF,* 40). Initially, Ralph and Jack hedge their bets by stating that even if there was a beast, they would hunt and kill it. The mysterious disappearance of the boy who had seen the "snake-thing" compounds with the fall of snakelike creepers from an exploding tree and adds fuel to fear. In their beach huts the "littluns" are plagued with nightmares. And in pace with the growing sense of strangeness, the island environment itself becomes equivocal and menacing: "Strange things happened at midday. The glittering sea rose up, moving apart in planes of blatant impossibility; the coral reef and the few, stunted palms that clung to the more elevated parts would float up into the sky, would quiver, be plucked apart, run like raindrops on a wire or be repeated as in an odd succession of mirrors. Sometimes land loomed where there was no land and flicked out like a bubble as the children watched" (***LF,*** 63).

Yet this strange transformation of the natural fabric of the coral reef is rationally explained by Piggy as a mirage. But such is the general uncertainty now of what is real and unreal that the fall of darkness is unwelcome. The equivocal nature of familiar things is constantly in view: "If faces were different when lit from above or below—what was a face? What was anything?" (***LF,*** 85). The "littluns" are constantly attacked for their fearfulness. Jack calls them "babies and sissies" (***LF,*** 90). Piggy proclaims that if these fears continue, they'll be "talking about ghosts and such things next" (***LF,*** 91).

But no sooner has Piggy subdued his own and everyone else's doubts by advancing a scientific approach to reality than Phil, another "littlun," speaks of seeing "something big and horrid" in the trees (***LF,*** 93). Although Ralph insists that he was experiencing a nightmare, Phil maintains that he was fully awake at the time. Then Percival says he has seen the Beast and that "it comes out of the sea" (***LF,*** 96). Thus, doubt and hesitation increase. Maurice says: "'I don't believe in the beast of course. As Piggy says, life's scientific, but we don't know, do we? Not certainly, I mean—'" (***LF,*** 96). Then Simon amazes the older boys by admitting that "'maybe there is a beast'" (***LF,*** 97). Here, Simon elliptically hints that the Beast might be them: "'We could be sort of . . .' Simon became inarticulate in his effort to express mankind's essential illness" (***LF,*** 97). The boys even vote on the issue of whether ghosts inhabit the island. Only Piggy fails to lift his hand. Yet Piggy's claim that ghosts and suchlike do not make sense brings its own fearful counter: "'But s'pose they don't make sense? Not here, on this island? Supposing things are watching us and waiting?' Ralph shuddered violently and moved closer to Piggy, so that they bumped frighteningly" (***LF,*** 101).

Schoolboy nerves are further jangled by what follows: "A thin wail out of the darkness chilled them and set them grabbing for each other. Then the wail rose, remote and unearthly, and turned to an inarticulate gibbering" (***LF,*** 103). But this noise turns out to be Percival reliving his own personal nightmare. For the moment there is the relief of natural explanation. The Beast from Air we know to be a dead parachutist, shot down over the island while all but Sam and Eric are asleep. This figure is uncannily animate, moving in the wind:

> Here the breeze was fitful and allowed the strings of the parachute to tangle and festoon; and the figure sat, its helmeted head between its knees, held by a complication of lines. When the breeze blew the lines would strain taut and some accident of this pull lifted the head and chest upright so that the figure seemed to peer across the brow of the mountain. Then, each time the wind dropped, the lines would slacken and the figure bow forward again, sinking its head between its knees.
>
> (*LF,* 105)

Sam and Eric who are guarding the fire on the mountain hear the strange popping noise of the chute fabric in the wind. Here, hesitation between a supernatural and a natural explanation to the Beast from Air belongs only to the characters. They return and tell the others of the beast on the mountain. Despite a natural though uncanny explanation being available to us, we cannot fail to empathize with the subsequent fear and hesitation experienced by the characters: "Soon the darkness was full of claws, full of the awful unknown and menace" (***LF,*** 108). However, the disturbing fact that the only beasts on the island are the boys themselves begins to gain ground: "Simon, walking in front of Ralph, felt a flicker of incredulity—a beast with claws that scratched, that sat on a mountain top, that left no tracks and yet was not fast enough to catch Samneric. Howsoever Simon thought of the beast, there rose before his inward sight the picture of a human at once heroic and sick" (***LF,*** 113).

Our own hesitation and uncertainty as readers has begun to shift more clearly toward a natural yet uncanny explanation that the boys are their own monsters. But the breaking of this central hesitation, as to the nature of the Beast, does not exclude further peripheral uncertainty between natural and supernatural events. Apart from the fact that we participate vicariously in the hesitation of Ralph and Jack as they hunt down the figure on the mountain, a "great ape . . . sitting with its head between its knees" (***LF,*** 136), the pig's head or "Lord of the Flies" remains on the border between reality and unreality. It is animated: "the Lord of the Flies hung on his stick and grinned" (***LF,*** 152). It appears to be a focal point of something supernatural—Evil, the Devil, Satan. Here, peripheral uncertainty is maintained. We hesitate between formulating natural or supernatural explanations. There is a definite sense of the "Lord of the Flies" as a possessed object, and this possession is registered through the visionary viewpoint of Simon. Though Simon has repeatedly been described as mad, hesitation remains as to whether the strange conversation he has with the "Lord of the Flies" is a fit-induced psychosis or not; indeed, we hesitate to ascertain whether psychosis disallows vision. This threshold between Simon's sanity or insanity—a hazy world of split personality, psychosis, and dreams—magnifies fantastic uncertainty, as does, in a more marginal way, the "doubling" of the twins, Samneric. Simon's "madness" has its base in both Todorovian "themes of the self" and carnival foolery. Ironically, it is the death of the equivocal and mysteriously spiritual Simon that erodes fantastic hesitation. His "madness" may also mark the beginnings of Golding's perennial questioning of religious authority throughout his work, a critique most powerfully achieved in ***The Spire.***

A final break of the core hesitation concerning the nature of the "Beast" occurs when in Simon's eagerness to explain the human nature of the phenomenon, he unwittingly becomes the "Beast" and is murdered. An exchange of beasts occurs. At this point, we become fully aware of the boys as beasts, in their vicious murder of Simon. This most poignant and telling delivery of an uncanny explanation breaks fantastic hesitation most completely. Then, by way of contrast, the harmless, dead Beast from Air exits the island, though, for the characters, its exit remains a supernatural phenomenon.

The shift, then, is from a predominant hesitation about the nature of the Beast to an uncanny explanation that the boys, and humans in general, project fear onto other groups, individuals, or objects. Even so, the uncanny resolution of who or what really is the Beast on the island remains somewhat equivocal. We are still unsure of a background supernatural activity or influence. The natural and the supernatural seem to coexist, a realm perhaps more akin to Todorov's "fantastic uncanny." Supernaturality is still registered, for example, in the description of Simon's body, which, like that of Lycaon in Homer's *Iliad,* is devoured by "sea monsters."[14]

The characters continue to fear an external beast, with Jack's gang having already tried to propitiate the Beast by making an offering of the pig's head, deciding to "keep on the right side of him" (***LF,*** 177). Even rational, scientific Piggy ends up thinking strange sounds outside his hut are made by the Beast: "A voice whispered horribly outside. 'Piggy—Piggy—' 'It's come,' gasped Piggy. 'It's real'" (***LF,*** 184). Of course, the sounds are those of Jack and members of his gang stealing the remains of Piggy's glasses. Again, the shift from character hesitation to uncanny natural explanation is effective. Notions of "beast" are transposed onto Jack's gang.

With Piggy's murder, and the "pig hunt" of Ralph under way, clarification of the human nature of the Beast is intensified. The natural as opposed to supernatural interpretation of events is given its final and fullest exposition. Yet, even so, the uncanny does not completely override the supernatural. The pig's head remains strangely animated, as when the hunted Ralph strays upon it: "[T]he pig's skull grinned at him from the top of a stick. He walked slowly into the middle of the clearing and looked steadily at the skull that gleamed as white as ever the conch had done and seemed to jeer at him cynically. An inquisitive ant was busy in one of the eye sockets but otherwise the thing was lifeless. Or was it?" (*LF,* 204).

Effectively, the fantastic elements in ***Lord of the Flies*** operate in tandem with those of carnival: they combine to disturb us and subvert dominant cultural notions of the superiority of civilized English behavior. These are the kind of assumptions that buoyed the complacency of England, and indeed other Allied nations, namely, that the atrocities perpetrated by the Nazis were an exclusively German phenomenon. Within the fantastic framework, it is the break from potential supernatural explanation to the chilling and uncanny reality of natural explanation that disturbs us: that the Beast is human, Nazi-like, and English. We participate in the shock that this shift in perspective brings. Instead of externalizing and projecting evil onto objects, phantoms, and supernatural beasts, we confront the reality of human destructiveness. This is registered in both a universal or "perennial" frame and a specific "contemporary" frame, polemicizing the English capacity for Nazism, especially in the light of its exclusionary class system. Although the novel is set in the future, the surface detail, as discussed by earlier critics such as James Gindin, corresponds to World War II. In effect, the fantastic interrogates the postwar "reality" of Britain and its Allies. Yet it does not do so alone.

The shift from the fantastic to the uncanny amplifies carnivalesque elements in the text that symbolically subvert, turn upside down, the vision of civilized, ordered, English behavior. In combination, these elements are the structures through which ***Lord of the Flies*** disturbs. Yet such is the inherent irreversibility of the narrative structure—its dependence upon hesitation or suspense of explanation—that we cannot read ***Lord of the Flies*** and register the peculiar shock it delivers a second time.[15] Indeed, there is something particularly "evanescent" about the pure fantastic, not as a genre, but as an element.[16] Ultimately, the shock recognition of the negative, transgressive, "evil" side of not simply human behavior but the behavior of English boys is what is disturbing about ***Lord of the Flies.*** Such shock recognition is effected by the combination of fantastic and carnival elements. Because of the fantastic's evanescence, we need to recall our first reading when we reexamine ***Lord of the Flies:*** we must remember our initial shock. We find no relief in the novel's coda at the end of the book when the boys are "saved" by an English naval officer. Our unease shifts from the carnival square of the island to the wider adult world—a world at war for a third time, a world in which the theater of war greatly resembles, in its detail of a paramilitary fascist group, machine-gunning and, in its dead parachutist, the familiar Second World War. It is a world of continuing inhumanity. This open ending is typical of "the satirist's representation of evil as a present and continuing danger."[17] The naval officer marks the gap between ideal British behavior and reality: "'I should have thought that a pack of British boys—you're all British aren't you?—would have been able to put up a better show than that—I mean—'" (*LF,* 222). The substantiation of the children as British subjects is not superfluous to the novel's meaning. It is fundamental to this novel's ethical interrogation of England, Britain, and its Allies at a specific juncture in history.

One of the most powerful carnivalesque elements in ***Lord of the Flies*** is that of the pig, which Golding uses symbolically to subvert dominant racial assumptions, in particular toward the Jews, and, universally, toward those humans considered alien or foreign to any grouping. This has alarming relevance to the atrocities committed against the Jews in World War II, yet has been overlooked by Golding critics who have not interpreted Golding's merging of the pig hunt with the human hunt, and the racial significance of eating pig flesh at carnival time.

The pig symbol is developed in ***Lord of the Flies*** as the pig of carnival time. It is a major motif: as locus of projected evil; as food for the schoolboys; as propitiation to the Beast; but more than anything, as the meat the Jews do not eat. This link between pig flesh and the Jews is reinforced by Golding's choice of the novel's Hebraic title. "Lord of the Flies," or "Lord of Dung," as John Whitley renders it, comes from the Hebrew word *Beelzebub.* As I noted earlier, Peter Stallybrass and Allon White argue that the eating of pig meat during carnival time is an anti-Semitic practice. It is an act of contempt toward the Jews for bringing about the Lenten fast. White asserts: "Meat, especially, pig meat, was of course the symbolic centre of carnival (*carne levare* probably derives from the taking up of meat as both food and sex)." That the pig becomes human and the human being becomes pig in the frenzied, carnivalistic debauchery of Jack and his totalitarian regime is important. The shadowing of pig hunt and human hunt, ending with Simon's and Piggy's deaths, and almost with Ralph's, signifies the link between the pig symbol and the extermination of those considered alien or outsiders. The name "Piggy" does not merely imply obesity. It is the lower-class Piggy who is always on the periphery of the group of schoolboys, always mocked, never quite belonging. As Virginia Tiger points out, "Piggy is killed . . . because he is an alien, a pseudo-species."[18] Piggy is alien or foreign, and, as such, he is a focus for violence based on the sort of racial assumptions found in Ballantyne's writing, but it is important to clarify the precise nature of his outsider status. The character name "Piggy" does not, unlike that of Ralph and Jack, feature in Ballantyne's *Coral Island.* Piggy is Golding's creation—a creation that suggests a Jew-like figure: "There had grown tacitly among the biguns the opinion that Piggy was an outsider, not only by accent, which did not matter, but by fat, and ass-mar, and specs, and a certain disinclination for manual labour" (***LF,*** 70). We find something of the Jewish intellectual in this description of the bespectacled Piggy, with his different accent and physical feebleness. The stereotype of Jewish feebleness has been a stock in trade of anti-Semites and peddlers of degeneration theories.[19] It is here that we witness the anti-Semitism of carnival. In essence, Golding utilizes the imperial tradition of pig sticking to suggest a continuum between English imperialism and fascism.

Jack's gang persecutes Jew-like Piggy and those it considers outsiders. As a carnival mob they break the normal rules of authority with a willful, transgressive violence that marks a shift from liberal democracy to fascism and anti-Semitism. We witness the demise of Ralph's parliament and the ascendancy of Jack's totalitarian, primitive regime based on savagery, hunting, and primal drives. There follows aggressive sexual debasement and frenzy in the killing of the carnival pig, mimicking anal rape by sticking the spear "'Right up her ass'" (***LF,*** 150):

> [T]he sow staggered her way ahead of them, bleeding and mad, and the hunters followed, wedded to her in lust, excited by the long chase and the dropped blood. . . . [S]he squealed and bucked and the air was full of sweat and noise and blood and terror. Roger ran round the heap, prodding with his spear whenever pigflesh appeared. Jack was on top of the sow, stabbing downward with his knife. Roger found a lodgement for his point and began to push till he was leaning with his whole weight. The spear moved forward inch by inch and the terrified squealing became a high pitched scream. Then Jack found the throat and the hot blood spouted over his hands. The sow collapsed under them and they were heavy and fulfilled upon her.
>
> (***LF,*** 149)[20]

The transgressive connotations of this act are amplified by Robert and Maurice's mimicry of the event. In effect, the whole scene is one of a carnivalesque focus on the lower body parts, particularly that "low" orifice, the anus. As Allon White points out: "Orifices, particularly the gaping mouth, emphasize the open, unfinished, receptive nature of the body at carnival, its daily proximity to flesh and to dung." We may further note scatological details of the "littluns'" toilet habits or Jack's orgasmic fart. Later we witness the "befouled bodies" (***LF,*** 172) of Piggy and Ralph. The orifice as mouth or anus is found in several descriptions in ***Lord of the Flies.*** Arnold Johnston considers that Golding's Swiftian scatology strengthens an accusation that the contemporary world evades home truths about human nature such as the killing of six million Jews.[21] We have the foul breath from the mouth of the dead parachutist and the vast gaping mouth of the pig: "Simon found he was looking into a vast mouth. There was blackness within, a blackness that spread" (***LF,*** 159). The theme of "lower body parts," symbolic of misrule, is replicated elsewhere in the novel, as in Ralph's derision of Piggy's asthma: "'Sucks to your ass-mar'" (***LF,*** 156). Here, we find the connotations of anal damage or marring and "sucking ass." In the mock pig killing that follows, Robert ends up with a sore backside. The transgression of sodomy is further evidenced in the likely spear rape of Simon on the beach implied by the kind of elliptical references expected of sexual taboo. Although no explicit reference is made to such actions, we must bear in mind previous pig-killing ritual and play:

> "Don't you understand, Piggy? The things we did—"
>
> "He may still be—"
>
> "No."
>
> "P'raps he was only pretending—"
>
> Piggy's voice tailed off at the sight of Ralph's face.
>
> "You were outside. Outside the circle. You never really came in. Didn't you see what we—what they did?"
>
> There was loathing, and at the same time a kind of feverish excitement in his voice.
>
> "Didn't you see, Piggy?"
>
> (***LF,*** 173)

We must read this transgressive violence in political terms. Golding is explicitly linking extreme violence with anti-Semitism and the kind of "sadomasochistic homosexuality" that Wilhelm Reich and Erich Fromm considered integral to fascism.[22] Of course, we might argue that Reich and Fromm's analysis is misplaced or erroneous, yet Golding adopts this kind of popularized image. As Roger Eatwell notes: "Images of fascism are part of our culture. For most people, the word 'fascism' conjures up visions of nihilistic violence, war and *Götterdämmerung*. 'Fascism' has a sexual side too: but it is the world of Germanic uniforms and discipline, of bondage and sadomasochism, rather than love."[23] Whether or not "sadomasochistic homosexuality" is a definitive aspect or style of fascism, Golding certainly appears to have drawn on such popularized theories and images, even though such an analysis is ultimately contradictory in terms of the Nazis' exclusionary acts toward homosexuals. Yet it makes sense in that what is feared is persecuted in others.

Jack's gang descends into a meat and sex society, rejecting the liberal democracy of the conch-invoked meetings. Their carnival is filled with dance, chanting, fire, "fun," and irresponsibility—of general festivity. Those routines that reflect responsible society, such as keeping a fire going on the mountain, are neglected. They wear masks and painted faces. They dress and present themselves as a choir, an oxymoronic combination in light of their actions. The rules are challenged, turned upside down—as we have noted, Jack cries "Bollocks" to the rules. They are the "painted fools" of carnival, part of a masquerade (***LF,*** 197). Of course, such imagery may equally apply to the imperialist notion of descent into savagery, both carnival "painted fool" and "savage" being "low domains." Golding provides a dystopian representation of carnival that dwells on the pessimistic, violent, and racist seam that has had its place in the history of carnival crowd behavior. He makes a strong connection between this history and contemporary fascism. This aspect of the carnivalesque cannot be appreciated by those "critics who remain purely within the celebratory terms of Bakhtin's formulation," nor those who universalize transgression.[24]

Golding's dystopian representation incorporates noncelebratory carnival decrowning, where a king figure is parodied and derided as the played-out subversion of hierarchical society. This is evident in Jack's thrusting of a pig's decapitated head on a double-pointed spear, as propitiation to the Beast. Such an oxymoronic symbol, referred to in the title of the novel as "Lord of the Flies," reflects the enactment of misrule, the turning upside down of order and authority, of what is crowned. What is "lord" is lord only to flies—those insects of the scatological. This symbol is both fitting to the overall dark or dystopian misrule of carnival in ***Lord of the Flies*** and the etymological base of "Lord of the Flies" as meaning Beelzebub or Devil.

We may view Golding's use of carnival in ***Lord of the Flies*** as registering his deeply felt unease about the nature of English "civilization" in light of the events of World War II—of totalitarianism and genocide: a "civilization," among others, that is primed for the total wipeout of nuclear apocalypse. The misrule of carnival in contemporary history is presented as integral not simply to Nazis or other totalitarian regimes but also to England with its divisive and cruel class system. Golding lays bare an alternative view to civilized English behavior, one that counters accepted, familiar, erroneous complacencies. In the isolated focus, in the "carnival square" of Golding's island, carnival affirms that everything exists on the threshold or border of its opposite.[25] In effect, Golding explodes a Nazi-English or them-us opposition.

So, to summarize, noncelebratory or Juvenalian satire with its combined fantastic and carnivalesque in ***Lord of the Flies*** subverts the view that the "civilized" English are incapable of the kind of atrocities carried out by the Nazis during World War II. These modes are deployed in the novel as an attack on what Golding deems to be a complacent English democracy, and its masculinity and classist attitudes in particular, in relation to the rise of National Socialism. . . .

In ***Lord of the Flies*** and ***The Inheritors,*** it may be that Golding wished to avoid effecting any kind of representation of the Holocaust that might appear to be what Lawrence Langer calls an "unprincipled violation of a sacred shrine."[26] Or maybe Golding was aware of the difficulty of "presenting the unrepresentable." Hence, his reference is somewhat masked by a universal or fabular setting of these novels. He does, however, strengthen his reference to broad or popular conceptions of fascism and the totalitarian personality in ***Pincher Martin, Free Fall,*** and ***Darkness Visible,*** perhaps to compensate for making too oblique a reference in these early more fabular novels. Yet even so, as we shall see, the later novels only barely connect with the "Final Solution" as such.

In conclusion, then, Golding surely knew that his representations of the Holocaust, and indeed fascism, were necessarily limited and partial. Yet he obviously wanted to make some kind of intervention with what he perceived as complacency among the English in particular about their moral distance from Nazism. This focus on English complacency is evident in Nigel Williams's comment on Golding's view of ***Lord of the Flies:*** "He once said to me that one of the main aims of his book was to tell the story of the breakdown of English parliamentary democracy. 'Don't make them into little Americans, will you,' he added." Golding does not attempt to be comprehensive or detailed in his reference to the Holocaust as he needs only to suggest the conceptual territories of this genocide and fascism to effect his satire. Golding knew that, like himself, the postwar reader would have sufficient familiarity with German prison camps and the Holocaust through a plethora of accounts. Like Clamence in Albert Camus's *La Chute* (1956), Golding did not need to play the historian here: "We children of this half-century don't need a diagram to imagine such places."[27]

In terms of the Holocaust, Golding placed himself within what Langer calls the "culture of dread" as opposed to the "culture of consolation." We cannot accuse Golding of any sentimental aestheticization of the Holocaust or the Nazi "Final Solution." We may accuse him of being a "long-distance" writer like Sylvia Plath, D. M. Thomas, and William Styron, but not a barbaric one. Indeed, as Berel Lang admits rather reluctantly, there is some justification in the "barbarism" of imaginative writing about the Holocaust, even "bad" or "false" contributions, "as a defence against still greater barbarism—against denial, for example, or against forgetfulness."[28] Golding's early fiction offers a defense against this barbarity of amnesia and denial. His later fiction moves away from what may be thought of as a grief response and encrypts the Holocaust in his reflection on "post-Auschwitz" life and meaning. Having instantiated the massive "seismic" force of the Holocaust in his early fiction, he traces its aftershocks or aftermath as they threaten comforting epistemologies and rationality itself with further collapse and fragmentation. Indeed, the arch-relativization of meaning we call postmodernism has spawned a concerted attack on the historicity of the Holocaust. The Holocaust is treated as merely textual, as something that can be deconstructed. Part of this effort involves the extreme claim by deniers of the Holocaust that the mass killing of Jews in World War II was a hoax. In this sense, we might consider the Holocaust as heavily influencing the postwar skepticism that eventually developed into what we broadly call postmodernism yet subsequently fell foul of its more hard-boiled deconstructive and antifoundationalist pronouncements. Or, in other words, the Holocaust intensified the climate for its denial.

Notes

1. For a useful summary of critical positions that support or oppose the notion of "escape" in the fantastic, see Siebers, *The Romantic Fantastic,* 43-45.
2. Sinfield, *Society and Literature, 1945-1970,* 35-36; McEwan, "Schoolboys," 158; Boyd, *Novels of Golding,* 10-11; Morrison, *The Movement,* 77.
3. Boyd, *Novels of Golding,* 40-42. See Langer, *Literary Imagination,* 43-49. Langer asserts: "To establish an order of reality in which the unimaginable becomes imaginatively acceptable exceeds the capacities of an art devoted entirely to verisimilitude; some quality of the fantastic, whether stylistic or descriptive, becomes an essential ingredient of *l'univers concentrationnaire.* Indeed, those who recorded details painstakingly in an attempt to omit none of the horror may have been unwittingly guilty of ignoring precisely the chief source of that horror—existence in a middle realm between life and death with its ambiguous and inconsistent appeals to survival and extinction, which continuously undermined the logic of existence without offering any satisfactory alternative" (43).
4. Oldsey and Weintraub, *Art of Golding,* 173. Oldsey and Weintraub consider the branding of Golding's vision "by acts of superior whites in places like Belsen and Hiroshima" as the core unifying thesis behind his early novels (45). Dick suggests that Golding's focus on the evil side of humankind in *Lord of the Flies* resembles media presentations of Nazi atrocities that do not tell the whole story (*William Golding* [1967], 34-35).
5. On the paradox of timeless novels that remain contemporary, see Oldsey and Weintraub, *Art of Golding,* 11, 43-45, 173; and Josipovici, *World and Book,* 236. Dickson, developing the work of Edwin Honig and Angus Fletcher, evaluates allegory along the lines of what Scholes has termed "modern fabulation," which "tends away from the representation of reality but returns toward actual life by way of ethically controlled fantasy" (see Dickson, *Modern Allegories,* 1; and Scholes, *The Fabulators,* 11-14).

6. According to Crompton: "The book originally began with a description of the atomic explosion [cut prior to publication] out of which the children escaped, an event recapitulated exactly but in miniature by the fire that is destroying the island at the end of the book" (*View from the Spire,* 96). This is ratified by Golding who told John Haffenden that the "picture of destruction" in the fire scene "was an Atomic one; the island had expanded to be the whole great globe" ("William Golding: An Interview," 10).

7. S. Laing argues that "the reversal of texts of high bourgeois optimism" in Golding's early work, and focus on the irrational, follows Golding's participation in and reflection on World War II. He refers to Golding's revelation of "history as nightmare" ("Novels and the Novel," 241).

8. MacKenzie, "The Imperial Pioneer and Hunter and the British Masculine Stereotype in Late Victorian and Edwardian Times," 188.

9. See Dawson, *Soldier Heroes: British Adventure, Empire, and the Imagining of Masculinities.*

10. Gindin, *William Golding,* 22; Hodson, *William Golding,* 32. See also Medcalf, *William Golding,* 10, 13. Dickson, *Modern Allegories,* 24-25. McCarron has written that the novel "would not have been written had Belsen and Auschwitz never existed, or indeed had Dresden never been bombed by the Allies" (*William Golding,* 4). Mackenzie, "Return of the Natives," 40; see Rupert Butler, *The Black Angels;* Haffenden, "William Golding: An Interview," 11; see E. W. W. Fowler, *Nazi Regalia,* 150; Nolte, *Three Faces of Fascism,* 39.

11. The significance of male youth to fascist movements has been noted by historians and theorists of totalitarianism. See Hannah Arendt, *The Origins of Totalitarianism,* 227, 366, 377, 399; Renzo de Felice, *Interpretations of Fascism,* 179; Nolte, *Three Faces of Fascism,* 618; Noel O'Sullivan, *Fascism,* 74-75; and Alice Yaeger Kaplan, *Reproductions of Banality: Fascism, Literature, and French Intellectual Life,* 22. For a detailed examination of the importance of young male gangs to fascism, see Silke Hesse, "Fascism and the Hypertrophy of Male Adolescence," 157-75. She writes: "I would suggest that, rather than patriarchy, the very different structure of a gang of adolescent youths is the model of Fascist society" (172).

12. Hesse, "Fascism and Male Adolescence," 172, 175; Saul Friedlander quoted in Gerhard Rempel, *Hitler's Children: The Hitler Youth and the SS,* 1; Mosley, *Rules of the Game: Sir Oswald and Lady Cynthia Mosley, 1896-1933,* 211; Skidelsky, *Oswald Mosley,* 317; Pritchett, "Secret Parables," 37.

13. Hitler described the Jews as bloodsucking vampires (see *Mein Kampf,* 296).

14. See *The Iliad* 21.135-40: "Lie there, Lycaon! let the fish surround / Thy bloated corse, and suck thy gory wound: / There no sad mother shall thy funerals weep, / But swift Scamander roll thee to the deep, / Whose every wave some wat'ry monster brings, / To feast unpunish'd on the fat of kings" (in Pope, "The Dunciad," 466).

15. Todorov, *Fantastic,* 89.

16. Brooke-Rose, *Rhetoric of the Unreal,* 63.

17. Connery and Combe, *Theorizing Satire,* 5.

18. Whitley, *Golding: "Lord of the Flies,"* 43; see Stallybrass and White, *Politics of Transgression,* 54; White, *Carnival, Hysteria, and Writing,* 170; Tiger, *Dark Fields,* 63.

19. See Sander Gilman, *Franz Kafka: The Jewish Patient.* See also Gilman, *The Jew's Body.*

20. Stallybrass and White note that the Latin etymology of pig, *porcus* or *porcellus,* refers to female genitalia and that in Attic comedy, prostitutes were called pig merchants (*Politics of Transgression,* 44-45).

21. White, *Carnival, Hysteria, and Writing,* 170; see Johnston, *Of Earth and Darkness,* 38, 45.

22. See James A. Gregor, *Interpretations of Fascism,* 50, 55, 68, 74.

23. Eatwell, *Fascism: A History,* xix.

24. Stallybrass and White, *Politics of Transgression,* 191, 19. For early examples of crowd violence in carnival, see Ladurie, *Carnival in Romans;* Buchanan Sharp, *In Contempt of All Authority: Rural Artisans and Riot in the West of England, 1586-1660;* and Charles Tilly, *Charivaris, Repertoires, and Politics.* It is important to note the relevance of crowds or masses to theories on fascism. For a summary of the work of Gustave le Bon, José Ortega y Gasset, Emil Lederer, Sigmund Neumann, Eric Hoffer, Hannah Arendt, and William Kornhauser on the phenomenon of crowds or masses, see J. Gregor, *Interpretations of Fascism,* 78-127. See also Eatwell, *Fascism,* 4-10.

25. On the carnival square, see Bakhtin, *Problems of Dostoevsky's Poetics,* 128-29, 168-69.

26. Langer, *Admitting the Holocaust,* 76.

27. N. Williams, *William Golding's "Lord of the Flies,"* ix; Camus, *The Fall,* 92.

28. Langer, *Admitting the Holocaust,* 9; Lang, "The Representations of Limits," 317.

FURTHER READING

Biographies

Lamber, Bruce. Obituary. *New York Times,* (20 June 1993): 38.

Gives an overview of Golding's life and career.

Wood, James. "Religious Insight of a Man Apart." *Manchester Guardian Weekly* (29 September 1991) 25.

A tribute to Golding, written on the occasion of his eightieth birthday.

Criticism

Gindin, James. "Background Themes: The Propellants." In *William Golding,* pp. 8-19. Houndmills, Basingstoke, Hampshire: Macmillan, 1988.

Discusses underlying themes and literary influences for *Lord of the Flies* and *The Inheritors.*

Hodson, Leighton. "The Metaphor of Darkness: *Lord of the Flies.*" In *William Golding,* pp. 19-38.

Contends that Golding's intention in his body of work is to show the darkness in the soul of humanity and the salvation of self-awareness.

Hollahan, Eugene. "Running in Circles." *Studies in the Novel* 2, no. 1 (spring 1970): 22-29.

Examines circle motif in *Lord of the Flies.*

Rahman, Khandkar Rezaur. "Early Period." In *The Moral Vision of William Golding,* pp. 33-48. Dhaka, Bangladesh: Dhaka University, 1990.

Chronological examination of Golding's works.

Redpath, Philip. "Doorways Through Walls: *Lord of the Flies* and *The Inheritors.* In *William Golding: A Structural Reading of His Fiction,* pp. 78-98. London: Vision Press Limited, 1986.

Posits the lack of definition in *Lord of the Flies* and *The Inheritors* leaves both books open to myriad interpretations.

Sternlicht, Sanford. "Songs of Innocence and Songs of Experience in *Lord of the Flies* and *The Inheritors.*" *The Midwest Quarterly* 9, no. 4 (July 1968): 383-90.

Argues that it is in The Inheritors that Golding writes about the loss of innocence, not in *Lord of the Flies.*

Tiger, Virginia. "Lord of the Flies." In *William Golding: The Dark Fields of Discovery,* 38-64. London: Calder and Boyars, 1974.

Discusses several standard interpretations of *Lord of the Flies* and then her own view of its symbolic structure.

Additional coverage of Golding's life and career is contained in the following sources published by the Gale Group: *Authors and Artists,* Vols. 5, 44; *Beacham's Encyclopedia of Popular Fiction: Biography and Resources,* Vol. 2; *Beacham's Guide to Literature for Young Adults,* Vol. 2; *British Writers Retrospective Supplement,* Vol. 1; *British Writers Supplement,* Vols. 1; *Concise Dictionary of British Literary Biography,* 1945-1960; *Contemporary Authors,* Vol. 5–8R, 141, *Contemporary Authors New Revision Series,* Vols. 13, 33, 54; *Contemporary Literary Criticism,* Vols. 1, 2, 3, 8, 10, 17, 27, 58, 81; *Dictionary of Literary Biography,* Vols. 15, 100, 255; *DISCovering Authors; DISCovering Authors: British Edition; DISCovering Authors: Canadian Edition DISCovering Authors Modules: Most-studied Authors* and *Multicultural Authors; DISCovering Authors 3.0; Encyclopedia of World Literature in the 20th Century,* Ed. 3; *Exploring Novels; Literature and Its Times,* Vol. 4; *Literature Resource Center Major 20th-Century Writers,* Eds. 1, 2; *Novels for Students,* Vol 2; *Reference Guide to English Literature,* Ed. 2; *St. James Guide to Horror, Ghost and Gothic Writers; St. James Guide to Science Fiction Writers,* Ed. 4; *St. James Guide to Young Adult Writers; Twayne's English Authors; Twentieth-Century Romance and Historical Writers; World Literature and Its Times,* Vol. 4; and *World Literature Criticism.*

Megan McDonald
1959-

American author of children's novels, readers, and picture books.

INTRODUCTION

McDonald has earned an international reputation for her range of picture books, story books for early readers, and chapter books for middle-grade readers. Often combining engaging storylines with educational information, McDonald's works attract young readers through her use of lively protagonists in such works as *The Potato Man* (1991), *Beezy* (1997), *The Night Iguana Left Home* (1999), and *Judy Moody* (2000). Best known for her recurring Beezy and Judy Moody series, McDonald also explored the myths and traditions of indigenous Americans in *The Bone Keeper* (1999).

BIOGRAPHICAL INFORMATION

Born on February 28, 1959, McDonald was raised in Pittsburgh, Pennsylvania, the youngest of five girls. Her father, John, was regarded as great storyteller and loved to tell his tales at family dinners; several of them provided inspiration for McDonald's children's works. During primary school, McDonald wrote her first short story for a school newspaper in which she detailed, in first person, the life of someone who ate pencil shavings all day. She began her post-secondary education at Oberlin College, graduating with a B.A. in 1981. After graduation, McDonald enrolled at the Center for the Study of Children's Literature in Boston, receiving a B.A. in children's literature. McDonald continued her training at the University of Pittsburgh where she obtained her M.A. in library science. She worked as a children's librarian at the Carnegie Library in Pittsburgh between 1986 and 1990, later working at the Minneapolis Public Library and the Adams Memorial Library. In 1987 McDonald became interested in writing children's literature after hearing children's book editor Richard Jackson speak at a conference. She eventually sent Jackson the manuscript for *Is This a House for Hermit Crab?* (1990), which became her first published work.

MAJOR WORKS

McDonald's picture books focus primarily on combining elements of natural science with entertaining fantasy. *Is This a House for Hermit Crab?* originated as a story for a puppet show that McDonald had composed during her tenure as a children's librarian. The title character is based on one of her own pets, a hermit crab who got loose and eventually found a hiding place in McDonald's shoe. The book follows Hermit Crab, who has outgrown his old shell, forcing him to search for a new home. He tries on many different new houses—none of which suits him—while trying to avoid the dreaded pricklepine fish. Before the pricklepine fish can catch him, Hermit Crab discovers a sea snail shell that fits him perfectly. Covering similar subject material, *Whoo-oo Is It?* (1992) recounts a mother owl's contemplation of a strange noise she hears during the night. The mother owl makes several guesses before figuring out that the sound is coming from her own baby owl, hatching from its egg. In addition to her works that focus on animals and nature, McDonald has also written a number of books based on stories originally told to her by her father. One of these tales, *The Potato Man,* is narrated by a young boy who observes a strange-looking man with only one eye and a lumpy face which makes him look like a potato. The Potato Man's odd appearance scares little girls and causes him to be relentlessly taunted and teased. Throughout the narrative, the Potato Man catches the narrator causing trouble three times, resulting in punishment, but the narrator continues to view the Potato Man as a gentle and understanding soul. McDonald wrote a sequel to *The Potato Man* in 1992, *The Great Pumpkin Switch,* which describes an incident where the narrator accidentally destroys his sister's prize pumpkin and has to enlist the aid of the Potato Man to save the day.

The 1997 easy reader book *Beezy* christened one of McDonald's most popular recurring series. Each Beezy story contains three short stories about a little girl named Beezy, her friends, and her dog Funnybone. In the three stories collected in *Beezy,* the title character meets Funnybone for the first time, makes a new friend, and stays indoors during a hurricane. The subsequent titles in the series include *Beezy at Bat* (1998), *Beezy Magic* (1998), and *Beezy and Funnybone* (2000). A departure from McDonald's previous works, *The Bone Keeper* melds images from a mixture of cultural mythologies to create an archetypical Wise Woman character. Set in a desert environment and utilizing the structure of a tone poem, the story follows the title character as she collects old bones from the desert floor. She eventually performs a ritualistic dance around the bones which brings them back to life as a wolf. McDonald returned to the genre of nature-fantasy picture books—which she first explored in *Is This a House for Hermit Crab?* and *Whoo-oo Is It?*—with *The Night Iguana Left Home.* The protagonist, Iguana, resides in Schenectady, New York, where she has her own e-mail address and subsides on a diet of anchovy pizza. However, Iguana longs to travel to Florida and, one night, she runs away and takes a bus to Key West. For weeks, she lives a life of indulgence until her money runs out, and she realizes that she needs to find a job. After a variety of bad job experiences, Iguana decides that she misses Schenectady. As a result, she finds a new job at the post office and mails herself home. Torn between her desire to be in both places, Iguana solves her problem by spending part of the year in each location and traveling between the two.

Spotlighting the trials and tribulations of a grouchy pre-teen, McDonald's middle-school chapter books about Judy Moody have proved to be one of her most successful and popular series. The first book, *Judy Moody,* establishes the protagonist as a young girl who seems to be perpetually stuck in a foul mood. Her displeasure is further aggravated when her little brother manages to ruin the collage she made for a homework assignment. In the end, Judy figures out how to save the assignment, though it hardly changes her grouchy outlook. Judy's life has been further documented in *Judy Moody Gets Famous* (2001), *Judy Moody Saves the World* (2002), and *Judy Moody Predicts the Future* (2003).

CRITICAL RECEPTION

McDonald's easy-reader books have become popular with both students and teachers, with the *Judy Moody* series drawing particular attention for its humor and unique characters. Reviewers have also lauded McDonald's science-picture books for their combination of educational information and entertaining narratives. Elizabeth S. Watson has commented that, in *Is This a House for Hermit Crab?,* "Hermit Crab's search for a new house is told simply and very effectively with a wonderfully alliterative, rhythmic refrain." Watson further commended McDonald's skill with descriptive language in *Whoo-oo Is It?,* noting that, "[t]he mysterious sound will send delicious shivers up little spines, but the final tender family scene will relieve any lingering concerns." McDonald's Potato Man books have also been praised for their imaginative phrasing and evocative illustrations. Additionally, the Beezy series has received similar critical acclaim, with the critic for *Publishers Weekly* asserting that, "[McDonald's] ear for the way children speak is on target." However, McDonald's *The Bone Keeper* has been met with a decidedly mixed critical reception, with some commentators expressing both admiration and confusion about the book's narrative. Some critics have found the work to be evocative and dream-like, while others have complained that the story is overly puzzling and borderline incoherent. Susan Dove Lempke has commented that, "[*The Bone Keeper*]'s austere quality will not be to all tastes, but the words and pictures together create a spooky, thought-provoking experience." McDonald's Judy Moody books have been her most favorably received works to date, with Janie Schomberg complimenting Judy as "a delightful new character for beginning chapter-book readers." Audiences have also embraced the series' sly humor and recurring commentary on the perils of pessimism. Junko Yokota and Mingshui Cai have noted that, "[t]he moody yet spirited protagonist [in *Judy Moody*] is as lovable as the story is enjoyable. Teachers will admire her intelligence in dealing with challenges in school."

AWARDS

McDonald received the Children's Book Award from the International Reading Association for *Is This a House for Hermit Crab? The Bridge to Nowhere* (1993) won the Judy Blume Contemporary Fiction Award from the Society of Children's Book Writers. *Judy Moody* was named a Best Book of 2001 by the American Library Association, and *Judy Moody Gets Famous* received the same honor in 2002 as well as being named a *Boston-Globe Horn Book.* Several of McDonald's other books were on the American Booksellers Pick of the List and received citations for Best Book of the Year from the *School Library Journal.*

PRINCIPAL WORKS

Is This a House for Hermit Crab? (picture book) 1990
The Potato Man (picture book) 1991
The Great Pumpkin Switch (picture book) 1992
Whoo-oo Is It? (picture book) 1992
The Bridge to Nowhere (young adult novel) 1993
Insects Are My Life (easy reader) 1995
My House Has Stars (picture book) 1996
Beezy (easy reader) 1997
Tundra Mouse: A Storyknife Tale (picture book) 1997
Beezy at Bat (easy reader) 1998
Beezy Magic (easy reader) 1998
Bedbugs (picture book) 1999
The Bone Keeper (picture book) 1999
The Night Iguana Left Home (picture book) 1999
Beezy and Funnybone (easy reader) 2000
Judy Moody (easy reader) 2000
Lucky Star (easy reader) 2000
Judy Moody Gets Famous (easy reader) 2001
Reptiles Are My Life (easy reader) 2001
Shadows in the Glass House (historical fiction) 2001
Judy Moody Saves the World (easy reader) 2002
Baya, Baya, Lulla-By-A (poetry) 2003
Judy Moody Predicts the Future (easy reader) 2003
Shining Star (easy reader) 2003

AUTHOR COMMENTARY

Megan McDonald (essay date March 2000)

SOURCE: McDonald, Megan. "Bones of a Story." *Book Links* 9, no. 4 (March 2000): 22-3.

[*In the following essay, McDonald reflects on the creation of* The Bone Keeper.]

Bones. My first experience with bones was eating one. In my family of older sisters, we still tell the story of being given holy relics from Rome, by an uncle of mine who is a priest. Each ornate case was rumored to contain the bone of a saint. My sisters convinced me, the youngest, that if I smashed my case and swallowed the tiny bone inside, I would be holy forever. Without hesitation, I smashed the jeweled case and swallowed the tiny bone. I don't know that it made me holy! But, it did begin my fascination with bones, with things that once were.

As a child, I was famous for collecting—bones, skulls, fossils, shells, skins of snakes and bugs, and charcoaly leaf-prints pressed between layers of Pennsylvania shale. Even scabs—and baby teeth I could not surrender to the Tooth Fairy. What do we know of bones in our culture? There is the Halloween skeleton, the Thanksgiving turkey wishbone, and the museum artifact. Scary. Wishful. Old.

A few years back, my young niece arrived at the family farm after a 13 hour road trip. She stepped out of the car, took a look around the farm, and asked, "You got any old bones around here?" Bones signify age, wisdom, and a connection with the past. Her interest reminded me that bones inspire a child's natural curiosity about things that came before us, about things that may have existed. When I visit schools and tell young people that I've written a story about bones, I get many emphatic responses of "YES!"

Bones, to me, are anatomy and history. They are haunting, lonely, and lovely. Think for a moment of Georgia O'Keeffe's paintings of blue sky seen through the "window" of a pelvic bone, or her juxtaposition of roses against cow skulls. Through her eyes, bones can be seen as form and contour, shape and composition. Bones become, in a word, art. It was her work that first had me connect bones with the desert, first let me see. And, in the words of that great painter, "to see takes time."

It took time to see this story. Like ***The Bone Keeper***'s creation, many pieces had to come together. I had never been to the desert until my husband and I came across Nevada in the heat of an August, traveling what's called the Loneliest Road in America. It is. This gave me the setting for ***The Bone Keeper.*** More important, it offered me the feeling of loneliness and isolation I needed to write about the desert, rather than just imagining it.

I never knew my own grandmothers, so I invented an old woman. She's an every-grandmother, the book's single character, the collector of bones. It had to be someone wise. Images of the archetype of the old woman are ancient and many: the crone, grandmother, wise woman the Greek deity Hecate, the Russian witch Baba Yaga, Italy's Strega Nonna, India's Kali, and the Hopi Spider Woman, to name a few. I borrowed attributes from mythology for my own composite. For example, Hecate, in Greek mythology, is said to have three heads, tame wild animals, turn invisible, and be able to see past, present, and future, like Bone Woman in my story.

The Bone Keeper is not based on any one individual tale. I remembered coming across oral tales in which storytellers spin yarns about bones that come back to life. I consulted a friend of mine with extensive background in mythology, who excitedly informed me that these bone stories appear in virtually every culture around the world. My curiosity had me racing to the library, heading first for mythology and folklore. To my delight, I discovered tales of bones coming to life from Africa to India, Greenland to New Guinea, Australia to Iran. From the American Sonoran and Chihuahuan deserts to the Arabian Rub'al Khali and the Takla Makan of China. I found bones that jump from fires and deep wells, animals that leap from skeletons, earths and mountains created, and heroes born from a single swallowed bone.

I read everything I could get my hands on about deserts all over the world. I discovered a strange and unique ecosystem where eerie rock shapes loom, sands sing, and silence is deafening. I researched desert plants and animals. I imagined a place where mammoths, sloths, and camels once roamed. I pored over books with animal skeletons and studied the facts and names of bones. The small collarbone of an owl is called a wishbone; snakes have 400 vertebrae.

I made lists! Yucca and catclaw, ocotillo, ironwood and smoke tree; bat and badger, kit fox and kangaroo rat, rattlesnake and ring-tailed cat. None of my research was wasted; it did more than provide the "bare bones" of the story. It was like learning a new and foreign language. Its words and sounds created a rhythm, became part of the poetry, giving the story its otherworldly quality. "One by one by one / she collects / each lonely bone."

Early attempts at finding an illustrator for the story turned up sketches and drawings that were scary and dark and disturbing. This was not at all what I intended. I wanted mystery, magic, creation—as with castles from sand, sculptures from clay, stories from words—a wolf from bones.

Illustrator Brian Karas understood my intentions. He says, "There is a stillness when you come across a bone. You think about origins, the post and the future. The stillness . . . is where the book takes place."

Listening to a group of third-graders at the Wild Rumpus bookstore in Minneapolis give a choral reading of ***The Bone Keeper,*** I was surprised by that stillness, the spell that was cast over the room. Read it aloud to a classroom full of sixth-graders and you'll feel it: The hush. The stillness. The magic of bones.

Megan McDonald (essay date 27 February 2002)

SOURCE: McDonald, Megan. "Homepage." 27 Februray 2002 <http://www.meganmcdonald.net/about.htm (9 August 2003).

[*In the following essay, McDonald talks about why she became a writer.*]

Becoming a pencil sharpener was my first experience as a writer.

I was in fifth grade when I wrote the story for my school newspaper. In first person, it detailed a life of eating pencil shavings all day.

Since then, I've been a hermit crab, a one-eyed potato man, and a girl who loves insects. I've been to Alaska and Florida—places I've never actually visited—lived in a Mongolian yurt or a Philippine houseboat under the stars, and peered through the eye of a hurricane. I even know what it's like to drive off a bridge!

Growing up was filled with box-turtle races, chasing the ice cream truck, searching for nickels hidden by my father in the mossy insides of a certain tree stump. But always the dinner bell rang from the back porch, calling my sisters and me home to the circle of the kitchen table, where we'd carved our names with the tines of forks.

"Abba-no-potata-man!" my father called after dinner. A story would begin, about the scary old one-eyed huckster from his neighborhood who later became the inspiration for ***The Potato Man*** and ***The Great Pumpkin Switch.*** His stories were funny and dangerous, from squeezing an orange in his brother's hair to stowing away in the rumble seat of an old Model-T.

With four older sisters, I couldn't get a word in edgewise during those dinner-table conversations. I'm told I began to stutter in elementary school. My mother bought me a small notebook, and I began writing everything down in true Harriet-the-Spy fashion.

I'm often asked how I remember all those things from my childhood—tricking my sisters with a plastic ice cube that had a dead fly in the center, hatching praying mantises in my sock drawer a la Amanda Frankenstein, or drinking a dozen glasses of water like Hallie in ***A Bridge to Nowhere*** because I was convinced I had rabies.

I'm not a writer because I had an adventurous childhood. I'm a writer because of what I choose to do with remembering. I'm a writer because I imagine.

What made me want to write? Reading. Did I always want to be a writer? Deep down. How did I become a writer? I'm still becoming one.

I'm lucky to be a writer. I spend my days thinking like a mouse. Or pretending I have taste buds on my feet, like a butterfly. I spend my days looking at things sideways, questioning, always wanting to see the inside.

Megan McDonald (interview date 27 February 2002)

SOURCE: McDonald, Megan. "Homepage." 27 February 2002. <http://www.meganmcdonald.net/about.htm (9 August 2003).

[*In the following self-interview, MacDonald answers questions children often ask her.*]

Where were you born?

I grew up in a house full of books in Pittsburgh, Pennsylvania, the youngest of five girls. My father, an ironworker, built bridges all across the city, including the real Bridge to Nowhere. Known among ironworkers as Little Johnny, he was a great storyteller. My mother, a social worker, was a very good listener.

Dinnertime took place at a large round table in the kitchen, where the seven of us gathered nightly, talking and telling stories. With four older sisters, I couldn't get a word in edgewise. I'm told I began to stutter. That's when I first started writing things down.

What was your childhood like?

What I remember of childhood is summer—the woods, the creek, the goldfish pond. Skinned knees from climbing in tree wells. Picking blackberries. Searching for nickels in old tree stumps, where my father used to hide them. Chasing after the ice cream truck.

What is the first story you remember writing?

A story in grade school called "The Plea of the Pencil Sharpener," told from the point of view of a pencil sharpener!

Did you have a favorite book as a child?

A biography of Virginia Dare, the child from the Lost Colony at Roanoke [in Virginia], until I was banned from taking it out of the library, in order to give other kids a chance to read it.

Where did you go to school?

Oberlin College. And the University of Pittsburgh, where I got my M.L.S. [Master of Library Sciences degree].

Did you always want to be a writer?

Deep down, I did. In the meantime, I've had jobs as a park ranger, chambermaid, cook, tour guide, and storyteller. I've worked in bookstores, libraries, and schools, a children's theater company, a children's museum, and a museum full of old cars and fire engines!

How did you become a writer?

I'm still becoming one.

What made you want to write?

Reading. Love of language. Childhood. Imagination. Belief in the transformative power of story.

When did you know you wanted to write books for children?

The exact moment? In 1987, when I heard Richard Jackson, my editor, speak at a conference. It took me two years from that time to work up the courage to send him a manuscript. When I finally did, it got lost in the mail . . . two times!

How do you get your ideas?

Ideas are like secrets waiting to be told. An idea begins as a tiny seed, then swells inside me until it captures my imagination, makes me laugh, or strikes me deeply. Ideas come from inside out and outside in. An idea may enter with the surprising force of a thunderclap or slowly, gradually shape itself over time.

You write about animals. Do you have any pets?

Over the years, I have had goldfish, newts, turtles, snakes, mice, lovebirds, canaries, finches, parakeets, and—yes—hermit crabs. Right now I have two dogs named Banjo and Fudgie, two adopted horses, and 15 wild turkeys that hang out on the roof of my house.

How did you get the idea for your first book, **Is This a House for Hermit Crab?**

It grew out of a story told with puppets to children at the library, based on an incident where my pet hermit crab got loose and hid in my tennis shoe. Its alliterative sounds, its rhythm and repetition worked so well with children that I imagined it as a picture book, in hopes that it might find a wider audience.

GENERAL COMMENTARY

Janet Schnol (essay date 21 December 1990)

SOURCE: Schnol, Janet. "Flying Starts: New Faces of 1990." *Publishers Weekly* 237, no. 51 (21 December 1990): 13-18.

[*The following essay, Schnol gives an overview of McDonald's early work.*]

A crab hand puppet and a children's story hour inspired librarian Megan McDonald to create the tale of a crustacean in search of a new home in ***Is This a House for Hermit Crab?*** When she decided to use the puppet as a visual aid, and couldn't find a book starring a hermit crab, McDonald remembered a story she had written more than 10 years earlier, in college. With a few alterations to the old story and some props of possible homes, McDonald told the children in her library the tale of the hermit crab looking for a place to live. Afterwards, when people asked where they could find the book, McDonald decided to write it.

Though she had thought about writing for children while in college, McDonald says, "When I felt the story worked with kids, it was the first time I believed in my own work." Even so, when she decided to take a leave of absence from the library to concentrate on writing, McDonald was too nervous to tell anyone she was using the time off to write a book. "Everyone kept asking if I was pregnant," she recalls.

McDonald had previously met editor Richard Jackson of Orchard at the Pittsburgh Fall Festival of Books. She was so taken with his encouragement of new writers that when the manuscript was finished she sent it directly to him. Jackson accepted it, though McDonald says it wasn't until she saw illustrator S. D. Schindler's drawings for the story that reality began to sink in.

The Potato Man, McDonald's second title, is due from Orchard next March. There are two more picture books under contract as well: ***Whoooo Is It?,*** inspired by a nature program on television (from which McDonald learned that barn owls can hear their babies crying inside the egg); and a sequel to ***The Potato Man.*** McDonald has just received a grant from the Society of Children's Book Writers, the Judy Blume Contemporary Fiction Award, and she is currently working on a novel for 11-to-13-year-olds called ***The Bridge to Nowhere.*** "It's about a girl and her relationship to her father, an unemployed bridge builder," which McDonald says is semiautobiographical.

Though she says she was prepared for bad reviews and low pay, McDonald has been happily surprised—***Is This a House for Hermit Crab?*** recently went into its second printing. Now a part-time librarian at the Minneapolis Public Library, McDonald says she is also surprised by the different ways the story affects readers. She has heard about the book being used in science classes, and received a touching letter from a boy whose family moves often and who felt he could relate to the hermit crab in search of a home.

Not only is McDonald's reputation growing, but she is gaining confidence as a writer. When asked what advice she would give to other newcomers, McDonald's first response is, "The most important thing is to try to believe in your writing."

TITLE COMMENTARY

IS THIS A HOUSE FOR HERMIT CRAB? (1990)

Elizabeth S. Watson (review date March 1990)

SOURCE: Watson, Elizabeth S. *Horn Book Magazine* 66, no. 2 (March 1990): 222.

Hermit Crab's search for a new house [***Is This a House for Hermit Crab?***] is told simply and very effectively with a wonderfully alliterative, rhythmic refrain: "So he stepped along the shore, by the sea, in the sand . . . *scritch-scratch, scritch-scratch.*" Rejecting in turn a rock as too heavy, a tin can as too noisy, a pail as too deep, and several other equally unsuitable habitats, Hermit Crab finally finds his new home in the nick of time, just as he is about to be eaten by the dread prickle-pine fish. The pictures are realistic yet spare—appropriate for a sea-swept beach. The sand is textured so well that one must touch and touch again before believing that the page is really smooth and not grainy. The text has movement, repetition, drama, and a time-honored, comforting conclusion: "It was not too heavy, not too noisy, not too dark, and not too deep. It was not too crowded and did not have too many holes. At last, Hermit Crab had found a new home. And it fit just right." Goldilocks would love it, and the young listener will, too. ***Hermit Crab*** will fit just right into summer story hours and family suitcases.

Susan Scheps (review date April 1990)

SOURCE: Scheps, Susan. *School Library Journal* 36, no. 4 (April 1990): 94.

Across flecked, sand-colored pages [***Is This a House for Hermit Crab?***] crawls Hermit Crab—"scritch-scatch, scritch-scratch"—hunting for a new house. He tries a rock, some driftwood, a plastic pail, and a net. Nothing suits him until, washed to sea by a great wave, he *must* find a place to hide from his enemies. An empty sea snail's shell provides the perfect home. Schindler's pastel illustrations provide the perfect visualization of the text. Hermit Crab and his enemy, the prickle-pine fish, appear so realistic that children will want to reach out and touch them. Prints in the sand left by Crab's moving "houses," foamy waves breaking on the beach, the vastness of the ocean floor and its quiet greenness—all can be felt in [S. D.] Schindler's pictures. The bits of repetition in the text are pared with the visual continuity of sand and sea and the outgrown shell left on the sand as Hermit Crab tries on each prospective home. This wonderful marriage of words and illustrations is destined to become a well-loved storyhour tale.

THE POTATO MAN (1991)

Diane Roback and Richard Donahue (review date 14 December 1990)

SOURCE: Roback, Diane, and Richard Donahue. *Publishers Weekly* 237, no. 50 (14 December 1990): 66.

When the Potato Man came to East Street, a white-haired man tells his wide-eyed grandchildren, bad luck came with him [***The Potato Man***]. Back then, the narrator was a boy in knee pants and the street, with its endless stream of hucksters, was an exciting place. But then the one-eyed, lumpy-faced old Potato Man arrived, scaring the girls and prompting taunts from the boys. Three times the Potato Man caught the narrator making mischief, and three times the boy wound up with extra chores at home. Finally, "I figured three times bad luck was enough for me," the narrator relates, and on the first day of winter the boy finds a way to make peace with the Potato Man. McDonald (***Is This a House for Hermit Crab?***) and [Ted] Lewin (*Tiger Trek*) have created a lovely, evocative period piece. The artist's horse-drawn wagons, rugged faces and turn-of-the-century kitchen are perfectly matched by the gentle homespun writing style. Like the narrator's grandchildren, who beg him to "tell us another one about when you were a boy," readers will eagerly await more from this team.

Mary Lou Budd (review date February 1991)

SOURCE: Budd, Mary Lou. *School Library Journal* 37, no. 2 (February 1991): 72.

Children will seldom turn down a good story of the "olden days" from a grandfather, and this one [***The Potato Man***] gives a vivid glimpse into the early part of our century. Scissor grinders, organ grinders, and peddlers' wagons creaked through the streets and alleys in those days with things or services to sell. Mr. Angelo, with a face as lumpy as his potatoes, is just such a huckster and it seems natural that he should be the butt of the neighborhood boys' pranks. But he is the ultimate winner of these "battles" through his use of gentleness and understanding. The exceptional, realistic watercolor artwork fairly leaps from the pages with its portrayal of emotions and action. It is so evocative that readers and audiences are swept into and held to the action of the intriguing story. The manageable text contains so much descriptive phrasing that action is brought immediately to the mind's eye. With a fine balance between text and illustration, this is picture book reading at its best, revealing a genuine cohesion of word and picture. And, as all "Grampa" tales should, it gives vitality to a long-ago era, as well as subliminally teaching something of compassion, understanding, and remorse. Whether read to a group or on an individual basis, this will be a popular choice for a wide spectrum of ages.

Mary M. Burns (review date May 1991)

SOURCE: Burns, Mary M. *Horn Book Magazine* 64, no. 3 (May 1991): 318.

An incident from Grampa's boyhood [***The Potato Man***] told to his two attentive grandchildren transports the reader back in time to an era when Stanley Steamers were still in vogue and peddlers with horse-drawn carts brought their wares and services directly to neighborhoods. Of these hucksters, the Potato Man makes the greatest impression on the narrator, for he seems to be the harbinger of bad fortune. Injured in "the Great War," he has only one eye and a face "as lumpy as a potato"—which terrifies most of the children and causes others to tease him. The boy finds himself catapulted from one scrape to another—from stealing potatoes to breaking a neighbor's window—and each time the source of the problem seems to be the fearsome old Potato Man. But an opportunity comes one snowy day at Christmas time for the boy and his nemesis to reach out to each other and resolve their differences. The text, a slice-of-life evocation of a past era, sets forth conflict and solution without moralizing. The tone suggests an underlying sentiment but not sentimentality, matched by Ted Lewin's handsome, glowing watercolors. Ranging from expressive portraits to interiors, from studies of laden wagons to a breathtaking impression of a snow-shrouded street, they add dimension and verisimilitude to the story. The conclusion suggests that Grampa may have still more memories to share. Let's hope so.

🕮 *THE GREAT PUMPKIN SWITCH* (1992)

Susan Scheps (review date August 1992)

SOURCE: Scheps, Susan. *School Library Journal* 38, no. 8 (August 1992): 143-44.

McDonald's storytelling skill is once again very much in evidence in this sequel [***The Great Pumpkin Switch***] to ***The Potato Man*** (1991). This time Grampa tells of the time he and his friend Otto accidentally cut the stem of his sister's prized pumpkin, causing "Big Max" to tumble down 34 front steps and smash. With some quick thinking and the help of Mr. Angelo, the Potato Man, the boys are able to bring about a happy ending. Although the story is set in the early part of the century, this very realistic tale involves typical childhood dilemmas and will not seem the least bit old-fashioned to today's readers. [Ted] Lewin's outstanding watercolor paintings add even more flavor and appeal to the well-crafted text. Especially noteworthy is the composition of each illustration and his use of perspective and bold color highlights to define the focal points. This perfect melding of words and pictures is a shining example of the finest in picture book production.

🕮 *WOO-OO IS IT?* (1992)

Hazel Rochman (review date 1 February 1992)

SOURCE: Rochman, Hazel. *Booklist* 88, no. 11 (1 February 1992): 1041.

From twilight through the darkness to dawn, a mother owl hears secret, half-familiar sounds in the night [***Whoo-oo Is It?***]. Is it the *whoosh* of a dragonfly's wing? The *tat-a-tat-a-tat* of the woodpecker? [S. D.] Schindler's fine, textured pastel drawings—brown, gray, black, and white on colored paper—combine a mood of mystery with precise observation, extending the images, sensations, and movements of the silence. As our eyes grow accustomed to the dark, we're drawn into the pictures, and we notice details of the barn, a stone wall, a raccoon in shadow, a distant fence. The surprise of the story is that all this whispery life is coming from the birth of the owl's new nestling. The crack of the egg, "fine as the vein of a new leaf," is part of a wide, natural universe, lit by the first splinter of light at dawn. Like McDonald and Schindler's ***Is This a House for Hermit Crab?*** this would make a fine read-aloud, with lots of audience help in re-creating the sounds.

Susan Scheps (review date April 1992)

SOURCE: Scheps, Susan. *School Library Journal* 38, no. 4 (April 1992): 96.

McDonald once again combines story and nature lesson in this sophisticated piece of prose [***Whoo-oo Is It?***] that incorporates some nighttime sounds. Mother barn owl, sitting on her eggs in the eaves of the barn at sundown, hears some familiar noises and flies off to investigate. Observant children will quickly connect the odd noises to the eggs shown in an early illustration, yet the first glimpse of an owl hatchling holds an element of surprise. [S. D.] Schindler illustrates this soft, sometimes poetic piece in a style similar to that in his earlier collaboration with McDonald, ***Is This a House for Hermit Crab?*** (1990). Most of the realistic pastel drawings rendered on earth-toned papers are dark scenes of barn interior and woods, with an occasional sand or gray-bordered scene for contrast. The format is quite attractive. Although this quiet story with its unfamiliar sounds is not exactly exciting fare, it will make a satisfying read-aloud selection for classrooms and story hours.

Elizabeth S. Watson (review date May 1992)

SOURCE: Watson, Elizabeth S. *Horn Book Magazine* 68, no. 3 (May 1992): 331.

The author-illustrator team of ***Is This a House for Hermit Crab?*** has produced another handsome book [***Whoo-oo Is It?***]. This one asks a new question: Who or what is making the noise—"*whhh, whhh, whhhhh* . . . no more than a whisper"—that troubles Mother Owl as she sits on a clutch of eggs? Ruling out a small mouse on the barn floor, a puppy barking, a kitten crying, the creaking of the barn floor, a snake, and a raccoon, the worried mother "circled the fields and returned, out, over, away, and back. Sweeping, swooping, through the trees she searched, then flew back to her eggs, her nest. Wondering. Waiting." All is well when the noise is discovered to be the first owlet emerging from its shell. The illustrations are as dark as the barn night, but perfectly discernible. The velvety pastels create texture and depth, making the white features of the barn owl all the more dramatic. The mysterious sounds will send delicious shivers up little spines, but the final tender family scene will relieve any lingering concerns.

THE BRIDGE TO NOWHERE (1993)

Susan Oliver (review date April 1993)

SOURCE: Oliver, Susan. *School Library Journal* 39, no. 4 (April 1993): 143.

In a story [***The Bridge to Nowhere***] almost as fragmented as the family at its center, readers get a glimpse of hard reality in tough economic times. Hallie's father was laid off from his job building bridges and his disintegrating emotional health has begun to tear at the other members of the family. The young teen feels abandoned by her older sister, away at college, and by her mother, who is struggling to support the family and maintain its facade of normalcy as her father disappears more and more into his basement workshop and out to his last, unfinished bridge. Hallie struggles—with junior high school, with her gossipy best friend, and with a budding romance with an incredibly sensitive teenage boy—as anecdotes take a troubled family to a dramatic climax, if not to resolution. Rich in metaphor, slim in character development, this is a moving, but not fully satisfying, slice of life, sure to inspire more questions than answers.

Deborah Abbott (review date 1 April 1993)

SOURCE: Abbott, Deborah. *Booklist* 89, no. 15 (1 April 1993): 1424-425.

Seventh-grader Hallie O'Shea [***The Bridge to Nowhere***] tries desperately to close the ever-widening gap between her and her father, who was laid off two years earlier from his job as a bridge builder. It makes no sense to anyone—especially Jim O'Shea, whose only passion in life has been the intricate construction of iron and steel webs that span rivers in Pittsburgh—that a bridge should be left uncompleted, a bridge to nowhere. Hallie's mother nervously watches her husband's mind deteriorate, and Hallie's sister, Shelley, away at college, is unwilling to see the real picture at home. Hallie turns to Crane Henderson, two years older, who offers a fresh perspective and warmth, kindling Hallie's first boy-girl relationship. In the typical fits and starts common to new friendships, Hallie learns a lot about herself. When her father unexpectedly travels the bridge to nowhere and ends up in the hospital, she finds a new strength and the ability to cope. This welcome first novel by the author of several picture books (among them, ***The Great Pumpkin Switch***), offers realistic characters, an attention-holding plot that blends Hallie's normal teen concerns with her worry about and anger at her father, and an upbeat ending.

Publishers Weekly (review date 19 April 1993)

SOURCE: *Publishers Weekly* 240, no. 16 (19 April 1993): 63.

Despite this first novel's [***The Bridge to Nowhere***] firm sense of place—Pittsburgh—its grasp on time, narrative structure and characterization remains rather shaky. A pivotal event, in which protagonist Hallie's father "flies" his car from an unfinished bridge across the Allegheny River, is—according to a note in the text—based on an actual incident in 1964. McDonald does practically nothing to anchor the story in that period. She sets the scene for a problem novel rife with dramatic possibilities—embittered unemployed father, mother struggling to support the family, older sister with dark secret, a seventh-grader's first love—but she constantly misses the payoffs. Her troubled family is miraculously fine again after Hallie's father suffers amnesia following his car stunt, Shelley has only to sniffle a little to be straightened out, and Hallie's fears of physical intimacy with older admirer Crane melt away with a mere hug. Lack of a satisfying resolution makes this an uncompelling read.

INSECTS ARE MY LIFE (1995)

Publishers Weekly (review date 16 January 1995)

SOURCE: *Publishers Weekly* 242, no. 3 (16 January 1995): 454.

Pigtailed and bespectacled—and with a freckled, round face and turned-up nose—Amanda Frankenstein looks like a junior pedant [***Insects Are My Life***]. And perhaps she is. Crazy about insects, the strong-willed girl dumps her brother's fireflies out of the jar and informs him, "Bugs are people, too, you know." Amanda amasses a huge collection of bugs ("Dead ones, of course"), is proud of the number of mosquito bites on her leg (22) and utters the dramatic claim stated in the book's title. Incessantly talking about (and even acting like) various insects, she antagonizes her brother and classmates. The plot wears thin, although some of Amanda's antics are engaging and many of McDonald's (***Is This a House for Hermit Crab?***) lines are quite funny (when the aspiring entomologist puts her feet on the kitchen table because, she announces, butterflies have taste buds in their feet, her mother orders her to "please keep your taste buds on the floor"). [Paul Brett] Johnson's (*The Cow Who Wouldn't Come Down*) animated watercolor, colored-pencil and pastel illustrations depend on exaggeration for their humor; even so, they are truer to life than the text in their depiction of ordinary feelings.

Virginia Opocensky (review date March 1995)

SOURCE: Opocensky, Virginia. *School Library Journal* 41, no. 3 (March 1995): 183-84.

Amanda loves bugs [***Insects Are My Life***], a fact that no one else seems to appreciate. She examines them, collects them, protects them, and imitates their behavior. She even gets into trouble at home and at school because of them. Kids tease her, and one in particular, Victor, makes her life miserable. In one humorous exchange she calls him ". . . a stinkbug on the leaf of life." Then she discovers Maggie, a classmate who has a passion of her own—reptiles. Factual tidbits slipped surreptitiously into the appealing text add information to this spirited tale. It's refreshing to have nonsqueamish female characters who are willing to take on all adversaries in defense of their causes. Full-page and vignette illustrations rendered in soft-hued watercolors, colored pencils, and pastels complement and add humor to the story. They are energetic, engaging, and entomologically correct. ***Insects Are My Life*** is an almost-perfect specimen.

Stephanie Zvirin (review date 1 March 1995)

SOURCE: Zvirin, Stephanie. *Booklist* 91, no. 13 (1 March 1995): 1249.

Amanda Frankenstein adores insects [***Insects Are My Life***]. She collects them ("dead ones, of course"), observes them, reads about them, and even writes poems about them. But nobody seems to understand her fervor, not her mother or her brother, and certainly not the kids at school—that is, for except Maggie, whose green scuba goggles betray her dearest love: "Reptiles are my life!" Amanda's discovery of a new friend comes a mite too abruptly at the close of the story, but McDonald beautifully captures kids' wonderful ability for all-encompassing devotion and offers children reassurance that it's perfectly OK to be different, [Peter Brett] Johnson's pleasingly unsaccharine illustrations, rendered in a combination of watercolor, pencil, and pastel, catch sometimes sour Amanda at her willful, stubborn, preoccupied best.

Margaret A. Bush (review date March-April 1995)

SOURCE: Bush, Margaret A. *Horn Book Magazine* 71, no. 2 (March-April 1995): 185.

Megan McDonald, whose previous books have been picture-book nonfiction such as ***Is This a House for Hermit Crab?*** and ***Who-oo Is It?*** adroitly blends humorous human nature and respect for natural science [***Insects Are My Life***]. Life among humans is not always easy for Amanda Frankenstein, whose passionate interest in insects is not shared by family and classmates. Amanda sets free the fireflies her brother has captured in a peanut-butter jar. She examines live bugs and collects dead creatures. In her avowed role as a bug's best friend, Amanda not only goes to great lengths to protect insects and invite them into the house, but she also gets even with her detractors. "And you, Victor, are less than a flea. You are a stinkbug on the leaf of life." Amanda's devotion to insects causes problems as other class members begin to ostracize her, but all ends unexpectedly well when she is sent to sit next to newcomer Maggie—who loves reptiles. Paul Brett Johnson's crayon and pastel illustrations, which sometimes border on caricature, aptly convey the emotional ups and downs of all concerned as Amanda explores nature and aggravates folks at home and school. Megan McDonald's single-minded, sometimes naughty heroine evokes chuckles with her feisty independence, and she will surely have special appeal for readers possessing their own personal passions.

MY HOUSE HAS STARS (1996)

Publishers Weekly **(review date 26 August 1996)**

SOURCE: *Publishers Weekly* 243, no. 35 (26 August 1996): 97-8.

McDonald (***Is This a House for Hermit Crab?***) turns to geography here [***My House Has Stars***], showing vastly different houses from around the world which all have one feature in common: the "roof" of stars that hangs over them. Eight colorful, dense vignettes feature a child describing his or her home ("My house has walls made of sheep's wool and a real door in the front of the tent that squeaks like a crybaby"). The "tour" of each dwelling, be it houseboat, igloo, skyscraper, yurt, etc., concludes with a reference to the stars above; for example, a child in a pueblo says, "I see stars, like tiny handprints, where Coyote scattered the mica dust and stars were born!" Unexplained facts and referents abound, tantalizing readers but also likely to frustrate them: What is a jeepney? Why does the Weaver Princess star go to meet the Ox Boy star? [Peter] Catalanotto's (*Who Came Down That Road?*) diffused watercolors show the children in their environments. Facing art, beneath the blocks of text, clues readers into the characters' locations: a hazy map of the world, with the child's homeland circled. The impressionistic style of the pictures suggests as much as it represents. Unfortunately, this approach exacerbates the gaps left in the vignettes. At best this is a lyrical invitation to a scavenger hunt on the reference shelf; otherwise it is essentially a cliff-hanger.

Sally R. Dow (review date October 1996)

SOURCE: Dow, Sally R. *School Library Journal* 42, no. 10 (October 1996): 102-03.

Children from widely different cultures have one thing in common—all of their homes have a view of the night sky [***My House Has Stars***]. From the roof of his mud-walled house in Nepal, Akam sees stars; Carmen watches them from her houseboat in the Philippines; Abu sees the night sky from his village in Ghana; Mariko looks out of paper windows from her house in Japan. In an adobe pueblo, Chili can see the stars when he climbs to his flat rooftop; Oyun sees the heavens above her yurt in the Mongolian desert; Sergio goes out on the roof of his Brazilian city skyscraper to see the night sky, and Mattie views the winter night from her igloo in Alaska. The concept of one earth, one sky unfolds in poetic imagery embracing the universality of people everywhere: "Our house, the earth. Our roof, the sky." Full-page watercolor paintings in soft, misty colors reflect the awesome quality of the universe as viewed by youngsters throughout the world.

Carolyn Phelan (review date 1 November 1996)

SOURCE: Phelan, Carolyn. *Booklist* 93, no. 5 (1 November 1996): 508.

In the framework story [***My House Has Stars***], a mother tells her daughter that "night is falling somewhere. And now. And now again. Night is coming to this sky. To houses everywhere. This house. / And there are stars." In the pages that follow, eight children around the world tell about their homes at night a houseboat in the Philippines, a mud house in Nepal, a group of round huts in Ghana, a Japanese house, an adobe pueblo, a Mongolian yurt, a sky-scraper apartment in Brazil, and a house on the Alaskan tundra. Each child, each culture views the night sky and the stars in a slightly different way, yet as the book's point of view pulls back visually in the last pages, it is clear that earth is home to all, and the roof above our heads is the same sky. [Peter] Catalanotto's impressionistic watercolor paintings capture each culture's individuality yet maintain the same soft-focus view of the world after darkness falls. Although the scenes take place at night, each is full of light: firelight, starlight, moonlight, city lights, the northern lights, and even the light of glowing silkworms. All add to the sense of wonder created by the well-crafted words and art in this purposeful yet impressive picture book.

Publishers Weekly (review date 18 June 2001)

SOURCE: *Publishers Weekly* 248, no. 25 (18 June 2001): 83.

McDonald turns to geography in this picture book [***My House Has Stars***], showing vastly different houses from around the world which all have one feature in common: the "roof" of stars that hangs over them.

BEEZY (1997)

Stephanie Zvirin (review date 15 September 1997)

SOURCE: Zvirin, Stephanie. *Booklist* 94, no. 2 (15 September 1997): 235.

Enlarged type, lots of leading, and amiable watercolor illustrations give this book for new readers [***Beezy***] plenty of visual appeal. McDonald's stories are pleasant, with two of the three (Beezy finds a dog and Beezy makes a new friend) solidly anchored in everyday life. The third (actually the first in the collection) is a bit more dramatic four "friends" sit out scary hurricane winds together, telling stories by candlelight. Kids who take things literally may be a little confused by Beezy's seeming unconcern about the predicament ("Maybe we will have another hurricane tomorrow"), but they'll have no trouble understanding the idea of friends helping one another during difficult times.

Publishers Weekly (review date 29 September 1997)

SOURCE: *Publishers Weekly* 244, no. 40 (29 September 1997): 89.

A trio of breezy tales fills this beginning reader [***Beezy***], which stars the peppy title character and her easygoing best buddy, Merlin. McDonald (***The Great Pumpkin Switch***) shrewdly gives each selection a theme or setting loaded with child appeal: in **"Eye of the Storm,"** the lights go out, candles make spooky shadows and the two youngsters listen to tales of a long-ago hurricane; Beezy secretly hopes no one will respond to her notice about a stray dog she has found in **"Funnybone"**; and in the third, she and Merlin make friends with a new girl, **"Sarafina Zippy,"** whose parents are circus performers. The author's cleverly subtle repetition of words and phrases, often appearing in the punchy dialogue among the young characters is well suited to beginning readers. And her ear for the way children speak is on target, as when Beezy tells Sarafina that she has known Merlin her "whole life," or at least since the age of two, "except for one week when I was mad at him." In step with the stories' energetic stride, [Nancy] Poydar's (*Cool Ali*) cheerful, brightly hued pictures imbue Beezy and her companions with an extra measure of personality.

Barbara Elleman (review date November 1997)

SOURCE: Elleman, Barbara. *School Library Journal* 43, no. 11 (November 1997): 92.

In three short stories styled just right for the beginning-to-read crowd [***Beezy***], Beezy waits out a Florida hurricane with her Gran; adopts a homeless dog she names Funnybone; and befriends newcomer Sarafina Zippy, whose parents are the Flying Zippys in the Pickle Circus. McDonald uses lots of word repetition and short sentences, injects dialogue in a natural way, and repeats story elements within the plot, which will be helpful for problem readers, without losing any punch to the narrative. Poydar follows suit: the full-color illustrations are delivered with zest and are integrated into the text for an easy flow between word and image. McDonald delivers another winner.

TUNDRA MOUSE: A STORYKNIFE TALE (1997)

Jane Marino (review date October 1997)

SOURCE: Marino, Jane. *School Library Journal* 43, no. 10 (October 1997): 42.

A multilayered but often confusing tale within a tale [***Tundra Mouse***]. Older sister Elena repeats a family holiday story to her little sister, Lissie, using words, sounds, and "storyknifing," described in the book's foreword as a Yup'ik Eskimo technique of drawing pictures while telling a story. Elena recounts how Tundra Mouse is accidentally picked up in Grandmother's gunnysack and taken into the house, where she meets the House Mouse, who takes her into his own nest. When a huge, sparkling spruce tree appears, the two mice spend the nights before Christmas spiriting away the tinsel and ornaments. By Christmas morning, the tree is bare. Grandmother explains the disappearing decorations as the work of the *cingssiiks,* tiny, magical people. When a pipe bursts and drives the mice back into the fields, they build a nest for their new family with the tinsel, which the girls discover out in the fields one day. Although this picture book celebrates family tradition and the pleasure taken in a story remembered, lapses in logic, unexplained elements, and amazing coincidences, along with Lissie's interruptions and interjections, overwhelm the narrative. The expertly rendered, colored-pencil illustrations have a scratchboard look; the brown paper that surrounds each one shows the small storyknife figures and gives the story a rustic air. A package with many appealing elements, but they don't come together to create a satisfying whole.

Publishers Weekly (review date 6 October 1997)

SOURCE: *Publishers Weekly* 244, no. 41 (6 October 1997): 55.

A felt-like, mouse-brown background sets the mood for this original "storyknife" tale [***Tundra Mouse***], traditionally relayed by Yup'ik Eskimo girls, who use a knife's tip to scratch pictures in the mud or snow while storytelling. Sprinkling her tale generously with Eskimo terms, Elena tells of a mouse who was transported from the Arctic prairie to her grandmother's home, where it met a mate and filched their Christmas tinsel to feather its nest—a nest which mysteriously reappears many weeks later back on the tundra (filled with baby mice). Storyknife symbols (rendered by a Yup'ik elder) encircle [S. D.] Schindler's softly realistic colored-pencil illustrations in a tender wreath of authenticity.

Susan Dove Lempke (review date 1 January 1998)

SOURCE: Lempke, Susan Dove. *Booklist* 94, no. 9 (1 January 1998): 824.

As she tells a story about ***Tundra Mouse*** to her sister, Lissie, Elena uses her storyknife to scratch pictures in the mud that represent the mouse's adventures. When her cozy home is disturbed, Tundra Mouse hides in Grandmother's gunnysack and winds up journeying to a place with delicious tastes but frightening sights and sounds. Diving into an open silverware drawer, she meets House Mouse. Together, they work to improve House Mouse's messy home by stripping a Christmas tree of its tinsel, cookies, and candy canes, and when Elena and Lissie wake up on Christmas morning, the tree is empty. The mouse's adventures are in roman type, the girl's comments appear in italics, and the storyknife pictures are in the page borders. The illustrations, on warm brown paper, look like scratchboard art and ingeniously echo the scratches of the storyknife. The book nicely captures the style and tone of the Yup'ik people's storytelling, at the same time giving children a glimpse of contemporary Yup'ik custom and some laugh-out-loud fun.

🕮 *BEEZY AT BAT* (1998)

Pam Hopper Webb (review date September 1998)

SOURCE: Webb, Pam Hopper. *School Library Journal* 44, no. 9 (September 1998): 176.

Youngsters who are already familiar with the unflappable heroine, introduced in ***Beezy*** (1997) and ***Beezy Magic*** (1998), will enjoy these new adventures [***Beezy at Bat.***]. In the first chapter, Beezy, her Gran, and neighbor Mr. Gumm spend a summer evening "cracking" riddles as they crack nuts. The next episode features the girl and a friend who is so troubled about snakes that he can't pick blackberries. The third chapter finds Beezy and her companions playing a sandlot baseball game during which they recruit a mysterious right fielder with an alligator-tooth necklace and a unicycle. Sarafina Zippy takes center stage in this episode, and while she is a spirited character, readers may wonder who she is and where she came from, and question her fielding techniques. What makes the book so appealing is that all of the characters and situations are child centered and fun and the plots use familiar settings with innovative devices. Subtle humor and softly colored, though slightly washed out, gouache illustrations make this title a suitable addition to the early-reader shelves.

Hazel Rochman (review date 1 November 1998)

SOURCE: Rochman, Hazel. *Booklist* 95, no. 5 (1 November 1998): 508.

In the third easy chapter book about Beezy [***Beezy at Bat***], she plays baseball, scares her friend with a snake, and cracks riddles with Gran on the porch.

The riddles are silly, but they are a playful way to enjoy words; the baseball action has a nice turnaround when the clumsy kid learns to catch; and the snake episode is just on the edge of shivery. Cheerful gouache illustrations show Beezy and her friends having fun in the Florida sunshine.

Horn Book Guide (review date spring 1999)

SOURCE: *Horn Book Guide* 10, no. 1 (spring 1999): 58.

In this third chapter book about Beezy [***Beezy at Bat***], she trades riddles with Gran and Mr. Gumm, finds a snake while picking berries with her friend Merlin, and gets an unusual new unicycle-riding player for her baseball team. The stories and their cartoon-style illustrations are amusing enough, but readers who don't know the previous books might feel a little lost.

BEEZY MAGIC (1998)

Jackie Hechtkopf (review date April 1998)

SOURCE: Hechtkopf, Jackie. *School Library Journal* 44, no. 4 (April 1998): 104.

In the first of three easy-to-read stories [***Beezy Magic***], Beezy decides that her name is uninteresting, but when her grandmother tells her the story about how her nickname came about, she is delighted with it. In the next chapter, Gran tells Beezy and her friend Merlin a humorous trickster tale of a clever rabbit who outmaneuvers a panther. Unfortunately, this segment takes readers too far away from the characters for too long, giving the book a disjointed tone. In the final story, Beezy's dog jumps into a pastry shop window to eat his favorite food, key lime pie. The reaction to his foaming green mouth is very funny. Fans of ***Beezy*** (1997) are likely to enjoy this title more than readers not previously introduced to this charming character. Only one of the three chapters puts her in a starring role, which serves to distance readers. [Nancy] Poydar's gouache paintings have a great deal of energy and child appeal, but they don't elevate the book enough to make it a first choice for beginning-reader collections.

Stephanie Zvirin (review date July 1998)

SOURCE: Zvirin, Stephanie. *Booklist* 94, no. 21 (July 1998): 1891.

Lively, carrot-haired Beezy returns in another collection of "adventures" for young readers [***Beezy Magic***]. In the first, Beezy learns about her nickname; in the second, Gran tells about a tricky rabbit besting a panther; in the last, Beezy's dog goes on a hunt for its favorite treat, key lime pie. There's enough commotion and variety to keep readers interested; the artwork is adequate; and the text, which is mainly dialogue, is printed in easy-on-the-eye, extra-large type. Children who like Beezy will enjoy this as well.

BEDBUGS (1999)

Kirkus Reviews (review date 15 July 1999)

SOURCE: *Kirkus Reviews* 67, no. 13 (15 July 1999): 1141-142.

Getting ready for bed is a challenge if there's an ostrich in the bathtub [***Bedbugs***], and everyone knows that it's hard to brush teeth with a shark in the sink. Both parents and children will identify with Susan's clever attempts to put off going to sleep and will chuckle at the illustrations showing the transformation of everyday objects into creatures unlikely to reside in any normal family's home. [Paul Brett] Johnson is fearless in his depictions of the creatures, imaginary and real, residing in Susan's home, and the ongoing conversation between father and daughter is one children will recognize and relish.

Ginny Gustin (review date September 1999)

SOURCE: Gustin, Ginny. *School Library Journal* 45, no. 9 (September 1999): 194.

A little girl's active imagination slips into high gear as bedtime approaches [***Bedbugs***]. Suddenly, a moth becomes a bat, a mop an octopus, a pair of furry slippers a bear . . . until the bedroom resembles a miniature wild kingdom. The child's father nonchalantly reassures her, viewing her panic as a tactic to delay bedtime. Eventually, he plays along with the frenzy and she must reassure him. The final pictures raise questions about imagination versus reality. The book's charm lies in the unrestrained line-and-wash illustrations that depict common household objects transformed into menacing creatures. Unfortunately, the text isn't as strong as the pictures. While the rhyming verse echoes a child's world, it is too forced and awkward to be truly effective. The narrative flaws keep this title from being a first purchase.

Jennifer M. Brabander (review date spring 2000)

SOURCE: Brabander, Jennifer M. *Horn Book Guide* 11, no. 1 (spring 2000): 19.

Susan puts off bedtime [***Bedbugs***] by conjuring up a series of imaginary distractions in the form of animals—a moth becomes a bat, a mop is an octopus, and so on. Her father patiently plays along, and soon she's all tucked in. Though sometimes awkward, the rhyming text aptly conveys a child's creativity. Amusing illustrations show the various animals, invisible to Daddy, traipsing around the house.

THE BONE KEEPER (1999)

Chris Sherman (review date January-June 1999)

SOURCE: Sherman, Chris. *Horn Book Guide* 10, no. 2 (January-June 1999): 259.

In words sounding like an incantation, the text [***The Bone Keeper***] describes a desert-dwelling woman who "searches the sand, / searches and sifts / for bones, bones." Piecing together bones from various animals, she brings a wolf to howling life. Spare pictures capture the parched setting as well as the story's mysterious mood. The story is evocative but somewhat puzzling, as readers are left wondering exactly who the enigmatic conjurer is.

Janice M. Del Negro (review date March 1999)

SOURCE: Del Negro, Janice M. *Bulletin of the Center for Children's Books* 52, no. 7 (March 1999): 245-246.

This lyrical tone poem [***The Bone Keeper***] brings us the bone keeper, a creator figure who gathers bones from the desert sand and breathes life into them: "Some say she has three heads, / past, present, and future. / Some say she carries the snake, / walks with the wild hare. // Some say Bone Woman brings the dead back to life." McDonald's Bone Woman sifts and searches the sand for remains ("One by one by one, / she collects / each lonely bone"), reconstructs the creature they come from, and dances, chants, and moans the bones to life. Mythological images combine into an original creation story of power and force. [G. Brian] Karas' mixed-media illustrations are pseudocave paintings, sepia variations on primitive themes, with dark brown lines against sand backgrounds limning the outline of the bent old Bone Woman, the curve of white bones seemingly scraped into stone walls and white lines scratched into thick dark paint to indicate an emerging wolf. There is a primal feeling to Karas' illustrations that suits the evocative nature of McDonald's text; combined, they conjure ancient images and archetypal possibilities.

Susan Dove Lempke (review date 15 April 1999)

SOURCE: Lempke, Susan Dove. *Booklist* 95, no. 16 (15 April 1999): 1531.

In this picture book for older readers [***The Bone Keeper***], a rhythmic, lulling text almost chants as it speaks of the Bone Woman: "She is Hunter. She is Gatherer. She is Keeper of the Bones." She moves through the desert sifting sand, gathering bones, and taking them back to her cave: "One by one by one, she collects each lonely bone." As the bones are assembled, a wolf comes together, then springs to life and goes off howling. Karas' illustrations reflect the moody mysterious text, showing, in a range of browns, the dry desert setting. At the same time, they reveal only the essence of the words, never overexplicating their meaning. The book's austere quality will not be to all tastes, but the words and pictures together create a spooky, thought-provoking experience.

Rosalyn Pierini (review date May 1999)

SOURCE: Pierini, Rosalyn. *School Library Journal* 45, no. 5 (May 1999): 93.

An eerie tale with mythical qualities [***The Bone Keeper***], set in the Southwestern desert. The protagonist is an elemental creature referred to as the Bone Keeper and additionally as Owl, Rattlesnake, or Bone Woman. This ancient entity wanders through the desert alternately laughing, singing, and chanting while collecting bones from the sand. She gathers her finds deep in a cave and then calls together the desert animals for a show of sorts—that of a skeleton maker. When at long last she has assembled her creation and performed the appropriate rituals, a flesh-and-blood wolf emerges. The process by which this miraculous transformation takes place is mysterious to say the least. Young readers will be puzzled by the text's enigmatic description of the Bone Keeper's supernatural machinations, as well as the illustrations. Artwork resembling primitive petroglyphs employs "a variety of materials, conventional and otherwise," to achieve a grainy and highly textured appearance. Most of the figures depicted are obscure and shadowy. The effect of both text and art is to create more mood than substance. There is too much left unspoken, perhaps lost in the sands of time, to convey a coherent story.

Book Links (review date March 2000)

SOURCE: *Book Links* 9, no. 4 (March 2000): 23.

This intriguing tale [***The Bone Keeper***] takes the reader on a mythological journey of an old woman called the Bone Keeper. She meticulously combs the desert for animal bones and carefully reassembles them. After the assembly is complete, she performs a rhythmic chant, accompanied by a hypnotic dance, which ultimately transforms the bones into a new living creature. Earth-toned and textured illustrations bring ***The Bone Keeper*** to life without unmasking her mystical persona.

THE NIGHT IGUANA LEFT HOME (1999)

Kirkus Reviews (review date 1 August 1999)

SOURCE: *Kirkus Reviews* 67, no. 15 (1 August 1999): 1229.

It's not that Iguana is angry or anything [***The Night Iguana Left Home***]. After all, she has her own e-mail address and all the anchovy pizza she wants; she loves her human pal, Alison, who treats her as a best friend should. Iguana pines for the sun and surf and as many miles as she can get between herself and Schenectady, New York, where the winters know no mercy. So she grabs a bus to Key West, where she lives the good life until her allowance runs out. Then she has to wash dishes in a restaurant, and on the night the restaurant serves a special iguana, Iguana lights out for a stamp-licking job at the post office, then tucks herself into a parcel addressed to Schenectady. The warm south is in her blood (this comes as no surprise, given [Ponder] Goembel's wry, alluring scenes of the place) and she heads back to Big Pine Key, commuting back to Alison for anchovy pizza when it beckons. McDonald's story is wonderfully alive, with the iguana a bit of a cool cat, and the Keys exotic but available. It is full of love, independence, and natural law, and the slice of biogeography can't hurt.

Gay Lynn Van Vleek (review date September 1999)

SOURCE: Van Vleek, Gay Lynn. *School Library Journal* 45, no. 9 (September 1999): 195.

Alison's pampered iguana longs for warm weather perks [***The Night Iguana Left Home***]. One day, the lizard travels from Schenectady, NY, to Florida via bus where her attempt at living "the high life" meets with mixed success. For a while, the creature sunbathes, swims, and surfs, but soon her money runs out and she is forced to find work. Another problem is that the two friends miss one another. Eventually, the animal finds a job licking stamps at the post office and the two are able to find happiness through a compromise of e-mail and semiannual visits. [Ponder] Goembel's dynamic drawings done in sepia ink with watercolor washes produce portraits of the lonely child and sunbonneted iguana with equal panache. Although young listeners may need explanations for a few of the words and phrases in the text (forwarding addresses, priority mail), this inventive tale will guarantee grins.

Kitty Flynn (review date September-October 1999)

SOURCE: Flynn, Kitty. *Horn Book Magazine* 75, no. 5 (September-October 1999): 596.

When Iguana's dewlap droops, her skin peels, and she craves seaweed [in ***The Night Iguana Left Home***], it's time to leave her comfortable life with her human friend and "almost sister," Alison Frogley. Iguana boards a bus to Key West, where she basks in the sun and enjoys the high life until her allowance and luck run out. Text and illustrations contain a slyly humorous balance of fantasy and realism, making the surreal seem plausible. While Iguana has an e-mail address and library card, the text portrays her as (relatively) true to her species: she needs calcium and a heating pad; dogs are her enemy. (Young iguana experts, however, may have trouble reconciling liberties taken with other facts.) Using spare cross-hatching and shading to good effect, the detailed ink-and-watercolor-wash artwork give scenes an almost stage-lit quality at times. Like a movie camera, the front matter scenes move progressively closer to the Frogleys' snow-covered house; though the text never mentions that the tale starts in winter, [Ponder] Goembel has provided a context for Iguana's physiological and emotional state. Despite some anthropomorphized facial expressions and a penchant for colorful scarves, Iguana looks realistically reptilian. With a well-developed character on an intriguing odyssey, ***The Night Iguana Left Home*** will stir the imaginations of armchair travelers.

John Peters (review date 1 November 1999)

SOURCE: Peters, John. *Booklist* 95, no. 5 (1 November 1999): 540.

Though Iguana is happy living in the bedroom of her good friend Alison Frogley [***The Night Iguana Left Home***], she needs something more, and so leaves Schenectady for the sand and surf of Key West. It's an idyllic life, until the money runs out and Iguana discovers, almost too late, that the eatery where she lands a dishwashing job specializes in "Gallina de Palo"—iguana stew. In [Ponder] Goembel's illustrations, done with a bold, hilariously enhanced realism, Iguana (only slightly less than human size) basks in scaly resplendence beneath pink shades and stylish neckwear, her great tail sweeping out behind her in strong, graceful curves. After a narrow escape, Iguana settles down on another Key, supporting herself as a stamp licker for the local post office, keeping in touch with Alison via e-mail, and, twice a year, mailing herself to Schenectady for tête-à-têtes over "the best anchovy pizza in the world."

BEEZY AND FUNNYBONE (2000)

Carolyn Phelan (review date July 2000)

SOURCE: Phelan, Carolyn. *Booklist* 96, no. 21 (July 2000): 2045.

This volume [***Beezy and Funnybone***], the fourth in the Beezy series, features three stories about a little girl and her dog, Funnybone. In the first, Funnybone is slow to learn to fetch, but once he grasps the concept, he fetches more than his owner ever wanted. In the second, he digs up some flowers, leading Beezy to an interesting discovery about the word *spat.* In the third, Beezy and her friends jump out of a hot-air balloon gondola just before it rises into the air, taking Funnybone on his first flight. Well designed for young readers, these mildly amusing tales are enhanced by [Nancy] Poydar's appealing gouache paintings of Beezy, her dog, and her friends.

Maura Bresnahan (review date September 2000)

SOURCE: Bresnahan, Maura. *School Library Journal* 46, no. 9 (September 2000): 204.

Beezy is back for another set of adventures, this time with her canine companion [***Beezy and Funnybone***]. As this easy chapter book opens, Funnybone is learning how to fetch. Unfortunately, he carries this new game a bit too far. In the next lighthearted escapade. Beezy and her classmates unsuccessfully search for the meaning of the word "spat"; even a trip to the library proves fruitless. Not until Funnybone digs up the garden and they notice a slug on the flowers, do they learn from Gran that a "spat" is a baby snail. In the last chapter, the pup takes an unexpected trip in a hot-air balloon when he accompanies Beezy to her friend's birthday party. The simple sentence structure will encourage children to practice their new skills. The gouache illustrations match the warm and friendly tone of the stories and provide visual clues.

JUDY MOODY (2000)

Kirkus Reviews (review date 15 April 2000)

SOURCE: *Kirkus Reviews* 68, no. 8 (15 April 2000): 564.

Changeable skies arch over a third-grader's moodscape in this easy-reading chapter book [***Judy Moody***] from the versatile McDonald (***The Night Iguana Left Home,*** 1999). Whether it's having to sit next to Frank "Eats Paste" Pearl on the first day of school, having a toad relieve itself in her hand, or playing the role of a cavity at the Brush Your Teeth Week assembly while her little brother Stink gets to tour the White House, something is always putting Judy into a grouchy mood, at least for a while. The author casts her appealing protagonist with equally appealing friends, plus a brother who not only holds his own, but also has a redeeming ability to take a practical joke. She brings the episodic story to a satisfying climax in which Judy, instead of throwing a tantrum, resourcefully rescues her homework, a painstakingly constructed collage, after Stink accidentally splashes it with purple juice. [Peter] Reynolds's black and white washes are perfectly placed to track Judy's ups and downs, though parts of the full spread scenes do vanish into the gutter. Surefire fare.

Janice M. Del Negro (review date May 2000)

SOURCE: Del Negro, Janice M. *Bulletin of the Center for Children's Books* 53, no. 9 (May 2000): 324-25.

Third-grader Judy Moody lives up to her name in this beginning chapter book [***Judy Moody***]. Judy is moody about the first day of school after summer vacation, moody about being in a different class with a different teacher, and moody about her autobiographical "Me collage" assignment (she doesn't have anything to put in the "THE WORST THING THAT EVER HAPPENED TO ME" space). Ably assisted by best friend Rocky, "pest friend" Frank, and younger brother Stinky, Judy navigates the moody muddy waters of third grade with a fair amount of grace. The humor is third-grade funny (the establishment of the TP Club requires an initiation that will have readers howling) and Judy, despite (or because of) her many moods, is a character with sass and style. Each chapter is amiably illustrated with black-and-white mixed-media (pen and ink, tea, watercolor) full-page and spot art that extends the friendly feeling of the humorous text. The catchy cutout cover and overall book design (large fonts, wide leading, generous borders) will appeal to young readers, and adults will welcome Judy to the readaloud shelf.

Shelle Rosenfeld (review date July 2000)

SOURCE: Rosenfeld, Shelle. *Booklist* 96, no. 21 (July 2000): 2028, 2030.

Judy Moody is in a bad mood the first day of school, certain third grade won't be as fun as second. Being assigned a front-row seat, beside yucky Frank "Eats-Paste" Pearl, isn't encouraging, although things improve when her teacher assigns an intriguing "Me" collage, and Judy gets a new pet, a Venus Flytrap. There's always some trial to contend with, from pesky brother Stink to being the only girl at a birthday party, but sometimes the worst events—or people—turn out better than expected. Deceptively hefty, this beginning chapter book features large type; simple, expressive prose and dialogue; and plenty of child-appealing humor. Children will enjoy lively Judy and her diverse hobbies and adventures with best-friend Rocky. They'll also like the witty, detailed drawings (especially the picture of Judy's unique collage, a nice activity idea), contributed by Peter Reynolds. An entertaining story that portrays challenges and pleasures from a kid's perspective, and shows how making the best of things can have surprising rewards.

Janie Schomberg (review date July 2000)

SOURCE: Schomberg, Janie. *School Library Journal* 46, no. 7 (July 2000): 83.

Judy Moody is grumpy. She hates the thought of summer ending and dreads starting third grade, until her new teacher asks each student to create a "Me" collage to share with the class. Then she can't wait to tell about her new pet—a Venus flytrap that eats bugs and hamburger, the T.P. (Toad Pee) Club initiation, and how she ate a shark over the summer. Judy's second-grade brother Stink and her friend Rock are major figures in the story as is her nemesis, Frank Pearl. Judy is independent, feisty, and full of energy, a delightful new character for beginning chapter-book readers. [Peter] Reynolds has captured her personality in his humorous illustrations done in watercolor, tea, and pen and ink.

Horn Book Guide **(review date fall 2000)**

SOURCE: *Horn Book Guide* 11, no. 2 (fall 2000): 308.

Judy Moody discovers that being in third grade brings a new set of challenges, including the creation of a "Me collage" that showcases her feelings, family members, and favorite activities. McDonald's offbeat humor coupled with expressive black-and-white cartoonlike illustrations make Judy, her family, and her friends both appealing and realistic.

Junko Yokota and Mingshui Cai (review date September 2001)

SOURCE: Yokoto, Junko, and Mingshui Cai. *Language Arts* 79, no. 1 (September 2001): 80.

Judy Moody starts third grade in a bad mood. Summer ends too soon with no adventures to show off, and she hates having to sit by her "pester friend" Frank. But she cheers up as she thinks about herself being the star of her "me" collage. Judy has a best friend, Rocky, and a pesky, second-grader brother, Stink, who is the cause of the "Worst Thing Ever" and "Funniest Thing Ever" in her collage. Her relationships with Rocky, Stink, and Frank furnish one comic episode after another in this hilarious story. The moody yet spirited protagonist is as lovable as the story is enjoyable. Readers will admire her intelligence in dealing with challenges in school.

🕮 *LUCKY STAR* (2000)

Maura Bresnahan (review date March 2001)

SOURCE: Bresnahan, Maura. *School Library Journal* 47, no. 3 (March 2001): 194

In [***Lucky Star***], Star accidentally damages her library book. When her attempts to repair it are not successful, she and a friend start weeding a neighbor's garden to earn money to replace it. This inspires them to have a sidewalk sale for money to buy toys. Young readers will identify both with Star's concerns and her friendship. The illustrations are filled with subtle humor, especially those chronicling the attempts to remove a pizza-sauce thumbprint from the page of a book.

🕮 *JUDY MOODY GETS FAMOUS* (2001)

Kirkus Reviews **(review date 15 June 2001)**

SOURCE: *Kirkus Reviews* 69, no. 12 (15 June 2001): 867.

Envious of classmate and spelling-bee champ Jessica's picture in the local paper, the irrepressible third grader introduced in ***Judy Moody*** (2000) tries for her own 15 minutes of fame [***Judy Moody Gets Famous***]. As she quickly discovers, it can be elusive. Like its predecessor, a disarming plot and likable characters are matched to an equally appealing format: small pages, generously spaced and sized type, die-cut windows in the dust jacket, and frequent ink-and-wash illustrations featuring smiles and high spots inside. In the end, Judy Moody earns her write-up inadvertently, after spiriting away a bagful of battered dolls from a hospital's playroom, refurbishing them from her large private collection of loose doll parts—plus hospital gowns made from an old sheet and little casts of "oogey wet newspaper"—then returning them anonymously. "Phantom Doll Doctor Strikes County Hospital," reads the headline. Only she, her affectionate nuclear family, and her likely-to-burgeon fan base know the truth. New chapter-book readers will enjoy watching Judy's moods, and the ensuing complications, unfold.

Diane Roback, Jennifer M. Brown, and Jason Britton (review date 30 July 2001)

SOURCE: Roback, Diane, Jennifer M. Brown, and Jason Britton. *Publishers Weekly* 248, no. 31 (30 July 2001): 85.

This sequel [***Judy Moody Gets Famous***] to ***Judy Moody*** handily matches the original in zip and wit, portraying the spunky Judy in her quest for recognition. Famous for her changeable moods, the third-grader wants to become just plain *famous* after her arch rival, Jessica, wins a spelling contest to earn the title of Queen Bee, an honor accompanied by a bejeweled tiara and a front-page headline in the local newspaper. In contrast, green-eyed Judy "felt about as famous as a pencil." When it becomes clear that her spelling prowess will not pave Judy's way to fame, the resourceful child tries to pass off a hammered cherry pit as one from George Washington's ill-fated tree—a ruse that bombs when a boy mistakes it for an M & M and swallows it. Judy's cat, Mouse, makes another appearance, helping the heroine attract the spotlight when it wins second place in a pet contest; but the newspaper photo shows only her elbow, and her name appears as "Judy Muddy." McDonald provides an inventive conclusion to her tangy tale, as an altruistic undertaking on Judy's part garners her fame (hint: her medical school aspirations once again come into play)—but anonymously. Even Judy could spell two words that describe both the plot and its heroine: f-r-e-s-h and f-u-n-n-y. Here's to her quick return.

Martha V. Parravano (review date September-October 2001)

SOURCE: Parravano, Martha V. *Horn Book Magazine* 77, no. 5 (September-October 2001): 589.

In this sequel to ***Judy Moody*** [***Judy Moody Gets Famous***], the irrepressible third grader—envious of goody-goody classmate Jessica Finch, who gets a tiara and her picture in the paper when she wins a spelling bee—is in the mood to get "F-A-M-O-U-S." Her relentless and indiscriminate pursuit of fame yields few results, however. She tries to pass off a cherry pit as belonging to George Washington, but a little kid swallows it before she can attract reporters; she manages to win second place in a pet contest (her cat makes toast), but only her elbow makes it into the newspaper photo. Worse, when she recruits the gang to try to set the world record for farthest human centipede walk, her friend Frank ends up in the hospital. When she eventually does make it into the newspaper, it's anonymously, as a secret philanthropist—but it's for a cause she really cares about, and it makes her feel "famouser" than even George Washington. The ending may leave some readers bemused—it's not really clear why Judy's lust for fame is satisfied by her anonymous rehabilitation of the hospital dolls—but the force of Judy's personality and the story's great energy and humor should carry the day. Everything about these ***Judy Moody*** books—from the liberally illustrated, spaciously designed, accessible format to the believability of Judy's third-grade worldview—spells G-O-O-D N-E-W-S for early chapter book readers.

Sharon R. Pearce (review date October 2001)

SOURCE: Pearce, Sharon R. *School Library Journal* 47, no. 10 (October 2001): 124.

Third-grader Judy Moody is back in her second adventure for the young chapter-book crowd [***Judy Moody Gets Famous***]. She has a mood for all seasons, and this time it is jealousy. She thinks everyone else is famous except for her—even her parents and brother all have claims to fame. Sure that she'll be a winner when her cat makes toast for the "Famous Pet Contest," she loses to a boy whose chicken plays "Three Blind Mice" on a toy piano. In the end, Judy becomes famous anonymously after she steals some broken dolls from the hospital, fixes and cleans them, and mails them back, and the local newspaper picks up the story. To her surprise, she finds her secret even more satisfying than having everyone know who did the good deed. Funny black-and-white cartoons appear throughout. Dialogue is right on target for the character's age and feelings. The child's self-centered attitude may be tiresome to some adult readers, but kids will relate to her every concern. Look for future adventures of this feisty heroine, and don't miss her time in the spotlight.

REPTILES ARE MY LIFE (2001)

Kirkus Reviews (review date 1 July 2001)

SOURCE: *Kirkus Reviews* 69, no. 13 (1 July 2001): 943.

Non-stereotypical hobbies and sprightly writing keep this routine tale [***Reptiles Are My Life***] of a friendship's collapse and regrouping afloat—but barely. Insect-lover Amanda and Maggie, mad for reptiles, are as close as "two bugs in a rug, two crocs on a rock," until new classmate Emily, another reptile-phile, shoulders in. Suddenly Amanda's out in the cold, watching Maggie and Emily bond and seeing her own overtures to join in ignored or scorned. Only when Amanda steps up to save the "Snake Sisters" from a reprimand by explaining to a teacher that they weren't sticking their tongues out to be rude does the ice suddenly melt, and without further ado the trio becomes "three bugs on a rug, three crocs on a rock." The plot's not going to sell many readers, nor will the art; though he catches a guilty look on Maggie's face once, by and large [Paul Brett] Johnson depicts a set of indistinctly drawn, stiff-faced children walking through a series of conventional school and playground scenes. The children do impart snippets of fact about the creatures to which they're devoted, but the brio and good humor of ***Insects Are My Life*** (1995) is missing from this follow-up.

Linda M. Kenton (review date August 2001)

SOURCE: Kenton, Linda M. *School Library Journal* 47, no. 8 (August 2001): 156.

Readers first met Amanda and Maggie in ***Insects Are My Life*** (1995). The ups and downs of their friendship are the focus of this story [***Reptiles Are My Life***]. Maggie adores reptiles and she and Amanda share their respective passions by doing the sorts of things good friends do—they change their names, reptile and insect related of course, and enjoy a secret hiding place. Things are perfect until a new girl, Emily Elligator, joins their class. Maggie gravitates to Emily, another reptile aficionado, abandoning her friend. Amanda is left out of their games, and friendship, until she defends them against the accusations of a classmate and "From that day on, they were as together as three bugs in a rug, three crocs on a rock." The story accurately portrays the roller-coaster ride that some friendships take, and the language is filled with delightful metaphors. [Peter Brett] Johnson's impressionist acrylics depict a multicultural cast of characters and a host of creatures.

Jill Quisenberry (review date mid-summer 2002)

SOURCE: Quisenberry, Jill. *Childhood Education* 78, no. 5 (mid-summer 2002): 307.

Amanda and Maggie are best friends [***Reptiles Are My Life***]. Amanda is an insect enthusiast and Maggie feels the same about reptiles. They are an inseparable pair until Emily comes along. Emily loves reptiles as much as Maggie does; the two pair up and exclude Amanda, driving her "buggy!" Friendships have strong roots, though, and this story helps young readers see that three's not always a crowd. The story is full of great insect and reptile references.

SHADOWS IN THE GLASS HOUSE (2001)

Kristen Oravec (review date February 2001)

SOURCE: Oravec, Kristen. *School Library Journal* 47, no. 2 (February 2001): 118.

Set in 1621, [***Shadows in the Glass House***] begins when 12-year-old Merry is kidnapped from London and forced to suffer a grueling journey by ship to the New World. Upon her arrival in the Jamestown settlement, she is promptly sold into indentured servitude and forced to work in a glasshouse. There, Merry works under the tutelage of kindly Franz, the master glassblower. A mystery ensues when someone begins to sabotage the operation and tries to steal the formula for *cristallo,* a valuable clear glass from Italy. The historical descriptions of Jamestown and especially glassblowing are detailed and lively enough to hold readers' interest. While the mystery element is somewhat predictable, it adds another level to the historical detail. "A Peek into the Past" section describes the era and includes appropriate photographs, reproductions, and drawings. A quick and fun read for those who have outgrown the "American Girls" books.

JUDY MOODY SAVES THE WORLD (2002)

Shelle Rosenfeld (review date 1 September 2002)

SOURCE: Rosenfeld, Shelle. *Booklist* 99, no. 1 (1 September 2002): 125.

The third title in the Judy Moody series [***Judy Moody Saves the World***] finds the spunky third-grader in a save-the-world mood. Judy would like to enter an adhesive bandage design contest, but she doesn't have any ideas. Then a class environmental preservation project inspires her creativity, as well as a new mission. But it's not long before Judy discovers that saving the world isn't easy, whether she is trying to convince her father not to drink rainforest bean coffee or her mom to dispose of a rubber toilet plunger. However, Judy persists, and while bandage-art fame eludes her, she does come up with a class recycling project that makes a difference. It also puts her in a very good mood. This charming read features characteristically snappy, humorous prose; expressive, witty, black-and-white illustrations; and some great ideas for classroom or home projects. The book stands alone, but fans will enjoy familiar, distinctive characters and references from previous titles.

BAYA, BAYA, LULLA-BY-A (2003)

Publishers Weekly **(review date 30 June 2003)**

SOURCE: *Publishers Weekly* 250, no. 26 (30 June 2003): 77.

McDonald's (***Judy Moody***) lilting poem [***Baya, Baya, Lulla-By-A***] tells parallel stories about a mother baya bird weaving a nest "strand/by strand / by willowy strand" and an Indian mother weaving a safekeeping blanket "thread / by thread / by whispering thread." McDonald's languorous and graceful text flows with satisfying imagery. The mother carries her baby "heartbeat to heartbeat, / through the pale green / haze of desert," and "she sings to you morning after morning, / like a sleepy cricket. / Kira, kira. / Your heart answers, a small drum. / Dholak, dholak." The rhythmic repetition of Indian words lends a peaceful, somnolent tone to the narrative (the words are translated in an appendix). After the two stories merge and baya bird helps save the baby from a cobra, however, the narrative meanders between lullaby and story, and loses some of its effectiveness. [Vera] Rosenberry's (*Savitri*) framed watercolors in jewel-like colors recall the stylized perspectives and, occasionally, the motifs of Hindi paintings. The portraits are not always consistent in their portrayal of the characters, but the landscapes and the textiles are intricately detailed. One painting, which invites comparison of the elaborate designs of the mother's scarves with the stars of the night sky, presents the mother almost like a goddess, with four arms: she tends the baby while at the same time plucking the moon from the sky and presenting a yellow garland to the bird. This cross-cultural venture will delight the ear—and intrigue young readers with its exotic introduction to the customs of another country.

JUDY MOODY PREDICTS THE FUTURE (2003)

Publishers Weekly **(review date 21 July 2003)**

SOURCE: *Publishers Weekly* 250, no. 29 (21 July 2003): 197-98.

Judy Moody Predicts the Future in the famously temperamental third-grader's fourth adventure by Megan McDonald, illus. by Peter H. Reynolds. Here Judy, equipped with a mood ring, convinces herself and her classmates of her clairvoyant capabilities. Fans can track their own mood swings with ***The Judy Moody Mood Journal***; the paper-over-board volume, with lined pages and Reynolds's occasional spot art, sports a spinner set into the cover, whose arrow (when spun) lands on one of 10 possible Judy moods. Sections such as "Favorite Pets" suggest prompts and provide quotes from the books to spark budding writers' entries.

SHINING STAR (2003)

Gillian Engberg (review date July 2003)

SOURCE: Engberg, Gillian. *Booklist* 99, no. 21 (July 2003): 1899.

In this Step into Reading title [***Shining Star***], Star and her friend, Blister, discover the joys of "duck" tape. In the first episode, Blister has a hole in his bike tire. After chewing gum fails to patch the leak, the friends turn to duck tape, and then, in a frenzy of duck-tape fever, they repair everything from a backpack to a doghouse. In the second story, Star's older sister, Ivy, notices that Star's paintings resemble the styles of Picasso, Matisse, and van Gogh. Determined to make her art her own, Star adds cluck tape to her final masterpiece. In the last episode, the friends take their taped flashlight out for an evening of stargazing. The duck-tape references get old, but the art information and warm friendship between Blister and Star distinguish these stories, which will help prepare children for chapter books. Appealing watercolor art illustrates the rhythmic text, which is filled with enticing sounds and repetition.

FURTHER READING

Criticism

Children's Book Review Service, Inc. (March 2000): 86.
Review of *The Night Iguana Left Home.*

Flynn, Kitty. *Horn Book Guide* 11, no. 1 (spring 2000): 45.
Review of *The Night Iguana Left Home.*

Horn Book Guide 11, no. 2 (fall 2000): 295.
Review of *Beezy and Funnybone.*

Additional coverage of McDonald's life and career is contained in the following sources published by the Gale Group: *Contemporary Authors,* Vol. 135; *Literature Resource Center;* and *Something about the Author,* Vols. 67, 99.

Janet S. Wong
1962-

(Full name Janet Siu Wong) American children's poet and picture book writer.

INTRODUCTION

Wong is an Asian American children's poet whose works employ a variety of voices and poetic styles to explore her own heritage. Born in the United States, Wong is the daughter of a Korean-born mother and a Chinese-born father—all three cultures have found a place in her works. Although she was an adult before she came to appreciate poetry, Wong became such a fervent advocate of the form that she gave up her career as a corporate lawyer to become a children's poet. Her verse has won praise for its unique structure and phrasing as well as its variety of thematic material—typically explorations of cultural heritage and everyday life. In an interview with *Something about the Author,* Wong commented that, "I like poems that are not afraid to talk about painful things. I like poems that make you laugh, or cry; poems that grab you and make you read them again; poems that make you think." Wong has also fostered a reputation as an author of juvenile picture books, beginning with the publication of *Buzz* in 2000.

BIOGRAPHICAL INFORMATION

Wong was born on September 30, 1962, in Los Angeles, California. The mixed heritage of her parents and the cosmopolitan nature of Los Angeles exposed Wong early to a environment rich with cultural diversity. She attended the University of California in Los Angeles as a history major, but spent her junior year in France studying art history at the Université de Bordeaux. Upon her return, Wong founded the Immigrant Children's Art Project, a program focused on teaching refugee children to express themselves through art. She graduated summa cum laude from the University of California in 1983 and enrolled in the Yale School of Law, receiving her J.D. in 1987. While at Yale, Wong was the director of the Yale Law and Technology Association and worked for New Haven Legal Aid. After obtaining her law degree, Wong worked as an attorney in Los Angeles, practicing corporate and labor law for GTE and Universal Studios until 1991. In 1991 Wong attended a workshop about writing for children which featured a reading by the poet Myra Cohn Livingston. Wong had such an intense emotional response to the reading that she subsequently chose to abandon her law career to pursue professional writing, although she continued to work as an arbitrator until 1995. Her first book of poetry for young adults, *Good Luck Gold and Other Poems* was published in 1994, receiving a warm critical reception. Wong followed *Good Luck Gold* with several additional works of poetry, exploring themes related to her life and multiethnicity. In 1995 Wong served as Writer in Residence to the University of Southern California Writing Project, and in 1997, she served as a Visiting Author to the Singapore Society for Reading and Literacy. In April 2003 Wong was invited to read from her work at the annual White House Easter Egg Roll.

MAJOR WORKS

In Wong's first two collections of poetry for young adults—*Good Luck Gold and Other Poems* and *A Suitcase of Seaweed and Other Poems* (1996)—the author explores her mixed ethnic background by utilizing a child's point-of-view. The poems examine themes of family, a child's burgeoning sense of self-identity, and cultural traditions. *A Suitcase of Seaweed* is divided into three separate sections—Korean, Chinese, and American—with a short personal memoir introducing each segment. Another of Wong's recurring subjects throughout her verse is the complex relationship between mothers and their children. In *The Rainbow Hand: Poems about Mothers and Children* (1999), Wong creates a subtle portrait of how the pressures of the modern world can make children question the strength of the maternal bond. In a similar vein, *Behind the Wheel: Poems about Driving* (1999) collects a series of poems inspired by the myriad errands that are typically part of a busy American mother's daily routine.

Wong branched out into a new literary genre with *Buzz,* her first picture book for young children. The story recounts in simple text all of the things that go "buzz" in a little boy's world—the alarm clock, his father's electric shaver, the blender, the doorbell, and so on. Returning to Wong's prevailing themes of family and culture, *The Trip Back Home* (2000) recalls a childhood journey to visit Wong's grandparents in rural Korea. The narrative follows her family as they plan for the trip—picking out what gifts to bring their relatives—and as they try to adjust to the routines of their grandparents' household—going to the market, feeding the pigs, playing cards, among other activities. Told in the first person, *Apple Pie 4th of July* (2002) is concerned with what it means to be an American citizen. Set on the Fourth of July in a Chinese restaurant, the Chinese American daughter of the owners tries to persuade her parents that "[n]o one wants Chinese food on the Fourth of July." However, her parents insist on preparing food for the day. After the big holiday parade passes by, crowds of onlookers come into the restaurant, convincing the young girl that "egg rolls are part of America too." The book ends with the family watching the annual fireworks display from their rooftop.

CRITICAL RECEPTION

The favorable critical response to Wong's poetry for young adults has established her a solid reputation among children's librarians and scholars. One of her poems—"Albert J. Bell" from *A Suitcase of Seaweed*—was selected to appear on posters in the New York subway as part of the city's "Poetry in Motion" program. Many critics have praised the universality of Wong's poetic themes, lauding her portrayal of commonality through diversity. Hazel Rochman has asserted that, "[t]he poems [in *A Suitcase of Seaweed*] overlap their ethnicity and subject of course, and young people will recognize many of the situations, whether Wong is imagining her parents 'Love at First Sight' or chaffing at their high expectations and their disappointment." Reviewers have also commended Wong for her evocative forays into the genre of picture books. In the review for *Buzz, Horn Book Magazine*'s critic commented that, "[n]ot every writer can make a smooth transition from one genre to another, especially when there's a vast difference in intended audience, but here an established poet for young adults proves that she is more than able to do so with her first picture book for preschoolers." *Apple Pie 4th of July* has been praised for its sensitive and emotional examination of a child's understanding of racial and national identities. Alicia Eames has stated that, "[t]his simply told story [*Apple Pie 4th of July*] explores a child's fears about cultural differences and fitting in with understanding and affection."

AWARDS

Wong has won numerous awards and citations for her work, including the Stone Center Recognition of Merit for *Good Luck Gold. A Suitcase of Seaweed* received a citation from the New York Public Library as a Book for the Teen Age and was named a Notable Trade Book in the Field of Social Studies from the National Council for the Social Studies and the Children's Book Council in 1996. *A Suitcase of Seaweed* also received the Stone Center Recognition of Merit from the Claremont Graduate School and was included in the William White Award Master List of 1998 and 1999. *The Rainbow Hand* was honored with the Lee Bennett Hopkins Award from Pennsylvania State University. In addition to these accolades, Wong is the recipient of several Best Book Awards from the *New York Times, The Los Angeles Times, School Library Journal,* and *Book Links.* She has also received the International Reading Association's Celebrate Literacy Award in 1998 for exemplary service in the promotion of literacy and was appointed to two terms on the Commission of Literature by the National Council of Teachers of English.

PRINCIPAL WORKS

Good Luck Gold and Other Poems (poetry) 1994
A Suitcase of Seaweed and Other Poems (poetry) 1996
Behind the Wheel: Poems about Driving (poetry) 1999
The Rainbow Hand: Poems about Mothers and Children (poetry) 1999
Buzz (picture book) 2000
Night Garden: Poems from the World of Dreams (poetry) 2000
The Trip Back Home (picture book) 2000
Grump (picture book) 2001
This Next New Year (picture book) 2001
Apple Pie 4th of July (picture book) 2002
You Have to Write (picture book) 2002

AUTHOR COMMENTARY

Janet S. Wong (essay date 1999)

SOURCE: Wong, Janet S. "Homepage," 1999, <http://www.janetwong.com/poems/index.cfm (15 February 2004).

[*In the following essay, Wong talks about how her early memories influence her poetry.*]

One of my strongest childhood memories takes me back to holiday dinners at my grandparents' house, where we would sit and drink tea, long after dinner was done, listening to my grandfather tell stories. GongGong loved to tell stories about his boyhood in China, about life on the farms in Northern California during the Depression years, about the escapades of his dog Susie. I grew up hearing these stories over and over, year after year—his and the stories of my grandmother and mother and father, too. Now, when I read the poems I wrote about these stories, I hear their voices again.

I like to sandwich my poems in story, to show how the poems come from my life. Hopefully, when you read my poems, you will be reminded of your own stories: how you baked cookies with your grandmother, your birthday parties, your old friends. So when you share my poems with children, you can sandwich them in your own stories, connect them to your own life, too.

Janet Wong, Junko Yokota, and Stephanie Sanderson (interview date January 2000)

SOURCE: Wong, Janet, Junko Yokota, and Stephanie Sanderson. "Talking with . . . Janet Wong." *Book Links* 9, no. 3 (January 2000): 57-61.

[*In the following interview, Wong discusses the meaning poetry has for her.*]

Janet Wong is the author of five books of poetry for young readers. When she visited schools, universities, and bookstores in the Chicago-area last-spring, Junko Yokota, an associate professor of reading and language arts, and Stephanie Sanderson, a middle-school language arts and humanities teacher, engaged in the following conversation with her, following a writer's workshop with Sanderson's middle-school students at Baker Demonstration School of National-Louis University.

[*Sanderson*]: *How did you decide to become a poet?*

[Wong]: Eight years ago I was a lawyer, the director of labor relations at Universal Studios Hollywood. One night I said to my husband, "Glenn, I think I'm becoming a mean person." I decided I wanted to do something good with my life—something of importance. And, decided, I can't think of anything more important than working with kids. So, I tried writing picture books for a year—really simple picture books for the very, very young. At the end of a year I decided I loved it, so I kept doing it.

[*Yokota*]: *Would you tell us what you remember from your childhood experiences that might have influenced your eventual path to writing poetry?*

When I was in fourth grade, I decided I hated poetry—that's true—and in no way was I ever going to write a book of poems! In fact, as a child, I never really enjoyed writing at all. I don't remember my creative writing exercises as being fun or interesting, although I'm sure many of them were. When I worked at my writing, it was because I knew I needed to get good grades to make my parents happy, but writing didn't bring me much joy. It was such work!

My attitude toward poetry didn't change until I was an adult. My accidental introduction to Myra Cohn Livingston led me to studying poetry. When I heard Myra speak, I was amazed by what she could do with just eight lines. She could make me blink back tears.

If Myra Cohn Livingston had taught a class in writing the novel, would I be writing novels today? I don't think so. I have a hard time sticking with novels, simply because they are so long. One reason I like to write poems is that I'm lazy. Poems are short and they're very manageable. I can write one quickly, get down what I need to say. Later I'll revise it, and I love to revise. Revision is a very easy thing to do with a poem, especially a short poem. You can tackle a revision in 10 or 20 minutes and put it aside. Two hours later, you can try another revision. I might do 50 versions of a poem in the course of a month's time—10 minutes here, 20 minutes there. That's part of the appeal of poetry to me. It's manageable. Broken up into small bits, it's never boring.

[Sanderson]: Many of my middle-school students are intimidated by reading longer texts.

Some reluctant readers have a hard time reading for various reasons. Perhaps they have short attention spans or their skills are not up to a certain level. But when they look at a poem of mine, a short poem, they see all that white space around it, and it's not intimidating. It doesn't scare them. They look at it and say, "That's only 10 lines. I can read that." One of the first compliments I got on ***Good Luck Gold*** was from a woman in the children's literature world who had bought the book for herself. She said her 13-year old granddaughter who hates to read took that book off the shelf and sat in her house and read it from start to finish in an hour and said, "Wow, Grandma, I just read this whole book!" And there was an enormous sense of accomplishment in reading something that wasn't a baby book. Here was a 13-year-old who hated to read, but she was able to do it; she was able to zip through it. This woman told me, "My granddaughter never finishes a book. This is amazing. I guess I'll just have to give her poetry."

[Yokota]: You mentioned that you "accidentally" fell into Myra Cohn Livingston's class. Tell us a little more about this important turning point in your writing career.

I was at a one-day seminar at UCLA Extension on everything you need to know to write and sell your children's book. Because I knew so little about the world of children's literature, I didn't think I needed to know how to write a children's book. I thought all I needed to know was how to sell a manuscript. It was there that I heard Myra speak for the first time. I had no idea who she was, but she stood up and recited poems by other people from memory with such elegance and clarity that I was impressed. I thought, "Wow! This woman really is smart!" And then she read her poem "There Was a Place," which is in the book by the same title. There's a part of that poem that goes something like this:

> There was a place we'd always walk
> Look at the sky, have a long talk
> Sit on a bench, drink a few Cokes
> Listen to Dad telling some jokes
> Now the sky's dark
> Can't see his face
> Can't hear the jokes
> There was a place.

That last stanza really knocked me over and it made me think of how my grandmother looked when she was in the hospital dying. It made me think of my father and the long trips he used to take. The sheer power of that poem made me think, "Wouldn't it be terrific to be able to write something so small that can affect you in such a great way?" Thank goodness I was at that seminar trying to learn how to sell a book.

[Yokota]: What are examples of personal experiences that you express through poetry?

In writing the poem **"Immigrant Boy,"** I started with the memory of being in college in a French class and having the teacher ask me to help this new Vietnamese girl who had come to the class late in the term. The teacher was constantly asking me to help Lan. Lan and I were not friends; we didn't even sit next to each other. I felt myself thinking, she's asking me to help this girl because we're the only two Asians in the class. I don't even know her. Why is she lumping us together? Lan's French was good enough—better than mine. She didn't need help. I didn't understand what the situation was, and I was very resentful. I treated Lan very poorly because of these feelings. When I sat down to write that poem, I wanted to write it from my own perspective. I wanted to say, "She and I are not the same. Look, I was born here, right?" But then I realized, in writing the poem, how incredibly obnoxious I had been. And it wasn't Lan's fault. I felt so guilty I decided to change the voice in that poem. I even changed the gender of the child. I wrote:

> He and I are not the same,
> Though we look alike to you.
> He was born here. I am new.
> just three months ago I came.
> I followed him around today.
> He does not like me to be near.
> I wonder-had I been born here,
> would he want me to play?

The process of writing that poem was a wonderful experience for me because it sensitized me to how awfully I had acted toward this girl. The immigrant child is saying, "We're not the same, so don't lump us together because he [the American-born child] doesn't even like me."

In my poem **"Speak Up,"** I created a conversation in which a person says to me, "You're Korean, aren't you?" and I say, "Yeah." I'm then asked, "Well, say something Korean." And I reply, "I don't speak it." (It's true—I can't speak Korean. I wish I could. I can't speak Korean except for little words and phrases that my mother taught me like "Come here," "Eat more.") I end that poem, "I was born here." So here we have this distancing of ourselves—that one Asian was born here, and is different from the Asian who has just come to America.

Yet in another poem about a year and a half later, **"Other,"** from ***A Suitcase of Seaweed,*** I'm breaking down that difference. I'm saying, "We're the only two Asians in the room and I notice her and I feel an affinity for her. I feel that we have something in common. Immediately we connect. It doesn't matter that I'm fat; it doesn't matter that she's thin and tall. We connect. I look at her and I see myself as if I'm looking in a mirror." Some people have asked me, "Isn't this inconsistent? How can you be upset that people are lumping you together when you lump yourself with others?" I think the difference is that in one case it's people—other people—looking at us and lumping us together and in the other instance I'm doing it myself. I'm recognizing it. Maybe that doesn't seem like a big difference but it's a question of self-definition versus being defined and limited by others.

[Sanderson]: You grew up in the midst of different cultures. Although you didn't speak Korean during your childhood, you've expressed that you wish you spoke more today. How did your family's cultural differences define your identity and the language that you used growing up?

I grew up speaking English because my mother spoke Korean and a little bit of English (but no Chinese), and my [Chinese American] father spoke English and a little bit of Chinese (but very little Korean). English was the common language. But also, I didn't really want to speak Chinese or Korean, because as a very young child I remember thinking, "I don't like it when people make fun of me for being Asian. Why would I want to be even more Asian?"

My parents didn't teach me Chinese or Korean because they felt that it was "the American way": being born in America, they wanted me to have all possible opportunities, and making me as "American" as I could be would give me more opportunities. The irony of it is that I'd have more opportunities today if I spoke those languages!

How has language defined who I am culturally? If I spoke Korean, undoubtedly I would be more Korean, because the Korean community in most parts of America is very tightly knit, and if you don't speak Korean, you don't fit in.

I remember going with my mother to Korean shops, both as a young child and as a teenager. When she spoke to the Korean shopkeepers, they responded to both of us. I would look at them blankly, and I could tell they were saying something like, "What's the matter with her? Doesn't she speak Korean?" And my mother would apologize profusely in Korean. "Oh, no, no, no. She doesn't speak." And I would hear her explain how I could speak French and German. They would look at me strangely, and I felt embarrassed for my mother. When I was in high school, I remember saying, "Maybe I should just not stand by you. Or, you could pretend that I'm deaf-mute or something." She didn't think that was very funny. I wish I had learned the language, now, because it would allow me to feel more completely linked with a whole other culture.

[Sanderson]: Would you respond to a few of my students' questions about your writing? They ask, "How do you get started, writing poetry, and once you get started, how do you do this figurative language stuff?"

I think you have to begin with reading. That's the way Myra taught me. She used to nag at me, "Read, read, read. You need to read more books." I would reply, "Yes, I'm reading. I'm reading a lot." And she would say, "You need to read even more." At one point, while I was studying with Myra, I would check out 40 books a week from the library and read them quickly, trying to digest as much as I could. I was reading to expose myself to what was out there, hoping to absorb some sense of how people put music in language. In the beginning, I focused on David McCord. I also read John Ciardi, Lilian Moore, Valerie Worth, Arnold Adoff.

[Yokota]: It seems like you're going right down the list of poets who have won the NCTE Excellence in Poetry Award.

By reading a ton of poems, I saw how people could write about the same thing in totally different ways. For example, I might be reading a Gary Soto poem, and, all of a sudden, I will think, "Well, when I do dishes, it's not quite that way. When I do dishes, we stand there afterward and we compare the lines in our hands. Our shriveled-up red hands." Reading a poem, someone else's poem, can take me back to one of my own experiences.

One thing I like to tell kids is—and I try to show this by example—the language doesn't need to be fancy. If I have a choice between a one-syllable word and a four-syllable word I'll often use the one-syllable word. Instead of saying bawl or whimper, I'll use cry. I like the language really plain.

When I do workshops in schools, I focus on metaphor and simile because I think that children are naturally good at writing them. It's something that a child in kindergarten can do and also something that is still interesting to a senior in high school. But I don't want them to come up with unnatural images. I want them to pluck images from their own world.

[Yokota]: Would you describe how you work with students in a writer's workshop?

I want them to work quickly, not to have time to worry about writing. After sharing examples of what I want them to do, I give them one minute to come up with a mental image and a second minute to draw the image. Drawing is a great prewriting tool, especially for reluctant writers. After they've had a chance to come up with an idea, some students will share their ideas. Then, it's time to write. I give students permission to copy other students' ideas, because of the time limits I put on them; besides, when two or more students write on the same idea, they'll almost always come up with totally different poems, and it's good for them to see this. We all write for five minutes. I write with them, so they can see me struggle, too. My teaching style is very direct and rather demanding. I truly expect that they'll come up with good first drafts—at least drafts that are better than they thought they'd be! And the students always come through.

[Sanderson]: What can we look forward to seeing in publication next?

Coming out in October 1999 is ***Behind the Wheel,*** a collection of poems about driving. The first poem in that book is called **"Ask a Friend."** It goes like this:

> You don't always need
> to go it alone.
> Ask a friend
> to give you a ride,
> to help you out,
> to get you home.
> When you've found some better times,
> you won't forget, you'll pay him back.
> Let your friends be good to you.
> Go along for the ride,
> face in the wind.

I like to think of myself as a very independent person. But one small way in which I think I'm finally growing as a person is that it has become easier for me to say, "I don't have to do everything in the world." I can let others help me, and then I can pay them back.

I'm hoping that students and teachers will realize that they don't have to "go it alone." Perhaps we can relate this concept to poetry and realize that we can use words to reach out to others.

Janet S. Wong and David Marc Fischer (essay date 8-22 April 2002)

SOURCE: Wong, Janet S., and David Marc Fischer. "Take a Ride with Janet Wong and Get on the Road to Poetry." *Scholastic Scope* 50, no. 15-16 (8-22 April 2002): 24-6.

[*In the following essay, Fischer interviews Wong about her views on poetry.*]

For many years, Janet S. Wong steered clear of poems. "I used to hate poetry, and now it's practically all I write," Wong tells *Scope.* "I think I hated poetry because I thought of it as difficult. I especially hated trying to 'find the meaning' in poems."

So what sparked Wong's drive to be a poet? One day, she heard a poem called "There Was a Place" by Myra Cohn Livingston. It almost made her cry. "Right then, I realized how simple yet powerful a poem can be," she says. The experience sent Wong on the road to writing four poetry books, including ***Behind the Wheel: Poems about Driving.***

"[P]oetry is perfect for me because I'm busy," Wong tells us. "Writing a poem can be fast work. I usually try to write a first draft in just five minutes. [I take] five minutes for a second draft, and five minutes for a third draft, and I've got something good."

Wong also loves the freedom of poetry writing. She rhymes only when she wants to. "Anything goes in poetry," she says. "There are rules, but you don't need to know them; even if you know them, you can break them."

At times, Wong's poetry even resembles real-life speech. "Some of my poems do sound like regular talk, and I tried hard to make them read that way," she says. This is especially true in poems about her Chinese grandfather, she says. "I wanted to capture 'his voice,' his own way of talking. I think of those poems as 'word photographs'—words that capture a particular moment."

Wong gets most of her ideas from life experiences, such as "childhood memories, or a story a friend told me, or what I ate for breakfast," she says. But she doesn't let real-life facts get in the way of her freedom.

"I usually like to change some facts, to make the writing even more fun. That's the great thing about writing. You can take the worst thing that happened to you last week, and change the ending."

Kathleen Odean (essay date July-August 2003)

SOURCE: Odean, Kathleen. "Unanimous Verdict." *Book* (July-August 2003): 31.

[*In the following essay, Wong comments on her change of career from lawyer to poet.*]

Janet S. Wong, who left a four-year law career to write kids' books, does have a regret: "I miss my expense account," she quips. The author of thirteen books, including the new ***Minn and Jake,*** Wong practiced just long enough to pay off her student loans before taking time off to write, with the encouragement of her attorney husband. A year and a half later, she had a book accepted. "Twenty-five rejection letters later, I finally clicked," says Wong, who is forty. "And now I'm paid to daydream and write." Is she happier as a writer? "As a lawyer, I felt like I was becoming a mean person," she says. "I wanted to do something important with my life, and I can't think of anything more important than writing books for kids." Case closed.

TITLE COMMENTARY

GOOD LUCK GOLD AND OTHER POEMS (1994)

Hazel Rochman (essay date 15 November 1994)

SOURCE: Rochman, Hazel. *Booklist* 91, no. 6 (15 November 1994): 600.

Fresh, honest, and not at all reverential, these poems [***Good Luck Gold and Other Poems***] are simple dramatic monologues about growing up Asian American. The lines are short and very easy to read; the voices are strongly personal. The ethnicity is strongly individualized, but whether the subject is food, family, or immigration, Wong moves beyond stereotype. This Asian isn't quiet and good at math ("Me. I like to shout"). The pain of being an outsider and the sting of bigotry are both individual and universal ("Ching chong Chinaman / Those kids over there / are laughing at me"). In a scene in a railroad cafe, where no one will serve a Chinese child and her father, she pulls him by the hand to get out of there. "We're not equal. We're better," she says.

Barbara Chatton (essay date January 1995)

SOURCE: Chatton, Barbara. *School Library Journal* 41, no. 1 (January 1995): 133.

Most of the 42 poems in this collection [***Good Luck Gold and Other Poems***] give readers insight into the experiences of Chinese-American children. Starting with the **"Good Luck Gold"** of charms on a bracelet, they explore feelings about food, language, shopping, the importance of grandparents, and holidays. A number of the selections reflect on serious themes such as racism, the death of loved ones, divorce, and illness, all of which represent universal experiences. A variety of poetic forms are used, including rhymed poetry and free verse, a vivid haiku about a family eating with chopsticks, a dialogue between a Korean-American and another child about being American, and a question-and-answer poem in which a grandmother talks about why she wears jade. Children who live in cities with Chinese-American populations will recognize some of the images described—the ducks hanging in grocery-store windows, dim sum stands, parades with firecrackers and dragons. For others, these pieces provide an introduction to the sights and sounds of Chinese-American neighborhoods.

Sylvia M. Vardell, Nancy L. Hadaway, and Terrell A. Young (essay date April-May 2002)

SOURCE: Vardell, Sylvia M., Nancy L. Hadaway, and Terrell A. Young. *Book Links* 11, no. 5 (April-May 2002): 53.

Wong takes the experiences that came with growing up Korean, Chinese, and American and fuses them in her poetry for children [***Good Luck Gold and Other Poems***]. She captures moments with her Asian grandfather or with English-speaking classmates with powerful feeling and simple language, such as in the poem **"Speak Up."**

A SUITCASE OF SEAWEED AND OTHER POEMS (1996)

Hazel Rochman (essay date 1 April 1996)

SOURCE: Rochman, Hazel. *Booklist* 92, no. 15 (1 April 1996): 1362.

As she did in **Good Luck Gold** (1994), Wong writes in simple, casual free verse about herself [***A Suitcase of Seaweed and Other Poems***]. This time she has divided the small collection into three parts: Korean, Chinese, and American poems. At the start of each section is a page of autobiography as interesting as the poems. Her Korean mother met and married Wong's father when he was in Korea with the U.S. Army. He is Chinese but came to this country when he was 12. Wong was born here. Some of the poems are flat, but the best of them show a mix of feelings. Koreatown is growing, spreading—and "splitting."

Korean women, furious with their families, come to the beauty salon to change their "stubborn, straight, heavy hair" and get themselves a perm. The poems overlap their ethnicity and subject, of course, and young people will recognize many of the situations, whether Wong is imagining her parents' **"Love at First Sight"** or chafing at their high expectations and their disappointment.

Nancy Vasilakis (essay date July-August 1996)

SOURCE: Vasilakis, Nancy. *Horn Book Magazine* 72, no. 4 (July-August 1996): 475-476.

Wong's mother is Korean, her father is Chinese, and she herself has grown up in this country, as she explains in the brief biographical essays that preface this collection's [***A Suitcase of Seaweed and Other Poems***] three sections: "Korean Poems," "Chinese Poems," and "American Poems." The quiet, lyric poems acknowledge proudly, subtly, and with occasional touches of irony and humor the distinct strands within the weave of cultures of which she is a part. Her mother is the commanding figure of the Korean poems, first introduced as a laughing village girl meeting the man she will marry, then shown praying, styling hair, and toasting marshmallows—or perhaps grasshoppers!—around a campfire. In the other two sections the author reveals more of her inner self at epiphanous moments: while pouring tea for her grandfather "like an offering to the gods," for example, or upon recognizing another Asian face in a room full of strangers. A few of the poems are set in rhymes, but the best of them are written in free verse that is wistful, revealing, and direct: "Our family / is a quilt / of odd remnants / patched together / in a strange / pattern, / threads fraying, / fabric wearing thin—/ but made to keep / its warmth / even in bitter / cold."

Sharon Korbeck (essay September 1996)

SOURCE: Korbeck, Sharon. *School Library Journal* 42, no. 9 (September 1996): 237.

Wong was born in America of Chinese and Korean heritage, but the basic subjects she addresses [***A Suitcase of Seaweed and Other Poems***] in neat stanzas of free verse aim at the heart of any family, any race. The quiet, touching poems are divided into three sections, each honoring another part of her ethnicity. The Korean section deals with such diverse topics as hospitality, acupuncture, or the spicy *kimchi* that was a frequent dinner food. The author learned about Chinese culture from her father's parents, whose presence plays a large role in these poems of family. As an American, Wong writes poems of realization and identity. Whether the words are about customs or careers, they provide a sense of who the author has become because of her pride in her bloodlines. People may ask Asian-Americans "Where are you from?" This collection, appropriate for YAs of any culture, may make this question less relevant and important as they realize the commonalties among cultures.

BEHIND THE WHEEL: POEMS ABOUT DRIVING (1999)

Roger Sutton (essay date November 1999)

SOURCE: Sutton, Roger. *Horn Book Magazine* 75, no. 6 (November 1999): 755.

It's difficult to believe that the theme of driving offers much range for a single-author poetry collection, particularly when, as here [***Behind the Wheel: Poems about Driving***], the mood is predominately reflective and the flashes of humor, gentle. But despite the occasional patch of fog, the mostly free verse is conversational and unfussy, as when the poet compares herself to her trusty Honda: "You don't have to pamper me. / Don't have to worry / someone will steal me away." The timeworn idea that "driving is like life" is simply a given here, and Wong relies on telling particulars rather than heavy universals, as in a poem about family: "Sometimes you wonder if they care. / But when you mess up—WOOMPH!— / they're there, like air bags, / in your face." Several of the poems feature the poet's grandmother; one of the best in the collection, **"Neighbors,"** compares the tight-knit quality of Grandmother's village to the isolation of the speaker's contemporary suburb, where "the good quiet neighbors . . . follow us home/down our hill. / Their headlights/throw shadows, / our big empty heads / bobbing on the dash."

Sharon Korbeck (essay date December 1999)

SOURCE: Korbeck, Sharon. *School Library Journal* 45, no. 12 (December 1999): 162.

Wong presents driving as a metaphor for life [***Behind the Wheel: Poems about Driving***]. She makes the rather obvious analogy in the poem **"Behind the**

Wheel": "Everything you need to know / you learn right here / behind the wheel. / Watch out for the other guy. / Keep your eye on your rear. / Thank the old lady who lets you in. / Don't steal someone else's spot. / When you rush to park and end up hopeless, crooked— / just start over." Many of the poems are simply memories of driving-related events, e.g., taking grandma to the store, a first hitchhiking attempt, and dreaming of luxury cars at the auto show. These glimpses are a bit distant, not really enticing readers to slip inside the memories. The metaphors continue throughout the book, often becoming tiresome. In **"Restraint,"** parents are compared first to seat belts, and then to airbags: ". . . when you mess up— WOOOMPH!— / they're there, like air bags,/in your face." There is the obligatory, somewhat preachy poem about drunk driving, a little too light to have much impact. Not entirely convincing, these poems don't succeed as extended views of life.

Gillian Engberg (essay date 1 January 2000)

SOURCE: Engberg, Gillian. *Booklist* (1 January 2000): 913.

"Forget kindergarten, / sharing. / Everything you need to know / you learn right here / behind the wheel." As in her previous poetry collections, Wong uses simple, personal free verse to explore the spaces between family and self, this time through distilled moments in the car and on the road [***Behind the Wheel: Poems about Driving***]. In one poem, a grandchild connects a car crash with the financial crash that took her grandmother's savings; in another, a daughter criticizes her father for picking up a hitchhiker and, in her sullenness, realizes she looks "not at all like my father's daughter" The poems are mostly intimate, first-person monologues, but there are some narrated vignettes and very funny radical suggestions for reshaping the rules of the road (in **"Insurance for Teenage Drivers: A New Plan,"** the speaker suggests that, as punishment for violations, young offenders should: "Direct traffic, / head shaved bald . . . flanked by parents / dressed in pajamas"). Wong's brief, clear lines will be accessible even to the most reluctant poetry readers, and readers of all ages will be moved by the intersection of poignancy and humor as she describes the thrilling freedom of the car and an emerging adult's awareness that, although she's traveled, her road still leads to home.

🕮 *THE RAINBOW HAND: POEMS ABOUT MOTHERS AND CHILDREN* (1999)

Sharon Korbeck (essay date April 1999)

SOURCE: Korbeck, Sharon. *School Library Journal* 45, no. 4 (April 1999): 128.

Like the presence of a mother's hand, Wong's thoughtful and reflective volume [***The Rainbow Hand: Poems about Mothers and Children***] is comforting and easily accessible. The poems are solid and steady reminders of the connections between mothers and children. In the brief lines, which are boldly paired with [Jennifer] Hewitson's striking and colorful scratchboard illustrations, children see only glimpses of life, but meaningful ones. A daughter notices, and loves, her mother's white hairs that ". . . grow back like daisies / poking through dark mulch." A mother cradles her child with ". . . her fingers curved / like a rainbow." In **"Mother's Day"** a boy gives his mother a hastily wrapped rock as a gift, and the caring woman immediately finds a purpose for it. Upon hearing her mother say, "When I was ten . . . ," a girl wonders, "When she was ten, could she have been / such an amazing freak?" Universal love, discipline, strength, and emotion are all in evidence here.

GraceAnne A. DeCandido (essay date 1 April 1999)

SOURCE: DeCandido, GraceAnne A. *Booklist* 95, no. 15 (1 April 1999): 1412.

These 18 short poems [***The Rainbow Hand: Poems about Mothers and Children***] are limpid reflections on mother and child, some from the mother's point of view, some from the child's. All of them hold a kernel of truth that readers of all ages will recognize. A child walking **"In Mother's Shadow"** delights that she stops to rest "the very moment / my shoes grow / heavy." In another, a child compares plucking her mother's white hairs at her mother's request to plucking daisies. A tiny poem compares mother to an onion: golden good for you, sometimes surprising in sweetness, or making you cry. A mother breathing slowly in sync with her infant or shielding her baby's eyes with "fingers curved / like a rainbow" are poems lovely in their simplicity. Jennifer Hewitson's illustrations are both sweet and powerful-strong scratchboard lines with pastel washes that make arresting images. The mother and child in **"Smother Love"** are a sculptural single shape; in the **"Rain-**

bow Hand" image, the lines of the mother's and baby's faces and the curves of the mother's hands echo the rhythm of the poem. Children from tots to teens, and beyond, will find their own tangled feelings here.

Publishers Weekly (review date 3 May 1999)

SOURCE: *Publishers Weekly* 246, no. 18 (3 May 1999): 78.

Janet S. Wong draws from her experiences as both child and mother in ***The Rainbow Hand: Poems about Mothers and Children,*** illus. by Jennifer Hewitson with boldly graphic color scratchboard renderings. Whether or not the poems allude to her Chinese- and Korean-American heritage, their focus on the ambivalence and tension found in the most fiercely loving relationships extend the perspective to the universal.

Horn Book Guide (review date fall 1999)

SOURCE: *Horn Book Guide* 10, no. 2 (fall 1999): 376.

Eighteen free verse poems about mothers and the experience of motherhood [***The Rainbow Hand: Poems about Mothers and Children***] are told from the perspectives of both parent and child. The author's mother inspired the poems, but they transcend any particular relationship to become an honest portrayal of mother/child universalities. Stylized scratchboard and watercolor illustrations complement the poems.

🕮 *BUZZ* (2000)

Carol Ann Wilson (essay date May 2000)

SOURCE: Wilson, Carol Ann. *School Library Journal* 46, no. 5 (May 2000): 158-59.

Buzz is the sound of a bee outside a little boy's window as he awakens one morning. It's also the sound of his parents alarm clock, his father's shaver, the blender whirring his banana shake, and myriad other activities that culminate in the doorbell's "Buzz" that announces his Grandma's arrival and Mommy's swift departure "so she can fly BUZZ outside like a busy bee." From the black-and-gold striped endpapers to the bold typeface of the oft-repeated sound, and right down to the mother's bee-striped socks, the concept underlying this book will be apparent to even the youngest listeners. The comfort that is derived from the familiar and routine is reflected in the retro-looking illustrations (created with a variety of printmaking techniques) that have the flat, bold quality of graphic art. While the text is simple and straightforward, it drives the story along and occasionally offers moments of whimsy and lyricism. The lifestyle portrayed here is decidedly middle class, with its coffee grinders, gardeners, and automatic garage doors, but this child savors the morning's events in a way that is universally appealing. Storytime audiences will "buzz" right on cue with this charming vignette of one family's bustling a.m. schedule.

Horn Book Magazine (review date May-June 2000)

SOURCE: *Horn Book Magazine* 76, no. 3 (May-June 2000): 304-05.

Not every writer can make a smooth transition from one genre to another, especially when there's a vast difference in intended audience, but here [***Buzz***] an established poet for young adults proves that she is more than able to do so with her first picture book for preschoolers. Wong's poetic vision serves her well in this story of early-morning family rituals written from the point of view of a young child. Everyone, it seems, is in a hurry to get somewhere—all except the narrator, who opens the story by leisurely observing a bumblebee buzzing around the garden outside his bedroom window. Next it's his parents' alarm clock buzzing, then his father's razor buzzing, and then the kitchen blender buzzing as he and his mother make a banana shake for breakfast. The boy gets into the spirit of things by buzzing his toy airplane around the breakfast table. Wong has selected just the right onomatopoeic word to reflect the mechanics of a busy morning. She artfully brings the conclusion back to the original image of the bumblebee when the mother rushes out for work "like a busy bee"—in black-and-yellow-striped socks. Beginning with a window-screen background on the book jacket and black-and-yellow-striped endpapers, Chodos-Irvine effectively uses pattern and color in a flattened perspective to balance the sounds and sights of the child's morning. While her bold style suggests picture books of an earlier era, it works remarkably well for this obviously modern family that includes an Asian mother and a white father living life in the fast lane.

Publishers Weekly (review date 5 June 2000)

SOURCE: *Publishers Weekly* 247, no. 23 (5 June 2000): 92.

Wong turns from the nearly surreal, hypnotic world of ***Night Garden*** to this wide-eyed, cheerful tale [***Buzz***] offering a boy's view of a busy weekday morning. From the opening spreads, an industrious bee acts as the guiding spirit and its buzz as the leitmotif: the boy translates its hum to the "BUZZZbuzzzBUZZZbuzz" of his parents' snores, an alarm clock, a coffee grinder, a doorbell and his toy airplane's ill-fated flight over the breakfast table; bold type emphasizes the onomatopoeia. It's a hectic household, but Wong's story emphasizes the boy's reassuring routine in her insistent staccato prose: "BUZZZ I run to the front door when Grandma comes and I kiss Grandma hello and I kiss Mommy goodbye so she can fly BUZZ outside like a busy bee." In her first children's book, [Margaret] Chodos-Irvine combines the appealing blocky shapes of cut-paper collage with the delicacy of woodcuts on backgrounds such as the parents' clothing and the wallpaper. She knowingly shows a boy managing his world, whether it is in the image of his small body's outsize shadow filling the door of his parents' bedroom as he shouts "Wake up!" or the boy aping his father as he shaves (using a toy car as his razor). This joyful book will strike a resonant chord—especially for the many children with two working parents.

Kathy Broderick (review date July 2000)

SOURCE: Broderick, Kathy. *Booklist* 96, no. 21 (July 2000): 2044-045.

A young child relates [***Buzz***] the simple morning events that happen in his house, all of which seem to make a buzz. There's the bee outside, the alarm clock. Daddy's electric razor, the neighbor's lawn mower, the blender, the garage door, the coffee grinder, the clothes dryer, Mommy's blow dryer, and finally the doorbell. Then Mom flies out the door, buzzing like a busy bee. [Margaret] Chodos-Irvine uses various print-making techniques, including one that produces a collage effect, to make her fine, rerro-looking illustrations come alive. The writing flows, the pages turn naturally and easily in a good rhythm, and there is great movement on each double-page spread. Beginning and ending the book with a bee is a nice touch. A great sensory experience for very young children.

Janice M. Del Negro (review date July-August 2000)

SOURCE: Del Negro, Janice M. *Bulletin of the Center for Children's Books* 53, no. 11 (July-August 2000): 420.

A little boy comments on the busy morning [***Buzz***] minutes when he and his parents are getting ready for their day. The boy is the first one awake, and he notes that outside his window "a bee eats breakfast in a big red flower," while his parents' alarm clock ("BUZZZbuzzzBUZZZbuzzz Mommy and Daddy snore") announces that it's morning. From the buzzing of "Daddy's silver razor" to the buzzing of the gardener, who "mows grass across the street," to the buzz of the blender as it whips up a banana shake, the little boy contentedly organizes his day around familiar morning sounds. The end circles back to the beginning as the boy kisses Grandma hello and Mommy goodbye "so she can fly BUZZ outside like a busy bee." [Margaret] Chodos-Irvine's use of various print-making techniques results in illustrations that are strongly geometric and graphically clean, in springtime colors that suit the cheerful tone of the text. The humor in both text and pictures contributes to the light-hearted atmosphere, and the gentle predictability of the chronology of events is reassuring. Participatory buzzing is optional.

🕮 *NIGHT GARDEN: POEMS FROM THE WORLD OF DREAMS* (2000)

***Kirkus Reviews* (review date 15 December 1999)**

SOURCE: *Kirkus Reviews* 67, no. 24 (15 December 1999): 1966.

From Wong (***The Rainbow Hand***), a collection of 15 soulful poems [***Night Garden: Poems from the World of Dreams***] that commands attention and keeps until the end, with a canny, singular take on the familiar imagery of dreamtime.

These are episodes of remembrance and genesis, falling and flying, of speaking an unknown language with facility, of the bite of an inexorable nightmare. Short and vivid, the poems urge readers to "pull / at the air around you / when you wake, / pull and gulp it down" to keep alive the presence of the departed who have just visited the dreamer. Wong can be skip-quick to suggest evanescence, or her words can flutter with fear; she can be exquisitely funny, as when a sibling eavesdrops on a sister who is talking and laughing in her sleep—about the eavesdropper. [Julie] Paschkis is equal to the task of illustrating these poems, with two-page spreads presented as mirror-image two-toned diptychs, bursting with glyphs and portents across dream-crazed backgrounds, with the text scrolling across one page and the full-color image undulating from the other.

GraceAnne A. DeCandido (review date 1-15 January 2000)

SOURCE: DeCandido, GraceAnne A. *Booklist* 96, no. 9-10 (1-15 January 2000): 920.

This collection of 15 poems [***Night Garden: Poems from the World of Dreams***] takes on the distorted and sometimes dark world of dreams. Wong, an accomplished and versatile poet, finds dream images that children will know: dreaming about flight (**"Flying"**) or being afraid of things on TV (**"Nightmare"**), Sometimes, friends who have almost been forgotten appear (**"Old Friend"**). The illustrations are magnificent: gouaches that are equal parts William Morris pattern and Magritte/Bosch surrealism. Each poem faces an illustration by Julie Paschkis on the opposite page; both poem and picture are placed on a double-page spread of wild pattern echoing the images of the poem.

Barbara Chatton (review date March 2000)

SOURCE: Chatton, Barbara. *School Library Journal* 46, no. 3 (March 2000): 232.

In the title poem [***Night Garden: Poems from the World of Dreams***], Wong compares the bed in which dreams happen with the tangled roots and blooms of a garden bed. The 14 poems that follow are about the people who appear in dreams, eating, swimming, flying, running, and falling. The poems use sound qualities—repetition, alliteration, and occasional rhyme—to capture each dream. Even poems about nightmares and anxieties are couched in gentle language that evokes wonder and thoughtfulness rather than fear. Paschkis's paintings highlight the gardening metaphor. The selections are set against background frames of earth-toned colors, filled with animals, humans, and plants reminiscent of the organic creatures of Hieronymus Bosch. The frames are symmetrically balanced to enclose a small painting on the left-hand page and a similarly shaped space for the poem on the right. Pictures of children of many cultural backgrounds add to the universal quality of the book, as does the last poem, **"There Is a Place,"** which suggests that a storyteller lies inside each of us and comes out as we sleep. Children will enjoy capturing their own dreams and giving them shape and meaning after they have experienced these poems. This is a particularly fine collection for libraries in which young writers and painters are encouraged.

Publishers Weekly (review date 13 March 2000)

SOURCE: *Publishers Weekly* 247, no. 11 (13 March 2000): 84.

In this absorbing volume [***Night Garden: Poems from the World of Dreams***], Wong (***A Suitcase of Seaweed and Other Poems***) and [Julie] Paschkis (*Play All Day*) examine the familiar yet surprising qualities of dreams. The poems recall a weightless feeling of flying, an anxious sense of being late or an unexpected visit from a dead or living acquaintance ("I had forgotten you, friend. / Is that why you came / into my dream?"). **"Gently Down the Stream"** alludes to the phrase "life is but a dream" and describes swimming in clear water; the accompanying illustration pictures a sinuous orange-and-turquoise fish with a peaceful human face. Wong seldom abides scary dreams, but she does include "a news-at-seven true nightmare," which Paschkis supplements with beastly imagery of snakes and howling sleepers. Paschkis's gouaches at times suggest an illuminated manuscript, elements from medieval tapestries or elaborate Arts and Crafts-era wallpaper. The artist responds to each poem with a multicolor image framed within a monochromatic, repetitive motif. She creates a host of weird creatures, from a hunched man in a long-nosed white mask to a turnip-headed being with pea-pod arms; to indicate the mysterious workings of the imagination, she shows strange flowers sprouting from a restful figure. Paschkis's swirling imagery and Wong's quiet yet haunting words skillfully simulate the reveries they recount.

Cyndi Giorgis and Nancy J. Johnson (review date March 2001)

SOURCE: Giorgis, Cyndi, and Nancy J. Johnson. *The Reading Teacher* 54, no. 6 (March 2001): 633-34.

Janet Wong's mode of expression is enchanting poetry. ***Night Garden: Poems from the World of Dreams*** takes readers from the depths of the earth with dreams waiting to bloom, to the heights of soaring birds flying free. It tells tales of fears in the night that are offset by dreams of "soft and fuzzy things." The 14 poems are illustrated by Julie Paschkis, who brings a mystical quality to the verse with her surreal characters and monochromatic, repetitive motif found on each double-page spread. The dream poems illustrate the power of imagination—even when asleep.

Kathleen Armstrong, Mingshui Cai, Cyndi Giorgis, and Kathryn Mitchell Pierce (review date March 2002)

SOURCE: Armstrong, Kathleen, Minshui Cai, Cyndi Giorgis, and Kathryn Mitchell Pierce. *Language Arts* 79, no. 4 (March 2002): 352.

Dreams sprout and grow wild like dandelion weeds in the night garden of a girl's mind [***Night Garden: Poems from the World of Dreams***]. In her blooming dreams she sees the face she wears inside, savors her favorite turnip cake, swims gently down a stream like a fish, or runs away from scary scenes on TV. Her subconscious is like a museum housing thousands of paintings "seen nowhere else in the world" or a library "filled with brand new books" to tell stories only she could know. With phantasmagorical images and freely flowing rhythms, this night garden of dreamy poetry invites readers to take a walk through intricate paths and be mesmerized by its visions. The surrealistic touches of gouache illustrations create a mysterious ambient and add another fascinating dimension.

THE TRIP BACK HOME (2000)

Ellen Mandel (essay date 15 November 2000)

SOURCE: Mandel, Ellen. *Booklist* 97, no. 6 (15 November 2000): 651.

Recalling her childhood trip to rural Korea with her mother to visit her grandparents and aunt, [***The Trip Back Home***] Wong measures her words to reflect the simple pleasures of the reunion. The pages reveal the farmers' way of life: Grandfather makes the charcoal that heats the house through tunnels under the floor; Grandmother markets in outdoor stalls and cooks in a stove lit with pine branches. The foods and their preparation, including persimmons stored on the roof, are described, as are the leisure-time activities—telling stories, playing cards, reading. There's no hustling to tourist attractions, just time together, paced to the daily rhythms of the family from whom the author has been separated. The gifts given on leave-taking are all the more meaningful for the memories they trigger of the cherished visit—a charcoal drawing of the neighboring hills, a necklace of dried persimmons, and an original poem written in Korean. This tender story of family love is expressively pictured in bright watercolors: jewel-tone clothing, colorful vegetables, and homey objects sparkle against the grays of the hills and the browns of the fields and the house. Bridging cultural and generational gaps, this beautiful, lyrically written picture book has much to say to children, no matter their nationality.

Wendy Lukehart (review date December 2000)

SOURCE: Lukehart, Wendy. *School Library Journal* 46, no. 12 (December 2000): 128.

A gentle celebration of family bonds [***The Trip Back Home***]. Drawing on her own visit to her mother's homeland, Wong relates the excursion of a young American girl and her parent to stay with relatives in Korea. The travelers first carefully select gifts for their hosts: leather work gloves for grandfather, a pretty apron for grandmother, and an alphabet book for the child's aunt. In return, "they gave us hugs." The child participates in daily routines such as heating the house with charcoal placed in a floor tunnel, feeding the pigs, going to the outdoor market and playing cards-all in a warm, familial setting. Author and illustrator harmonize well, painting the patterns and flavors of rural life [Bo]. Jia's brown-and-gray watercolor backgrounds are punctuated by spots of bright color in the clothing, rows of vegetables, and in a few special treasures. In a bittersweet, circular closing, gifts are given to the travelers, and "we gave them hugs."

Judy O'Malley (review date December 2000-January 2001)

SOURCE: O'Malley, Judy. *Book Links* 10, no. 3 (December 2000-January 2001): 24.

Poetic text [***The Trip Back Home***] describes a young girl's journey with her mother to Korea, where her mother was born and raised. The pair's greeting by the family, and the day-to-day rhythms of life in a rural village, to which the young girl quickly becomes acclimated, offer many details about the culture, but the information is intrinsic to the family story, never seeming tacked on or intrusive. The art and text also weave together seamlessly, sharing a gentle, soft focus.

Horn Book Guide (review date spring 2001)

SOURCE: *Horn Book Guide* 12, no. 1 (spring 2001): 54.

Simple and poetic, this [***The Trip Back Home***] unadorned story of a young girl's trip to Korea to visit her relatives has an appealing circular structure in which gifts and hugs are exchanged at the beginning and end of the visit. The rural household is very traditional, with no hint of contemporary life. Based on Wong's own experience, the themes of family love and nonverbal communication are lovingly portrayed in the text and the quiet watercolors.

GRUMP (2001)

Kirkus Reviews (review date 1 January 2001)

SOURCE: *Kirkus Reviews* 69, no. 1 (1 January 2001): 60.

A weary mom and her tireless tot are the subject of Wong's (***This Next New Year,*** 2000) humorous and poignant tale [***Grump***]. The scenario is familiar: a mom, tired and slightly crabby, eagerly awaits baby's naptime. However, her energetic infant has other ideas. Lunch becomes a science experiment as baby mixes this and that, eventually deciding to wear the concoction rather than eat it. After an exasperated Mom cleans up, she marches baby upstairs for a nap. Naturally, just as mother reaches the nursery door, baby awakens. The conclusion is predictable—at least for sleep-deprived parents—and the mother falls asleep reading baby a story while baby remains cheerfully awake . . . until snuggling up on her lap for a comfy snooze. Wong hits upon a universal truth of motherhood: as mom's energy wanes, baby's waxes accordingly. Her short, gently repetitive verses neatly capture the swinging moods between infant and parent. Although young children are unlikely to catch the wry humor, beleaguered mommies may appreciate the jests. Wong's imagery has high giggle appeal for gleeful tots, making the poetry accessible for the littlest listener: "Mommy's stomping / Jumping, chomping / Long arms dragging like a chimp." Wallace's watercolors adroitly capture the nuances of the story, depicting both the increasingly frenzied dismay of mom as well as the sweeter, more sentimental moments. An enjoyable romp for little ones and a compassionate reassurance for their exhausted parents.

Diane Roback, Jennifer M. Brown, and Jason Britton (review date 1 January 2001)

SOURCE: Roback, Diane, Jennifer M. Brown, and Jason Britton. *Publishers Weekly* 248, no. 1 (1 January 2001): 91.

Mommy has reached the end of her rope [***Grump***]. She's "tired and frumpy / Grouchy chumpy / Oh, what a grump!" But Baby, of course, is just getting started, happily "making gravy / Applesauce and ketchup gravy" and dumping it on his head and the floor. Exhausted Mommy declares naptime—but Baby won't cooperate, at least not until Mommy herself drops off to sleep while reading Baby a book. This slice-of-life book should strike a chord with frazzled mothers of toddlers, especially the implacable expression of [John] Wallace's (*Tiny Rabbit*) Baby and Wong's (***Night Garden***) repetition of the line "Baby's going to take a nap now" three times in a row, as if saying it would only make it so. Toddlers may be too wrapped up in themselves to be charmed by the parental sense of irony that informs the book, but Wallace's delicate watercolor vignettes with their sunny translucency keep the mood upbeat.

Elaine A. Bearden (review date February 2001)

SOURCE: Bearden, Elaine A. *Bulletin of the Center for Children's Books* 54, no. 6 (February 2001): 241-42.

Wong focuses on a mother's long day [***Grump***]: "Look how tired this Mommy is / Tired and frumpy / Grouchy chumpy / Oh, what a grump!" "Smart, good Baby" may be happy, but he makes messes with abandon and then refuses to go to sleep: "Baby's eyes are getting heavy / Heavy sleepy baby eyes / Mommy starts to tiptoes out— / And oh of course that baby cries . . . *Play with me*!" Wong's minimal text (in tasteful baby blue) neatly accents [John] Wallace's sparse line and watercolor illustrations, both floating on a sea of white space in an attractive layout. Unfortunately, the expressions often don't synchronize with the text, and there's frequent visual repetition, dulling the impact of the art. Families will be familiar with this scenario, but since Wong writes for knowing adults, it is doubtful most toddlers will last past the first pages.

Hazel Rochman (review date 15 February 2001)

SOURCE: Rochman, Hazel. *Booklist* 97, no. 12 (15 February 2001): 1142.

New mothers will appreciate this [***Grump***] as much as their babies. Wong's very simple bouncing rhyme starts off far from the usual soothing lullaby. This mom is frazzled, "Tired and frumpy / Grouchy chumpy." Wallace's clear watercolor scenarios with lots of white space show Baby dumping his applesauce and gravy and making the mess that sees Mommy stomping, jumping, chomping as she cleans up all day. Then it's naptime and loving Mom reads to her baby, but it's not Baby who falls asleep. Both the situation and the words with their rhythmic bumps and gentle grumps are just right for lapsit sharing.

Joy Fleishhacker (review date March 2001)

SOURCE: Fleishhacker, Joy. *School Library Journal* 47, no. 3 (March 2001): 224.

A poetic yet accessible text [***Grump***] blends with appealing watercolor paintings to tell the tale of a bright-eyed baby and his exhausted parent. Poor Mommy is "Tired and frumpy / Grouchy chumpy / Oh, what a grump!" Baby, however, is busy "Making gravy / Applesauce and ketchup gravy" and then dumping it over his head. As his disgruntled mother scrubs the floor on hands and knees ("Sponging all the spots away / Wash and wash and wash / All day"), the child rides on her back and smiles. Finally, it's time for Baby's nap, but just as the mother is about to tiptoe out of the room, he starts to cry. The two sit together in a chair to share some stories, and before long, Mom is fast asleep. Quietly, the youngster settles more comfortably in her lap and closes his eyes. Filled with rhythm, repetition, and simple word-play, Wong's language is inviting and fun to read aloud. The illustrations consist of a series of vignettes that depict the interaction between mother and son set against plain white backgrounds. The bright colors and clean lines will capture the attention of young listeners.

Horn Book Guide (review date fall 2001)

SOURCE: *Horn Book Guide* 12, no. 2 (fall 2001): 244.

Tired and slightly grumpy Mommy tries to put her baby down for a nap and soon is asleep herself [***Grump***]. The rhythmic, alliterative text tells the gentle tale in a way that will captivate even a wide-awake toddler. Soft ink and wash illustrations capture Mommy's harried state and the sleepy bliss that she and her baby finally find together.

THIS NEXT NEW YEAR (2001)

Elizabeth Bush (review date September 2000)

SOURCE: Bush, Elizabeth. *Bulletin of the Center for Children's Books* 54, no. 1 (September 2000): 42.

A young boy catalogs his preparations for Chinese New Year [***This Next New Year***], a holiday that his family enthusiastically celebrates even though, as he explains, he is "half Korean." While his friend Glenn (French and German) marks the day with Thai food, and Evelyn (Hopi and Mexican) looks forward to "red envelopes stuffed with money from her neighbor who came from Singapore," the narrator focuses on all the rituals that will ensure good fortune in the coming year. He observes that his palms are itching (a sure sign that money's coming), helps his mother scrub the house "rough and raw so it can soak up good luck like an empty sponge," and even cleans the dirt out "from the corners of my big toenails so the luck can squeeze itself in here." Unfortunately, Choi's paintings aren't quite up to the standard set by the ebullient text; figures are stiff and doll-like, and her overuse of shortened foreground makes the scenes repetitively flat. Nonetheless, the narrator's joyous obsessions offer a delightful contrast to more staid primary-grade explanations of Chinese New Year, and listeners will chuckle at his ambitious list of good intentions that, like their own, is unlikely to last until the next new moon.

Kirkus Reviews (review date 1 September 2000)

SOURCE: *Kirkus Reviews* 68, no. 17 (1 September 2000): 1294.

The lunar new year doesn't begin on the first of January; it begins on the day of the first new moon [***This Next New Year***]. This celebration is commonly called the Chinese New Year but it is one celebrated by many cultures. A young boy (who is "half Korean") explains in a simple way his own family's traditions, which include a big bowl of duk gook, the Korean new-year soup, and then he tells about his friends. There's Glenn, "who is French and German" and "who celebrates . . . by eating Thai food to go." His other best friend Evelyn, "part Hopi and part Mexican," receives red envelopes "stuffed with money from her neighbor who came from Singapore." Going through his preparations, he literally cleans up the house, his clothes, and his own body, getting rid of all the bad luck to make room for the good. Wong's (***Night Garden,*** 1999) poetic voice creates art from the ordinary: "A river of leaves from the plant that died even thought I meant to water it soon—gone." A new year vow becomes, "I will not say one awful thing, none of that, *can't do, don't have, why me,* because this is it, a fresh start, my second chance." [Yangsook] Choi's (*Nim and the War Effort,* 1996) lively, two-page spreads in bright colors, perfectly complement the energetic text, adding visual reinforcement to the scenes described by the narrator.

Gillian Engberg (review date 15 September 2000)

SOURCE: Engberg, Gillian. *Booklist* 97, no. 2 (15 September 2000): 251.

A young boy prepares for Chinese New Year [***This Next New Year***] with rituals and wide hopes, in this illustrated, free verse poem. The narrator, who is half Korean, describes how he and his friends, like so many people in a multicultural society, celebrate the holiday with a modern blend of adopted and inherited traditions: the boy's mother makes traditional Korean new year soup; Evelyn, part Hopi and Mexican, loves the money-stuffed red envelopes from her

Singaporean neighbor; and Glenn, part French and German, "calls it Chinese New Year, too, even though he celebrates it at his house by eating Thai food to go." At home, the boy cleans the house, "so it can soak up good luck like an empty sponge," grooms himself, and pledges to be brave and positive—"none of that can't do, don't have, why me." [Yangsook] Choi's smooth, brightly colored paintings-filled with firecrackers, dragons, and other cultural symbols ably illustrate the optimistic activity and the yearning in the accessible, rhythmic text. Children of diverse backgrounds will connect with the boy's earnest desire to help change the family's luck and realize his own potential.

Anne Connor (review date October 2000)

SOURCE: Connor, Anne. *School Library Journal* 46, no. 10 (October 2000): 142-43.

A Chinese-Korean boy relates [***This Next New Year***] how he and his friends celebrate the "lunar new year, the day of the first new moon." One child celebrates the holiday with "Thai food to go," while a non-Asian child likes to get ". . . red envelopes stuffed with money from her neighbor who came from Singapore" The narrator's mother cooks a special Korean soup, and his family observes the traditions of house cleaning, lighting firecrackers, and being extra good to ensure a lucky new year. Wong carefully and clearly presents the reasons behind the rituals in a manner understandable to young children. She explains in an appended note about her own confusion as a child about the timing and meaning of the holiday. [Yangsook] Choi's vibrant, somewhat primitive paintings realistically capture the details of and preparations for this hopeful time of year. Youngsters will enjoy the bright colors and the sense of motion and activity conveyed as the boy helps his mother clean, flosses his teeth, and cringes from the noise of the firecrackers. A good choice for anyone getting ready to celebrate Chinese New Year.

***Horn Book Magazine* (review date November-December 2000)**

SOURCE: *Horn Book Magazine* 76, no. 6 (November-December 2000): 751.

In a spare, lyrical narrative a Chinese-Korean boy reflects on what the lunar new year [***This Next New Year***], otherwise known as Chinese New Year, means to him. He and his family have had their share of trouble ("our luck is long overdue"), but by sweeping last year's dust, mistakes, and bad luck out of the house, he hopes to make room for good luck and "a fresh start, my second chance." The concepts of renewal, starting over, and luck, which inform many of the rituals, will resonate with young readers, and the narrator's personal impression of the celebration makes this a refreshing departure from the standard nonfiction holiday-introduction fare. Though the boy mentions a few of his family's customs ("my mother cooks *duk gook,* the Korean new year soup") and the things his non-Asian friends do to acknowledge the new lunar year, this is primarily an imaginative appreciation of the emotional associations of the holiday. Choi's festive, richly colored but somewhat flat illustrations enhance the text's poetic language with unexpected, fanciful touches. An author's note provides additional facts about the lunar year and about some of the symbols associated with Wong's own half-Chinese, half-Korean family's new year traditions.

🕮 *APPLE PIE 4TH OF JULY* (2002)

Diane Roback, Jennifer M. Brown, and Jason Britton (review date 8 April 2002)

SOURCE: Roback, Diane, Jennifer M. Brown, and Jason Britton. *Publishers Weekly* 249, no. 14 (8 April 2002): 226.

The author and artist teamed for ***Buzz*** return for this carefully honed story [***Apple Pie 4th of July***] about a girl's experience as a first-generation Chinese-American. Readers first encounter the unnamed narrator as she looks unhappily out the glass door of her parents' market, open for business even on the Fourth of July. Hearing the "boom, boom, boom" of the approaching parade, sniffing the apple pie baking in a neighbor's oven, she is distracted by the cooking smells from the store's kitchen, where her parents are preparing chow mein and sweet-and-sour pork. "No one wants Chinese food on the Fourth of July," she tries to explain, and her prediction seems right as the afternoon lengthily unfolds with almost no customers. "My parents do not understand all American things," she reminds herself, "They were not born here." But the evening brings a steady stream of patrons, and the holiday concludes with the family watching fireworks (invented by the Chinese) and eating—what else?—apple pie. The well-paced text—heavily freighted at the beginning and swift by the end—reflects the girl's changing emotions and moods. The art resembles cut-paper collage. [Margaret] Chodos-Irvine deploys sharply defined objects in a range of colors and patterns to construct harmonious, forthright compositions that will likely prove inviting to readers of many backgrounds.

Alicia Eames (review date May 2002)

SOURCE: Eames, Alicia. *School Library Journal* 48, no. 5 (May 2002): 132.

This simply told story [***Apple Pie 4th of July***] explores a child's fears about cultural differences and fitting in with understanding and affection. A Chinese-American girl helps her parents open their small neighborhood grocery store every day of the year. However, today is the Fourth of July and her parents just don't understand that customers won't be ordering chow mein and sweet-and-sour pork on this very American holiday. As she spends the day working in the store and watching the local parade, she can't shake her anxiety about her parents' naivete. When evening arrives along with hungry customers looking "for some Chinese food to go," she is surprised but obviously proud that her parents were right after all: Americans do eat Chinese food on the Fourth of July. Nighttime finds the family atop their roof enjoying fireworks and sharing a neighbor's apple pie. Done in a "variety of printmaking techniques," [Margaret] Chodos-Irvine's illustrations are cheerfully bright and crisp, capturing the spirit of the day as well as the changing emotions of the main character. This second successful collaboration by the creators of ***Buzz*** is one you won't want to miss.

Gillian Engberg (review date August 2002)

SOURCE: Engberg, Gillian. *Booklist* 98, no. 22 (August 2002): 1963.

"No one wants Chinese food on the Fourth of July," says a young Chinese American girl, [***Apple Pie 4th of July***] sulking because she's stuck at her parents' food store, missing the parade and the holiday clamor. At first the day feels interminable: there are only a few customers, no one buys the homemade Chow Mein, and the girl thinks, "My parents do not understand all American things. They were not born here." But then, at dinnertime, hungry celebrators crowd in; they want Chinese food, and the line stretches down the block. Later, when the store is closed, the girl joins her parents on the roof for fireworks and a neighbor's apple pie. Wong's message is clear; Chinese food is American. But this powerful, simple reminder is gracefully woven into an appealing story with believable characters and emotions, written in the girl's spare, lyrical voice. [Margaret] Chodos-Irvine, who also illustrated Wong's attractive ***Buzz*** (2000), captures the story's uncluttered, elemental qualities in opaque prints that resemble paper cutouts. Vibrant, colorful spreads keep the focus on the girl, using body language to accentuate first her discomfort and boredom, and then her pride as she hands out cartons of takeout.

🕮 *YOU HAVE TO WRITE* (2002)

Julie Cummins (review date July 2002)

SOURCE: Cummins, Julie. *Booklist* 98, no. 21 (July 2002): 1841.

It's the dreaded class task [***You Have to Write***]: write something! "You have to write. You hate to write." Wong's poetic text, which encourages kids to use their own experiences, is practical and also sometimes amusing. The with-it rhymes set the tone while gouache illustrations depict four diverse kids as they sift through the advice, thinking and envisioning. One scene shows the students at their desks picturing different locations they might write about. A variety of page compositions effectively exemplify various choices by using overlapping scenes and album-like framed images. "Take your mind for a walk" and "think about the plain, the everyday." The direct, you-can-do-it approach will stimulate kids to write and also help them with that dismaying assignment. Lots of classroom teachers will find this a great motivator.

Adele Greenlee (review date July 2002)

SOURCE: Greenlee, Adele. *School Library Journal* 48, no. 7 (July 2002): 112.

This book's [***You Have to Write***] gentle but direct approach to creative writing may not appeal to all youngsters, but it may help some students to address some common struggles and to find their own voices. Through free-verse poetry, Wong targets a group of youngsters looking for good topics for a writing assignment. "You want it to be good,/to make us cry/or bust up laughing/when the room is quiet." They are encouraged to look around, and not to be discouraged by the worldliness or experiences of others. "Wait. Did you forget who you are? / Who else can say what you have seen? / Who else can tell your stories. . . ." A photo albumlike page shows a variety of pets, holidays, hobbies, vacations, and family outings that could be possible topics. "Reach inside./Write about the dark times. / . . . Write about the bright times. / . . . Take your mind for a walk / back to this morning, / back to yesterday. . . ." Examples are given of parents fighting, a wet library book growing mildew, childhood fears of storms, and taking out the trash. For "Weave / them together— / half of Draft 1, a word from Draft 4, / a whole line from number 5. / Try. Because you have to write, / and you want it to be good," the illustration shows each child laying out stretches of many drafts on the floor. The simple realistic gouache paintings are rather ordinary but appropriate for the "writing from life" philosophy that is espoused.

Laura Tillotson (review date December 2002-January 2003)

SOURCE: Tillotson, Laura. *Book Links* 12, no. 3 (December 2002-January 2003): 15.

Writers young and old will relate to this entertaining, hands-on exploration of the writing process [***You Have to Write***]. In poetic text along expertly focuses on the nitty-gritty frustrations and insecurities that come with writing. "No one else can say / what you have seen and heard / and felt." "Reach inside. Write about the dark times." [Teresa] Flavin's cheerful illustrations feature four young writers and lots of paper flying everywhere.

FURTHER READING

Biography

Wong, Janet. "Janet's Biography." www.janetwong.com/

Biographical essay on author's Website.

Criticism

Flynn, Kitty. *Horn Book Guide* 12, no. 1 (spring 2001): 53.

Review of *This Next New Year.*

Horn Book Guide 11, no. 2 (fall 2000): 259.

Review of *Buzz.*

Roberts, Rebecca Boggs. "Children's Books." *New York Times Book Review* (16 June 2002): 20.

Review of *Apple Pie 4th of July.*

Schliesman, Megan. *Book Links* 11, no. 5 (April-May 2002): 48.

Review of *Grump.*

Sherman, Chris. *Horn Book Guide* 11, no. 2 (fall 2000): 391.

Review of *Night Garden: Poems from the World of Dreams.*

Sinkler, Rebecca Pepper. "Wild Pig-Rats and Carrot-Headed Dogs." *New York Times Book Review* (19 November 2000): 46.

Review of *Night Garden: Poems from the World of Dreams.*

Additional coverage of Wong's life and career is contained in the following sources published by the Gale Group: *Contemporary Authors,* Vol. 166; *Literature Resource Center;* and *Something about the Author,* Vol. 98.

How to Use This Index

The main reference

Baum, L(yman) Frank 1856-1919 .... **15**

lists all author entries in this and previous volumes of *Children's Literature Review*.

The cross-references

See also CA 108, 133; DLB 22; JRDA; MAICYA; MTCW 1; SATA 18, 100; TCLC 7

list all author entries in the following Gale biographical and literary sources:

AAL = *Asian American Literature*
AAYA = *Authors & Artists for Young Adults*
AFAW = *African American Writers* (Charles Scribner's Sons, an imprint of The Gale Group)
AFW = *African Writers* (Charles Scribner's Sons, an imprint of The Gale Group)
AITN = *Authors in the News*
AMW = *American Writers* (Charles Scribner's Sons, an imprint of The Gale Group)
AMWR = *American Writers Retrospective Supplement* (Charles Scribner's Sons, an imprint of The Gale Group)
AMWS = *American Writers Supplement* (Charles Scribner's Sons, an imprint of The Gale Group)
ANW = *American Nature Writers* (Charles Scribner's Sons, an imprint of The Gale Group)
AW = *Ancient Writers* (Charles Scribner's Sons, an imprint of The Gale Group)
BEST = *Bestsellers* (quarterly, citations appear as Year: Issue number)
BLC = *Black Literature Criticism*
BLCS = *Black Literature Criticism Supplement*
BPFB = *Beacham's Encyclopedia of Popular Fiction: Biography and Resources*
BRW = *British Writers* (Charles Scribner's Sons, an imprint of The Gale Group)
BRWS = *British Writers Supplement,* (Charles Scribner's Sons, an imprint of The Gale Group)
BW = *Black Writers*
BYA = *Beacham's Guide to Literature for Young Adults*
CA = *Contemporary Authors*
CAAS = *Contemporary Authors Autobiography Series*
CABS = *Contemporary Authors Bibliographical Series*
CAD = *Contemporary American Dramatists* (St. James Press, an imprint of The Gale Group)
CANR = *Contemporary Authors New Revision Series*
CAP = *Contemporary Authors Permanent Series*
CBD = *Contemporary British Dramatists* (St. James Press, an imprint of The Gale Group)
CCA = *Contemporary Canadian Authors*
CD = *Contemporary Dramatists* (St. James Press, an imprint of The Gale Group)
CDALB = *Concise Dictionary of American Literary Biography*
CDALBS = *Concise Dictionary of American Literary Biography Supplement*
CDBLB = *Concise Dictionary of British Literary Biography*
CLC = *Contemporary Literary Criticism*
CMLC = *Classical and Medieval Literature Criticism*
CMW = *St. James Guide to Crime & Mystery Writers* (St. James Press, an imprint of The Gale Group)
CN = *Contemporary Novelists* (St. James Press, an imprint of The Gale Group)
CP = *Contemporary Poets* (St. James Press, an imprint of The Gale Group)
CPW = *Contemporary Popular Writers* (St. James Press, an imprint of The Gale Group)
CSW = *Contemporary Southern Writers* (St. James Press, an imprint of The Gale Group)
CWD = *Contemporary Women Dramatists* (St. James Press, an imprint of The Gale Group)
CWP = *Contemporary Women Poets* (St. James Press, an imprint of The Gale Group)
CWRI = *St. James Guide to Children's Writers* (St. James Press, an imprint of The Gale Group)
CWW = *Contemporary World Writers* (St. James Press, an imprint of The Gale Group)
DA = *DISCovering Authors*
DAB = *DISCovering Authors: British*
DAC = *DISCovering Authors: Canadian*

DAM = *DISCovering Authors: Modules*
DRAM: *Dramatists Module;* ***MST:*** *Most-Studied Authors Module;*
MULT: *Multicultural Authors Module;* ***NOV:*** *Novelists Module;*
POET: *Poets Module;* ***POP:*** *Popular Fiction and Genre Authors Module*
DA3 = *DISCovering Authors 3.0*
DC = *Drama Criticism*
DFS = *Drama for Students*
DLB = *Dictionary of Literary Biography*
DLBD = *Dictionary of Literary Biography Documentary Series*
DLBY = *Dictionary of Literary Biography Yearbook*
DNFS = *Literature of Developing Nations for Students*
EFS = *Epics for Students*
EXPN = *Exploring Novels*
EXPP = *Exploring Poetry*
EXPS = *Exploring Short Stories*
EW = *European Writers* (Charles Scribner's Sons, an imprint of The Gale Group)
FANT = *St. James Guide to Fantasy Writers* (St. James Press, an imprint of The Gale Group)
FW = *Feminist Writers* (St. James Press, an imprint of The Gale Group)
GFL = *Guide to French Literature,* Beginnings to 1789, 1798 to the Present (St. James Press, an imprint of The Gale Group)
GLL = *Gay and Lesbian Literature* (St. James Press, an imprint of The Gale Group)
HGG = *St. James Guide to Horror, Ghost & Gothic Writers* (St. James Press, an imprint of The Gale Group)
HLC = *Hispanic Literature Criticism*
HLCS = *Hispanic Literature Criticism Supplement*
HW = *Hispanic Writers*
IDFW = *International Dictionary of Films and Filmmakers: Writers and Production Artists* (St. James Press, an imprint of The Gale Group)
IDTP = *International Dictionary of Theatre: Playwrights* (St. James Press, an imprint of The Gale Group)
LAIT = *Literature and Its Times*
LAW = *Latin American Writers* (Charles Scribner's Sons, an imprint of The Gale Group)
JRDA = *Junior DISCovering Authors*
LC = *Literature Criticism from 1400 to 1800*
MAICYA = *Major Authors and Illustrators for Children and Young Adults*
MAICYA = *Major Authors and Illustrators for Children and Young Adults Supplement*
MAWW = *Modern American Women Writers* (Charles Scribner's Sons, an imprint of The Gale Group)
MJW = *Modern Japanese Writers* (Charles Scribner's Sons, an imprint of The Gale Group)
MTCW = *Major 20th-Century Writers*
NCFS = *Nonfiction Classics for Students*
NCLC = *Nineteenth-Century Literature Criticism*
NFS = *Novels for Students*
NNAL = *Native North American Literature*
PAB = *Poets: American and British* (Charles Scribner's Sons, an imprint of The Gale Group)
PC = *Poetry Criticism*
PFS = *Poetry for Students*
RGAL = *Reference Guide to American Literature* (St. James Press, an imprint of The Gale Group)
RGEL = *Reference Guide to English Literature* (St. James Press, an imprint of The Gale Group)
RGSF = *Reference Guide to Short Fiction* (St. James Press, an imprint of The Gale Group)
RGWL = *Reference Guide to World Literature* (St. James Press, an imprint of The Gale Group)
RHW = *Twentieth-Century Romance and Historical Writers* (St. James Press, an imprint of The Gale Group)
SAAS = *Something about the Author Autobiography Series*
SATA = *Something about the Author*
SFW = *St. James Guide to Science Fiction Writers* (St. James Press, an imprint of The Gale Group)
SSC = *Short Story Criticism*
SSFS = *Short Stories for Students*
TCLC = *Twentieth-Century Literary Criticism*
TCWW = *Twentieth-Century Western Writers* (St. James Press, an imprint of The Gale Group)
WLC = *World Literature Criticism, 1500 to the Present*
WLCS = *World Literature Criticism Supplement*
WLIT = *World Literature and Its Times*
WP = *World Poets* (Charles Scribner's Sons, an imprint of The Gale Group)
YABC = *Yesterday's Authors of Books for Children*
YAW = *St. James Guide to Young Adult Writers* (St. James Press, an imprint of The Gale Group)

CLR Cumulative Author Index

CLR Cumulative Nationality Index

ANTIGUAN

AUSTRALIAN

AUSTRIAN

BELGIAN

CANADIAN

CHILEAN

CHINESE

CUBAN

CZECH

DANISH

DUTCH

ENGLISH

Nationality Index

FILIPINO

FINNISH

FRENCH

GERMAN

GREEK

HUNGARIAN

INDIAN

IRISH

ISRAELI

ITALIAN

JAMAICAN

JAPANESE

CLR-94 Title Index

ISBN 0-7876-6787-0
90000
9 780787 667870